Toward Cinema and Its Double

Arts and Politics of the Everyday

Patricia Mellencamp

Meaghan Morris

Andrew Ross

Toward Cinema and Its Double

Cross-Cultural Mimesis

Laleen Jayamanne

INDIANA UNIVERSITY PRESS

Bloomington and Indianapolis

This book is a publication of
Indiana University Press
601 North Morton Street
Bloomington, IN 47404-3797 USA

http://iupress.indiana.edu

Telephone orders   800-842-6796
Fax orders   812-855-7931
Orders by e-mail   iuporder@indiana.edu

Manufactured in the United States of America

Library of Congress Cataloging-in-Publication Data

Jayamanne, Laleen.
    Toward cinema and its double : cross-cultural mimesis / Laleen Jayamanne.
        p.   cm. — (Arts and politics of the everyday)
Includes bibliographical references and index.
    ISBN 0-253-33982-0 — ISBN 0-253-21475-0 (pbk.)
    1. Motion pictures.   I. Title. II. Series.
    PN1993.5.A1 J37 2001
    791.43—dc21

                                                    2001000988

1 2 3 4 5 06 05 04 03 02 01

For Brian and Anusha Rutnam

Contents

Acknowledgments

I am grateful to the editors of this series, Meaghan Morris and Patricia Mellencamp, for their encouragement, patience, and sustained interest in my work. This book began with a suggestion made by Meaghan Morris in the early 1990s, and she ensured that it materialized by helping me from its very slow beginnings right up to the very end. Her astute scholarly advice on several of the chapters, her detailed editorial assistance, and her generous enthusiasm and mateship have made this book possible. I have benefited greatly from her mode of thinking and her skills as a teacher and mentor. And as far back as the late 1970s she helped create an Australian film culture milieu where one could begin to think about film and with film in an unabashedly intellectual manner. I wish to thank Tina Kaufman, a major figure in this milieu, for publishing my early writing on film and giving me a sense of the enormous pleasure in writing in the vernacular, which cut across several institutional spaces. I would also like to thank Steven Shaviro for his stimulating reader's report and Jelena Stojanovic for suggesting the title, which, as Adorno said, is often given or arrives like a gift. Many others have contributed to this work, especially my students in the Department of Art History and Theory at the University of Sydney. I thank them for their passionate interest in cinema, which has stimulated some of the work in this book; their mimetic perceptions keep me going. My colleagues in the department have provided a generous work environment where one is allowed to pursues one's interests untrammeled. And finally I am most grateful to Brian Rutnam, my husband, without whom I would not have dared to write in English at a time when Sinhalese was not an option, for sharing my interest in film, and Anusha Rutnam, my daughter, for activating the image of "the little girl" as an enabling figure for my work.

29 January 2001, Sydney

Introduction:
Criticism as "Exact Fantasy"[1]

This is a book of film criticism, nothing but film criticism. What this means is that the filmic object under consideration is of primary value. I should like to think that I have been faithful to the object in much the same way that a singer is true to the score in not singing a single wrong note. In the film criticism that I have come to practice over some twenty years, correct description is as necessary as hitting all the right notes. But then, getting all the notes right is not all there is to singing (as I realized when I fainted on finally hitting the high note successfully in Schubert's *Litany for All Souls' Day,* when I was a girl of fifteen), just as describing a film exactly is only the beginning of a certain kind of critical move. Description is critical, in the sense that it is through that move that a film is apprehended or not.[2] If the description does not move, then criticism is no more than a dull copy or repetition of the object. The kind of descriptive act required cannot be determined before the encounter with a particular object, but certain guidelines (at least those that work for me) seem to emerge through this writing. One is to ride an impulsive move toward whatever draws one to something in the object—a color, a gesture, a phrase, an edit point, a glance, a rhythm, a whatever. Enter the film through this and describe exactly what is heard and seen, and then begin to describe the film in any order whatever rather than in the order in which it unravels itself. Soon one's own description begins not only to mimic the object, as a preliminary move, but also to redraw the object. This is not a betrayal of the object through an enthroning of the primacy of the subject's narcissistic projection but rather the activation of an encounter, a means of entering the object, though not necessarily through the door marked "Enter." An eccentric, impulsive, descriptive drive will cut the film up and link the fragments differently from the way the film is itself organized. It is through this montage of description that a reading might emerge.

While it is true that I can get into a film and happily spend a good six months or more thinking about it, it is also true that recently I have found myself compelled by concepts too. This compulsion has been spurred by particular films (rather than by any prior program) in that I have needed to find ways of entering them and have had to look for concepts that would help me do so. Choosing a concept, or a cluster of concepts, is not always a neat and tidy process. Once, a concept hit me like lightning. Mimesis so hit me that, like Saul of Tarsus struck down and blinded by lightning on the road to Damascus, I must even as a lapsed Catholic confess that I believe in mimesis. If one does believe, then one must follow Theodor Adorno in *Aesthetic Theory*[3] and not use it as a category, but try to activate its bio-anthropological, impulsive, performative vitalism in the act of criticism itself. I learned this, however, from Michael Taussig's wildly wonderful exact relocation of the concept of mimesis in the colonial moment, in his *Mimesis and Alterity: A Particular History of the Senses*,[4] which generated my dramatic encounter with it. Taussig's book opened up in an almost magical way the Frankfurt School texts on mimesis, which had until then remained impenetrable to me. Mimesis is an operative concept and something of a guiding star for my book. A star, because mimesis in action has a mysterious aconceptual facet which makes it elude categorical thinking. It offers a means of retooling my senses and cognitive drive as well as a way of understanding the connection between these two as they encounter that elusive object, film.

In the programmatic statement of his inaugural lecture, Adorno speaks of the necessity of reviving an *ars inveniendi* (an art of coming upon something, invention) for contemporary philosophy. And he insists that

> the organon of this *ars inveniendi* is fantasy. An exact fantasy; fantasy which abides strictly within the material which the sciences present to it, and reaches beyond them only in the smallest aspects of their arrangement: aspects, granted, which fantasy itself must originally generate.[5]

Buck-Morss shows how Adorno was influenced by Walter Benjamin's thought on the mimetic. She says that Benjamin activated the idea of "exact fantasy" to highlight the nature of translation, and Adorno that of musical performance, as acts of mimetic transformation.

> Literary translation and musical performance did not simply copy the original; they maintained the "aura" of the original by transforming it, precisely so that its truth might be preserved. To mime the original in a new modality thus required "exact fantasy." As Tiedemann has noted in Benjamin's case, translation provided the model for this theory of

truth because it was "simultaneously reception and spontaneity: the translator needs the model, the original, and his task is to produce a new version."

She further adds that

> the transformational character of the mimetic moment in Adorno's theoretical method must be taken literally. The "inner logic" of objects (jazz music, a theater seat) was transformed into words and conversely, words (of a popular song, of a Kierkegaard text) were transformed into "images." Unlike that mere duplication of the "given" world which was the signpost of bourgeois theory, exact fantasy performed a metamorphosis, which, for all its enlightened reason, retained the faint image of a magic trick.[6]

There are, according to Raul Ruiz, two kinds of film critics. One sees a lot of current films and is able to respond to the moment on the run; the other spends a year or two on a few films. I am, alas, the latter kind of critic; hence the criticism in this book has taken nearly twenty years to write. In that time Australian cinema studies has undergone some changes, of which this book is a product, though it is not organized according to the chronology of those changes. Something about a film or a cycle of films, or their reception, prompted me to write, and, looking at the selection of films in this book, I can't say that in all instances I chose to write on such and such, for at times a film or its reception beckoned me, even forced me, to engage with it, despite whatever my personal tastes may have been.

In the material presented in Part One, which dates from the early 1990s, I was drawn to write about *The Piano* and *The Good Woman of Bangkok* by the very different natures of their public receptions, whereas I wrote about *Night Cries* to find out who Jimmy Little is and what he does in the film. As I did so, the fiction of a "Sri Lankan reading" gave me the poetic license that film theory never permitted.

Part Two gathers together my writing on my own film and video work within an idea of a "performance of narcissism," theoretically developed in relation to *The Piano*. While I have to thank Tina Kauffman, the editor of *Film News*, for the idea of interviewing myself (because she never interviewed me, as I had dreamed she would, on my film *A Song of Ceylon*), Anna Rodrigo, a fictional interviewer who bears the name of my late mother, is my own narcissistic projection (mimetic doubling, really) trying to fix a problem or two. The figure of the maternal haunts this section for good reason, and it, in its several avatars, and that of the little girl are enabling figures for this work.

Part Three, the middle of this work, is the real blast from my past (and the past of cinema studies as well), and the impatient western reader of this book will no doubt skip it, as it is about the little-known national cinema of a small island, overshadowed by the power of Indian cinema and now on the verge of disappearance under the pressure of new technologies and economic trends. The project of an ideological and historical analysis of my national cinema's myths of femininity has oriented me in more ways than one. While the project was begun in the late 1970s as my Ph.D. thesis, I have returned to it in the late '80s and early '90s to see how Sri Lankan cinema survives under irreversible technological and economic pressure. Chapter 9 in this section is the only polemical piece in this volume, first delivered as a public lecture in Sri Lanka, largely addressed to film critics and cinephiles and focusing on the perennial critical discourse on the Sinhalese cinema. It is my cinema, the one I grew up with (alongside Hollywood and Indian films) and the one that oriented me, both here (Australia) and there (Sri Lanka), in decisive ways and at the critical moment that I arrived in Australia from New York City, knowing that there would be no returning home. Apart from these biographical reasons for including these essays here, the Sri Lankan genre cinema's fantastical, allegorical narratives of class and gender, and what I call its "narrative prodigality," may interest the curious reader.

Parts Four and Five (with the exception of the chapter on Akerman, written in 1980) have been written with methodological tools I have tried to develop by using Gilles Deleuze's work on cinema,[7] but I have also used other thinkers' ideas when in need of concepts to make images yield both questions and possible answers and, equally important, to express the aconceptual yield of images as well. Put in general terms, these chapters mark the move from thinking of film as a textual system to thinking of it as an art of movement and of duration. And I am thrilled that the Akerman piece, written during the hegemony of *Screen* and *Camera Obscura* (to use a shorthand to designate the key determinants of a period of academic film studies in Australia), could be revised and expanded now, without changing much of its initial impetus and structure.

While my work has been strongly influenced by the experience of teaching for nearly twenty years in Australian colleges and universities, another vital influence must be acknowledged. Luckily, in Australia, film academics have been invited to participate in the wider public sphere of Australian film culture in the last several decades, including public lectures, film festival and art gallery forums, and radio discussions. How to speak to and write for a non-academic, general audience is one of the most valuable lessons I have learned from this public engagement. I cannot take the academic vocabulary for granted, and accessibility is as important a goal to me as theoretical rigor and empirical exactitude. This bridging of institutional spaces has been possible because of the strength of Australian public cultural institutions. And when one's somewhat obscure research links up with the interests of others in unpredictable ways, the linkage yields a sense of (extra-academic) legitimation, which is essential if one is to keep on working.

It is, I think, the mimetic faculty (in however atrophied a form it survives in each one of us) that helps one to perceive links or similarities between different elements of a film. If description, as I have sketched above, must be exact, then the move by which the descriptive passages are re-linked is best specified by the term "fantasy." I understand fantasy in terms of Walter Benjamin's theory of correspondences, which, according to his essay on the mimetic faculty,[8] is the capacity to perceive and create non-sensuous similarity, as well as in terms of Adorno's idea of musical performance. The idea of exactitude acts as a rein on the fanciful and capricious correspondences one may be prone to make, while the mimetic impulse that enables one to perceive correspondences is what individuates criticism. If one has the time and inclination to be with a film for a long time, first loving or hating it, as the case might be, then worrying over it meticulously and reading as much as possible on the lineaments of the concepts used as tools of entry and passage, then forgetting the film consciously, the chances are that something will emerge, which in its turn must be worked over thoroughly as well. So this is one way to go to work, perchance to dream.

The double, then, that emerges through these two procedures of exact description and uncontrolled, uncontrollable compulsion to make (or perceive) correspondences is not a copy or an imitation of the object, but a mimetic double of it. This is the kind of doubling I have striven after in this book, crossing cultures, cinematic and other.

Toward Cinema and Its Double

Part One
Two-Way Street: Three Australian Films

1 "Love me tender, love me true, never let me go": A Sri Lankan Reading of Tracey Moffatt's *Night Cries: A Rural Tragedy*

We have been herded as people of color to mind only our own cultures. Hence, Asians will continue to make films on Asia, Africans on Africa and Euro-Americans on the world.

—T. Minh-Ha Trinh[1]

We must assimilate all those systems we come across or admit defeat.

—Kumar Shahani[2]

When I was in Rome several months ago, I was talking with other Chilean exiles about how the feeling of schizophrenia is becoming stronger after seven years. One recalled that he had seen himself walking down the street, another saw himself drinking a cup of coffee, and I, who normally write the dialogue for my films in a Spanish that can easily be translated into French, saw my own handwriting in French. After that I began to write in French all the time. Another was in a tailor's shop surrounded by mirrors and saw a profile he could not identify; only after several minutes did he recognise himself.

—Raul Ruiz[3]

In framing my comments about *Night Cries* with those of three Third World filmmakers, I am not appealing to authority. I use these quotations here because they refer in different ways to conditions that are necessary for work to be at all possible, and they also imply ways of inventing methods. These conditions are not simply idiosyncratic needs of individual creativity (though they may be that too); they also link up with wider cultural processes in a neo-colonial and postmodern world.

An Australian friend encouraged me to do a Sri Lankan reading of *Night Cries.* What would a Sri Lankan reading be? This is the wrong question: you can't know what it is until you do it, because a reading is in part a deciphering and in part an invention, in the sense of making connections. How then would I set about reading the film as a Sri Lankan, as a foreigner, as one outside the cultural forces the film dramatizes in a highly distilled form?[4] But it is not only I who am foreign. *Night Cries* itself is utterly different in look and conception from much of Australian 35 mm cinema. It can, however, be located within the "popular culture-fiction tradition" of Australian independent low-budget experimental filmmaking which Adrian Martin posits in his typology of the field. The energy of this tradition, according to Martin, lies in an "impulse to incorporate—in however dislocated or perverse a way—vivid fragments of the given cultural environment (television, music and the whole 'style' culture alongside cinema itself)." He further qualifies this impulse:

> The popular culture-fiction tradition differs from the agitational-deconstructive one in that there is less overt "critique" and more emotional indulgence; and it replaces the romantic imagistic plundering of the strange or dark "edges" of popular imagery with a greater sensitivity to and awareness of original cultural contexts and meanings.[5]

If *Night Cries* does in many ways belong here, there is also a sense in which it doesn't. This is because it looks glossy and breathtaking in the way big movies do. The ideology of experimental cinema, with its bias toward a rough and uncommodified look, may declare this glossiness suspect, but I would like to sustain a sense of strangeness in all these aspects even as I respond to parts of the film that are more accessible than others. This approach helps me to talk about the film, which, because it is a film by an Aboriginal Australian woman filmmaker, is otherwise difficult to do. In the early 1980s I faced no such trepidation in writing about, say, the work of the Belgian filmmaker Chantal Akerman, largely because her early films fitted into a feminist international theoretical agenda where questions of cultural, regional, and ethnic specificity weren't—or didn't seem to be—relevant (see chapter 11). But with Moffatt's work these questions cannot be elided. So, to my surprise, the scenario that should have been most accessible for feminist reasons—that of the maternal melodrama seen from the daughter's perspective—is opaque in certain crucial ways. Its universal aspect, the tension between the call of duty mixed with love on the one hand and the call of desire for another life on the other, is legible and wrenching. But it is from the film that I learned of the harrowing history of the assimilation policy of forced adoption of Aboriginal children and what it means in terms of lived experience between a "mother" and "daughter."[6] Also, the location of this tragedy, the outback ranch, is presented in a way which is partly familiar and partly opaque. At one level the Moffatt image is completely mediated by technology and therefore familiar to contemporary television and video viewers. This is interesting in the context of "big" Australian movies that celebrate the land and its putative pristine otherness in a transparent cinematography. Ross Gibson draws out the implications of this practice thus:

> The presented image of a landscape is necessarily a sign. And in the Australian setting, it is a sign of nature as opposed to a sign of a sign; Australian film culture remains "innocent" or "primitive," declining to graduate to the (post-)modernist worlds of second and/or third degree (re-) presentations of pre-existent social constructs.[7]

He does go on to show that this seeming naiveté is in the interest of producing a product marketable elsewhere. In opposition to this, Moffatt's setting is figured as a sign of a sign, marked by a specific cultural reference. It was from the film and the discourses around it that I learned that its art director, Stephen Curtis, and Moffatt wanted the film to have the color of the painting of Albert Namatjira, an Aboriginal artist of the Aranda watercolor school. To pursue the implications of this decision is to explore the very terms of Aboriginal tradition and modernity, and as an outsider I can only, with diffidence, cite a review article that seems to me to map out lucidly the terrain of both the art-historical and the cultural, political debates. Ian Burn and Ann Stephen, in their review of a book on Namatjira, discuss some of the reasons for the extreme popularity of Namatjira's work and for his rejection by the art establishment. The work was related to the tourist industry; the Aranda painters assimilated the pictorial idiom of the so-called gum tree school of regional landscape painting, which members of the Modernist critical establishment despised. Furthermore, they disliked the use of watercolor, an "amateur" medium. Burn and Stephen make the point that

> [a]rt historians would have had to qualify their Modernist viewpoints in order to acknowledge the significance of his art, particularly since the

work entailed other forms of innovation in terms of different subject matter, new types of landscape, using traditional forms as a vehicle for other meanings.[8]

They go on to say that the kind of Aranda work that entered the galleries in the 1950s did use watercolor, but in patterns that were more "primitive." Geoff Batchen has noted the cultural similarity between Namatjira and Jimmy Little, the Aboriginal singer who plays himself in *Night Cries*.[9] It is no accident, it seems, that Moffatt invokes both Little and Namatjira in her work. I agree with Batchen that this film "is all about the politics of imitation and assimilation," but would add that it is perhaps also about an aesthetics of assimilation. Apart from the thematic of assimilation within which the mother/daughter relationship is lived unto death, Moffatt also brings into play the idea of "assimilation" as a matter of method and of survival—survival not in a cultural ghetto but in the market, as well as in the domains of cultural visibility and legitimacy. The *Shorter Oxford English Dictionary* defines "assimilate" thus: "to make like, to adapt, to absorb and incorporate, to convert into a substance of its own nature; to absorb into the system." I also want to invoke the bodily connotations of the word, as when food is assimilated into the body, because I want to discuss how Jimmy Little performs in the film and how he in turn is performed by filmic operations such as editing and framing. Through the performance of Jimmy Little, Moffatt explores both the violent and the fluent aspects of cultural assimilation and taps into an Aboriginal cultural history which is neither pristinely indigenous nor completely other, a kind of mimetic zone. Jimmy Little is the first figure to appear in the film, and he also concludes it. Given that beginnings and endings are privileged moments, his presence at these points marks him as fundamental to the concerns of the film. The song he sings unaccompanied at the opening is given in its hit version, with all the brassy trimmings, at the end. And in addition to framing this seventeen-minute film, he appears in two crucial scenes within it. I will discuss these two scenes in some detail presently.

In recalling Jimmy Little to our memory, Moffatt is making an enabling tradition for herself to work in. At one level, then, I see this as a homage to a barely remembered Aboriginal showman who had his brief place in the sun with a single hit song, "Royal Telephone" (1964). Part of the film's magic is that even as one laughs at the pure cornball lyrics of the song, one is nevertheless engaged by Little's performance: the velvet texture of his voice, the movements of his hands, and the melody of the song. The overtly jarring effect of his songs (both heard and unheard), in the context of the tragedy between the mother and daughter, functions at another level. It would have been too easy to use him as a parodic figure and poke fun at his song to Jesus. This film does not work with parody, perhaps because its genre is tragedy. But what function does a singer have in a tragedy, especially a singer whose songs don't in any way set the mood but instead interrupt it? In this film, Jimmy Little's smoothness is not simply pitted against the harshness of the woman's story, though this does happen once and in an interesting way.

The Singer

Little reappears in the body of the film when the daughter cracks a whip outside the house while the mother, seated inside, registers each lash viscerally. There is no telling whether it is pleasure or pain or a bit of both that this aged body feels. This is a rare scene in Australian cinema for its perverse intensity. The laughter of the daughter as she cracks the whip is both utterly thrilling and chilling in its demonic, asocial force. It is this scene that Jimmy Little interrupts, and one wonders why. He seems to function as the third term necessary to break the dyad of the mother and daughter, but although he is a man, his presence is not phallic. As the whip cracks and the mother shudders, Jimmy Little is cut in. He is seen in a series of shots, putting the guitar strap over his shoulder, adjusting it, then adjusting his collar in an effort to get comfortable so as to perform, and the sound transmitted here is that of static electricity or "white noise." The song he then sings silently is Elvis's "Love Me Tender" ("love me true, never let me go"). Moffatt certainly takes this song to heart: she will not let him go. So he returns again to the beach scene of childhood. When the little girl is tormented by her two black male playmates and is also abandoned by the mother, who just disappears, leaving her on a rocky outcrop on a dark and hostile, thoroughly un-Australian beach, he returns. As the little girl cries in anguish, Jimmy Little sings, in extreme close-up, a silent lullaby which fails to lull the desolate, abandoned child. In this return, the previously benign smile takes on a sinister quality. There is a need here that this figure cannot now satisfy, a register of feeling that he cannot be a part of. But even so, at this critical moment too Moffatt fragments his body, and in so doing she opens up multiple and contradictory zones and temporalities in it and in his voice. The seamless ease of the performance is cinematically fragmented to create tender and terrifying zones and rhythms, and Jimmy Little is refigured under the sign of cultural ambivalence. Who is this Jimmy Little? He is a modern Aboriginal shaman/showman who sings Elvis, Harry Belafonte, and country and western, that quintessential Aboriginal music, who mediates several cultural forces via his body and voice. With style and panache he embodies cultural assimilation. Here the notion of assimilation may suggest the mimicry involved in camouflage, which is intended to keep others from knowing whether you are there or not. Now you are, now you are not; it all depends on how you look. Ambivalent, unsettling perception becomes necessary: the performer is working in a tradition which is not his but which he sings as his own.

The Mother: The Daughter

In the history of feminist attention to the mother/daughter dyad in cinema, *Night Cries* stands out for its completely unsentimental and yet emotionally charged exploration of this primal theme, in both its tender and murderous dimensions. *Night Cries* is a powerfully gripping film both aurally and visually. It leaves a series of sharp impressions on the viewer: the daughter biting into an apple with all the ferocity of her contained energy as she dreams of an elsewhere to escape to; the sullen, acerbic desperation of her gaze and the sensuality of her full body. Marcia Langton, playing the daughter, has a physicality and an emotional richness such as one usually associates with an Anna Magnani or Smita Patil, and are rare in my experience of Australian cinema. These qualities are not "primitive emanations" from her body (though there is a voluptuous pleasure to be had in the fragmentation of the daughter's body). They are, rather, in part a result of the intensity of her desires, which are in fact quite modern. In opposition to the daughter's corporeal weight and voluptuousness, the maternal body is withered, just skin and bone. Moffatt heightens this opposition to a point of excruciating pain by giving us close-ups of the mother's face, so that her sightless gaze seems to pierce us; the profile with the toothless mouth is held for what feels like an eternity. These images of a body's vicissitudes and traumas make me want to cry out "No more, no more," and yet I watch, in horror. This visual insistence is shocking in our (Australian) culture, where death, old age, and bodily decrepitude do not usually figure so forcefully in the cinema. Something, however, changes this opposition when the daughter washes the mother's feet, soon after the whipping scene. One can't quite forget the sound of the whip when looking at the twisted and gnarled feet in extreme close-up. But the soft sound of the water pouring over the feet and the gentleness of the daughter in washing them create a new mood. The mood shifts again in the next scene, when they both sing "Onward, Christian Soldiers." The continual shifting of emotional tone and register in such a short film is in part achieved by the suggestive power of a minimalist use of sound and color. The tableau compositions, as well, are pared down and thus intensified.

A Black Void[10]

Night Cries: A Rural Tragedy begins with an emblematic sound of modernity, that of a train, almost imperceptibly becoming a cry. This doubling and forking of the sound lacerates a black void which the title then emphatically stamps and causes to vanish. A black space mediates between this title shot and the first appearance of Jimmy Little, functioning as a momentary pause. We hear his song over this blackness before we see him. Because the formal presence of the black space marks the entire film, it may be thought of as a fluid matrix. Jimmy Little emerges from it, often positioned on the left side of this generously empty black space. The two tableaux of the mother and daughter consoling each other are also placed in this black void, though positioned differently. They seem to be set within it (a function of screen position and lighting), while Jimmy Little seems to be more on the surface. The daughter lamenting the mother's death recedes into the vast expanse of the black space after being held by a tiny iris-in shot. Finally, the credits roll up the side of it, leaving a moment of empty space where Little was a moment before.

This black void is not just black leader, not just a bit of empty time. It has the weight of duration and a fluidity of movement because of the way sounds are played across its immeasurable form. Its contours change invisibly through the sounds that cut across it or play on it or in it (and these changes depend on the sounds and how we hear them). So the black void is not a nothing and is not an empty space. The flexibility with which it is used makes it formally possible for Moffatt to bring a residual figure like Jimmy Little from the forgotten past of '60s pop culture into a filmic economy of modernist rigor. Although the act of reviving Jimmy Little may seem anachronistic in such a context, the sense of "time lag" or "historical belatedness"[11] that marks the figure does not function as a sign of retardation. This is because he is refigured or performed by the filmic operations. The framing fragments his body just as the montage that intervenes between the voice and body puts them out of sync. His opening address to us is oblique: he is singing to someone elsewhere, not to us, the audience of the film. He is made to negotiate the other scene of this film before he can address us "directly." But even when he finally does so, his hit song is post-dubbed—he only lip-syncs it. So Jimmy Little mimics his own song, which assimilates its own history and performs its dual temporality (rooted as it is in both 1964 and 1989). The song is now shot through with the "unspeakable" historical tragedy he has witnessed and helped to signify.

The Shaman and the Showman

At one time, I programmatically refused to analyze the relationship between *Night Cries* and *Jedda,* saying that it was a "white man's burden" to do so. However, over the past eight years I have screened the two films together in a course I teach on cross-cultural perspectives on cinema, and I have became aware of a correspondence between two unlikely figures, Jimmy Little and Marbuk, the tribal Aboriginal man in *Jedda* played by Robert Tudawali. On the face of it they are not at all similar, because Jimmy Little's is an image of a successfully assimilated Aboriginal performer while Marbuk's is that of a "primitive" shaman, who is unassimilable. Certainly they both sing, a source of their power to enchant all who hear them, but their songs, their language, their modes of singing, indeed their performances as a whole mark them as absolute opposites to each other in the great divide between white Australian and Aboriginal culture. If anything, Jimmy Little's parallel in *Jedda* is the stockman Joe, the "half-caste" assimilated Aboriginal who narrates the film with a BBC accent and is the husband chosen for Jedda, the assimilated Aboriginal girl. So the kind of similarity the film enables me to see is not a natural, obvious, narrative one but a "non-sensuous similarity."[12]

In the many parallels drawn between the two films by critics, the enigmatic, uncanny, fleeting resemblance between Little and Marbuk, which (like Bergson's conception of the past) subsists and insists, has gone unnoticed. Two articles I have recently read have helped me to draw out the mimetic resemblance or correspondence Moffatt has created between Marbuk and Little. Meaghan Morris, in "Beyond Assimilation: Aboriginality, Media History, and Public Memory," makes the point that Moffatt's film "refers . . . to the work of three cultural mediators of race relations in Australia"—Charles Chauvel, the white Australian director of *Jedda,* and

Jimmy Little and Albert Namatjira, the two Aboriginal artists.[13] It is Morris's notion of a "cultural mediator" that I would like to take up via (Mudrooroo) Colin Johnson's article "Chauvel and the Centering of the Aboriginal Male in Australian Film."[14] In this article Johnson responds to an Aboriginal woman's sense of excitement on seeing *Jedda* ("Why don't they make films like *Jedda* any more?") and begins to explore the source of the film's fascination. The figure who still (after forty years) casts a spell on the viewer as he moves across the screen is certainly Marbuk. Because of the affective response that Marbuk evokes, Johnson says that Chauvel has made an Aboriginal text despite himself. While the white characters and the assimilated Aboriginal main characters, such as Jedda and Joe, operate as "flat" stereotypes, Marbuk, despite embodying the stereotypic traits of the "noble savage," emits an energy in his performance that stands out as unique in the history of Australian cinema, which, Johnson claims, has usually represented Aboriginal masculinity as emasculated. He is the dark figure that lures the assimilated Jedda from her adopted white culture through the power of his shamanistic song and dance. In a film that oscillates uneasily between a Hollywood B action scenario and a cultural debate on assimilation staged between Mr. and Mrs. McMahon, the real source of erotic vitality is Marbuk. How then can Jimmy Little have anything in common with such an intransigently unassimilable figure of vitality? Isn't Little more like Joe, part of an efficient, clean, sterile, white order?

Moffatt, the "assimilated" avant-garde Aboriginal artist, is loath to answer this question with an unequivocal "yes." In cutting up Little's hands in those enigmatic, rather uncanny close-ups even as he silently sings "Love me tender, love me true," she opens up a correspondence between Marbuk's and Little's bodies, despite their obvious dissimilarity. When Marbuk sings to charm Jedda he uses his arms and hands in undulating movements which are recalled through the movements, seen in close-up, of Little's hands. I have wondered for several years why those close-ups are there, and recently a similarity appeared (as Benjamin might say) "in a flash." But it is only by reading the Morris and Johnson pieces together that I am now able to articulate the remarkable work of cultural mediation performed by Moffatt through the figure of Little as mediator of a kinetic (Aboriginal) memory. Through those dismembering close-ups, Little himself is affectively recharged with an empowering sense of ambivalence. So if he seemed overly familiar, a little too nice, very much a part of the Christian family, those dismembering close-ups create a sense of unease, enabling the viewer to remember the vital force of the shaman. In making us perceive such a similarity Moffatt participates in assimilation on her own terms, aesthetically,[15] with the help of Little as an "indirect mediator."[16]

As noted earlier, though Little's presence is not phallic, he is certainly not emasculated in the way Aboriginal masculinity has been (according to Johnson's cogent analysis) in much of New Australian cinema. This is so precisely because of a correspondence drawn between the doomed "savage," Marbuk, and the urbane Little, still alive and singing. Moffatt recharges Little with a bit of mimetic capital[17] drawn from the body of the dead Marbuk/Robert Tudawali. And no doubt our senses also profit from this surplus value drawn from the "primitive" body. In performing this kind of complex mediation Moffatt is one of the most inventive and eloquent artists of reconciliation, even before the idea became state policy.

A film that can cut from the sweetness of a music-box to a whiplash and laughter, then to Jimmy Little singing "Love Me Tender," and not use one to parody the other, signals the presence of a certain unusual daring in Australian cinema. From her first work as a still photographer, through her numerous video works and *Nice Coloured Girls,* to *Night Cries,* Moffatt emerges ever more clearly as a fascinating, sophisticated talent in Australian cinema. As a Sri Lankan working here, I can only hope that the monocultural blandness of much of Australian cinema will be transformed by the force of mimetic forms.

2 Reception, Genre, and the Knowing Critic: Dennis O'Rourke's *The Good Woman of Bangkok*

Destabilization of the Knowing Critic[1]

When *The Good Woman of Bangkok* was first shown, at the Sydney Film Festival and then at a documentary film conference in Australia in 1991, it raised a great deal of controversy, and with its general release in March 1992 the controversy broke out in the mainstream media. I do not know of any other independent Australian film that has had such polemical media presence. In fact the reception of this film may be described as a small media event or phenomenon. Meaghan Morris describes the notion of "media event" in the following way, with reference to *Crocodile Dundee:*

> By phenomenon I mean what the advertising industry means: an *event;*
> a complex interaction between commerce and "soul"; or, to speak more
> correctly, between film text, the institution of cinema and the unpre-
> dictable crowd-actions that endow mass-cultural events with their
> moments of legitimacy, and so modify mass-culture.[2]

This description is useful to me because I want to talk about the function of criticism, or how criticism functioned in this film's contribution to the creation of a media event. Also, I want to be able to sustain a sense of the unpredictability, relative autonomy, and reciprocity implied in Morris's definition of reception in discussing *The Good Woman of Bangkok*. In this analytic process I do not, however, have an anonymous crowd in mind so much as the figure of the critic, including myself (of course) and also the crowd of critics who publicly struggled with this film and its director and the considerable subsequent conversation that picked up and elaborated the media fallout in some unpredictable ways.

Everything I write about this film is related to the destabilizing effects of its public reception. In fact my very desire to see it was kindled by the way it was talked about—attacked, praised, and so forth—in the Australian mass media. I had put this film into the category of "worthy but boring Aussie documentary" and avoided seeing it until I was invited—in fact, coaxed—to talk about it on radio with the director. My views were solicited because I am not only a film academic but also an Asian woman. How does a critic chart her passage through the maelstrom of responses to this film? There is also an ethical question—how shall this Asian woman critic speak about a film about an Asian woman prostitute? Will Aoi, the sex worker, simply be a silent muse presiding over my ability to speak about her? These questions are prompted by the peculiar historical relationship of prostitute to cinema. I am reminded of the early-twentieth-century male intellectuals who, in writing about the cinema in the days of silent film, were torn between their fascination with the prostitute in the audience and the spectacle on the screen and perceived these two commodities with some suspicion, but yet were able to write discourses of knowledge constructed by these forms of commercial pleasure.[3] Clearly, I want to be careful not to make Aoi my silent muse.

Genre and Reception

Dennis O'Rourke designates the genre of his film as "documentary fiction," which enables him to self-consciously and quite overtly transform that which he documents. He thus places himself within the "truth of cinema," which fictionalizes the real (like Lumière's ghost train arriving at a station we don't see, because we are in its place, so to speak). The fictional genre that O'Rourke creates can be further specified as part ethnography, part psychodrama—a strange dialogue between film director and actor, who are also client and prostitute.

Adrian Martin calls it a diary film or "personal cinema," filmmaking as therapy.[4] I am interested in how these formal and generic determinations of the film (which have been outlined in detail by Martin) may be interrupted or complicated by other factors; in how generic elements seem to mutate in the heterogeneous and unpredictable field of reception, under very specific pressures. So while I am certainly concerned with formal aspects of the film, I am equally interested in how and why these constraints do not solely determine how one might read this film.

Feminist responses to the film have been extremely diverse and polemical (and here I wish to identify myself as a feminist critic). The most extreme feminist view is determined by a knee-jerk response, which is at its base the old "cultural imperialism" thesis, on the grounds of the very nature of the project itself—a white, first-world filmmaker using a third-world sex worker in order to make a film. The project becomes a perfect model of national, racial, cultural, sexual, and linguistic exploitation. This view fails to read the structure of the film and consider how it works, and condemns it on the basis of a priori beliefs. It is similar to Laura Mulvey's reading of *Vertigo* in "Visual Pleasure and Narrative Cinema."[5] She uses the film to prove her thesis of male oppression of women via the controlling patriarchal gaze and fails to see that the film is about male subjectivity not in control so much as in extremis. Jimmy Stewart's Scotty is subject to vertigo: he swoons, he falls, without Madeline he is nothing. Like Scotty, O'Rourke seeks an image in order to reconstitute his sexual identity, shattered in the breakup of his marriage. To find in *The Good Woman of Bangkok* a textbook confirmation of a cultural-imperialist, postcolonial dynamic, as Jeannie Martin does,[6] is problematic because the critical assumptions here are so solidly in place that no film can ever shift them. This view does not test the film to see if it in any way departs from an imperializing mode—and to do this one has to read the film's enunciatory strategies. One of the major omissions of this approach is the erasure of Aoi's aunt from any discussion of the film. The figure of her aunt initiates Aoi's story and introduces her to us. She is a village woman who abstains from any moralistic condemnation of Aoi for the choices she has made. Structurally she is central to the film. Some of the most complex conversations in the film are between Aoi and her aunt. Here, for instance, they are discussing the filmmaker, O'Rourke.

> Aunt: Who is he?
> Aoi: He wants to make a film about me . . . (laughter)
> Aunt: You like him, don't you?
> Aoi: I don't know, we fight a lot, but I go along with him and don't quite know why.
> Aunt: He is not making those nude pictures?
> Aoi: No.

The analytic sophistication Aoi shows in her ability to speak her ambivalent response to her strange client has been sadly lacking in the fundamentalist feminist response, which attacked the film from high moral ground. This feminist superego discourse lacks an awareness of the unconscious and preconscious workings of desire. But the worst charge that can be made against this discourse is that it misogynistically attributes a simple passive state of victimhood to Aoi, who, on the contrary, speaks so well of the problematic of agency under the sway of desire. Feminist fundamentalism has referred to Aoi's expression of hatred of men as "words he has got her to speak."[7] To say that O'Rourke has put words in Aoi's mouth is to fail to hear how Aoi's mode of being/performing in the film is one of extended conversation, and the desire (often contradictory) that arises there is a result of a certain exchange. I will return to this performative aspect of the film in the final section of this chapter.

Another critical response to the film is encapsulated in Martin's statement that

> O'Rourke's justification of the film comes in several guises: that it is a provocation to Australian documentary cinema; that it is a daring self-revelatory project putting his own masculinity on the line (since the very idea was to let himself fall in love with Aoi, his "subject"); and that it is a work of art, in a specific artistic tradition. Clearly, *The Good Woman of Bangkok* is a film that deserves a lot more than a knee-jerk "lefty" dismissal. What it demands, on all its levels, is a *thoroughgoing, properly critical dismissal.*[8]

Although Martin has done a detailed formal analysis of the film, which differentiates his work from the fundamentalist feminist discourse, he comes to the same conclusion. While a feminist fundamentalism is unacceptable to me as a politics and a method, Martin's position poses a dilemma because I do agree with almost everything he says about the film in formal terms. But I differ from him in not being able to dismiss it, nor do I think it a reactionary film as he does. I myself publicly described the film as largely a bland, functional documentary without any visual fascination in its camera work and said that it is interesting despite O'Rourke's intentions, precisely because of Aoi and what she says and how she says it.[9] It is how she holds my interest (which cannot now be separated from how O'Rourke has presented her) and the interest that the film has caused that makes it impossible for me to dismiss it, despite its being, for the most part, formally dull. I therefore want to "judge the film without criteria, judge it without the underpinning of a general model" or a tradition of "exciting personal direct cinema." I want to make "discrete evaluations of particular relations of force with only opinion as guide."[10]

Martha Ansara opposes both of these critical views in her unconditional praise of the film on both aesthetic and ethical grounds. Ansara says that *The Good Woman of Bangkok* "is a challenge to the present state of documentary filmmaking. Its exploratory and subjective treatment of third world prostitution contrasts vividly with the moralizing thesis-driven approach of so many of today's social documentaries." She analyses the continuity in O'Rourke's work, which she characterizes as based on a "critique of imperialism and development in the Pacific," and she is able to show how *The Good Woman of Bangkok* is not an aberration but an exacerbation of the dynamics present in his previous work, such as *Half Life* and *Cannibal Tours* (the former is about the impact of atomic testing in the Marshall Islands; the latter, about German tourism in Papua New Guinea). Ansara concludes her review article with the following remark: "[W]hile I am hardly overjoyed that Dennis O'Rourke shares so many of the characteristics which make men difficult to live with, it gives me hope that at least one of them can produce a film on such a subject so thoughtfully and so beautifully realised."[11]

I disagree with Ansara's favorable assessment of the film on at least three counts. One has to do with the fearful symmetry created by the use of an operatic aria that is repeated three times in the film (at the beginning, middle, and end). The operatic effect that this creates saturates the image and creates a fatal scenario associated with opera and the undoing of women. "The film's frightful artistic coherence,"[12] as Adrian Martin calls it, is also seen in the neat fit between the film's structure and Aoi's own sense of karma, fatedness. The second point, related to this, is the "rescue fantasy" that drives O'Rourke's filmic practice, not unlike D. W. Griffith's rescue fantasies.[13] The logic of O'Rourke's fantasy requires a certain kind of woman. There is no way that the raunchy, gutsy prostitute of Mira Nair's film *India Cabaret* could be rescued by any man. It is only the "good woman" who can be rescued. However, like the "friendless one" in Griffith's *Intolerance,* Aoi refuses the role of the helpless victim. The third point is the facile city/country opposition that the film establishes, in a very naive manner (both semantically and filmically). The film is unable to show why Aoi might not want to go back to a Thai Buddhist village, even if she were given a rice farm for subsistence. This inability is related to a lack of a complex understanding of the nexus "women-tradition-modernity" that mutates in the modern Asian city. If O'Rourke knew how to cut, say, from a peaceful country scene (of a tree, a road, a pair of bulls, a paddy field) not to the heavy traffic of Bangkok but to two prostitutes talking over a meal after work, one could perhaps see how, for the modern Asian woman, the terrible price of independence cannot be measured on a simple binary schema of city versus country.

The final critical view I want to cite is what Sylvia Lawson calls the reduction of the work "to the filmmaker's biography."[14] According to her, the media usually took *The Good Woman of Bangkok* up in this way. The problem with this reduction, she says, is that the authorial discourse was considered the only important context of the film.

Several media performances by Dennis O'Rourke as auteur are worth discussing:

1. On radio Andrew Olle asked O'Rourke, "If you loved Aoi, why didn't you marry her?" O'Rourke answered that question by turning it on the interviewer, saying, "Have you married every woman you have been in love with?" Olle expressed concern at O'Rourke's confession that he had had sex with Aoi without a condom, and O'Rourke responded by saying that he wanted to subject himself to the same kind of risk as Aoi. Thus an accusation of irresponsibility toward public health was displaced by O'Rourke, who recoded the gesture as a democratic one of equalizing risk: a kind of lucidly mad act.[15]

2. In answer to a TV interviewer (a woman) who sternly asked him, "Why didn't you make a film about prostitution in Australia, say King's Cross?" O'Rourke replied, "Is there anything wrong in going to Thailand to make a film with a prostitute?" This answer links up with O'Rourke's previous work, all of which was made in the Pacific region. The empathy for, and fascination with, another culture central to O'Rourke's work was never mentioned.[16]

3. To Philip Adams's question "What do you think of prostitution?" O'Rourke answered, "I am not a specialist on it, I don't know much about it. I know Aoi and myself but I am no longer the same person who made the film."[17]

As these selective examples of the author's media construction show, O'Rourke has been able to play the media game rather well. He is presented as a figure of impropriety for having crossed certain borders, but this just makes him fascinating media material. This irreducible personal motivation, the obsessive desire of this middle-aged Australian man produced, for this middle-aged Asian critic, irresistible viewing and listening. His assertion of an intense individualism alive to its cultural contexts marked a small shift in a myth of Australian masculinity which hardly ever embraces dangerous, passionate, sexual love of the "unto death" variety. In this aspect I, unlike Lawson, had a high degree of tolerance for the O'Rourke "Author as Romantic Lover" phenomenon in the media.

White Clients as Native Informants

In an article titled "Personal Relationships and Sexuality in the Australian Cinema," Meaghan Morris observed the following:

> At the centre of the representation of sexual relationships in Australian cinema is the mark of an impossibility of some kind; in the study of the ways of the tribe personal differences and individual emotion have very little place.[18]

The perceptions of this paper, written in 1979, can be extended to the 1980s as well. Though efforts have been made to go into the mire of sexual and personal relationships, Australian cinema is at best embarrassed by this dimension, which Hollywood cinema, in contrast, thrives on. The award-winning 1991 film *Proof* is further evidence of this phenomenon. Sexuality and personal relationships can be handled only when the narrative is about their awkwardness.

The social and historical reasons for Australian cinema's embarrassment are perhaps located in its segregated colonial past and in the separatism wrought by feminism itself. In this filmic and cultural context O'Rourke's *The Good Woman of Bangkok* is, for me, a significant transformation of one of Australian cinema's myths of masculinity. Here the filmmaker, as a lover with a movie camera, deliberately creates an emotional event with his camera and lives out its terms with the rigor of a martyr. There are no martyrs to love in Australian cinema in the way that there are in, say, Sri Lankan cinema, which is littered with the corpses of those sacrificed to love. In creating a scenario where he is reconstituted as subject—marked by a transition from the "he" of the opening captions to the "I" of the end captions—O'Rourke activates the "you" without which he could not have reconstituted himself as subject. It is this "I-You" relationship, played out filmically across a series of registers both verbal and imagistic, that makes the film emotionally complex, showing a range of feelings, desires, and ambivalent responses, even contradictory ones that cancel each other out.

Within a national cinema context which in general is comfortable with sexuality only when it conforms to norms for social group behavior, *The Good Woman of Bangkok* offers a different kind of investment in sexual love. In the rigidly polarized world of Thai international sex tours the interviewees, all white first-world men (Australian, American, and European), appear to function as native informants. They inform us of the peculiar transnational male imaginary that sustains the sex industry in Thailand. I will only cite one ethnographic example of this phenomenon: the group of young Australian blokes who address the camera collectively. All the other white men function individually or in heterosexual couples, whereas the group of Aussie men, who salute both Mum and Australia in the same breath, are a precise example of conformity to group norms that govern the representation of Australian male sexual behavior on film.

That the most heatedly debated Australian film in recent times is a strange love story (and there are many who say that it is not a love story at all) between an Australian filmmaker and an Asian sex worker must surely mean that the film has touched us, wounded us, upset us, made us hopeful, destabilized our prejudices, etc., etc. *The Good Woman of Bangkok* is a serious attempt (however flawed) to create a personal sexual relationship across a sea of difference. In choosing the widest possible sea, the film is a narration and dramatization of a crossing—which is a continual effort to establish a relation. It shows and tells (and sometimes the showing contradicts the telling, as in the eating scene) that this is a fragile and perilous process. But the generosity (however constrained by a certain lack of imagination) of this Australian film lies in its ability to create a structure in which this perilous relationship can come to pass.

Mirror Conversation

The close-up image of Aoi narrating her story is really an image of an image—it is her mirror image. So Aoi is really talking to the mirror-self that is looking at its own image, i.e., herself. The filmmaker is "out of field." About a third of the film consists of this shot. It is not a stunning shot; it is flat, depthless, and not well defined, because it was video footage reshot on 35 mm film. It is a banal image, and yet it facilitates the very unusual narration of a life story. As well, it presents an image of a man and woman in conversation via the latter's own virtual image. This oblique conversation requires us to listen to what Aoi says—the quality of her speech, its slow rhythm, its long silences. Her tone, pitch, and timbre (unintelligible to non-Thai-speaking listeners) make these sequences very intense, almost Bressonian in effect and affect.

The subjectivity of the filmmaker and that of his object of desire are constituted by the mediation of Aoi's mirror face. This appears to be a mise-en-abîme construction and it is across this abyss that they converse—exchanging a volatile flow of speech, creating a problematic experience of ethnicity and gender in relation.

The images and sounds of this process made the film important for Australia of the early 1990s, as her political, economic, and cultural relationship to Asia was redefined by government policy. More immediately, as Lawson put it, "The film hit the Australian screens at a time when Asian-Australian relationships are high in the headlines; kept there by the Prime Minister." [19] In this kind of force field of desire the mirror image, which may seem nothing more than a boring talking head on TV and video, acquired a strange quality when watched publicly on the big screen. This mirror conversation certainly created a desire, a patience, and an ability to listen, at least among some Australians, and this was no mean achievement.

I want to end by describing a scene in the film and mentioning an anecdote. While O'Rourke was a good media performer, Aoi knew a trick or two herself; call this cunning, a form of knowledge. Aoi certainly had a sense of play, which is evident in her response to O'Rourke when he, as media man, asks that most media of questions, the one that often gets asked after unspeakable catastrophes have occurred. O'Rourke asks Aoi's friend, "How does it feel?" She replies, after a hard day's night, "No good, no good." O'Rourke (the media man here, not the lover) is unhappy with the answer, seeming to want something more—Aoi senses this and prompts her friend playfully, "Tell him sometimes good, sometimes bad," and then she laughs a kind of deliciously ironic laugh. Is it sometimes good because of the tip or because of the sex? We don't know—what we do know is Aoi's capacity, in this moment, to invent an answer to a question that's dumb and numbing. It is this position of playfully expressed knowledge that makes this such a memorable scene in the film, and it is in moments like this that the abject woman of O'Rourke's fantasy eludes that generic determination and shows herself to be an agile improviser with a sophisticated sense of play and humor—which I'd want to call a way of knowing, a making do.

Anecdote

Some twenty years ago a graduate student of drama at New York University, a reasonably articulate Asian woman student in her early twenties, became progressively aphasic—and it is important

for me, and I think not inappropriate to the concerns of a conference on Asian Cinema, that Aoi, my other, has enabled me to
speak here today. And that a sentimental (Aussie) bloke[20]with a
movie camera should have mediated my speech is a source of astonishment to me, because this shifts the representation of Australian masculinity in a small but significant way.

Postscript

I am struck by a particularly American form of cross-cultural
blindness that marks an essay by Karen Shimakawa.[21] The thrust of her
piece is to critique O'Rourke for not having signaled his national identity
unequivocally and for thereby functioning within what she calls an "un-
marked transnational" identity. Without being too pedantic, one might
say that it is a truism that certain cultural knowledges are necessary to read
films and only American cinema can take for granted its status as "universal language," which was Griffith's dream. For a Sri Lankan–Australian
such as myself the fascination of the film was in its effort to put into crisis
the very notion of national identity. The American identity politics that
determine the terms of Shimakawa's essay cannot begin to comprehend
the messy reality this film tries to negotiate, although she gives it good
marks for being properly self-reflexive. Shimakawa's own reflexive identification with Aoi "because we are both *culturally and politically constructed
as Asian women* by texts such as *The Good Woman of Bangkok*"[22] seems to
me to highlight the intellectual and ethical (not to mention aesthetic)
bankruptcy of her critical tools.

The American distribution company First National rejected Raymond
Longford's 1919 *The Sentimental Bloke* because it was marked by a "national ugliness." This was a reference to lead actor Arthur Tauchert, who
by American standards was thought to be "ugly." The standardized norms
set by Hollywood, or in this instance the American academic circuits, are
not interested in the micro-work that goes into the formation of cultural
work elsewhere. Raymond Longford chose Tauchert to play the bloke because he had the right appearance to transform "conventional narrative
types."[23]

When I was writing this essay at my sister's house in New Bedford, Mas-
sachusetts, in the summer of 1992, somewhere around three o'clock in
the mornin' (as they say in the blues), I caught a glimpse of a syndicated
news item on television that, as chance would have it, reported on Dennis

O'Rourke's film, then screening across the country. The commentator presented it as O'Rourke's *Pretty Woman* and of course didn't say where he came from. I was delighted that for once I was writing about a topical film. There is no common basis for comparing the intellectual capital one gains from such work to what Aoi earns from her international clients.

3   Postcolonial Gothic:
The Narcissistic Wound of
Jane Campion's *The Piano*

The primary meaning of the gothic romance, then, lies in its substitution of terror for love. . . . [It is] dedicated to producing nausea, to transcending the limits of taste and endurance, crimes to satisfy the hunger for "too-much" on which he [the author] trades.

—Leslie Fiedler[1]

Masterpiece Theater effect with Australasian twist, compounded by Visionary Art-House Maverick Factor.

—WHO[2]

On viewing *The Piano* I saw that it was no mere stately European art film, despite what its Cannes award had led me to suspect. Certainly its distribution and exhibition strategies, especially in America, and the Anglophone rhetoric on the film are those of art cinema; these have worked very well for it as a commodity, but not so well when one wants to think about the film in some detail.[3] So I have had to ask, what is the genre of *The Piano*? Something Holly Hunter, the actress playing Ada, said about the script of the film gives a nice clue, though of course there is plenty of evidence in the film's mise en scène and narration that it is a romantic Gothic melodrama. Hunter said that the script had "one ingredient that almost every script I read does not have: a vast dimension of things unexplained to the audience or even to the characters themselves—and that's just a real haunting part of the story, very, very haunting."[4] Also, the film's cinematographer, Stuart Dryburgh, said that the term "Gothic" was very much a part of its brief.[5]

One of the main features of the Gothic as a genre can be grasped through the distinction made between it and the genre of melodrama by Peter Brooks in his book *The Melodramatic Imagination*:

Melodrama tends to diverge from the Gothic in its optimism, its claim that the moral imagination can open up the angelic sphere as well as the demonic depths and can allay the threat of moral chaos.[6]

MaryBeth Inverso, in her book *The Gothic Impulse in Contemporary Drama*, elaborates on Brooks's distinction:

> While the Gothic tends to raise demons it can neither control nor exorcise, the melodrama, choosing the mode of fantasy and wish fulfillment, conjures demons, only to quash them with a thunderbolt from a morally operative heaven. Both modes evoke chaos, but only the melodrama achieves resolution. The Gothic tumbles us into a dizzying vortex; the melodrama grants us a quick, safe glimpse of the downward spiral while keeping us firmly anchored to the path of righteousness. In essence "Gothic melodrama" allows us to have our elixir and drink it too. Moreover, restabilization in melodrama is neither forced nor tacked on; it is implicit from the outset. Brooks' analysis enables us to see that the Gothic as a sensibility is capable of taking up residence in virtually any genre.[7]

The Piano, though a Gothic film, is inflected by a melodramatic impulse. I will explore this entanglement of two related and yet incompatible generic modes in terms of what they enable Campion to do. Thinking through the specific problems of genre will enable me to examine how narration, mise en scène, and gendered subjectivity are informed by generic imperatives.

I want to look at how different people (including Campion herself) have written and talked about this film so as to find out what it is in *The Piano* that strikes a chord for young women[8] and how this resonance is created through a cinematic rhetoric charged by a "Gothic will to form."[9] In using some of Campion's statements about the film and how the project was generated I am not simply bowing to the supremacy of authorial statements of intention, wishing to see them confirmed in the finished product. Rather, I am using these statements as points of entry and departure for my own reading. The fact of female authorship is also not without interest, given how few women (even today, at the end of this century of cinema) make big films that are both critically acclaimed and marketable, capturing the popular imagination.[10] In answering a question about the elaboration of late-twentieth-century affects in the guise of a nineteenth-century drama in her film, Campion says,

It's absolutely essential . . . to try to create new insights for people today when we see others in a situation set in the 1850s.[11]

I feel a kinship between the kind of romance that Emily Bronte portrays in *Wuthering Heights* and this film. Hers is not the notion of romance we've come to use; it's very harsh and extreme, a *gothic exploration of romantic impulse*. I wanted to respond to these ideas in my own century.[12]

While these comments have been quoted many times and a 1993 *Sight and Sound* piece even calls the film Gothic,[13] none of the articles I have read pursues the implications of such a designation at a formal and thematic level.[14] This may be because the Gothic in cinema is largely associated with the horror genre popularized by Hollywood and not with art cinema. And yet in their book *The Screening of Australia: Anatomy of a National Cinema* Susan Dermody and Elizabeth Jacka have identified in a small group of films something that they call an "Australian gothic," which they see as "a genuinely local aesthetic tendency, and one that has had some vitalising effects on the industry."[15] In discussing the Australian Gothic films, they refer to the elements of the fantastic evident in Jane Campion's early work, up to 1988. In her first feature film, *Sweetie* (1989), she confidently works with a Gothic mise en scène in a manner that gives her a place in the Australian suburban Gothic tradition of, say, the work of Jim Sharman and early Peter Weir. The terms within which Campion sets the Gothic melodrama of *The Piano* enable her to widen the scope of the Australian Gothic and express late-twentieth-century affects.

A Gothic performance of female narcissism: what might this be? Campion says,

It's unusual to have a woman exploring her libido without any kind of romantic attachment or sentimental quality, albeit briefly, as it is in this film. . . .

I wanted to tell a story around an object which would bring all the characters together and which would be the central mechanism from which the story would evolve.[16]

A simultaneous "gothic exploration of romantic impulse" and equally Gothic imperative to "explore her libido without any kind of romantic attachment" offer ample scope for dramatizing both terror in love and the trauma of narcissistic self-reconstitution.

Gothic Object

The piano itself is of course the most affectively charged object in this film, both as plot mechanism and as love object. Here I want to give the word "object" the affective weight psychoanalysis gives to the term. According to Freud, "the object of an instinct (as distinct from its source and aim) is the thing in regard to which or through which the instinct is able to achieve its aim."[17] The object may be a person, an attribute of a person, or a product of fantasy. Ada's piano, even in its concrete materiality, is a product of fantasy. Baines intuits this and finds it irresistible; Stewart is as yet unacquainted with a capacity for fantasy.

Ada's piano playing is described by Aunt Morag in the following way: "She does not play the piano as we do, Nessie . . . no, she is a strange creature, and her playing is strange, like a mood that passes into you. . . . To have a sound creep inside you is not all pleasant." The way in which the piano is performed, both by Ada and by the film's mise en scène, activates visual, tactile, kinesthetic, auditory, and even olfactory memory traces for the characters (the piano tuner smells the sea on it). It is therefore a multi-sensory object, and for Ada a prosthetic extension of her body, so to speak. Many examples of this link between the piano and her body have been noted, but the one I find most memorable is the two-shot of Ada gazing from a high cliff at her abandoned piano lying far below on the beach (seen in extreme long shot). A fragile (out-of-focus) and yet insistent, jagged, febrile, Gothic line created by the fluttering ribbon of her bonnet seems to touch the piano across a vast space, creating a tactile link between her body and the object of desire, enchantment, and longing. The piano, that quintessential European instrument of feminine domestic accomplishment and training, is set adrift in a strange Gothic universe to become an instrument of delirium serviceable to a female subjectivity in extremis. So if one hears something of Schumann's music in Ada's quiet playing, as some do,[18] the complex links between domesticity, intimacy, and madness may also figure, for those able to hear such rich dissonant textures.

Gothic Mise en Scène

The doom-laden apocalyptic Gothic coloration and figuration of land- and seascapes through which the piano passes, or in which it is marooned, animate it as much as does Ada's playing. The organic and the inorganic interpenetrate, obliterating the distinction between the two. This obliteration makes way for "the non-organic life of things"[19] to assert its Gothic energy; these "things" include the piano itself, but also the mud as it acquires a persistent force through its relationship to and counterplay with the human body.

Gothic Costume

If we approach the question of costumes in this film through the Gothic notion of drapery in relation to the human form, especially to the naked face, then we cannot simply say that Ada is oppressed by her Victorian clothes and install a certain feminist[20] or new-age[21] narrative of liberation of the body from constrictive codes of dress. In the Gothic idea of ornament the naturalism of the human face, its actuality, works in counterplay with the non-actuality of the drapery, which is conceived as "super-reality." Worringer describes this dynamic as "an artful chaos of violently agitated lines possessing an independent vitality and expressive power which in this connection are uncanny."[22] In the historical Gothic this counterplay produces a third term, the spiritual. Holly Hunter, playing Ada, has a very clear sense of this counterplay when she says, "The costumes helped me tremendously: the incongruity of having a woman in a really laced-up corset, huge hoop skirts, petticoats, pantaloons, bodice and chemise trying to gracefully maneuver her way through the bush was a real physical manifestation of Ada. There was an obvious physical fragility—and yet strength and stamina, as well as grace, were required to wear those clothes. That was an interesting dichotomy which that period offered me."[23] The performative dimension of costumes in this film clearly moves beyond historical exactitude and verisimilitude, and enables the emergence of a Gothic will.

Gothic Fantasy

The Gothic melodrama permits the piano to be played on two registers, so that while it works simply as an object, a piano, is a piano, it is also The Piano, the irreplaceable object of primary narcissistic investment. Here I shall simply avoid all the intricate psychoanalytic debates about primary and secondary narcissism and whether the former is an objectless state like sleep or intrauterine existence, thus indistinguishable from autoeroticism and absolutely separate from secondary narcissism, thereby making it difficult to move from one to the other.[24] Instead, I want to use primary narcissism to designate an early phase in or formative moments of the acquisition of a body image which is constitutive of the ego. In *The Piano* the image that Ada invests in is not primarily visual but crucially an auditory and tactile one. The amorous captivation of the "subject" in an auditory fantasy might produce a narcissism different from that modeled on the image of the mirror. I am not interested in being true to psychoanalysis as much as I want to see how this film can perform some of its concepts so as to find an exit for a female subjectivity in extremis, an exit which is not that of tragic death. Here too one may mark a difference between the nineteenth-century tradition of the Gothic, say of a *Wuthering Heights*, which reaches an intensity of passion on the other side of death, and the considered refusal of death in *The Piano*, which is part of its generic modernity. How else can one read that lucid, calm, splendid moment in which Ada is suspended under water, her breath bubbling as her will decides to choose life, than as a thoroughly considered refusal of death? For at this moment her father's description of her will (conveyed to us earlier via her phantasmic voice) comes perilously close to being realized: "My father says it is a dark talent and the day I take it into my head to stop breathing will be my last." The refusal of tragic death, which goes against a generic norm, makes this film a contemporary parable for women in a way not unlike that of *Silence of the Lambs*, with which it shares some family (Gothic) resemblance. In both, happiness and knowledge are wrested through a negotiation of Gothic terror.[25]

Campion is right; there aren't that many films exploring female narcissism and its mechanisms in multiple registers, where there is a veritable performance of it. Ada plays primarily for herself. She will play for another only under terrible duress. Hence I am not at all thinking of *narcissistic performance* but rather of *a performance of narcissism*, which is the same as a will to invent narcissism. Invent narcissism! Is that possible? The psychoanalytic narrative says that it is necessary for the infant as neophyte to go through certain immutable structures and processes in order to become a fully formed subject. *The Piano* tells us another story about subject formation under duress. I like to think that the film's modernity lies in its capacity to make one believe that narcissism can be invented or reinvented according to rules generated by the film itself. If this is so, then psychoanalytic truth figures here as the traditional heritage against which this film stakes out a psychic modernity for women. The public sphere and corresponding public memory created by feminist interdisciplinary labor and desires of the last three decades is the space-time within which such a project could be conceived and received.

Gothic Voice

At the very beginning of the film a voiceover, which is that of a little girl, tells us that "The voice you hear is not my speaking voice, but my mind's voice. I have not spoken since I was six years old. No one knows why, not even me. . . . The strange thing is I don't think myself silent, that is because of my piano. I shall miss it on my journey." The "interior" narrator,[26] a familiar Gothic device, is perversely used here, in that a woman's mind speaks as a little girl with no explanation at all. A certain sense of curiosity, a mood conducive to a quest or exploration, is thereby aroused by this device which exteriorizes interiority. This interior voiceover also resurfaces at the very end, seemingly to tie up the narration, but instead it takes us underwater to the piano, to which an image of Ada's floating body is attached via the umbilical cord of the rope. This scene ends the film with a verse that casts a Gothic shadow over the light of the previous scene in Ada's new suburban home. This phantasmic voice, of a girl of perhaps six, intimates a traumatic event, a loss, in the lightest of tones, tones reminiscent of Italo Calvino's puzzlingly marvelous description of melancholy as "sadness that has taken on lightness."[27] A question then for the critic is, how is the weight, the gravitational pull of traumatic loss, depression, melancholia, transposed into lightness?

Sadness Transposed: How Might It Sound?

Sadness is the fundamental mood of depression. . . . Sadness leads us into the enigmatic realm of affects—anguish, fear or joy. Irreducible to its verbal or semiological expressions, sadness (like all affect) is the psychic representation of energy displacements caused by external or internal traumas.

On the frontier between animality and symbol formation, moods—and particularly sadness—are the ultimate reactions to our traumas, they are our basic homeostatic recourse. For if it is true that those who are slaves to their moods, beings drowned in their sorrows, reveal a number of psychic or cognitive frailties, it is equally true that a diversification of moods, variety in sadness, refinements in sorrow or mourning are the imprint of a humankind that is surely not triumphant but subtle, ready to fight, and creative.[28]

For Freud, melancholia or negative narcissism, the mood of the black hole of nothingness, asymbolia, is the result of an oral disturbance: in short, a maternal failing. It is what Kristeva, following Freud, calls the "impossible mourning for the maternal object"[29]—impossible because of its inaccessibility to the signifier.

Mourning or Melancholia

What is the Gothic woman Ada's humor? Is she a melancholic? Ada certainly is not the subject of hysteria—the emblematic fate of some beautiful intelligent nineteenth-century women of Freud's case studies—because the hysteric's desire is the desire of the other. Ada, on the contrary, seems to be governed by an imperative foreign to the hysterical subject, for she seems at first to be totally impervious to the desire of the other. While the hysterical woman is at home in melodrama in her own uncanny (unhomely) way, the Gothic woman needs the appropriate mise en scène, a haunted house, a desolate moor, or an "untamed" colonial land, the space of alterity within which to explore her constitutive generic nature, which is a propensity to be haunted by a certain terror of otherness.

I want to think of her for the moment as a melancholy subject because she has been touched by a grave loss. Freud distinguishes mourning from melancholia in that the mourner consciously knows what has been lost, but the melancholy subject grieves at the loss of an object without knowing what it is. According to Freud, "it is an object loss withdrawn from consciousness."[30] This loss of the object is a double loss because of the attendant amnesia. But Ada, unlike the melancholy subject theorized by Freud, seems to know what it is that she has lost, i.e., her voice. And yet it is quite evident that what we perceive as a "loss" is not thought of as one by Ada herself: "I don't think myself silent," says Ada's phantasmic voice, adding "that is because of my piano." But in saying "I have not spoken since I was six years old. No one knows why, not even me" Ada does point to a loss that is truly forgotten, i.e., unconscious, and which is therefore an unspeakable loss of which her "loss of voice" is an index, not a symptom. A hysterical symptom is the somatic sign of the return of the repressed. There are no such symptomatic signs in this film. I want to argue that the indexical sign (a mark of contact) in this film bears witness to an operation of transposition[31] (in the musical sense) and that such an operation ought to be different from that of symptom formation.

The internal work of the melancholic, which Freud says is akin to that of mourning, consumes and depletes the ego. If indeed melancholia drains the narcissistic ego through the work of mourning, which internalizes the lost object, then the melancholic Ada's unassailable narcissistic strength becomes something of a Gothic mystery, and an irresolvable one at that, when looked at from a psychoanalytic point of view. In fact, Ada has all of the mythical enigmatic attributes of the narcissistic woman (self-sufficiency, inaccessibility, self-absorption, indifference), as delineated nostalgically by Freud.[32] I'd like to sustain this psychoanalytic impossibility (i.e., the simultaneous depletion and plenitude of the narcissistic ego) to see how it is made possible and credible in this film. There is no accessible primal trauma or seduction in this film, only fictional anecdotes told by the fanciful Flora, who loves telling stories about her mother's life. Perhaps it is the very displacement of a hermeneutic of a primal trauma that makes a Gothic performance of narcissism possible. A primal trauma and its attendant secrecy would lead to something like a compulsion to repeat, while the notion of "Gothic performance" might enable a performative transposition of the exhausted affect.

Because the work of this film is not the revelation of secrets but rather the transposition of trauma, it is perhaps more useful to think of Ada, the Gothic woman, not so much in the fixity of the designation "melancholy subject" (as I did earlier) but as responding to a "melancholy moment," which is defined movingly by Kristeva as "an actual or imaginary loss of meaning, an actual or imaginary despair, an actual or imaginary razing of symbolic values, including the value of life."[33] Ada's playing of the piano as tactile, aural object that constitutes her narcissistic bodily imago bears the trace of melancholy loss of the oral object. We are informed that her silence and her piano playing both began when she was about the age of six. Not only were the two acts (silence and playing) simultaneous, they also correspond in a mimetic way. This is why Ada's voice says, "I don't think myself silent, that is because of my piano." The senses that are normally separated and hierarchized in western culture are here made to interpenetrate and cooperate to transpose unbearable loss. So Ada's piano playing is at least several things at once, a work of mourning for an unspeakable loss—a wounded narcissism—through which a sublimation, or better still a transposition, of grief into a register of music, i.e., rhythm, melody, tonality, is effected. The pathological compulsion to repeat, which is said to be characteristic of mourning,[34] returns transposed as repetitive, minutely varied rhythms, each time enriched by the semiotic elements of the medium. The inability to concatenate said to be characteristic of melancholia[35] returns as endless concatenation (for one feels that the music Ada plays can go on and on; it does not conclude, it just stops). In this way loss is eroticized—temporalized in a non-climactic, non-cathartic, interminable music—and thereby made light. This playing is not narcisistically self-expressive, in the sense of the self-indulgent display usually associated with the term narcissism (in the banal sense), but is, rather, self-constitutive; out of the nothingness of melancholia a narcissistic oral/tactile/aural imago is created through the mediation of the piano.

Ridley Scott's *Thelma and Louise* (1990) is another recent film which refers to an unspeakable trauma suffered by a female subject.[36] Harvey Keitel (Baines in *The Piano*) plays the sympathetic detective, Slocumb, who is privy to the unspeakable thing that happened to Louise in Texas. Here the trauma is known discursively in a legal sense, though Louise cannot speak it, whereas in *The Piano* the trauma is unknowable, unpresentable. What is remarkable in *The Piano* is the refusal to pathologize the trauma or loss. This is why there are no symptoms to be deciphered here. The choice of Keitel to journey in this difficult and somewhat treacherous psychic terrain is full of a fascination which I will discuss in the final section of this essay.

When Baines takes Ada to her piano on the beach, she immediately starts playing it while Flora does cartwheels, and Baines walks around the piano registering with growing curiosity Ada's complete and absolute absorption in her playing; the camera encircles them all as though mimetically captivated by the multiple movements of bodies generated by the sound. Flora distracts her mother's attention and Ada willingly yields to her twice. Then with no transition at all two pairs of hands are shown in close-up, playing a duet. This is but one of many scenes of the "narcissistic rapture" shared by the mother and daughter, here very moving for its formality and restraint. The narcissistic dynamic between mother and daughter is mediated by the temporality of their playing. The film sets up a complex circuit linking the mother, the daughter, and the piano, for it is Flora who translates her mother's gestural signs into audible speech. The mother's abandoned voice has been replaced by the piano. While the daughter gives voice to the mother, the mother has taken on the voice of a little girl so as to be able to speak to herself. Thus the figure of the little girl is made serviceable to a maternal imaginary, which is not a common move in our popular culture. At a more immediate level the mother and daughter are also identified via their clothing. What is notable is that while in image they are immediately identified as doubles, on the aural register they do not echo each other: there is an asymmetry which enables each to fulfil different tasks in relation to the other. This slight dissymmetry (as I prefer to call it) is a crucial aspect of the film's performance of narcissism in a Gothic register. These doubles do not therefore haunt or kill the other: an unusual move, generically speaking.[37]

Gothic Action

The scenario of the maternal melodrama of love and betrayal of the mother by the daughter is deflected, however, because of the Gothic dimension. For it is Ada herself who first mutilates the piano, by removing a key from it to send to Baines as token of her love for him. And as though the key alone (so rich in exchange value and affect by now) were not sufficient, she also writes a sentence on it, seemingly duplicating the first gesture. These moves of the Gothic heroine are intriguing, intricate, precise operations, while still retaining a certain Gothic mystery. So it is imperative not to succumb to a commonsense explanation, for to do so would be to destroy the fascinating density of the Gothic action.[38]

If the piano has been figured as an object of primary narcissistic investment, as I have argued, then the removal of a key and the inscription of a sentence on it modifies the structure peculiar to that narcissism, which is its imperviousness to the other. The removal of the key wrecks the concatenation of music necessary for the integrity of Ada's selfhood, constructed under the duress of Gothic terror. It is as though she says, "It is necessary. I am it," transposing what Cathy says of her relationship to Heathcliff in *Wuthering Heights:* "my love for Heathcliff . . . [is] . . . necessary. . . . I *am* Heathcliff."[39] And yet, despite this knowledge, this Gothic act makes clear that Ada wants to drastically change her relationship to "it." In writing a full sentence, with an awkward mix of formality and erotic intimacy—"Dear George, You have my heart. Ada McGrath"—she decides to enter linguistic concatenation, with its clear separation between an "I" and a "you," so as to acknowledge that the "I" has erotically surrendered to the "you." She is learning how to signify loss without getting lost. Until this letter Ada's writing has been purely instrumental, functional, orders or exclamations. In the love letter she marks her loss in an unfamiliar code, hence its awkwardness. The shattering of the musical concatenation marks her decisive entry into heterosexual and linguistic concatenation, i.e., intersubjectivity. Through this ambiguous yet affirmative Gothic act Ada transforms herself from the (impenetrable, awesome) Gothic woman into one who is ready to take on the precarious dynamic of intersubjectivity.

Flora, the winged messenger of Gothic destiny (no longer the daughter), facilitates the metonymic exchange of objects of desire and terror, the piano key, the sentence, and the index finger, by carrying the appropriate signs to Stewart and Baines. Stewart, the patriarchal, Victorian, colonial man, knows only one kind of exchange, that of buttons, labor, guns, a piano, blankets, land: he can only read the writing causally, literally, and univocally as "betrayal"; he does not see the non-sensuous similarity or correspondence between the key and Ada's finger. In contrast, Baines can read correspondences among language, objects, and bodies, incommensurables all. Some such faith in Baines's capacity is perceptible in Ada's Gothic act of renouncing her impregnability. Such a perception entails a form of reasoning not alien to the mimetic faculty.[40] But more of that later.

Ada inscribes her message to Baines on the severed key and sends it to him via her daughter, knowing full well that though he cannot read the words (as he is illiterate) he is man enough "to read what was never written."[41] To read the unwritten, according to Walter Benjamin, is to see correspondences, similarities, or affinities between incommensurables. What Baines receives is her severed finger because for Ada the key corresponds to her finger; it is similar.[42] It shows in an almost unbearable way how her narcissistic imago was formed out of a tactile auditory labor, touch emitting sound. It shows how orality, tactility, and the aural are mimetically mobilized to form a delicate web of sound in the very place of loss. Baines can intuit this because he is "Harvey Keitel." More of this, also, later.

Gothic Stigmata

We can see all this and also note that, as it is Ada's index finger which bears the Gothic stigmata, it is rich in signifying possibilities. After all, it is the index finger that demarcates proximity and distance, nearness and separation; it is the pointer par excellence. So, at the moment of blasting open the continuum of her narcissistic impenetrability, the Gothic woman's body signifies in flesh and blood the cost of signification. Looked at in this way, Stewart's mutilation of Ada's hand is a literalization (a bringing into signification) of the narcissistic wound of melancholy, as well as of the libidinal cost of intersubjective erotics. The psychic wound is now presentable and open to the theatrics of fetishistic displacement, and the melancholy moment has been transposed not only on the piano but also on the body. In the register of the melodrama Stewart's is a villainous act, but in the register of the Gothic he is the helper of the Gothic woman who seeks an exit from her impenetrable narcissistic entrapment. That such an exit should be full of terror is a law of the Gothic genre. What is admirable and exemplary about the Gothic woman touched by a melancholy moment is that she is not evasive. She reaches the limits of terror, encountering Gothic sublimity through a certain curiosity, a certain will to knowledge. How else to describe the shot of Ada's foot being placed in the coil of rope even as it uncoils to take her and the piano into the depths of the deep blue sea?[43]

Gothic Sublime

While it seems a truism that the sublime is a masculine genre,[44] the Gothic sublime (a popular-culture spin-off of the magisterial eighteenth-century sublime) is functional for women. In Gothic fiction the relations of heterosexual power play and erotics warrant, necessitate, the evocation of the sublime as terror in love. Soon after Baines and Ada make love he trembles because he does not know where he stands with his dark, silent lover, so he speaks in clichés usually reserved for women in romantic narratives: "I don't know what you are thinking; do you love me?"[45] As he says this there is a quick close-up of Ada's urgent glance at herself in the mirror, and it is this mirror image that we see registering a moment of terror of the loss of the self. The montage of the ambivalence of the "you" and "me," when linked (as though over an almost imperceptible abyss) with the mirror image of Ada looking at herself, condenses in an instant the predicament of loss from which the Gothic woman protects herself. The repetition of Ada's gazing at herself in mirrors also marks this gesture as a moment of terror rather than of narcissism in the banal sense.

As Ada hurriedly gets ready to leave, Baines says something that always makes me laugh quietly. He says, "Now you are leaving and I'll be so miserable." Perhaps I laugh with pleasure because Baines's tender vulnerability makes him "beautiful," while Ada's dark, mysteriously intransigent silence is full of terror, thus inverting Edmund Burke's implied gendering of the concepts of the beautiful and the sublime.[46] In Burke's model of the sublime there is an implication that it is man who is sublime, capable of experiencing terror and the limits of reason, while woman is simply beautiful. The Gothic romance of *The Piano* does in fact set the scene for a sublime encounter between the sexes. In his book *Dickinson Sublime,* Gary Lee Stonum maps out the different moments of this encounter.[47] Joan Kirkby has pointed out the intimate links between Dickinson's poems and *The Piano:* the "two haunting piano solos which make up half of the soundtrack . . . have as their titles ("Big My Secret" and "The Heart Asks Pleasure First") lines from Emily Dickinson's poems."[48] Campion has quoted Dickinson in talking about *The Piano,* so there is something fitting about being able to bring the two together and discuss the structure of sublimity operative in their work.[49] According to Stonum, a sublime encounter of the Romantic variety always proceeds according to a three-phase sequence: 1. a normative phase, which is prior to the apprehension of alterity; 2. a traumatic phase of disintegration with the apprehension of an object, the intensity of which reduces the world to a dyadic relation of subject and alterity; 3. the final triumphal reactive or sublimatory moment of integration of the shattered ego.[50] The Gothic sublime seems to undermine the predictability of this threefold movement, which is often thought of as an Oedipal drama. In so doing the Gothic sublime enables the Gothic woman to negotiate terror without succumbing to it. I will demonstrate these assertions later, when I analyze the structure of the second attempted rape of Ada by her husband Stewart. Whether *The Piano* achieves something in simply reversing the gendering that is implied in the Burkean and Romantic sublime will also be dealt with later. Ada's wound and the severed key, both indexical signs of loss now open to the richness of excessive signification on the very site of loss, are not triumphal assertions of the mind's supremacy over the body (which is important to Burke's notion of the sublime as well as the Romantic sublime) but rather the determined undoing of that opposition through the intransigent embodied will of the Gothic woman. As Ada's Gothic encounter with death demonstrates, this undoing of the mind's supremacy over the body is achieved by eroticizing the terror itself through a voluptuous surrender to it. It is this performative relationship to terror that distinguishes the Gothic woman.

Gothic Will

The piano has enabled the melancholic female subject to carry out her work of mourning and transcend its gravitational pull. Toward the end of the film's dramatization of the dizzying twists and turns of narcissism's work of mourning and melancholia, Ada orders her piano to be thrown overboard. A Maori man concurs with, "Yeah she's right, . . . push the coffin in the water, let the sea bury it." This makes literal sense, of course, because its weight may unbalance the canoe. In addition to this, on the psychic level the work of the piano as the libidinally invested object of primary narcissism seems over and done with. But the Gothic link between the piano and Ada drags her into the depths of the sea. Is this Gothic poetic justice? Her generic punishment for wishing a happy ending? But instead of subsiding in a watery grave Ada decides to resurface and starts a new life. Is this the melodramatic resolution to the Gothic terror of the film? Does the Gothic woman thereby become the merely beautiful woman of melodrama, the potential hysteric? Instead of a polarized reading, could the last sequences be read as a negotiation between the Gothic and the melodramatic imperatives, i.e., an effort to make the will to knowledge (knowledge of the self, in the sense of its very formation) and happiness coexist? A negotiation, yes, but not a negotiated settlement, because Ada's quite considerable flaunting of her grotesque, hence Gothic, prosthetic finger as fetish,[51] as the emblem of her loss, her relishing of her consequent status as the town freak, and her attempt to enter spoken language on her own terms as primarily phonic, almost tactile, are not all.

At night she returns to (the memory of) the piano (now ruined), relinking herself to it to form a body image, a mnemonic trace. When the ending is read as a genre problem, the debates about whether it is a commercial cop-out happy ending or a proper feminist negation of high-romantic, passionate death as an anachronism may be displaced. These last sequences bring into high relief the uneasy marriage between the Gothic and the melodramatic impulses. Yet it is this very productive difficulty that enables Ada to have her daughter, her man, a piano, and the fetish. I feel this rather odd constellation[52] to be very late-twentieth-century. Certainly there are no echoes here of the impassioned archaic cry, "I am Heathcliff."[53] If indeed "the gothic felt for the first time the *pastness* of the past; . . . and tried to give . . . the sense of something lapsed or outlived or irremediably changed," as Leslie Fiedler claims,[54] then the abyss between the passionate Gothic intensity of *Wuthering Heights* and that of *The Piano* is temporal, not spatial. This is a temporality made possible by feminism.[55]

At the beginning of this chapter I said that it is the terms within which Ada's narcissistic drama and trauma are performed in a Gothic-melodramatic register that enable this nineteenth-century costume drama to express contemporary affect. In the following section I shall examine those enabling terms.

"Two-Way Street"

Campion has said, about one of the main impulses that led to the film,

> I had become intrigued over the years with the photographic section of the Turnbull Library in New Zealand which documents, from the earliest days of photography, the ways in which New Zealand became colonised. I was particularly taken by how the Maori people adapted to European clothes, in combination with their own dress, which became such a graphic metaphor for their understanding of Europeanism— and vice versa, in a way. There they were sitting in these photographs with great dignity, with such a fierce look at the camera. This sense of themselves was so powerful that it transcended anything that might seem ridiculous with the misappropriation of clothes.[56]

Mimetic Capital

Here Campion is registering what anthropology calls "first contact," or the colonial encounter. In her own film, however, she goes a step beyond and works within the moment of what Michael Taussig in his book *Mimesis and Alterity: A Particular History of the Senses* calls "second contact," which is in a sense the postcolonial moment already residing in the colonial moment. Taussig uses the term "second contact" to describe the process that occurs when the mythical one-way street of first contact gives way to the "two-way street" of mutual othering via a performative mimesis. This is the time of the metamorphosis of identity, both sexual and ethnic.[57]

Taussig's reading of Walter Benjamin's idea of mimesis (the Greek word for imitation) in relation to the colonial moment makes it useable in thinking *The Piano*. Benjamin, in his essay "On the Mimetic Faculty," defines mimesis as the "compulsion . . . to become and behave like something else."

> Nature creates similarities. One need only think of mimicry. The highest capacity for producing similarities, however, is man's. His gift of seeing resemblances is nothing other than a rudiment of the powerful compulsion in former times to become and behave like something

else. Perhaps there is none of his higher functions in which his mimetic faculty does not play a decisive role.[58]

There is a veritable flurry of mimetic behavior in the form of mimicry to be found in *The Piano,* such as the Maori men's mimicry of Stewart, the numerous acts of mimicry performed by Flora, Stewart's botched effort to mimic the love scene he has spied on (which turns into the attempted first rape), and so on.[59] Mimesis in the sense of mimicry may be seen as an effort to master, in a variety of performative modes, that which is other or different; it may be seen as rehearsal of mimetic apprehension of the other. So, following Taussig, it is possible to see forms of mimetic apprehension or cognition at work in the film:

> Benjamin's fascination with mimesis flows from the confluence of three considerations; alterity, primitivism and the resurgence of mimesis with modernity. . . .
> This resurgence is connected both to colonialism and to the invention of technologies of mass reproduction which have the capacity to activate mimetic modes of perception in which spontaneity, animation of objects, and a language of the body combining thought with action, sensuousness with intellection, is paramount.[60]

Taussig refers to a notion of mimesis as two-layered: "a copying or imitation, and a palpable sensuous connection between the very body of the perceiver and the perceived" (21). He calls it a "a sensuous knowing, a sensuous Othering" (68) and "a bodily involvement of the perceiver in the image" (21). Taussig also refers to Horkheimer and Adorno's concepts of "mimetic repression" and "organised control of mimesis" within fascism (68), concepts I would also like to use later in relation to *The Piano.* The reinvention of the idea of mimesis by the Frankfurt school theorists as a problematic of difference (otherness) and not of identity (sameness) implies that they are working against the Platonic notion of mimesis, which gives it no real epistemological status at all.[61] But, as many have noted, Plato did have an inkling of the terror of mimesis, which is why he would honor Homer but ask him to leave his Republic.

The colonial moment that releases a surplus of mimetic sensitivity for the white colonizers via the "primitivized" body of the colonized is not simply the background against which the main conflicts are dramatized in this film. As I shall argue, the colonial moment, understood as a "two-way street" of mimetic doubling, is absolutely integral to the negotiations of the main conflicts. It is also important to note that mimetic doubling is not a mirroring of the same, so that it is not about imitation and representation as it is in the mimetophobic Platonic tradition of theorizing mimesis. Rather, it is a way of understanding a crucial transformative moment in the encounter between subject and object. What defines this relationship is a tension between a sustaining and an opening-up, so that it is not a complete obliteration of identity but rather a moment when the secret of identity as constituted by difference is disclosed, not as revelation but as a perilous process.[62] This is what happens in the postcolonial moment of "second contact," and in placing her Gothic romance in such a space-time Campion is able to redefine the Gothic by widening its terms to include the ethnic other.

Mimetic Enchantment

The scene of the theatrical performance of the Gothic tale of "Bluebeard's Five Wives" within *The Piano* is the only one that shows the colonial community as a whole, both Europeans and natives, men, women, and children. So it is fitting that this scene is used to stage the mythical moment of first contact. It occurs when Bluebeard's fifth wife is to be decapitated for her act of curiosity in uncovering the severed heads of his four previous wives. The dramatic moment of decapitation is interrupted, as is the whole show, by a Maori man who rushes onto the stage to save the victim. This scene has been read by some as a bit corny or as racist, because the colonized man is shown to be unable to tell the difference between reality and image, original and copy.

I wish to displace this reading by transposing the primal scene of anthropological first contact onto the history of cinema itself and thereby examining what it achieves there. In the cinematic field, first contact is taken as the moment of contact between man and the image-making audiovisual machines of modernity. Campion is one among several distinguished directors who have created this moment of first contact as emblematic of the loss of a certain mode of spectatorship. Michael Taussig reminds us of a similar scene in Robert Flaherty's film *Nanook of the North* (1933), in which Nanook's mimetic sensitivity is dramatized for our benefit.[63] On hearing recorded sound for the first time, he tries to orally incorporate the very record. Through this scene the modern world gleans a little mimetic capital, which enables us to relive the magical moment of the creation of mimetically capacious engines of mechanical reproduction which by now have become everyday, therefore banal. So Taussig makes the point that the "primitive" is necessary to our modernity as a signal of a certain loss. Similarly, in the Sicilian episode of *Paisan* (1946) Roberto Rossellini shows us the black American soldier viewing a puppet play and jumping onto the stage to rescue the black Moor who is being vanquished by the white knight. *Paisan* too, in a way, is a film about a "first contact" of sorts, between American consumer culture and Italians derogatorily referred to as "peasants" by American soldiers. The soldier, though an American, is black and is therefore presented as a body that has not lost its mimetic faculty. Jean-Luc Godard, in *Les Carabiniers* (1963), reproduces several genres from "primitive" cinema, including the 1895 Lumière one-shot film *Arrival of the Train at the Station,* for Michelangelo, the "primitive" young soldier, to witness as his very first experiences of cinema. He too responds inappropriately—that is, mimetically—by trying to touch the image and jump into it. In all of these instances a body designated as "primitive" performs an encounter with an image (of one kind or another) in a manner which takes the image to be real, alive. The audience of the films and the diegetic audience are presented as more knowing, able to see that this apprehension is erroneous. In citing several films across the history of cinema that stage this metamimetic encounter, I am not saying that they are all the same. In fact, *Les Carabiniers'* staging of the mimesis of mimesis is so complex that the analogous scene in *The Piano* seems in comparison quite rudimentary in structure and effect.[64] Despite the varying degrees of sophistication in the construction of this primal scene of cinematic "first contact," of cinemimesis, across these different films, they all do signal for the audience "a nostalgia for a state of wonder."[65] The mimetic sensitivity of the "primitive," which we, the audience of the film and the diegetic audience, may have lost, is valorized. And in this valorization these scenes yield mimetic capital to the jaded, "civilized" vision for which an image is just an image, with no magic at all.

The Maori man who rushes onto the stage to save Bluebeard's fifth wife is incited to act by mere shadows projected on a white sheet (a sort of proto-cinematic shadow play) because his capacity for mimetic apprehension is still intact. In contrast, the down-to-earth Aunt Morag then introduces the Maori to the actors, hoping to dispel what she sees as the naive primitive man's mimetic delusion. The question is whether the film endorses Aunt Morag's mode of perception. In a film awash with mimetic forms of behavior which are efforts of cross-cultural cognition at a moment of violent confluence of cultures, Aunt Morag's behavior is held up to ridicule, played for laughs. This is because her simple-minded rationality is the virtue of a mimetically obtuse or atrophied person. The only kind of mimetic sensitivity that she can make happen is the parrot-like repetition of her self in Nessie, a sort of micro-fascist operation made laughable because of the parodic mode in which their performance is conceived. It is also worth noting how Aunt Morag covers up the traces of her outdoor urination with a gesture reminiscent of an animal's response gone awry. It seems unlikely, therefore, that anyone would have a compulsion to be like the overcultivated Aunt Morag. I contend that part of her function is to enable the audience to be more attuned to the high theatrical mimetic metamorphoses at the heart of this film.

Mimetic Metamorphosis

Campion has referred to the final scene of *Thelma and Louise* in the course of talking about *The Piano*. I want to link the two films in terms of an idea of mimetic metamorphosis. In the final scene of *Thelma and Louise* the two women rev up to fly over the grand canyon in a T-Bird convertible while Harvey Keitel[66] as Slocumb, the sympathetic cop who has been ordered to move out of the field of action (because he has become unprofessionally emotional), runs after the car in a last desperate bid to save them. Only one person in my extensive discussions of this film has ever asked the question "Whatever happened to Harvey?" and answered, "Well, he must have fallen into the abyss." Now this is terribly appropriate, for all through the film he has taken on the burden of the pathos of the women's lot while Thelma and Louise have moved into registers of feeling and action far removed from the pathetic. Slocumb's lyrical slo-mo run after Thelma and Louise, shot from the back, makes his stocky, suit-clad, and hence very awkward body take on the residual melodramatic pathos of the scene while the women vanish into the virtual space of the final white-out. To give these metamorphoses a Deleuzian formulation, while the women themselves become other, Keitel becomes woman (alas). Keitel's mimetic vulnerability is tapped by Campion in *The Piano*.

Harvey Keitel's American career also fell into a hole almost as it began, and it is only now, with his recent visibility in key roles in acclaimed low-budget films such as *Reservoir Dogs*, *The Bad Lieutenant*, and of course *The Piano*, that pop-culture magazines and film journals are assessing his long and somewhat obscure and eccentric film career.[67] After he came to prominence playing opposite Robert DeNiro in Scorsese's *Mean Streets* (1973),

DeNiro's career was marked by a meteoric rise just as Keitel's seemed to end. Thanks largely to his collaboration with Scorsese, DeNiro has created a form of psychotic masculinity that seems now to be very nearly branded on his flesh. Not so, Keitel. Thanks to his eccentric career (spanning both European and American cinema, big and low budget, and TV work) an image of the Keitel persona has emerged which is marked by a greater fluidity. Though he is a method actor, his body has not as yet become coded with method tics or mannerisms, which is working to his advantage. A recent article in *Sight and Sound* suggests that his career has in some way created a composite Keitel persona.[68] I like to use this compelling fiction and see how Campion draws on the cinematic "archive" in our bodies for memory traces created by certain previous roles in order to create George Baines of *The Piano*. The lineaments of this composite persona may be sketched roughly in the following list:

1. He portrays troubled masculinity in *Deathwatch* (1980, dir. Bertrand Tavernier) and *The Two Jakes* (1990, dir. Jack Nicholson).
2. He is a troubled authority figure in *Thelma and Louise* (1991, dir. Ridley Scott), *Bad Timing* (1980, dir. Nicholas Roeg), and *Reservoir Dogs* (1992, dir. Quentin Tarantino).
3. He displays a capacity for abjection in *The Bad Lieutenant* (1992, dir. Abel Ferrara).
4. He displays sexual and other perversity in *Taxi Driver* (1976, dir. Martin Scorsese), *Bad Timing*, and *The Last Temptation of Christ* (1988, dir. Martin Scorsese).
5. He is a reasonable Enlightenment man (Thomas Paine) in *La Nuit de Varennes* (1982, dir. Ettore Scola).
6. Playing the comic gangster Vince La Rocca, lover of the formidable Whoopi Goldberg, he displays a capacity for tongue-in-cheek comedy in *Sister Act* (1992, dir. Emile Ardolino).
7. In the extraordinary *Fingers* (1978, dir. James Toback), which might be described as "Martin Scorsese meets *The Piano*," he combines a neurosis which impedes his career as a concert pianist with equal ineffectuality as a part-time gangster.

In *The Piano*, though Baines is of Scottish colonial stock he has abandoned his cultural identity and become Maori mimetically, as the half-completed markings on his face and his interaction with the Maori indicate. The Maori themselves have created a hybrid identity out of bits and pieces of colonial forms of dress, disregarding as well their strict gender coding, so that when the Maori woman Hira wears a top hat she does so with a certain dignity which Stewart, fighting his way through the sub-tropical Gothic slush in one, lacks entirely. What distances this image of "becoming native" from its less savory instances within living memory is this two-way process of the performance of identity as mimetic exchange and contagion.[69]

Baines's capacity to become Maori mimetically enables him to be modern in several ways. Keitel as Baines is able to access traits from his composite screen persona, so that if we are tempted to see in him the new-age man seeking the primitive, memories of *Fingers, The Bad Lieutenant,* and *Bad Timing* can dispel such innocuous thoughts. As well, as Baines is the melodramatic opposite of Stewart's sympathetic "villain," his modernity (seen here as his fluid identity)[70] brings into relief Stewart's mimetically repressed, traditional, impermeable masculinity. Baines's capacity to be fascinated by Ada's fascination is facilitated by his prior mimetic sensitivity to the Maori culture. All of this is interesting but familiar terrain, showing what the "primitive" allows the modern to achieve, but with a new inflection.

Campion's originality (which gives her auteur status) lies partly in her ability to replay this great cliché of western modernity with a difference, so that a little time may rise between a man, a woman, and a child, the three primordial bodies[71] which cinema can reinvent for us, before they congeal within the family romance of melodrama. The space of alterity is absolutely essential to the reinvention of these figures. Ada, Flora, and Baines are Gothic melodramatic cinematic figures of romance who are able "to read what was never written." This capacity to read correspondences and create an exchange on such a basis is already a given in the relation between Ada and Flora, mother and daughter. In the relation between Ada and Baines it has to be learned through a rite of passage. This rite entails an agon between Gothic sublimity and mimesis.

Mimetic Contagion

But the terrifying generosity of the film is that Stewart also gets caught up in this uncontrollable process of mimetic contagion despite himself. This is evident in the extraordinary conversation he has with Baines (after he has mutilated Ada) about hearing her speak to him silently. Stewart says, as though it were both solace and terror, that he heard Ada speak, in his mind: "the words I heard were her words. She said, 'I have to go, let me go, let Baines take me away, let him try to save me. I am frightened of my will, of what it might do, it is so strange and strong." And then the mimetically repressed Stewart speaks of the terror of mimetic contagion: "She doesn't care for me. I wish her gone. I wish you gone. I want to wake and find it was a dream [and that is what I want. I want to believe I am not this man. I want myself back; the one I knew]."[72] This scene is extraordinary for its mise en scène as well. Stewart has come to Baines's hut with gun in hand to confront him but instead, disarmed by the magical force of mimesis, confesses how he has changed beyond recognition; and all the while the child Flora (the very figure of ontogenetic mimetic sensitivity, according to Benjamin) sleeps beside Baines after the trauma of delivering her mother's severed finger to him. But Stewart is terrified of his newly acquired mimetic vulnerability and longs to be the traditional impermeable Victorian man that he was at the beginning. The contradictory narrative functions of the Victorian patriarch, Stewart, also bring into focus the agon between the Gothic sublime and mimesis (the two antithetical forms of response to alterity) in this film.

Postcolonial Gothic

Because *The Piano* is set within the colonial moment refigured as second-contact, now time, I shall return to the issue of Gothic sublimity via Peter Otto's characterization of postcolonial sublimity:

> Throughout the nineteenth century and well into the twentieth, the language of the sublime was frequently invoked by travellers, explorers and writers as a discourse appropriate for an encounter with an alien land or people. . . . the sublime offers a powerful set of procedures for constructing a self in the face of external threat. It is in effect a defence reaction that preserves the self against alterity.[73]

I noted earlier that "the Gothic romance is a literary form that deliberately seeks to evoke the sublime,"[74] that it is an evocation of terror in love. Otto's definition of postcolonial sublimity as a procedure for fortifying the ego is therefore similar to the empowering Gothic sublimity dramatized in *The Piano*. According to Otto, in a colonial situation the sublime may be invoked to stage the colonial encounter, which is a problem ot the terror ot cultural difference and power, while in the case of *The Piano* Gothic sublimity is evoked to negotiate a problem of the terror of sexual difference and power. The sources of the threat (ethnic other and sexual other, respectively) are different, but the mechanisms of dealing with it have some common features. If the postcolonial sublime and the Gothic sublime are about the terror of otherness, then a great moment of triumph for Ada occurs when she deters her husband from raping her by simply casting a Gothic gaze at him. Ada's glance or look[75] is, however, not coded with the familiar affects of the Gothic horror look. The gesture of looking does not signify terror visibly, so we have to invent its meaning, as Stewart does by withdrawing from her. We are here in the realm of Gothic fairy tales, such as that of the man who rapes a captured Jewish girl and finds that he is stuck inside her, unable to pull out.[76] Similarly, Ada's impenetrable gaze mirrors the terror of mimetic contagion in which Stewart's fixed identity flounders. Unable to gain any mileage in his encounter with the sublime (because the third phase of the Romantic sublime encounter, the integration of the ego, fails to come), he is undone. It is his failure as agent of the sublime and subsequent master of terror that makes him mimetically sensitive to Ada's silent speech. His moment of disintegration is therefore also his salvation; mimetic retooling seems possible only on the condition of abandoning the fortified ego. Here too mimesis plays a crucial role, as it did in rewiring Ada's senses under duress. This second rape scene shows how the Gothic revision of the Romantic sublime enables the Gothic woman to accede to sexual power at a moment of terror.[77] However, if mimesis is a compulsion to become other, and if the sublime is about the terror of otherness (alterity), how is a romance between the mimetically sensitive Baines and the impenetrably self-sufficient (because mimetic) Gothic woman possible?

Gothic Allegorical Emblem

All of the people important to this drama are gradually eliminated from the image: the Maori woman who sings an elegiac farewell to Baines, Flora, and even Baines himself, so that the film may end on Ada's equivocal dream image underwater. This capacity to dream up the image of herself attached to the piano, now as a Gothic allegorical emblem (as a ruin in Benjamin's sense),[78] suggests that Ada has become adept at altering/othering herself mimetically yet again, this time by exiting her Gothic impermeability. This in turn suggests that the continuing romance between this man and this woman may now be possible only by not abandoning the piano.[79]

Gothic Anecdote

Because my objects of fascination are Ada the impenetrable Gothic woman and Baines the mimetically permeable man, I cannot end this piece as though I am an intact subject. Without getting either overly Gothic or melodramatic, I therefore wish to share with you an anecdote. While writing this piece I got up one fine morning in Sydney with an unaccountable pain in a finger of my left hand. Registering with dismay the onset of middle-age arthritis, I sought medical confirmation. No, there were no signs of arthritis there, and I had no memory of hitting my finger on something, either. Then in a flash I remembered Ada's severed finger, and was exhilarated and astonished by this sign of mimetic contagion. This may of course be a narcissistic delusion I need in order to sustain this writing. And now that I am near completing my labor, I do expect to get up tomorrow morning in Wellington and find the pain gone. But if I understand Taussig's reading, mimetic vulnerability offers no guarantee of a safe place.

Gothic sublimity does seem often to be on the brink of toppling into bathos and the ridiculous. For several Australians who (irrespective of gender) passionately loathe *The Piano,* it is already overladen with signs of tremulous awe and therefore too ridiculous to work in the register of sublimity. There is nothing one can say to this except that the Gothic as genre is writ large. I no longer know if I like the film or not, and the question is itself irrelevant.

Part Two
Performance of Narcissism

4   Speaking of *Ceylon:* A Clash of Cultures

AR: Have you forgotten your country?

LJ: *A Song of Ceylon* is in a way an attempt at not forgetting, among a few other things. Let's look at the other things, shall we, as the forgetting or not forgetting concerns only me and maybe you.[1]

In 1972 the island was officially renamed Sri Lanka.

Herr Rutman: Wo ist Ceylon?

Frau Lalune: Neither here nor there.[2]

In the absence of a relationship to the particularity of a beloved site, a land, a country, *A Song of Ceylon* generates itself by parasitically appropriating the title of Basil Wright's 1935 British documentary *The Song of Ceylon* and changing the article. Is this simply the appropriation of an erudite quotation, to be followed by further displays of knowledge of film history, or does it function as an index of some other process? If one has been possessed by cinema then it is necessary to exorcise it, especially when working within the problematic of quotation from canonical texts. In making this film, the question was something like how to use certain stills from classical films without simply reproducing them as quotations, and how to perform the text aurally without representing the madwoman.

Part One

The conjunction of feminism and cinema in the 1970s enabled forms of knowledge and ways of knowing hitherto unknown. I was not alone in sensing that knowledge, pleasure, and desire, experiences which had previously been painfully discrete, no longer needed to be so, thanks to the radical epistemological shift in the study of the humanities, marked by ambitions of interdisciplinary endeavor, which led to the constitution of the disciplinary field (disciplinary, unfortunately, in both senses) known as cinema studies. In this context the examination of the processes of the production of knowledge, of meaning, became central. We were methodologically equipped to inquire into the production of "the Feminine," the notion of "Woman" in cinema. It was not that something called "feminist content" lay hidden in films, to be uncovered by feminists, but rather that new methods of conceptualizing language and image, made possible by the conjunction of linguistics, semiotics, narrative analysis, and psychoanalysis, when brought to bear on cultural artifacts like film, enabled us to destabilize traditional meanings and interpretations which accrued to those objects. Methodologies with varying degrees of sophistication did produce new readings, ideas, values, and hopes.

> AR: Let's talk about the urbane drinking scene between the transvestite and the man in a suit.
> LJ: Did you like the kiss?
> AR: Yes.
> LJ: What about it?
> AR: The disjunction of intensity.
> LJ: What do you mean ?
> AR: The colours, textures and the light are sensuous, intense and produce a kind of erotic languor while the kiss itself feels like a gesture bereft of affect, not unlike some of the repetitions of hand gestures. The kiss should be intense but is not because it can't be . . .
> LJ: No, not in that mise-en-scene. Have you seen Dovzhenko's *Zvenigora*?
> AR: Years ago in the early 50s.
> LJ: Do you remember that marvellous drinking scene in the "mythical" section where the woman poisons her lover? It's done a bit like silent DeMille but even more formal, more ritualistically choreographed.[3]

Psychoanalysis as the theory of sexual difference was appropriated by feminists in order to understand the constitution of the gendered subject in extremis. Through feminist work with and on psychoanalysis, a sexual economy other than the hierarchized, oppositional conceptualization of sexual difference was made possible. This appropriation of psychoanalysis was methodological and strategic. "The Look," "Spectacle," "Suture"—a privileged cluster of concepts—were used to understand how they constructed the female form in classical cinema. "The Look" refers to that of the camera and the intradiegetic gaze as well as to that of the observer as it constructs sexual difference; "Spectacle" relates to the idea of mise en scène; and "Suture," to a particular mode of editing as well as a certain mechanism of identification. "The Look," its coding, its unconscious determinants, was used to understand how cinematic pleasure was linked to forms of gendered subjectivity. The development of these concepts was a real advance in knowledge, but it now seems unlikely that anything useful can follow from them, given the terms within which they have been theorized, which are largely those of psychoanalysis.

The blockage in the field is due to the fact that one can now [i.e., around 1987] only repeat the original insights through innumerable examples, through a simple model of application. The imbuing of these concepts with a form of puritan feminism has been unfortunate for feminist work in cinema. Also, the way in which the elusive Lacanian concept of the gaze has been appropriated by Anglophone film theory in the 1970s is, in my view, rather reductive. There is enough in Lacan's oblique theorizing of the distinction between the "look" and the "gaze" (a distinction that is not always adhered to in the Anglophone discourse) to generate cinematic work that can move beyond repeating ad nauseam the propositions "The Look is male, the Look is bad, down with The Look." The time is overripe for a practice which is not simply based on negating the classical paradigms on which much of the theorizing on the look, spectacle, and suture is based. It seems to me essential to maintain the difference between theoretical discourse and film work, so that feminist work in film does not dutifully set out to prove the propositions of theory, even feminist theory; the recent examples of such dutifulness have led, in my view, to an impoverishment of cinema, of its capacity to surprise in ways unknown and perhaps unknowable to theory.

> AR: You are not working within the tradition of a film like *Sigmund Freud's Dora*, are you?
> LJ: The image of someone being inoculated appeared on a leaflet soliciting articles for a publication. *Sigmund Freud's Dora* is a film in that tradition of cinema of inoculation—theoretical films which set out to illustrate a particular theory or at best take off from a theory. The least imaginative of these were crippled by servility to the idea of illustration. The best in this genre held at least a few cinematic surprises. I didn't want to make Obeyesekere's [the anthropologist] Somawathi [the possessed woman], even less "Jayamanne's Somawathi." It seems, now, that we were pursuing an idea of a more abstract body than that of an individual afflicted with hysteria, because the text was about the proliferation of bodies in the one body, many voices articulating it in a con-

stant motion of dissolution.

AR: Tell me about the supine bodies and also about the voices. It is the most appealing posture, especially for the men: voluptuous, strange to see them thus supine.[4]

This dutiful illustration of theory has led to a refusal to let films surprise and unsettle the feminist doxas, or those of film theory.[5] In some of the feminist writing on cinema a limited number of theoretical propositions are plastered onto a variety of texts, coming up with ever more of the same. The question of writing—how does one write about film?—also gets elided. It is in the context of a thorough dissatisfaction with this state of affairs that theoretical model films have been very intensely criticized in Australia, in conversations and in journalistic rather than in scholarly writing. This subservience to theory, this unimaginative relationship to it, is a failure of imagination and implies the return of the author as theory. This essay is not a criticism of theoretical work but an attempt to argue that we need a different kind of relationship of film and theory, so that we can overcome the poverty of reading.

Under the benign shadow of the death of the author (benign because it means, as Barthes suggested, the birth of the reader), this author-turned-reader would, however, like to hold on to a few vestiges of intentionality, if only to understand the ways in which authorial intentions get transformed and displaced, become irrelevant to any reading of the completed word. Authors too, like readers, must observe what it is that they have made and attempt to read it in the sense of inventing the text. My favorite example of such inventiveness in reading is the answer given to a question asked at a discussion: "Why do bodies droop, drop and swoon in *A Song of Ceylon*?" A man who saw the film said the bodies were falling as though unable to bear the weight, the intensity of the text. This was not the author's intention in directing bodies to fall into various extended arms, but as I said, intention pales in the face of the inventiveness of reading.

Part Two

AR: How did the process begin?

LJ: There were two prior uses to which I put this text, one being in my Ph.D. thesis on the "Position of Women in the Sri Lankan cinema, 1947–1979" and the other, a live performance in which it was heard as a sound tape for two voices. The third stage was to find images for it to make a film with. It was clear that the images would not illustrate or represent the drama and trauma of the possessed woman. The problem then was to work out images in which the body was in various forms of transport but in an entirely different register from the possessed body of the text, so that they could exist in parallel space/times without however being totally immune to each other. It was hoped that they would contaminate each other a little, for we did not want a voice-over effect but rather some idea of a tension where neither image nor text is slave to the other, where the relationships would be multiple, flexible. There is an attempt to explore the otherness of language to the body, to explore a bit the difficulty of that difference.

AR: In your writing on the Sri Lankan cinema there was a sentence about the "narrative prodigality" of that cinema. Were you thinking in those terms when you were structuring your film?

LJ: Though there is much that I loathe in my country's cinema, one of the things that I do love is its maddening "narrative prodigality"; the proliferation of sub-points and sub-sub-plots; arbitrary interruption; weak causal links and switching of modes. I have aspired to this mode of organisation in *A Song of Ceylon* but I am not sure if it really works as well as it does in the Sri Lankan generic film. The intention was certainly there, and maybe if it is not perceptible as such then something hasn't worked in the editing. Do you think it has a certain prodigality in its construction?

AR: Somawathi has a prodigal energy!

LJ: There is a segment in the film, not quite a scene, dimly lit, through which wisps of smoke rise vertically. It is over this image that the female voice says, "Do you know who this woman is? This woman is *soma, soma, somawathi, somawathi.*" This fragmentation of the name, its rhythmic stretching and variation is in the verbal register what this woman's body does in the register of gesture, a refusal of a unitary identity, a proliferation of bodies in the one body, voices speaking in different registers, tones, rhythms and accents. The film of course does not give the particularity of "this woman" for the viewer to see; instead it turns out that there is a Somawathi, a possessed body/*soma* in practically every sequence, though it is not very clear who is Somawathi, who is possessed. This contagion of possessed bodies is related to one of the structuring mechanisms of the film, which is to infuse the "native" with the "foreign," to never be able to see or hear the untraduced other in its pristine state.

AR: The figure of the transvestite is quite central to the film. How was s/he conceptualised?

LJ: At the time I was looking at a still from *Vertigo*, where James Stewart carries Kim Novak out of San Francisco Bay. Juan Davila, the Chilean-Australian artist was suggested because he had performed as a transvestite in *Spider Woman* and also because of his work with tableaux constructions of reversed pietas. We did not want that element of campy parody as in drag shows. We wanted some archaic echo or resonance between the textual figure of the transvestite priest and the visual figure incarnating the lineaments of classical femininity.[6]

Part Three

Puppets and Puppeteers, Actors and Lovers

AR: Is the disembodied third hand connected to the idea of the puppeteer?

LJ: If Dora's hysteria manifested itself in her throat, then here the zone of investment and terror, pleasure and pain is the hand: "My hands and feet grow cold. . . . " But the image does not simply mirror the text. I think it does a number of different things. Yes, the third hand is also the hand of the puppeteer-lover who holds, moulds, pulls, stretches bodies from beyond the limits of the visible frame. That is part of the desire that animated the film.[7]

LJ: Your painted teardrop does not draw tears from my eyes the way glycerine-induced tears do sometimes in the cinema. But I prefer the sign, the shape of sorrow to the obscenity of its stimulation, for it leaves me room for my own. The human body, in the agitation of performance or love, may aspire to the poised stillness of the puppet's body and face of papier-mache or wood. If such aspirations are sustained through a variety of tribulations both mundane and ecstatic, endemic to film and love, flesh and bone may then be moulded, held, stretched and surrendered to the pull of gravity without relinquishing grace.[8]

Rex Butler: You say in an interview that "the visual ideas for *A Song of Ceylon* began with looking at a few film stills, which is why the segments most indebted to certain film stills have taken the form of tableaux; the arrangement of bodies in static poses held for so long as to render the body ecstatic, to empty it. One of these tableaux is from Alfred Hitchcock's *Vertigo,* a moment that doesn't last more than a few seconds on screen, when James Stewart pulls Kim Novak from the water after she has attempted to drown herself. Literally here, you have held this still itself so long that it too becomes ecstatic, begins to blur, to move, it becomes *filmic.* In the sense Roland Barthes uses that word in his essay "The Third Meaning"—the filmic as precisely *the movement within the still.* Certainly, it seems you want to take us via the still, the tableau, *inside* the fragment, according to Eisenstein's final conception of montage that Barthes cites: "the basic centre of gravity is transferred to *inside* the fragment, into the elements included in the image itself. And the centre of gravity is no longer the element between shots—the shock—but the element "inside the shot"—*the accentuation within the fragment.* And it's this gravity, that of the Earth and the other, to which the bodies in your film are subject. You yourself say in the interview with Anna Rodrigo: "I wanted a gesture that was aware of the body as mass, aware of its precise gravity and weight. I wanted a gesture in which the body surrenders to gravity and to another, simultaneously." Could we generalise at this point and say that it was precisely this *motion already within the body* you wanted to discover in *A Song of Ceylon,* the fact that the body, like the still, is *already filmic;* that the "basic centre of gravity" and the montage are not outside the body but are within it, traversing it *from the beginning?* And that the task for you, as film-maker, was precisely to *accentuate this fragment.*

That is why it is so strange to see your film described in the Sydney Film Festival notes (1985) as "framed as a kind of self-contained, poetic response to Britisher Basil Wright's 1935 documentary classic *Song of Ceylon,* the film counterpoints Eastern and Western cultures in a challenging and mesmerising mix of sounds and imagery," when it would be the very status of such "framing" and "self-containment" you would be questioning in your film. To what extent, Somawathi [*sic!*], would it be possible to frame your own response when your own body is not even "properly" yours, when there is already a gravity at work which is taking it beyond itself, rendering it ecstatic? In short, can there be a frame drawn around the body, the still, the text? You seem to raise all these issues yourself in that interview when you draw a distinction between the theatrical and the filmic: "My greatest investment, in this film, lies in figuring the body. In live performance the possibilities are obviously different from those available in film. In film, lighting, editing, camera distance and movement are equally potent "performers," so that one could talk of filmic performance as including all these technical elements. These elements can transform the phenomenal body to such an extent that one could say that the body that cinema materialises did not exist prior to the invention of film." And could we talk here, following Eisenstein, of the filmic body as precisely *the space between* the various elements that make up a film—lighting, editing, camera distance, movement, etc.—precisely as a kind of *obtuseness* or resistance to them? Everything we would summarise by the separation of the body from the voice (something that existed even in silent films)—"the absence of the voice propels the body into registers of excess that draw from a variety of performance traditions," you say. A difference perhaps itself made possible only by film. You write: "The separation of the voice from the body is a venerable convention in puppet theatre both eastern and western, a source of its energy and formal sophistication. A voice unfettered by a too intimate proximity to the body may speak, sing, be silent . . . in a manner not unlike what the puppeteer makes the puppet do. This elegant and at times grotesque distance between the body and the voice, between parts even of the same body as well as between one body and another, is all possible thanks to cinematography, the etymology of which—"writing with movement"—is good to remember even as one trembles at the prospect of directing disembodied hands to trace gestural vectors over bodies rendered still." I ask all these questions in the context of *Vertigo* because there too, it seems to me, the body itself is affected by a kind of vertigo, which we might define, strictly speaking, as the *motion within the body* (the vertigo that affects your characters also as they "droop, drop and swoon"). For me that film is not so much about the psychological themes of fetishism and necrophilia—which are there precisely as *tableaux,* subject themselves to a kind of vertigo that displaces and abolishes them—but rather about a certain repetition or montage *that makes the still impossible.* That is, there can be no single image of Madeline (such as the locket or "still" of Carlotta): she is simultaneously all women (all women in their way resemble her: Judy, Carlotta, the women James Stewart mistakes for her on the street, even Madeline herself who is only acting out a part—she only *resembles* the *true* Madeline like all the others) and absolutely unique, unable to be repeated. In fact, she exists only as *an effect of those repetitions* (that is to say, Scotty only realises what was unique to her, what it was about her that could not be duplicated, when he is con-

fronted with her exact double, Judy). As you say in your own writing on
A Song of Ceylon, it is never a question of "mirror-gazing at identical
doubles held in the rapture of narcissistic identification." It is rather, an
ancient passion that the performer activates by gazing at her double the
puppet—the gaze between Scotty and Judy in *Vertigo,* between Ted
Culless and Juan Davila, the woman and her image in the TV screen,
between you and your performers (including yourself) in your film, the
gesture of opening the eye we see throughout the film. There is only the
puppet and the puppeteer, without knowing for a moment which is
which. The fact that we cannot move without being moved ourselves.
You said, "What animated her as director of bodies was the possibility
of holding, moving, pulling, stretching and moulding bodies; the actor
as puppet surrendering his neck, back, arms . . . to the puppeteer. It
seems rather difficult to move, hold, pull, stretch and mould without
being moved. . . . " But could we say, to complete our questioning
here, that your film tries to capture the still *and* the moving, the insepa-
rability of both—the stillness of theatre, of two-dimensionality, and the
movement of film, of three-dimensionality. As you write: "When two
travellers meet in transient spaces, certain ephemeral exchanges occur
that are (alas) impossible in more durational spaces. So, by staging the
mise-en-scene of this film (in part) in that space marked by a sense of
the passing of time, of the intensity of moments, of a sense of before
and after—the theatre, that denigrated space of the proscenium theatre
and its infamous wings where so much happens before bodies move
into the space of light and sound—by trying to traverse that space
filmically, one also wants to transform the more durational places; in
so doing one hopes to work in film without having to surrender the
pleasures learnt (standing in the wings, waiting with other bodies) in
the theatre." You link cinema etymologically with "writing with movement" and this seems to sum up very well all that I would like to ask
you here: a certain stillness indispensable for writing (that of the desk,
the letters on the page, etc.) and the movement without which writing
could not be read. And thus for film: the stillness of the individual
frame, the passing away of the film itself, its seductive body that is an
elusive body (Raymond Bellour), that can neither be readily quoted or
grasped.

LJ: *A Song of Ceylon,* it seems to me, displays a fetishistic delight in the
act of framing, cutting the object to fit to the measure of a certain desire, the classical lineaments of which have been described by Roland

Barthes thus: "The tableau (pictorial, theatrical, literary) is a pure cut-out segment with clearly defined edges, irreversible and incorruptible; everything that surrounds it is banished into nothingness, remains unnamed, while everything it admits within its field is promoted into essence, into light, into view."[9] As distinct from this, *A Song of Ceylon's* economy is post-colonial in the sense that it is enamoured of corruption, processes of contamination, hybridisation. The fetishistic over-valuation of framing is, however, undermined in several ways, not the least of which is the duration of shots, a propensity to long takes. This might make one feel that the weight of time makes the "still" image blur and move.

It seems to me that Barthes' observations on the film-still are not entirely sufficient to think through what is happening in this film. Barthes, in concentrating on what is *within* the fragment, forgets what might lie neither inside the shot (mise-en-scene) nor between shots (montage), but what the shot excludes: off-screen space, as well as the tensions and more transient movements that can be generated between on- and off-screen space.

This brings me to one of the main devices of activating the dead zones of off-screen space in this film; the third and fourth hands of the puppeteer-lover. In speaking about these bodiless limbs I will also discuss your notion that the centre of gravity lies within the still. With the appearance of these disembodied hands the integrity of the tab-leaux, the cut-out, is contaminated with intimations of something, some element, some movement outside the scene. These hands seem to do several things.

The disembodied hands of the puppeteer-lover first appear at the beginning of the film over the painting of the mother goddess Pattini. The gestures of these two hands indicate a structural principle of the use of gesture in the film as a whole. The right hand with its palm open and fingers slightly curved is a more or less naturalist gesture, while the left hand has the thumb extended away from the rest of the fingers, an altogether more formalised gesture relative to the other hand.

Also, these hands emerge from the "nothingness" of off-screen space, thus activating these "dead zones" banished from light and visibility. They are not god-like authorial hands, because they are not one, are of different shapes, sizes and energy. The vectors of energy they produce are at times articulatory and at times move to disarticulate the body of its canonical forms of the ecstatic. So in answer to your question "Can there be a frame drawn around the body, the still, the text?": *A Song of Ceylon,* it seems to me, generates at least a dual movement held in a certain state of tension: 1) a movement of relentless cutting into beloved fragments: bodies, objects, space; 2) movements (of light, camera, spaces, voices) which work away from the pressure and delimitation of the still, out out fragment.[19]

All ritual drama reenacts a murder, a sacrifice, not an existential death but the death of the drives, or a certain channeling of the drives, which is the same thing. The ritual of exorcism is a graphic demonstration of this. Though the film draws from anthropology, it is not an ethnographic film of the body, because the body it figures is not the preexisting naturalist body but a body made possible and desirable by film itself, a body that did not and could not have preceded the invention of film. This film may be thought of as a dance film if one includes the work on and with gesture and posture as a concern of dance. The film is enamored of the possibility of the non-standardized body, and inflects it gesturally. Very small movements imperceptible in the theater are here foregrounded not for their unequivocally significatory function, but because they render the body more contingent, more surprising, more tender, voluptuous. The clarity of iconic gesture is blurred by obsessive repetition rendered banal by non-obsessive performing. The almost mannerist inflection of gesture in group scenes may also be read as a certain dispersal of the unitary focus endemic to the notion of the Scene.

The urbane drinking scene with the man in the suit and the transvestite is a transformation of a histrionic scene from the Kim Novak vehicle *Jeanne Eagels* via a minimalist mise en scène—the abstract indeterminate space created by lighting, the solidity of the couple in that space, the static long take with the feel of a sequence shot, and the repetition of Purcell's duet for tenor and countertenor from *The Indian Queen.* A recognition of its Hollywood origin, though not necessary, would raise formal questions about mise en scène and performance, especially the gestural body.

> AR: There is quite a marked formal shift in the coda with the close-ups. The shift into the genre of portraiture brings the family to the fore, at the end, and connects with the ritual of swearing in the text.
> LJ: The ending was a real problem. For months after the official shoot the film still had no ending, it wasn't conceptually worked out. And then someone came up with this idea and it seemed fitting to invoke "the family" in its most canonical form of representation, portraiture.

Speaking of Ceylon   61

Slight movement was introduced to permutate the fixity necessary to portraiture. The smallest articulation of neck, eyes and fingers then developed into vectors of motion that passed from one still shot to another. The camera is static, the only movement being of bodies within the frame and the relay of movement and looks that pass from one shot to another. From one figure to another.

AR: Figure?

LJ: Figure rather than character because these bodies in close-up are not there long enough to establish identities necessary for the recognition of them as characters. The different postures and groupings are important, like the movement which changes the original configuration. Also they have all performed different functions in the scene in the music room. They are given oscillating functions, viewers of a spectacle but also figuring in it.

AR: How did you choose the actors?

LJ: I chose some for the way they looked, some because they just happened to be there and some for personal reasons that would not necessarily enter the realm of signification. Also there are several families involved in the film but never a complete family, at least one member is missing.[11]

"Why do I faint into his arms after singing the Schubert *Litany*?" She could have said, "Because I want you to, because I want you to calmly surrender your body into the arms of your son, my husband." Would that have been simpler than saying that it was not a question of rejecting Stanislavsky for Brecht because the gesture of surrender was no simple quotation of a reversed Pieta, nor a reversal of the climactic scene in any number of Hindi and Sri Lankan films where the adult son, bespattered with blood, finally manages to work his way into an erotic maternal embrace before he dies? The passions and exigencies of the puppet/actor can never coincide with those of the puppeteer/lover, the mover of bodies, but thankfully in cinema there are other elements which move alongside those of contingent individual passion.[12]

AR: It is a commonplace in cinematic history (Western) for the male director to direct his actress wife. Méliès/D'arcy; Bergman/Ullmann; Godard/Karina/Wiazemsky; Roeg/Russell come to mind. But I can't think of an example of the reverse. Is this for the first time?

LJ: You know how we Sri Lankans love the idea of "It's the first time
. . . " What is more resonant culturally, however (in the context of South
Asian cinema), is that a woman has directed another to surrender her
body into the arms of her son, her husband, and that she did it with
such grace. I am referring to that potent triangle in South Asian cinema,
of mother, son, and daughter-in-law. Let's talk about the white spaces.
AR: They seem to work in the way old-fashioned wipes used to wipe
the screen because they are mostly moving shots.
LJ: Like a space to rest in?
AR: Were you thinking of silent cinema when you were making the
film?
LJ: Why do you ask?
AR: Well, the static frames for one thing and then within that, gestural
inflections, which is very different from the great gestural flurry and
commotion say as in early Chaplin. But the principle is similar. The
mannerist posture reminds me of fashion photography.
LJ: Is that good or bad?
AR: I was not making a normative statement. I would also have liked
the editing to be a bit more . . . prodigal.
LJ: A better word would be . . .
AR: Aberrant?[13]

Drawing highly coded gestures and sounds from different traditions,
the film needed to find ways of disembodying the bodies and spaces which
are saturated with meaning and affect. Whether the film has been successful in realizing this ambition is of course another matter.

In staging the classical lineaments of the Feminine (narcissism, masochism, hysteria) as spectacle, the film is aware of the binary schemas
within which these pathological, pleasurable, traumatic states have been
theorized, imaged, and lived. If *A Song of Ceylon* offers an intimation of
certain movements through and around these bodily states by dissolv-
ing the gendered binary oppositions within which they have been conceptualized, then the film is a spectacle not only of but also for the body in
extremis.

AR: One last question, the hand scratching the belly of the woman in
the black and white segment, it is quite arcane, no?
LJ: I don't at all know what that gesture means, it is the only specifically
Australian gesture, a tribute to a dead Australian lover.[14]

Credits

A Song of Ceylon (51 min, 8 mm and 16 mm)

Director: Laleen Jayamanne.

Producer: Adrienne Parr.

Screenplay: Laleen Jayamanne (adapted from Gananath Obeyesekere, "Psychocultural Exegesis of a Case of Spirit Possession from Sri Lanka," in *Contributions to Asian Studies,* ed. K. Ishwaran (Leiden: E. J. Brill, 1975), 41–89).

Cinematography: Gabrielle Finnane, Anne Rutherford, Andrew Plain.

Editing: Geoff Weary, Laleen Jayamanne.

Art Director: Sheona White.

Sound Mix: Geoff Stitt, Adrienne Parr, Andrew Plain.

This film was funded by the Creative Development Branch of the Australian Film Commission, 1985.

5 Anna Rodrigo Interviews Laleen Jayamanne on *A Song of Ceylon*

"Do you think I am a woman, ha! Do you?"

AR: I would like to take up a point you made in our previous interview. You said, "Though the film draws from anthropology, it is not an ethnographic film of the body." Would you elaborate on that distinction?

LJ: Traditionally, ethnographic film has been the handmaiden of the master discourse of anthropology. Also traditionally, anthropology has been enamored of the Other, of another place and time. Film has been enlisted in a variety of ways to enhance this enterprise of rendering the other culture visible, legible, and therefore intelligible to the perceiver. Now *A Song of Ceylon* is not about a place, despite the title. While Basil Wright's *The Song of Ceylon* is not pure ethnography, it has elements in common with an ethnographic enterprise, that of rendering an ancient culture visible as it enters the rapid transformations wrought by the colonial processes of a plantation economy and international trade. The film is a tender tribute to a culture whose shape and movement are being irrevocably changed by modernization and colonization. It has therefore a certain romance of a "Virgin Land" and the land's people and beliefs. To me, as a postcolonial Sri Lankan working in a foreign land, Wright's title was a perfect element to hang on to, with modification of the definite article into the indefinite. Also, Ceylon does not exist as the official name of a country: it is a name erased from the map of the world. So this intertextuality, between a memory of a place-name and the title of a semi-ethnographic film, is used in order to develop a film whose main concern is with a certain experience of a body under duress, of a body which is neither here nor there, in the sense in which it could be said that "Ceylon" is neither here nor there.

The anthropological text deals with an experience of "possession," of a body being possessed by other bodies, of the voice being multiplied, so that there is more than one voice to the body. In western terminology this experience may be called a form of hysteria, the malady of femininity.

What is interesting is that the beings possessing Somawathi are both male and female.

This is why the image track of the film is based on tableaux vivants constructed not from films but by looking at stills from a selection of films. This film has tried to recreate certain classic postures and gestures of western erotic and romantic possession taken from film stills. So the body it has sought is an imaginary body that did not exist before the technology of cinema. This is where the film most sharply departs from the project of ethnographic film. But if it is in any sense an ethnographic film, it is so only insofar as it is an ethnography of a certain cinema and of its capacity to render the body erotic, tender, voluptuous, via fragmentation.

Having said this I would also say that there is a strong Sri Lankan ethnography of class in the chamber music scene at the end of the film, when a song which has been heard in snatches is finally sung in full to an audience gathered in a bourgeois living room with grand piano, harpsichord, and record player. This is a haunted scene, full of echoes, because the elderly woman who sings Schubert's *Litany for All Souls' Day* is accompanied by the recorded Elisabeth Schumann (so the voices are doubled), while the harpsichord and the piano are not in tune with each other, so there is an auditory doubling and dissonance. The visual dissonance is not only in the variety of clothes from different cultures worn by the actors but also in the juxtaposition of faces and bodies as they participate in a western musical ritual. The ethnography here is one of cultural hybridization, which, if viewed negatively, may be seen as dispossession of pristine cultural identities. A variety of codes, of dress and of facial, bodily, and gestural expression, clash in this scene, whose mise en scène is quite evidently staged. So, having said that it is not an ethnographic film in the traditional sense of referring to a real or a referent, I seem to have come to a position of redefining what ethnography might mean on film if it uses cultural forms such as cinema as its referent and its real.

AR: Obeyesekere's text is a fascinating document. I'd like you to discuss why you chose it and how you used it as an oral and aural text for the sound track of your film.

LJ: Obeyesekere's work is exemplary, remarkable for its departure from the canonical anthropological topics into terrains that are of great importance to feminists, such as pregnancy cravings, experiences of madness and cure, and ecstatic religiosity; he addresses questions of gender and examines some of the rituals of gender in extremis, or, if that is too strong a phrasing, then of gender formation under duress. Yes, I do find the text fascinating in the sense that though I am from the same culture, that experience is quite foreign to me, having been brought up as a Roman Catholic, as you know.

I had also studied Freudian psychoanalysis by the time I read the text and was fascinated by the way in which my culture dealt with hysteria in the form of a theatrical ritual, that is to say a public ceremony. I was also amazed at the spectacle of a woman going against the cultural norms that constituted her identity as a woman. Her verbal and gestural virtuosity, energy, and dexterity were truly astonishing to me as a middle-class woman. I was interested by the other patient who was being cured at the same ritual. Obeyesekere says that "on the night of Somawathi's exorcism there was another patient—a young attractive female typist, middle-class and English-educated, who worked in the Supreme Court in Colombo. Yet although she underwent the same ritual as Somawathi, her behavior was strikingly different: she was quiet, reserved, and displayed none of Somawathi's acting-out behavior."

Western feminists have done a lot of work on women and madness, and it is an interest in this work, as well as the obviously theatrical elements of the ritual, that led me to this text. In this ritual both the body and the voice "perform" the madness in the presence of a congregation which is absolutely necessary for its efficacy. I was also interested in the way in which Obeyesekere interpreted the ritual and the woman's madness from a classic Freudian perspective. But even more, I was interested in the problems of this particular form of interpretation vis-à-vis cinema.

Because psychoanalytically inspired feminist theory (both filmic and other) has led to a kind of reductive practice, I wanted to use Obeyesekere's interpretation in a mildly parodic sense, which is why Somawathi drowns the Freudian interpretation with her hooting. The strategy was to have three male voices perform the text. One is the voice of anthropology à la Freud, for which we chose an Australian voice; the second was the voice of description and narration, for which we chose a Sri Lankan voice which had a trace of a Tamil accent; the third was the voice of the priest (Kapurala), for which we chose a Sri Lankan voice which had a certain English quality but was in fact modeled on the voice of Lionel Wendt, who read the voiceover text in Wright's *The Song of Ceylon*. This was a way of opening up the text to bring out its different discursive, i.e., generic and rhetorical, operations. Within this ambience is introduced the voice of the possessed woman, which is also a Sri Lankan voice. That same voice also speaks the descriptions of tone and emotion given by the anthropologist, such as "she spoke contemptuously," "sarcastically," etc., but in a high-pitched monotone.

AR: The voice of the priest and that of Somawathi dramatize the text in a gesture of high theatricality, while the other voices have a certain neutrality. Is it true that your husband plays the role of the priest and that you give voice to Somawathi?

LJ: Yes.

AR: What are the implications of this?

LJ: For whom? For you or for me? For they can never quite be the same for both.

AR: Well, if the viewer knows this biographical data then it adds a level of complication because the dialogue is not only one of power but also one in which power and pleasure are so closely connected.

LJ: Yes, not unlike the couple Love and Marriage. The film is not interested in finding the "real Somawathi" and trying to represent her. What we loved in the text was her ability to continually displace that very attempt to pin her down to one identity, one pleasure, one reason. She is after all a body possessed by at least four other bodies and voices performing in a continual motion of displacement of a unitary identity; we sought to reproduce this dynamic through the properties that cinema offers. So, for example, we have Somawathi's opening words in the film describing to the anthropologist her experience of possession: "My hands and feet grow cold. It is as if I do not possess them. Then my body shivers, shivers, and the inside of my body seems to shake, this goes on and on, and if I hear someone talk I get angry. My rage is such that I could even hit my father and mother. . . . this is how the illness starts." In the film we have two voices speak these lines; one is male and the other female, they are slightly out of synch, and halfway through the passage the male voice disappears. This of course is not in the anthropological text, but it is suggested by the dynamic of the ritual. This strategy has been maintained at certain key moments of the ritual when the punitive measures of the priest are the strongest. So we have the marvelous lines "Do you think I am a woman, ha! Do you? Do you? Do you think I am performing some gimmick? Do you know me well?" which are also spoken by a male and a female voice. Here the male voice chosen was asked to speak English with a strong Spanish accent as a trace of some other possibility; it is the voice that keeps disappearing in mid-speech, as if the ritual cannot accommodate the multiplicity for long.

AR: The film works with two systems which are separated from the beginning. One is the sound track of the Sri Lankan ritual; the other is the images largely taken from western cinematic images of secular possession. What sorts of relationships did you map out between the two?

LJ: To call them eastern and western systems is not accurate because the anthropological text is already in English. And I have never heard or read it in Sinhalese (our mother tongue). So the codes of the English language mark my access to the Sri Lankan text. A key word such as "emphatically," which is important in asserting the authority of the priest, sounds odd in English, the translation seems inadequate—through no fault of the translator, it seems. Also in choosing to include elements of the anthropological exegesis in the film I acknowledge the hybrid nature of that text, marked by heterogeneous sources and discursive operations. There is no question of a simple opposition between a pristine Asian text and images taken from western cinema. It is true that the images are staged in the classical space of western representation, the proscenium stage. But this space, rather than the arena space in which the ritual of exorcism is performed, is the one that the postcolonial Sri Lankan theatergoer is most familiar with, so it is not a strange and exotic western space. What you called the two systems of the film are already not pure in their difference; they are already the result of processes of cultural hybridization and contamination, for better or worse.

AR: But surely the film has an investment in retaining certain cultural and gender tensions which that very process of hybridization via quotation, pastiche, collage, and montage may tend to harmonize, neutralize, and render placid.

LJ: Well, that is the big problem, to be able to devise ways which (while acknowledging the speed and inevitability of cultural hybridization in this age of electronic media) do not posit a bland equivalence between cultures but facilitate the articulation of certain differences, cultural specificities. The postcolonial inheritance is one of hybridization, despite the efforts of chauvinistic forms of nationalism to erase such heterogeneity and regress into some mythical ideal of pure identity, whether of nation or gender. We have seen the bloody aspect of this in the history of Sri Lanka in the last decade.

AR: I would agree with your comment that "one thrust of colonization is to homogenize, render readable all that is seen and heard as foreign." How is this space different from the space of postcolonial inscription?

LJ: The "colonizing" projects of anthropology and psychoanalysis are attempts to bring the object of study into a system of intelligibility based on one explanation, a unitary explanation. Psychoanalysis can only ever speak of the object of desire, in the singular; the colonial discourse in its strict dichotomy of Self and Other also works within a unifying logic. Obeyesekere stresses the importance of infantile trauma in the genesis of Somawathi's hysteria. The ritual of exorcism is marked by a cultural experience of contradiction and heterogeneity where Buddhist and Hindu elements are brought together in order to articulate this desire for a multiplicity of bodies and voices. The film is enamored of at least three elements simultaneously, i.e., the proscenium theater space, the voice (whether male or female) as pure affect and gesture (in the Brechtian sense of conveying attitude through timbre, tone, pitch, and rhythm), and the feminine. Now certain usages have exhausted these elements, and if one wants to reuse them for a different purpose away from the unitary economy of the colonizing process then I think it necessary to have an investment in a certain opacity, an unreadability.

The bodies and faces in the film are as inscrutable as puppets are. The bodies are still and are manipulated by hands or voices emerging from the off-screen spaces.

The postcolonial can also move toward a hegemonic purism, as certain fundamentalist trends in various cultures are doing now. But one can also acknowledge and use the messy inheritance that is exacerbated by the introduction of electronic media into postcolonial societies. One could work intelligently with the conflicting codes and discourses, genres, and rhetoric that one finds without calling for a cultural vice squad to purify the culture of all "alien" elements so that we are left with something called a pure identity, which is a myth. This is a powerful myth, which can incite relatively normal, humane people to take, in word and deed, a bloody stance against those thought of as outside that purity, those others who are said to threaten that purity. Cinema is a happy medium to be working in, in these bloody times, because it is difficult to refer to something pristinely national in the cinema, though it has itself, in the case of Sri Lanka, constructed one of the most powerful images of Sinhalese, Buddhist, village femininity, which groups of real women have begun to embody in their everyday life, endorsed by political parties.

AR: On the point about the pristine image of Sinhalese, Buddhist, femininity, can we discuss the ways in which Somawathi goes against some of its most sacred norms?

LJ: How I would love to see her dance! I can only imagine her bodily vitality on the basis of the anthropological descriptions, which are very vivid. As for her verbal and oral virtuosity, we have enough to go by. Let's start with the non-verbal registers of the voice which she activates in the course of the ritual; the hooting and laughter are the most remarkable.

AR: From where did you get the hissing, whispering, and wailing which are there on the sound track?

LJ: The hissing sound is our translation of the laughter of the possessed woman. Obeyesekere is careful to record these extra-verbal emissions of the voice. We felt that we could not reproduce the laughter but wanted a sound that had the same indeterminacy as laughter.

AR: Indeterminacy?

LJ: You know how laughter can function in lots of different ways, that it is not very easy to decode, that it has the potential to be an equivocal sign. I remember certain feminists being annoyed at other feminists who laughed during a particularly painful scene in a German feminist film about fascism. During the discussion the irate feminists demanded an explanation of why some others laughed. This sort of policing of laughter, in order to enforce one meaning, indicates that it can have more than one. I also like that anecdote about the woman who laughed at Brecht's funeral, who turned out to be Helene Weigel, the famous Brechtian actress who was also his wife. So, to come to our example, we discovered that when seated at a microphone and hissing into it one could produce a sound that was the equivalent of laughter in its ambiguity and also had a certain physical intensity and violence. The pleasure in producing it was connected with the kind of muscles it activated in opening the mouth and throat wide to exhale. A nice complement to the possessed woman's other gesture, which is the fantasy of incorporation: "I will eat you up, eat you, *kanawa*. . . ."

AR: So you were in a sense performing the anthropological text like a score, introducing pitch, rhythm, and other such musical elements?

LJ: Yes.

AR: The hooting and the whispering, are they in the text?

LJ: The hooting is most certainly there as one of the key signs of the violation of gender identity. Good Sinhalese girls never hoot, must never hoot, for it is the prerogative of the male, usually used against her in public. The whispering was introduced by us in order to create a sense of suspense, as when the possessed woman says, "And this is how the illness starts," creating a sense of a hermeneutic, luring the viewer/listener into the performance of hysteria. I strongly feel not only that this text is about hysteria but that it is also a hysterical text, which is to say a text in a mode of excess. What is in excess is most often the voice, which refuses to be pinned down to one register of utterance and meaning, which constantly attempts to displace the unifying function of the ritual whose aim is to restore the naturalist body and voice to the possessed woman. And as we were working with an audiovisual medium, we wanted to multiply the effects through the technological means available to us.

AR: Talking of the technological means, the color and lighting in the film add a lot to the spectacular effect of an erotic ritual. Why did you have a black and white segment in a predominantly color film?

LJ: The anthropological text has no discourse on color and light, which are no doubt important (especially for a ritual which lasts from dusk to dawn), just as the sense of smell is. I used black and white because the original images from which this section is constructed are from a black and white film, *A Married Woman,* by Jean-Luc Godard.

There is the possessed woman's marvelous ploy to displace attention onto a man in the audience, whom she smells out because he is supposedly carrying pork fat. This invocation of smell shows how the ritual permits several senses to be activated in a play of affective intensity where pleasure and violence are coupled, as when the possessed woman is dragged into the dancing arena by her long hair, or beaten on her back with a stick. I suppose we should talk about the dancing here, because that is the dominant movement pattern in the entire ritual and its vital core: this is not only a talking cure but a dancing cure.

AR: Yes, in your film you make a gesture toward the possessed woman's dancing by staging a dance on the limited space of a chair. Why?

LJ: We did not want to simulate the madwoman's dance, which I am quite capable of doing in an open space. Instead we wanted the most restricted of spaces in which to dance, because the illusion of freedom in the dance movements is always maintained within the authoritarian command of the priest who says, "Yes, I will give you permission to dance for as long as you wish." The chair was chosen because it is a major object in the ritual; at a climactic moment the woman Somawathi has to crawl under it, as directed by the priest. Instead of going through that ritual of Oedipalizing and channeling recalcitrant energy, we wanted a more defiant gesture, which was not, however, a naive feminist gesture of breaking out or liberation, either. We wanted to shift the register of the gesture from a punitive one to something slightly funny in a sardonic, wry sort of way. Because the body is truncated, one never sees the face of the person whose hands and feet are in torsion. I think this makes the image of masochistic pleasure quite powerful. The body of the dancer is costumed in a hybrid manner, a South Indian sari worn in the manner that working-class Indian women wear it but the feet in Cuban tap dancing shoes, while the dance itself starts as a cha-cha that goes berserk when one hand starts hitting the other and the energy of the movement rocks the chair. The dance is conceived as the nearest thing to a static dance, a contradiction in terms, whereas Somawathi's ecstatic action-dance covers space and so provides a catharsis. We repeat this chair dance three times in images that accelerate the motion of the hands. I find it painful to watch, the twisted hands, one hand hitting against the other, despite the humor in the costume and the mise en scène. The kind of fragmentation of the body that framing, lighting, and camera movement permit on film is of course not present in the ritual.

AR: Would you say that you not only performed the anthropological text but also deformed it?

LJ: Yes, insofar as the image track and the sound track can, thanks to montage, say one thing and show another which might contradict or displace the verbal utterance. We have let ourselves be fascinated by the priest as much as by Somawathi, for they are both possessed bodies but she is possessed (*aruda*) by demons and *pretas* (dead relatives who return as lesser beings), while he is possessed (*akarshana*) by the gods, so there is a hierarchy and difference between them both linguistically and in their respective forms of bodily travail. We listened intently to the narration, which says, "He shakes, he shivers, he chants *gathas.*" From this moment on we bring forward the male bodies.

We also try to confuse the gender identity of the bodies, which is of course possible for cinematography, that great machine of illusions. Insofar as there is no one Somawathi in the film, but there may be a possessed body in each segment of the film, the burden of possession is spread democratically across gender boundaries. There is, however, no drive to specify who is possessed and by whom.

In fact what appealed to us about using human actors as puppets with invisible puppeteers manipulating them was precisely the fascination of not quite knowing who moves whom in moments of intensity. When the narrator says, at the very end of the film, "The girl dances for a few seconds within the circle and falls down in a faint," the image we have is of a woman who has been engaged in a series of movements (which include getting up from a supine position, getting up from a seated position, moving from a standing position, and encircling a certain space) turning and glancing at something beneath the frame, which is revealed to us in the next shot to be that of a supine, bare-bodied man with his eyes closed. It is this man who was previously involved in a ritual of seduction with the transvestite woman. That scene also ended with him in a supine posture shot from above, the only difference being that he was clad in full western suit and tie. If one also knew that he is the man who gives voice to the priest, it would surely be pleasant to see such a figure of authority brought down to such a posture of erotic languor, redolent of a certain passive competence, for he does open his eyes and slowly turn his head toward the viewer. He, like all the actors in the film, is a mute puppet. The voices are disembodied and the bodies must be animated by a caress of the hand or glance of the eye.

AR: Is the transvestite figure in the film an attempt to connect with the transvestite priest?

LJ: Yes. We wanted a man to embody the most classic lineaments of the feminine in order to observe the rigors of its demands, in order to render it slightly absurd and yet retain some of its ridiculous appeal. Because the film ends with the girl encircling the supine male body, the final triumphant words of the priest have a different resonance in the film than in the ritual text: "Thus it ends. Leave, you who inhabit this mortal body, and go back to those who brought you here. Emphatically, never again will this girl be beset with such misfortunes as long as her body lasts, therefore, emphatically, all the misfortunes caused by demons and demonesses are over. Watch these things with pleasure and expectation."

AR: It sounds like there will be another episode.

LJ: The return of the demons!

6 Anna Rodrigo Interviews Laleen Jayamanne on *Row Row Row Your Boat*

The project looks for the structures we rely upon to make sure "reality" flows by us invisibly, that we flow within its stream. It achieves this in part by working with children, because they are not quite us and not quite other. They are becoming us or they are becoming other. They are at a dangerous point.

—Lesley Thornton, on her film *Peggy & Fred in Hell*[1]

Row, row, row your boat,
Gently down the stream,
Merrily, merrily, merrily, merrily,
Life is but a dream.

Part One

AR: Why did you want to shoot your daughter?

LJ: It was a pure accident.

AR: Ah really!

LJ: Well, the first shots were quite by chance.

AR: At what point did it seem necessary?

LJ: When I saw the results of the random shots. Seeing that they formed little sequences of movement, I thought it would be nice to put them together, in some form.

AR: I see; so there is a shift from the "me and my baby" family-album genre to something that might interest anyone concerned with movement.

LJ: I am hoping that there will be something in it even for those who are "anti-children." I could of course have chosen the movement of some other creature, a horse, a man, or a woman, but none of these, I'm afraid, would have interested me in quite the way these snapshots did.

AR: You mean the narcissistic investment would be absent.

LJ: Absolutely. But of course the movement is not the only thing that interested me, though without it there wouldn't have been anything else.

AR: So there is a personal biographical element and a formalist element. Is that all?

LJ: There is a fictional aspect as well. The pregnant belly in one shot is not mine, for example. Also all the personal stuff is intercut with bits from Powell's *Thief of Baghdad* and the TV footage of the Gulf crisis.

AR: Why that particular film?

LJ: Because Anusha loves it. At first I wanted to cut in bits from all her favorite videos, but that would have resulted in too much of a collage effect. The restraint needed to work with just one major intertext is a good one. So we were then free to choose our favorite bits from it. Also, the film has a multicultural cast: the Indian child actor Sabu (whose life, by the way, ended tragically in Hollywood), Conrad Veidt of *Caligari* fame, and of course the British actors and the men, probably Indian, who play "the people." The film is also so appealing because one would have to try really hard to find an Oedipalizing narrative within it. All those viciously marvelous swords and scenes of beheading are not acts of castration but acts of political violence. It's also a film that displays the magical tricks of cinema to marvelous effect.

AR: Weren't you afraid that your snapshots would fade in the intensity of the Powell image?

LJ: Yes, terribly; it is an act of pure hubris and we will be punished each time we cut from *The Thief* to our snapshots by the groans of the viewer, but we are hoping that the sound track will just hold the two sets of images.

AR: Let's return to the micro-documentary thrust of the project, catching your daughter's fleeting gestures, movements, facial expressions, vocal emissions, prelinguistic babble, glossolalia, etc. Do you have all the documents you want?

LJ: No.

AR: What's missing?

LJ: Ah! The tenacity of the Michael Powell surrogate in *Peeping Tom* (played by the director himself). Do you remember what he did? He wired his house in order to record his son's voice up to about seven years and he also filmed, with relentless cruelty, his son's reactions to terror, loss, and intensity. I'd go for something less dramatic—a video camera placed in one place to get images as Anusha passed by. Had I not been distracted out of my mind, I would have done that and installed a tape recorder as well, just to record her movements and voice. As it is I have only very incomplete documentation.

* * *

The Thief of Baghdad
by
Ludwig Berger, Michael Powell, and Tim Whelan

ABU: the thief of Baghdad
AHMAD: the king of Baghdad
JAFFAR: the evil usurper of the throne of Baghdad
PRINCESS: the daughter of the Sultan of Bazra, loved by both Ahmad and Jaffar
DJINN: the black giant who has been imprisoned in a bottle for two thousand years
A OO SHA: the little Indian girl who flies with Abu on the magic carpet in *Row Row Row Your Boat*.

* * *

AR: How about the family archive, is that adequate?
LJ: What I miss most is not being able to recall, in the sense of hallucinate, the voices of my father and mother, voices that first intimated pleasure and fear, not to mention terror. There are so many images of them but not a single recording of their voices. This sense of loss is accelerated with a child in the first three years because they grow so fast and their bodies and voices go through such extraordinary transformations that we barely see or hear because of the pressure of the daily routine.
AR: So if you were given one wish—to choose between having a recording of the voice of the loved one or an image—which would you choose?
LJ: Oh, the voice, because hearing is like smelling, it activates memory and fantasy more immediately and intensely than seeing.
AR: With the photographic image "time returns to us brushed by death" (Bellour); with a vocal trace what is it that returns?
LJ: The body, perhaps, because the voice is "lined with flesh" (Barthes), and also time as pure intensity, duration. This is what Durand calls a vertical connection between incompatible elements, an instantaneous connection.
AR: To pursue the documentary impulse a bit further—there is that one image you have returned to over and over again since about 1979, when

you first used it in your piece *Holey Family*, done for Vivienne Binns's project *Mothers' Memories, Others' Memories* at the University of New South Wales.

LJ: Yes, you might call that my "primal scene"—the maternal tableau taken around 1910 in Ceylon. Every time I am stuck I go back to it. So in this sense it is enabling, but I must confess to a nagging feeling that this incessant return may also imply a certain impoverishment of the imagination. But I still harbor a fantasy of inserting it into the 35 mm film I hope to make one fine day in Sri Lanka. I would love to see it blown up to gigantic proportions—the virtual space that seems to open up from the dead woman's face, the melodramatic condensations of birth and death in the one image, and the lineaments of the faces of my dear departed, I still find fascinating. So though I call it my "primal scene," it is not so in the psychoanalytic sense. It is an image that helps me to go off in a few different directions—it never seems like a return to the same—this has something to do with the medium I happen to be working in, and also sound changes it.

AR: Is there an equivalent to this image in the aural register?

* * *

AHMAD: There was once a king, son of a king and of a hundred kings. His subjects countless, his wealth untellable, his power absolute, and this dog was not a dog.

DJINN: Dog of an unbeliever, you shall see and you shall believe.

* * *

LJ: Most certainly, but it is only in this project that I have been able to work with it. It is hearing two voices speaking to each other without the speakers being visible to me—they must have different kinds of voices and it is essential that I do not actually hear what they say.

AR: The play of voices in an unseen space, the pure texture of tones?

LJ: Of intimacy.

AR: Would more than two people in a room do just as well?

LJ: I don't think so, no. It is not about loneliness, exclusion, or eavesdropping (the equivalent of peeping through a keyhole). Kluge's film *The Occasional Work of a Female Slave* has an equivalent to what I am trying to say, but in the visual register: the breakfast scene in Roswitha's rather awful nuclear family—it's to do with how Kluge films the family having breakfast, the interstitial comes into fleeting and poignant visibility and one has an acute sense of why Roswitha is going through all that shit to keep her family together.

* * *

PRINCESS. Who are you?
AHMAD: Your slave.
PRINCESS: Where have you come from?
AHMAD: From the other side of time, to find you.
PRINCESS: How long have you been searching?
AHMAD: Since time began.
PRINCESS: Now that you've found me, how long will you stay?
AHMAD: Till the end of time. For me there can be no more beauty in the world than yours.
PRINCESS: For me there can be no more pleasure in the world than to please you.

* * *

AR: Why the title *Row Row Row Your Boat*?
LJ: A proto-TV-toy of Anusha's first gave me the idea, and it is connected to how children are so hooked on repetition. Though I know it is important for their mastery of certain kinetic and vocal skills, it is infuriating to my adult sense of economy and tolerance, except when it is structured, as in a nursery rhyme or whatever.

* * *

OLD KING: Hail, little prince.
ABU: Where am I?
OLD KING: This is the land of legend where everything is possible when seen through the eyes of—
ABU: Father of the great beard
I am not a prince
I am only a thief.
I am Abu the thief.
Son of Abu the thief.
Grandson of Abu the thief.
With ten cents for the hunger that yawns day and night.

DJINN: In a moment I will lift my foot and crush you! Insect, weevil, worm that you are. Are you afraid?
ABU: Yes, terribly.
DJINN: Why don't you run away?
ABU: I want to look; I've never seen a genie before.
Wait! Before I die, may I ask one question? How did you get into that bottle?
(The Djinn gets into the bottle.)
DJINN: Oh great and merciful master, let me out and I'll grant you three wishes.
DJINN: Free, free, free,
Ha ha ha!
Free after two thousand years.

*   *   *

AR: What made you want to bring in the TV news footage of the Gulf crisis?
LJ: When we were working on the piece the Gulf crisis broke out (for us, on TV), and I started taping news footage, thinking maybe I could use some of it, because of the literal connection between the intertext *Thief of Baghdad* and the site of the crisis. Also the title *Row Row Row Your Boat* meant that I could formally include any kind of boat footage, even warships. But the real reason, to tell you the truth, may be the nagging feeling that making a publicly funded video about one's child is too wanky (autoerotic) for words, and that aspect had to be linked with or juxtaposed to something else, something big. As a middle-aged mother I felt I had to be somewhat socially responsible and curb, or dampen a little, the romance of the mother-daughter dyad genre. Thanks to the warships, I can get away with a few things.
AR: After Mary Kelly's *Post-Partum Document*, need one feel so bashful?
LJ: I guess despite its pioneering work I have two difficult local memories to deal with: the virulent anti-child ethos of a certain feminism that had feared and loathed the maternal function, perhaps for very good reasons, on the one hand, and the euphoric celebration of the maternal in a certain body of Australian feminist cinema, on the other. That denigration and valorization are part of the local feminist context in which I work. The celebration of *Post-Partum Document* within a feminist international

arena does not in any way disturb the two difficult and intolerable memories available here. The video can be thought of as a child's imaginary (fictional) passage into the symbolic: a maternal fantasy. The effort to work through an experience of the maternal function as a form of social and intellectual retardation is another aspect of the piece, which may, however, not be visible.

*   *   *

JAFFAR: Who are you?
PRINCESS: I don't know. I've forgotten (smiles sweetly).
JAFFAR: Why have you suffered?
PRINCESS: Have I suffered? I don't remember; it seems I was in love.
JAFFAR: Whom did you love?
PRINCESS: I cannot tell, I don't know any longer (looks bemused).
Blue roses! The blue rose of forgetfulness!
JAFFAR: Every thing of the past is forgotten. You have been in love with me, you are in love with me, you will always love me.
PRINCESS: Every thing of the past is forgotten. I have been in love with you, I am in love with you, I shall always love you.
JAFFAR: Who are you?
PRINCESS: I cannot tell, I don't know any longer (looks bemused).

*   *   *

Part Two

"Take me to your cinema"

AR: Let's discuss the figuring of the maternal in Michael Powell's *Peeping Tom* (1960).
LJ: Why?
AR: Because it has either been passed over or misread.
LJ: Perhaps because the psychoanalytic concept of lack (both sexual and symbolic) informs most readings of the film, which is in many ways a rich dramatization of psychoanalytic concepts like sadism, voyeurism, scopophilia, fetishism, exhibitionism, etc.
AR: Yes; *Peeping Tom* even has a Viennese-sounding psychoanalyst giving a spiel to Mark Lewis, the murderer and peeping Tom, on "scopophilia" as the "morbid urge to gaze," in of all places a movie studio, where a gorgeous color film is being shot and a murder has just been committed. His pro-

fessional services are being solicited by the police, who suspect that this is no run-of-the-mill murder.

LJ: After the film was rejected by the whole British critical establishment as nasty and perverted, Powell's career also hit rock bottom. But since the late 1970s his work has been reassessed and *Peeping Tom*'s importance has been established. Feminist critics have been drawn to the film because, in the words of Kaja Silverman,

> *Peeping Tom* gives new emphasis to the concept of reflexivity. Not only does it foreground the workings of the apparatus and the place given there to voyeurism and sadism . . . [it also] deploys the film-within-a-film trope with a new and radical effect, making it into a device for dramatizing the displacement of lack from the male to the female subject.

She goes on to explain this film's importance for a feminist perspective on cinema:

> Because *Peeping Tom* evacuates woman from the center of Mark's horror film, it permits the female viewer to see what her voice and image have been made to conceal and adopt a different position in front of the cinematic "mirror" from that prescribed for her by Hollywood.[2]

AR: I'd agree with most of this except the move of pitting all of Hollywood against a European reflexive film.

LJ: Let's see how *Peeping Tom* has been discussed in terms of the allegories of spectating it offers women. Silverman says,

> Helen and her mother dramatize two of the possible discursive relationships opened up for the female spectator. Mrs. Stephens' response falls under the category of refusal; having grasped the pathological bases of Mark's cinema she turns away from both it and him, urging him to get "help." Helen, on the other hand, is possessed by the desire to understand the ways in which male subjectivity has been organized. She continues going to the cinema, because she knows the symptoms she is looking for are there, and in the darkened theatre she never removes her eyes from the images. However, she talks to herself incessantly during the screenings, interrogating, interjecting, interrupting, until the familiar grows strange, and the strange familiar. . . .
>   I am, of course, talking here about myself as much as about Helen—

like her book, mine is motivated by the desire to look beyond the sounds and images that have constructed my subjectivity to what those sounds and images serve to conceal, male castration. (41)

Silverman is one of the few feminist critics who have examined in detail films of male subjectivity in extremis (for example, Liliana Cavani's *Night Porter*). But insofar as they invariably seem to lead to a scenario of castration, the films seem to leave very little room for another economy.

AR: Mrs. Stephens, Helen's blind mother in *Peeping Tom*, seems to bypass the logic set up by the film and therefore, even though the film is not centrally about her, she is necessary to it.

LJ: Ever since I first saw the film on TV I've been drawn to Mrs. Stephens, the blind mother, but haven't been able to say quite why, which is what I want to work out with your help.

AR: How about Helen, the daughter?

LJ: As Silverman says, if the blind mother and the seeing daughter offer two modes of spectatorship, I'd go for the blind mother.

AR: Why?

LJ: Why, indeed, is this daughter's epistemophilia so unappealing? Why is her response to Mark's father's film—a documentary in which Mark as a child is terrorized—so grating?

AR: What's important is not only what Helen says as she views Dr Lewis's documentary—"Please help me to understand this. All right, now, what was all that about? Can't you try to explain, I like to understand what I am shown"—but how she says it.

LJ: Exactly! Her voice is shrill, and though grammatically her utterance is a request, it functions as a command in its enunciation. This aspect of tone gives me the impression that this mode of spectatorship can never understand the scenario it so earnestly wants to have knowledge of, because it goes about it the wrong way.

AR: How is Mrs. Stephens's response as a spectator different from her daughter's?

LJ: To determine the difference we have to analyze the scene in Mark's private screening room. Mark returns home from his date with Helen to screen his own documentary footage of his most recent murder, done on camera, when he suddenly senses that there is someone there. Switching on the light, he sees, to his horror, Mrs. Stephens assuredly poised in a corner. What she then says corroborates her ease in this space of darkness and terror. (Let's not forget how Helen stumbled around when she first came into the room at Mark's invitation in a previous scene.)

AR: She says, "Good evening, Mark. I feel at home here. I visit this room every night. The blind always live in the rooms they live under. Every night you switch on that machine. What are these films you can't wait to look at? What's the film you're looking at now; why don't you lie to me, I'd never know?" and Mark replies, "You would know at once."

LJ: And then she says "Take me to your cinema." Now Silverman reads this utterance in the following way: "Since she [Mrs. Stephens] is blind, her search is necessarily mediated by language. 'Take me to your cinema,' she commands Mark" (42). Certainly grammatically Mrs. Stephens's sentence is in the imperative mood, but its enunciation (tone, timbre, pitch, etc.) speaks another discourse, so that in fact it doesn't function as a command. The contrast between the mother's and daughter's voices is sharp.

It seems to me that there is a mode of experiencing cinema which the daughter has yet to learn. What's more, of the two it is the seeing daughter who cannot at all do without language in relation to the image—it is as though she can't, even for a moment, be silent in the face of its palpable effects. In contrast, it is the blind mother who actually leads Mark to his cinema, though Mark holds Mrs. Stephens by her arm. It is she who is ahead of him, almost drawing him forward. As Mark is held by the image on the screen, Mrs. Stephens says, "What am I seeing, Mark? Why don't you answer?" As Mark moves closer to the image, abandoning Mrs. Stephens's arm, she raises it, moving it around as though to touch the image which is now projected partly on Mark's body and partly on hers.

AR: It's after this scene that Mrs. Stephens talks to Mark about how she became blind, a totally unsolicited speech.

LJ: This is such a lengthy scene and so much happens in it.

AR: She says, "Instinct's a wonderful thing, isn't it, Mark; a pity it can't be photographed. If I'd listened to it years ago, I might have kept my sight. I wouldn't have let a man operate on me I had no faith in. So I'm listening to my instincts now. All this filming is not healthy. You can't see Helen until you get some help, or else we'll move."

LJ: What follows is absolutely central to the film's dual economy. Mark leads Mrs. Stephens downstairs, back to her apartment, and while they stand on the landing, she holds and touches his face with both hands in a searching gesture to which Mark yields for a moment by closing his eyes and saying, "Taking my picture? It's a long time since anyone did that."

This speech links her gesture with that of his father, who filmed him in states of terror so as to write a scientific treatise on the effects of fear on the nervous system.

AR: But there is a difference between the two modes of touching: the photographic requires spatial distance while Mrs. Stephens's act involves the elimination of distance.

LJ: Yes, but both forms generate knowledge.

AR: Then what's the difference? For there is a stark difference.

LJ: Is it that the respective forms of cognition are put to different use?

AR: What proves to be lethal in Mark's father's deployment of knowledge is the brutal severing of the experiential from the cognitive, while for Mrs. Stephens there is no knowledge without experience and, by extension, in the cinema too no knowledge without experience.

LJ: But you are surely not suggesting that she's the maternal as intuition incarnate.

AR: Of course not. But we need to see how Mrs. Stephens functions in the narrative in order to argue that she is not used to create the disjunction between the imaginary (intuitive) and the symbolic (discursive) and that she is not the embodiment of the imaginary.

LJ: Let's start, then, with the choice of the actors. Maxine Audley's mother is clearly contrasted with Anna Massey's daughter. Do you remember how Mrs. Stephens is introduced to us?

AR: It's an unforgettable shot—a fluent fragmented gesture of a hand pouring scotch. It's two shots later that we are given the establishing shot of her in profile, but it's in a still later sequence that we realize that she is blind.

LJ: In a subsequent sequence, we are given a close shot of her counting stitches with her knitting needles while listening to Helen read a newspaper report of Mark's most recent murder. Of course they don't know it was Mark, but we do.

AR: So there is an ease and precision in Mrs. Stephens's gestures. She has a rich physicality enhanced by her voice, which is distinct from the highly sexualized victims of Mark's obsession.

LJ: In contrast, the daughter is definitely asexual or presexual, her speaking voice rather nasal. These traits are effects of the choice of actresses as much as they are of the roles they play.

AR: Helen is associated with milk—Mark offers her a drink and ends up giving her milk.

LJ: In fact, Helen is linked to Mark's dead mother (the woman with no name). Helen happens to occupy the dead woman's room, and much is made of this.

AR: All we are shown of Mark's mother are the two lifeless arms of her corpse cropped at the elbow, with one palm facing up.

LJ: With Mark looking on blankly as his father films the scene.

AR: An image of utter desolation, the maternal as absence and loss, this disempowered mother is the pure object of Mark's love.

LJ: So via the different imagings of hands, Powell gives us two versions of the maternal, one socially absent, the other very much present but socially (not biologically) impaired.

AR: What form does her social presence take?

LJ: This question brings us back to the question of "intuition" we raised earlier.

AR: If the blind mother is not like the dead mother, nor like the sexualized victims of Mark's murderous obsession, nor like the asexual daughter—is she then the phallic mother?

LJ: That would be the most literal way to read the scene in Mark's screening room, wouldn't it?

AR: The phallic mother with powers of divination, because Mark says she can't be lied to, that she will know "at once"!—it's a knowing not dependent on vision. Mrs. Stephens doesn't know that Mark kills his victims on camera and that the murder weapon is a knife concealed in a leg of his tripod, nor that a distorting mirror attached to the camera reflects onto the victim the lineaments of her own terror at the very moment of murder —but she has a sense that "all this filming can't be good," which suggests that she knows the power of cinema.

LJ: And of course her walking stick, her phallic weapon, which in fact she uses "pointedly" to ward Mark off.

AR: It seems almost an exact equivalent of the murder weapon concealed in one of Mark's tripod legs.

LJ: If so, it would be such a neat psychoanalytic case study on film of the male fantasy of the phallic mother. But Powell's film figures the maternal in a manner that is unknowable to psychoanalysis. Mrs. Stephens's mode of viewing is different from what psychoanalytically based modes of spectating could permit.

AR: What she says is "Take me to your cinema," not "All right, now, what was that all about?"

LJ: To take something one has to touch it. Even at the most desperate moment of the film, when Mark is about to kill himself in the manner in which he has killed the "sexy women," Helen, who has seen the incriminating film, can only say, "Tell me, tell me, it's only a film, isn't it?" One could say that she already knows but only wants to be reassured. But her skepticism about the cinematic image at this point aligns her with the cops outside the building, who react to Mark's filming them from his building with "Oh, it's only a camera," unaware that it's a murder weapon. Mrs. Stephens, in contrast, knows that images and sounds have direct effects on bodies. By the time the daughter says to Mark, "Tell me what you did to those girls? Show me—otherwise I'll remain frightened for the rest of my life," it's already much too late for both of them. She is now ready to understand the difference between "telling" and "showing," but it's too late.

AR: You said, "To take something you have to touch it." Mrs. Stephens registers the gaze as a form of touch. When Mark looks into their living room through a window Mrs. Stephens recoils from his gaze and registers it as an intrusion on her body.

LJ: When Helen asks her, "How did you know he was there?" she replies, "The back of my neck told me" and then mutters to herself, "the part that I talk out of."

AR: That's a nice qualification of Mrs. Stephens, because it is a refusal to separate absolutely the discursive from the non-discursive (intuition). She does say, "It's a pity it [intuition] can't be photographed," but she strives to articulate it within discourse after having suffered as a result of their separation.

LJ: And most interesting of all, when Helen introduces Mark to her mother their handshake is accompanied by an amplified sound of Mark's heartbeat, creating a bizarre acoustic effect heard only by Mrs. Stephens. While it is realistically motivated by Mark's having run to meet Helen, so as not to be late, it nevertheless characterizes Mrs. Stephens's synesthetic capabilities (touch emitting sound), her ability to convert a social impairment into a gain of sorts.

AR: Mrs. Stephens has a way of knowing that is related to touch and hearing.

LJ: She compensates for her socially inflicted blindness by a highly developed kinesthetic and acoustic sense which she deploys cognitively for survival (her daughter's as well as her own). Her capacity to register the gaze as a form of touch means that for her the sense of touch itself is highly differentiated; she is both recipient and donor of that faculty. This is not the feminization of touch suggested by the notion that woman is closer to touch by virtue of biology. Touch in this film functions as a way of knowing as varied as sight, which includes to look, to stare, to gaze, to glance, and much else. Mrs. Stephens signals a mode of "seeing" whose cognitive attributes do not destroy the object but provide passionate diagnostic understanding. This most unusual avatar of the maternal disturbs the neat (albeit reflexive) psychoanalytic schema of the film's structure.

AR: While a film like *Psycho* (contemporaneous with *Peeping Tom* and often compared with it) subsumes the maternal within the son's pathological (murderous) fantasy.

LJ: The monstrous maternal.

AR: The modern Kali.

LJ: Did you see that fine documentary on Powell released soon after his death?

AR: No.

LJ: I must tell you about a scene obliquely relevant to what we've been talking about. At the beginning Powell walks up to a table covered with a white sheet on which we see a portrait of a woman and a box camera. Powell glances at the portrait, saying, "Hello, Mum," and proceeds to tell us how his mum took good photos from a box camera like the one there. He then proceeds to look through the viewfinder. This is cut to a lovely shot of a boy with a pony.

AR: Presumably Powell shot by Mum!

LJ: That Powell should choose this to represent his biography is delightful in its lightness, especially given that he has dramatized for us the weighty paternal legacy of imaging so harshly in *Peeping Tom*.

AR: It is curious that while Mark Lewis as a child is played by Powell's own son, the grown-up son is played by a German actor, Carl Boehm, who looks and sounds non-English, while his father, played by Powell himself, sounds very English.

LJ: I wonder if the adult psychopathic son was made to "appear" foreign so as to make the film more accessible to British good taste. But luckily Powell hasn't said why he did this, so we have to imagine it.

AR: It is marvelous that the very English Powell made such an un-English film.

LJ: By making his fictional son, Mark Lewis, foreign, Michael Powell provides an allegory of the film's disastrous reception as a thoroughly un-English piece of work.

Part Three
Melodramatic Femininity in Sri Lanka

7 Myths of Femininity in the Sri Lankan Cinema, 1947–1989

Myth must be understood as ideological dynamics.

—Adrian Martin[1]

Myths embody the conflicts and aspirations of a collective anguish; they compress, transfigure and objectify areas of distress and yearning which society cannot bear to confront directly; and they manifest only as much reality as a common level of consciousness can bear.

—John Flaus[2]

"Daddy, can we go and see a picture today?" Recurrent question of a girl-child growing up in a semi-feudal, English-speaking, Sinhalese, middle class family in Sri Lanka of the 1950s; a request posed to a father. The seeing of films, then generally referred to as "pictures." The desire to see, addressed to the father because he paid for the tickets and drove us to the cinema. The seeing was difficult if not impossible without him. The father was central in the exchange of money as well as the exchange of meanings and therefore of desire. Whenever something was not clear in a "picture," I, seated between my father and mother, would lean toward my father rather than my mother, and ask softly what it meant. And he would explain.

The linear exchange between father and daughter came full circle in the private viewing of the films which form the body of this thesis, where an often dozing father (close to death) would wake up and loudly ask for an explanation of something in the film from an irritable daughter who no longer wanted him to mediate, in any form whatever, between her and the screen.[3]

Impulse to Study

Both as a naive spectator of our cinema when I was a little girl and later as a more critical one, I have felt the lure (surprising as it may seem) of this cinema, its invitation to be a certain kind of woman. When watching several films a day, over weeks extending into months, I became aware, with some alarm, of the kinesthetic effect they had on me. I found myself moving, speaking, and regulating my gaze in the manner of the "good girls" of the Sri Lankan cinema, without consciously intending to. So the lesson is clear to me. The pleasures of seeing and hearing are invested with highly sexualized energy by the Sri Lankan cinema. The task for feminists is not to denounce the pleasurable but to try to call for, work for, new kinds of pleasures that are not oppressive. Some developments in western feminist cinema have demonstrated only too well that puritanical feminist paranoia does not go well with cinema. We do not need to repeat these developments, but should rather try to generate new meanings and pleasures such as are only sporadically glimpsed in the history of our national cinema.

Background

Sri Lankan cinema's short history, dating from 1947, coincides with the history of Sri Lanka as an independent nation. Two major factors must inform the analysis of generic cinema in Sri Lanka: first, that Sri Lankan cinema derives its formal and narrative conventions from Indian cinema (Hindi and Tamil); second, that Sri Lanka is a third-world capitalist country where feudal ideologies and practices still play an important role. The conjuncture of these factors has had a determining influence on the cinema.

Of the four Indian genres identified by Paul Willemen, the family melodrama is the one which has become the dominant, if not the only, genre in the Sri Lankan cinema.[4] The mythological genre of predominantly Hindu India is absent in predominantly Buddhist Sri Lanka. There are no more than five thrillers in the entire history of the Sri Lankan cinema. The genre of social problems does not exist as an independent category, although its elements can be found within the family melodrama. The centrality of the family is a significant factor in almost all Sri Lankan films. The filmic construction of the family and the positioning of women therein will be the focus of this chapter.

Melodrama in early usage meant a stage play in which songs were interspersed, and in which orchestral music accompanied the action. Now it usually means a dramatic piece characterized by sensational incidents and violent appeals to the emotions, but with a happy ending. What is specific to South Asian melodrama, which is derived from Indian cinema, is the combination of songs, dance, and music with action that can be both comic and tragic. Narrative economy is also problematic in an underdeveloped capitalist economy with strong feudal remnants. Ashoka Mammen's gloss on Indian cinema has some applicability to Sri Lankan cinema too:

> For better or for worse, indigenous cultural traditions, many still anchored in feudal social relations, are not subjected to the same intense pressures towards "modernisation" and the creolisation that could be seen at work in Japan or Hong Kong since the last world war. Consequently Indian cinema enjoys a measure of freedom as to which aspects of Hollywood cinema it absorbs and how these are to be articulated within Indian traditions of representation. One major result of this peculiar place Indian cinema occupies vis-a-vis the dominant face of world cinema, i.e., Hollywood, is the relative inaccessibility of Indian genres and aesthetic conventions to Western audiences. Another aspect of this same feature is the mismatch between, e.g., European-American genres and Indian ones which are difficult to distinguish according to Western criteria. There is a relation of imitation, even outright plagiarism, as well as a relation of uncompromising difference between the two types of cinema.[5]

Unfortunately, in the case of the Sinhalese cinema, which is directly dependent on Indian prototypes and even conditions of production (the first Sinhalese films were in fact produced in South Indian studios), the inventiveness of Indian cinema is very rarely in evidence. Sri Lankan film criticism refers to the phenomenon of slavish dependence on Indian originals by the derogatory term *vattoru,* which means a medical prescription or formula, and has consistently condemned the formula film. The relatively sporadic and yet passionate critical literature on the Sinhalese cinema (largely journalistic, and written exclusively in Sinhalese with the exception of the work in the *Lanka Guardian* in the 1970s and '80s) has over the decades called for its liberation from dependence on the Indian formula, by means of greater realism. I will demonstrate how Sri Lankan cinema has taken up this critical challenge in relation to the representation of femininity.

In the first part of this chapter I will analyze a small sample of genre films to explore how certain representations of femininity have been produced by this cinema through a variety of codes, both narrative and visual. I will follow the narratives of adultery and those of seduction across the decades to see how they are represented within different cinematic economies and how their representations affect the representation of Woman, and I will discuss changes in the ideological implications of these representations. One of the main ideological narratives of this cinema is constructed on a simple, mythical, binary schema which may be mapped out in the following way:

Rich	vs.	Poor
City	vs.	Village
Bad	vs.	Good
Westernized	vs.	Traditional

The sign Woman is mobilized to articulate this schema.

In the second part I will briefly locate the work of three major directors of the 1980s, Dharmasiri Bandaranayake, Vasantha Obeyesekere, and Sumithra Peries, in relation to the generic field via the image of a single actress, Swarna Mallawarachchi. I've chosen to do this because it is generally accepted that Swarna Mallawarachchi brought something qualitatively new to the Sri Lankan cinema—a set of visual traits and possibilities (narrative, emotional, intellectual) that help problematize the mythical schemas of the generic cinema. I will follow the vicissitudes of the "good woman"/"bad woman" opposition to see how the very structure of simple oppositions is rendered inoperative in the more sophisticated films of the 1980s. The path toward this important complexity in the representation of Woman had already been prepared by the best work of earlier auteurs Lester James Peries and Dharmasena Pathiraja, of the 1970s New Wave.

Out of about four hundred films made within a period of thirty-two years (1947–1979), I have viewed and studied 102, of which 78 can be classified as belonging to the genre of family melodrama. These 78 films can be subcategorized in the following way:

(i) 35 have a plot based on marital conflicts, chiefly adultery.

(ii) 30 have a plot based on the boy-meets-girl formula and conflicts which ensue from it.

(iii) 13 have neither of these plots; they also belong to the genre but are thematically different from the others.

The remaining 24 films are by the auteurs of the Sri Lankan cinema. They are significant partly because they rework elements of the genre cinema within a realist aesthetic. I have chosen to focus on how they rework myths of femininity rather than deal with the importance of their work in transforming the Sri Lankan cinema. In particular, I have chosen to focus on films with marital conflicts and on some atypical boy-meets-girl narratives.

The Formula of Marital Conflicts

Samiya Birindage Deviyuy (The Husband Is the Wife's God, dir. W. M. S. Thampo, 1964)

The credits of the film are accompanied by the theme song, sung by a chorus of men and women:

> There is one heaven for woman,
> in that heaven there is one god,
> that god is her husband/owner,[6]
> Ah ah ah.

The film ends with a male voice declaring, "For the good woman who preserved her virginity, the husband is the wife's god," followed by a repetition of the opening song. The film is a melodramatic reinforcement of this maxim. I will analyze its narrative structure and construction of iconography to foreground the structuring of the feudal maxim.

Rukmani Devi, the earliest superstar of the Sri Lankan cinema, plays the role of Chandra, who was duty-bound to marry the son of her father's boss in order to save her father from going to jail. For the sake of the family honor she dutifully sacrificed her love for a young doctor. The film opens with a chance encounter between Chandra, her husband, and her abandoned lover. The husband has been stricken with the disease in which the doctor is a renowned specialist. These highly contrived chance encounters and twists of plot are the very stuff of melodrama.

While the husband is hospitalized, Chandra and the doctor have a confrontation which the husband overhears, in typical melodramatic style. We learn that the doctor is still in love with her and treasures her photograph, which he says is the only comfort in his sad life. Her reply, overheard by the eavesdropping husband, is a perfect encapsulation of feudal wifely ideology.

Chandra says, "As a wife who asks you to care for her husband's life, as a wife of a critically ill patient, as an obedient wife of a beloved husband, I ask you to return my photograph. Your duty is to dry my tears and not destroy my reverence for my husband/master." The final term is my translation of a key phrase used in this scene: *swami bakti*. *Swami* has feudal connotations of "master" and also means "husband," while *bakti* means religious worship or reverence. Thus the very words used reinforce the inequality between man and woman. The operative word in the wife's rhetorical outburst is "duty," a feudal virtue. "Life is not built on the foundation of love. My duty now is to be a good, obedient wife. The heart is a sacred place and for a married woman the only god who owns it is her husband." This dialogue is intercut with a close-up of the husband, looking very pleased by this demonstration of his wife's virtue. The rhetoric, the artificial cadence and pathos of this language, are all melodramatic values that Sri Lankan film criticism has understandably abhorred in a call for a vernacular speech, real locations, and credible plots.

The climactic illustration of feudal wifely ideology occurs at the bedside of the husband on the eve of his major operation. The husband summons both the doctor and his wife, who stand on either side of his bed in medium shot. The magnanimous husband asks the doctor to take care that his wife does not remain a widow if he dies (Chandra is not asked if the plan suits her). Her response is a song: "Do you ask me to be caressed by another? Tell me, my golden one, oh tell me. You have made this bride into an obedient wife, I have done no wrong."

Chandra, in her earlier speech to the doctor, does not say that she does not love him. All she speaks of is the necessity of doing one's duty. The last line of this song, "I have done no wrong," suggests a degree of anxiety on the part of the good wife which will be referred to later. The husband's last wish is to see his wife dressed in her bridal sari, which she dons and sings,

> Oh, why have you asked me to come in my bridal dress?
> Do you remember my beautiful figure as you saw it then?
> I will come behind you.
> I will come to where you go.

Why is this the dying husband's last wish? What does it signify? How is it different from other, almost mandatory, formulaic scenes which represent the bride as icon? The dying husband desires to see his wife in her virginal state and the complying wife fulfils his desire without quite knowing why he desires it. She conjectures in her song: "Do you remember my beautiful figure as you saw it then?" Her desire is to activate his; his has more to do with his anxieties of potency and masculinity, which the virginal image helps to alleviate. The fact that they do not have children is conveyed, though not verbally, by Chandra's visits to a little girl in the same hospital, to whom she is shown to be very maternal. A childless couple is culturally seen as lacking, less than happy. In this scene, then, the bridal image of the wife works as a fetish which activates the husband's fantasies. This kind of symptomatic reading is warranted because of the ellipses in the narrative, which is melodramatically undermotivated.

The most puzzling of such scenes occurs when the doctor announces to the good wife that her husband has pulled through the operation. Hearing the good news she drops dead, subverting her earlier statement to the doctor that she would take her life if her husband should die. In fact, as a dutiful wife she should have, instead, broken into a song of joy and been full of gratitude to the doctor who saved her husband.

The last scene, in the clouds, shows the apotheosis of the virtuous wife, looking stoically tragic and silent with her loose hair blowing in the wind, accompanied by the little girl from the hospital, who has also died. Chandra's death and final apotheosis are very intriguing. Why do they happen? Why is she grimly silent in the last image? To answer these questions it is necessary to go back to an earlier scene between the husband and wife. In this scene, the husband hears that the doctor is refusing a very lucrative marriage proposal brought by his mother, because he is still pining for the woman who jilted him. The good husband does not know at this point that the woman concerned is in fact his wife.

> Husband: What a wretched woman she is, loves one man and marries another. It is unfortunate when an intelligent young man loves a fickle woman.
> Wife: That girl-child could be a good person, don't you think?
> Husband: How can that be? If she really loves him with a permanent kind of love, then her love for her husband is a false one. If she loves her husband now, then her former love for the doctor was a false love. Why are you crying; is it because I am finding fault with women? I consider you a pure jewel.

The premise of this argument is such that the woman's position is contradictory; she has no way out, she is guilty by definition, by the terms in which the patriarchal logic is articulated. All that the cornered Chandra can manage is a tentative suggestion, which is smothered by the power of the male discourse. Then her only outlet is crying, at which response the paternalistic husband calls her a "pure jewel."

Myths of Femininity in the Sri Lankan Cinema, 1947–1989   97

The peculiar logic of this melodramatically sensational plot does conform to a logic of unconscious fantasy or wish fulfillment. It brings into play individual desire and the claims of duty in a manner that neither the characters nor the narrative itself can directly articulate. The fact that the husband tries to organize the union of the two lovers in the event of his death could be seen as a mechanism for releasing unconscious feelings hitherto repressed. This official sanction and the possibility of its realization, coupled with her own internalized feudal notions of dutiful wifeliness, create too many contradictions for either the character or the narrative to cope with. The only way out of the contradictory situation is to kill the heroine and then deify her.

The last image of Chandra on a cloud with the little girl (a symbol of virginity) seems to reinforce the male fantasy of the virginal mother, the woman who is desexualized and therefore poses no threat to male sexuality. This film thus constructs woman as a sign which is circulated from feudal patriarchal father to feudal patriarchal husband, and finally as a feudal icon of femininity only realizable in death, through the death of desire. Woman as a desiring being is troublesome for the film text; the tension between wifely duty and sexual desire cannot be made explicit. The only resolution for the text lies in the death of the good wife, who in her death preserves her virtue as well as the power structures of the feudal patriarchal family.

Duhulu Malak (*Floating Flower,* dir. Vijaya Dharmasri, 1976);
Akke Mata Avasara (*Sister, Your Permission,* dir. W. Silva, 1979);
Induta Mal Mitak (*A Bouquet for Indu,* dir. S. S. Yapa, 1979).

In these three films, the tension between duty and desire within bourgeois marriage is made more explicit than in *The Husband Is the Wife's God. Floating Flower* is perhaps the first Sri Lankan film to represent adultery in a manner that makes it seem visually pleasurable. The fact that the adulterous wife is not punished by the narrative can be considered an advance on the previous moralistic resolutions. Previously, romantic depiction of love was reserved for the blossoming of young love, but *Floating Flower*'s extended formulaic sequence of the bored middle-class housewife/mother singing and dancing in the woods with her young lover constructs a romantic space and time for adultery. Because of this it aroused critical controversy, although it was popular. While some critics praised the film for its daring subject matter and greater technical sophistication than the average Sinhalese film, others condemned it for falsely representing a non-existent woman:

> Why does Nilupa commit adultery with Rohan? The film does not
> provide convincing reasons why a woman who has a loving husband
> and a delightful daughter would want to enter an illicit relationship.
> The film does not provide reasons for her frustrations and displeasure
> with her present life. Is she represented as a real middle-class mother?
> She is always dressed and waiting for someone to appear. Hence she is
> more like a film star ready to appear in a film than a middle-class house-
> wife.[7]

Another critic attempts to understand the film's popularity thus:

> It is the surface appearance of *Floating Flower* which has attracted the
> audience. New hairstyles, fashion, pop songs, puppy love. This is why
> working women and middle-class women go after the illusion presented
> by the film. It is true that there is a question. But is it a sexual problem?
> In other words, *Floating Flower* does not even give an inkling of the real
> problem.[8]

This narrative begins where a large number of Sri Lankan films end: when girl meets boy and gets married to live happily ever after. The doubts about the film's realism and the existence of women just like Nilupa miss the point of the film. What is important is that the film provides a narrative of a wife who, for no apparent reason, leaves her husband in order to have a romantic affair. The only reason which might be culturally tolerable would be, perhaps, extreme brutality on the part of the husband, or that he is a midget, as he is in *Sikuruliya*. Yet reasons such as boredom are very much on the visual surface if viewed through a feminist optic. Perhaps the (male) critics unaware of the insights of feminism failed to see these reasons. It is worth noting that at least until 1980 the term "boredom" had, to my knowledge, no real Sinhalese equivalent.

However, the film itself is only dimly aware of this problem. The terms in which Nilupa's sexual desire is aroused outside marriage and then brought within its regulation do not offer the bored housewife the possibility of understanding the limitations of her life, her narrow containment within affluent domesticity. Thanks to the construction of the woman as a pleasurable image clad in a variety of clothes, with all the leisure and wealth the majority of Sri Lankan women can never have, the film works seductively for women. The state of useless dependence is represented pleasurably and thus acts as a mechanism of containment for women, encouraging them to aspire to the status of beautiful image. The real problem is both sexual (affective) and political, but because the film defines female sexuality in terms of romantic love (singing in cars and dancing in beautiful surroundings) it forecloses the possibility of articulating a female desire which cuts across traditional definitions of femininity. In the sequence where the wife returns to her husband from her lover, a fantasy sequence from the husband's point of view is inserted. He imagines killing the unfaithful wife. The viewer is startled. Is this butchering real or is it a fantasy? The next sequence assures the viewer that it is fantasy. The film thus provides the audience with an imaginary gratification of its moralistic sentiments, after which the bad wife is accepted by the good husband and the family is restored.

The Boy-Meets-Girl Formula: An Atypical Example

Para Satu Mal (Another Man's Flowers, dir. Gamini
Fonseka, 1966)

This film was voted one of the ten best films in the fifty-year history of the Sinhalese cinema and has been described as a powerful representation of feudalism and its decline through the life and death of a feudal landlord. What is of interest for my purpose is the manner in which the film triangulates the simple binary opposition between the "good" woman and the "bad" woman by introducing two "bad" women. This innovation introduces greater complexity into the formulaic boy-meets-girl narrative of seduction and resistance. The film narrates a paradigm of class and sexual relationships within a feudal patriarchal village. I shall not just go along with this narrative but cut across it, using psychoanalytic concepts, so as to ask questions pertaining to the structure of male fantasy. Using this analytic strategy, I will examine the positioning of the three main female characters in the narrative through the narration of male desire: Bonnie's desire for women, and most particularly his desire for the one woman he can never have, the good woman, Kamala. Why does the narrative signify some women as "good" and others as "bad"? What is it that articulates this binary grid, and how, and why? These are some of the questions I shall pose and attempt to answer.

Bonnie speaks to the musical troupe he has hired about his desire: "I want a woman. Without her I have no longing for the arts. I can't exist without loving. There is a girl I love with a pure love [Kamala], but she doesn't love me. You must write a song for me about her sleeping in a cemetery and how I will go to England and bring a nightingale to wake her up." What does this fantasy signify? Why does he fantasize that Kamala (who is shown to be an industrious woman) should be sleeping in, of all places, a cemetery, and that he should be the one to wake her? That this bizarre sentiment should be articulated in a song is not strange, given the function of songs within the formula. Hopes and desires which cannot be realized are, quite often, expressed in songs. The music expresses and contains the energy which the narrative is incapable of articulating. A clue to deciphering Bonnie's morbid desire is to be found in the scene where he visits Kamala's house, toward the end of the narrative, after having accepted the fact that he will never obtain her. He has sanctioned her marriage to Sirisena, his guard, by offering Kamala his family heirlooms (presumably inherited from his mother). He says, "After my mother died while I was a child, this [pointing to Kamala] was the first female face I saw. I have done dirty things. I sacrificed a great love because I had no love. Love is like godliness; Sirisena has it and so has Kamala. We must all offer praise to it like beggars. I ask your forgiveness." Here, Bonnie explicitly draws a connection between his dead mother and the woman he loves "with a pure love." Purity is defined as that which is asexual, and is directly opposed to the lust he feels for both Nony and Maggy, women he has seduced and raped by using his position of power as a feudal landowner. Why does Bonnie desire Kamala to be asleep in a cemetery? Does she awaken in him his desire for his dead mother? If so, what does this do to the woman he loves, who is not his mother? It clearly desexualizes her; she is contrasted with Maggy and Nony, who are sexually active and therefore defined as "bad." The maternal is also desexualized because a sexualized mother would be profoundly problematic to patriarchal definitions of gender identity, which pivot on the phallus and its material correlate, the penis, and the threat of castration.

Bonnie desires to awaken a sleeping (dead?) woman in a cemetery (where his dead mother is) through the song of a nightingale he brings from England. The memories of the maternal and the real woman are thus spatially identified in his fantasy. Nightingales are to be found closer than England, but in the realm of fantasy the logic of common sense does not operate. What matters is the desire to actively arouse a dead/sleeping woman/mother despite the threat of castration. In making Kamala reject him, the narrative shows the impossibility of that desire. It is impossible not just materially (the dead don't rise from the grave), but also socially. The son cannot desire his mother, therefore he desires an ideal woman whom he constructs as the mother substitute, who then rejects him. This rejection drives him to drink and, finally, death. The sexually active women, Maggy and Nony, do not satisfy him because they do not fit in with his fantasy of the asexual, virginal mother. These contradictory male desires for the lost object place the three women in the narrative in a series of oppositions made complex by the feudal class relations within which they are set.

The film is also atypical in that there are oppositions between the two "bad" women, Maggy and Nony, who are throughout opposed to Kamala, the "good" woman. When Bonnie first seduces and rapes Nony, she says, "How can I afford to become pregnant, we are poor." Despite her initial fear and resistance she shows, through a slight smile, some measure of erotic feeling as she reclines on the bed and moves out of frame. The accompanying music underlines the sad mood. In due course she does become pregnant, and Sirisena, Kamala's lover, is implicated, though in fact it is Bonnie who is the father of the child. In another scene, Bonnie accosts Nony in a room which she is cleaning. She tells him, "I don't love Sirisena," aware that Bonnie intends to blame Sirisena for her seduction. He asks her, "Then whom do you love?" Her reply strikes a discord which reverberates across the history of Sinhalese cinema: "I don't love anybody." She lies on the bed and touches her breasts and pregnant belly while Sirisena peeps through the window and sees both her and Bonnie. The look of the voyeur, the look of Bonnie, and that of the viewer converge on the pregnant woman touching her body after having declared that she does not love anybody. The voyeuristic power structuring the scene is minimally shifted by her declaration of resistance to feudal power relations and her expression of a pleasure that is not heterosexual but autoerotic.

Bonnie drinks heavily, falls ill, and is bedridden after Kamala rejects him. Nony comes to his house with her father and her infant girl, seeking refuge. There is an extreme close-up of her touching Master Bonnie's feet, a gesture which affirms feudal class relations, and she sings a song lamenting her plight while carrying her illegitimate daughter and walking through the master's house. As she sings, the image cuts several times to close-ups of Nony and the moon. Bonnie's image functions as the source of Nony's present misfortune while the image of the moon seems to signify, in the context of a lament, that which is unattainable for her. The title of the film is voiced in the song:

The past scent of the faded flowers. Another man's flowers scatter away.
The tender smile on my daughter's face lightens my heart as the day
breaks. How shall I find bangles for your hand? How shall I find bangles
for your feet? How shall I find chains for your waist? What help is there
for a daughter other than in her mother?

Darkness flows, loneliness,
Between risings of the sun.

The mother's pleasure in having a daughter is circumscribed by her fear
for the future. If the child were male she would not have to worry about
finding the jewelry thought to be necessary for a girl. The extended lament
constructs woman as helpless victim and rouses masochistic pleasure in
the viewer, and yet the lyrics have a brute realism new to the genre.

Nony's attitude toward Master Bonnie creates the opposition between
Maggy and Nony. When the ailing Bonnie asks Nony for a glass of water,
she refuses to obey his orders and is very rough with the dying man.

> Bonnie: Why are you so rough with me; is it because I accepted you into
> this house?
> Nony: What could you have done without accepting me?
> Bonnie: I can chase you out even now.

Nony, in asserting her individual rights, cuts across feudal notions of gratitude for services rendered. Master Bonnie finds solace in a photograph of
Kamala, even on his deathbed.

> Bonnie: When I see this picture of Kamala I don't even want food.
> Nony: Shame on you, breathing your last and yet your mind is full of
> dirty thoughts.
> Bonnie: I don't have these thoughts when I look at this picture. I had
> them when I looked at you; now I am pure.

This male logic is fascinating because blame for "bad thoughts" is laid
on the woman who (unwittingly) stimulates them rather than on the man
who thinks them. Man thus becomes pure by defining woman as impure.

> Nony: I stole the picture from Sirisena and wore it next to my body;
> that is how I respect it.
> Bonnie: Bitch! It is because of my sense of justice that I brought you
> here. Ask forgiveness of this picture or I will . . . I will . . .

Bonnie, very weak, collapses and asks for help, at which point his faithful servant enters and scolds Nony for her heartlessness. Then Bonnie says, "Don't scold Nony; I am at fault. Don't be angry with me, Nony, I won't abandon you." The bad feudal lord thus appears better than the bad poor woman, who is stereotyped as a "bitch." So in this scene the difference between Nony and Kamala is articulated in highly melodramatic terms to suit Bonnie. The virgin is put on a pedestal and the patriarch orders the "whore" to worship the "virgin," both creatures of his fantasy. The opposition between Nony and Maggy is heightened when the latter comes to nurse the sick master.

> Maggy: Where is the master?
> Nony: Don't think this is a rest-house for everyone to creep into.
> Maggy: Whatever happens, we treat Master as a god. If there is no one else to take care of him we will do so.
> Nony: There is no need for that; I will take care of it all.
> Maggy: We have more duties than you, don't we, son? (addressing her infant son)

The opposed responses of two women to the same situation, of having been sexually exploited by a rich landlord, make this film more complex than the average formula piece. Maggy's assertion that she and her son have a greater duty toward Bonnie suggests that a male child has a greater claim on the father than a female child. Of the three women, Nony has the most insecure position. Kamala marries the ideal male, and Maggy marries a man and has a son; these are forms of security. In contrast, Nony has no man and is left with a daughter for whom she has to find jewelry. The woman who desires sexually, and who criticizes the feudal power structure within which desire is articulated, is left high and dry by the narrative. There can be no narrative resolution for the articulate woman who questions the status quo, who says, "I do not love anybody," who finds some pleasure in her infant daughter. There can be no resolution in this narrative because the terms in which it is articulated are the terms dictated by male fantasy. Female desire creates problems for the narration of male desire, but the problem is pushed to the periphery by the bad feudal lord's change of heart, a narrative strategy which makes him a good feudal lord and thus gains him the viewer's sympathy. The fact that the film was directed and the role of Bonnie played by Gamini Fonseka, the most popular male actor in Sri Lanka at the time, adds another dimension of sympathy for the dying feudal lord and the film retrospectively presents his wickedness as weakness. The villain thus becomes a hero through the narrative strategy of producing a bad woman and by the fact of this star's playing the role. The title, a cliché that presents women as flowers that belong to another man, precisely indicates the unconscious meaning which structures the film. The definition of femininity, though not a patriarchal "plot," is most certainly worked out in terms of male fantasy. The degree to which the viewer is invited to be fascinated with the idealized woman Kamala, and revolted by Nony in her "bitchiness" toward the dying man and the "good" woman, is a measure of how much the female unconscious is determined by cinematized patriarchal values.

Lester James Peries

Peries is Sri Lankan cinema's pioneering auteur, who with *Rekava* (*Line of Destiny*, 1956) established an idiom for a vernacular cinema distinct from the South Indian generic model to which the national cinema was slavishly bound. In 1967 he made *Ran Salu* (*Golden Robes*), the only one of his films in which the auteur Peries had no control over the story or the screenplay based on it. Both were written by P. K. D. Seneviratne, who also wrote *Another Man's Flowers*.

> The pattern had already been set by the script writer, P. K. D. Seneviratne; at its simplest terms, it was a contrast in white and grey—the boy and the girl who had all the virtues and the other boy and girl, easygoing, fun-loving, and irresponsible. The central character was Sujatha. The story was an examination of her gradual withdrawal from life as she knows it among the wealthy upper class.[9]

The standard generic oppositions of the boy-meets-girl plot structure appear in *Golden Robes,* but with noteworthy differences which establish Peries's authorial intervention. While previously the idealized Sinhalese woman had for the most part been located in the village, this film represents the icon within an urban, upper-middle-class milieu. Sujatha, the only daughter of a rich family, is engaged to Cyril, a playboy. Though she speaks in Sinhalese she addresses her parents with the English words "mummy" and "daddy," which in the generic cinema often connotes badness. Cyril and Sujatha have a mutual friend, Saroja, who is contrasted with Sujatha. Saroja is playful and sexually promiscuous, while the latter is more serious-minded.

The young people visit Sujatha's father's estate, where an old servant is humiliated by Sujatha's rich friends. This incident becomes the turning point for her disenchantment with her rich set. A Buddhist nun visits her house, and the two women exchange ideas. This scene is constructed by a medium two-shot with both women seated, talking to each other while looking in different directions:

> Sujatha: Did you become a nun because you were disillusioned?
> Nun: No, it was not because of a disillusionment.

Then each face is given in frontal close-ups, and back again to the original medium two-shot. The shot-reverse-shot convention of Hollywood cinema, with its eye-line matches, does not operate here, nor do the codes of the genre cinema. This conversation, marked by indirection (two people talking to each other in the same shot without really looking at each other), introduces one of the most engaging realist tropes of Peries's cinema as a whole. It is as though he has noted how rural people do in fact speak to each other, without direct eye contact, and then transposed this into an aesthetic form.

Cyril and Saroja have an affair and go to the movies to view a generic formula film where the lovers sing and dance, thus signaling to the viewer *Golden Robes*'s difference. The lovers in this film do not sing and dance; in even more striking contrast to the generic cinema, we see them lying in bed (with sheets covering them discreetly) and looking at each other. This was the nearest that a Sri Lankan film had then (1967) come to actually representing copulation. This scene of illicit premarital sexuality is represented in a non-moralistic manner which is pleasurable mainly because of the energy in the looks of the performers as they gaze into each other's eyes without doing much else.

Under the influence of the nun, Sujatha experiences a change of heart and image. This is represented in a rare cinematic sequence enacted in front of her dressing-table mirror. A medium shot of her seated with her face directed downward is cut to one of her hand masking half of her face, which registers a look of dissatisfaction with what she sees, the bejeweled image of an upper-class woman. The camera dollies back and forward to register her movements as she opens her fingers to frame her eye between her thumb and index finger. Camera movements create a slow, steady rhythm as she slowly and deliberately takes off her jewelry and elaborate hair ornaments. The shot scale varies from medium shot to extreme close-up, giving each gesture a weight. This is a rare scene in the

Sinhalese cinema in its self-conscious enactment of a critique of a certain image of femininity. Her fiancé registers her new image of unadorned simplicity with surprise and displeasure. Sujatha remains in full control of the situation, while her parents attack her for deliberately trying to turn Cyril away from her. Just as Cyril moves away from her life, another man, the medical student Senaka, who has been watching her from the house next door, starts visiting her and expresses his appreciation of her new look.

> Senaka: A great change. One can't be simple if one does not have a progressive mind.
> Sujatha's mother: We have no intention of making Sujatha into a nun.
> Sujatha: Do you think I will become a nun?
> Mother: You don't dress in a manner appropriate to the city.
> Senaka: It is now that her beauty is revealed.

The change is thus legitimized through the gaze of the ideal male observer, despite the resistance of the mother.

This scene is cut to Saroja and Cyril in a car. Saroja is seen applying lipstick, thus drawing a contrast between the ideal, simple woman and the westernized, bad woman. Sujatha's parents, who cannot understand the change in their daughter, confront her:

> Mother: What has happened to you?
> Sujatha: Nothing.
> Father: Do you intend to become a nun?
> Sujatha: I have no such intention, at least for the time being.
> Mother: Any day in the future?
> Sujatha: Who can tell?
> Mother: Why doesn't Cyril come?
> Sujatha: Yes, that's true. He hasn't come here in a long time.
> Father: Tell us why he hasn't come.
> Sujatha: While the nun comes here, he said, he will not be coming.
> Father: Is he afraid of the nun?
> Mother: What a stupid thing to say. We will go to meet Cyril.
> Sujatha: Why should you go after him?
> Father: Why can't you be the way he wants you to be?
> Sujatha: Let him come if he wants to.

What emerges clearly from this dialogue is that in the parents' eyes nothing at all (not even the religion that they, as well as their daughter, profess) competes in importance with their daughter's desirable marriage; her suitor's wishes must be regarded as the final determinant of her behavior.

Cyril impregnates Saroja and abandons her for a rich woman. Senaka comes to her help when her child dies.

What makes this narrative opposition of the good girl and the bad girl different from the generic formula is Sujatha's feelings for Saroja even after she has violated their friendship by having an affair with Cyril. She tells her parents, "Whatever happens, I am fond of Saroja." Their meeting is arranged by Senaka and the two women embrace each other in medium shot.

> Sujatha (tenderly): Sara.
> Saroja: I have done a lot of wrong.
> Sujatha: No, Sara.
> Saroja: Is it a nuisance, my being here?
> Sujatha: No; if you had not come, I would have had no rest.

The two actresses, Anula Karunatilleke and Punya Heendeniya, played similar roles in *Another Man's Flowers,* but in that film there was no point of contact between the "good" and the "bad" women, because they were mediated by the feudal lord. Here they do meet, and through the meeting Saroja becomes a Buddhist nun. At first she watches Sujatha humming, serenely arranging flowers and worshipping the Buddha. This is cut to a close shot of Saroja's hand with flowers held in a gesture of offering, and then to a shot of her looking at the Buddha. This is one of the earliest films to introduce the theme of renunciation of life as a narrative resolution for emotional or sexual trauma. The ideal man (who is originally from a village) and woman are marked out by their strong allegiance to simplicity. The very rare scene of a daughter questioning parental authority is articulated in terms of the daughter's new Buddhist values, which cut across her parents' class interests. What is represented as appealing and good in the upper-class daughter is her traditional goodness, which is reinforced through her association with the Buddhist nun, who is instrumental in her "conversion." Deviance in a daughter can be accepted by the parents and is idealized by the narrative insofar as it sustains traditional values. Sujatha is not a prodigal daughter like Saroja, who can only find peace by renouncing the secular life. The good/bad opposition is made considerably more complex, but the image of idealized Sinhalese Buddhist femininity is rewarded through the appearance of the ideal man, which is still the greatest benefit a good heroine can desire.

There is a continuing subtheme in Sri Lankan cinema's representation of the relationships between women. This subtheme could provide an alternative to the Oedipalizing of desire and its violent consequences—structures and processes that future work can draw on. Within the overall category of relationships between women three subcategories stand out: 1. friendship between women (within or outside class divisions); 2. the relationship between mother and daughter; 3. the power relations often enforced by a mother, to which the main female character submits while another resists them.

(i) In *Bouquet for Indu* the relationship between Indu and Nisa contains elements which are within patriarchal definitions as well as elements which resist and playfully ignore patriarchy's demands. In several scenes the audience is made aware of Indu's husband as a voyeur, the outsider in a scene of female pleasure. The element of defiance becomes explicit when he asks his wife to come to him and she refuses, preferring to stay with her friend.

Nalangan (*Dancing Girl,* dir. L. S. Ramachandran, 1960), *Pipena Kumudu* (*Opening Flowers,* dir. Ruby de Mel, 1967), *Sikuruliya* (*Ill-Fated Lass,* dir. H. D. Premarathna, 1978), *Gahanu Lamai* (*Girls,* dir. Sumithra Peries, 1978), and *Golden Robes* all represent a relationship between women of different classes. In *Ill-Fated Lass* and *Opening Flowers* the women's friendship illustrates the satisfying populist myth of sisterly love transcending class, but in contrast to the myth of heterosexual love's triumph over class barriers, the poor women in these two narratives bear the consequences of the happy narrative resolution for the heroines. In the case of *Ill-Fated Lass,* the working-class woman offers to be tied up so that Namali can escape with her true love. In *Opening Flowers* the rich sister boards a plane to go to England for university studies, while her poor sister is offered the prospect of a lucrative marriage to her former rapist, who has had a change of heart. In *Girls* the friendship between the rich and poor girls is represented both physically and emotionally. The rich girl stands firmly by the poor girl when she is taunted for being a vegetable seller's daughter. But halfway through the film the rich girl leaves the narrative after having articulated strong feelings against traditional views of marriage and obedience to elders, to which her poor friend is about to succumb. There is here no clear narrative resolution of the friendship between women of different classes. In *Dancing Girl* Leela, the unloved wife, shows all the harshness of an upper-class woman to her woman servant, but her relationship with the dancing-girl-turned-nurse is represented tenderly. The populist resolution of the union of true love beyond class is achieved through the melodramatic death of the unloved wife. In *Golden Robes*, a non-moralistic relationship is developed between Saroja and Sujatha, where the good/bad opposition is made problematic by Sujatha's love for the "immoral" Saroja. However, the narrative is resolved through their parting; Saroja renounces the world and its desires while Sujatha finds happiness in the arms of the perfect Sinhalese man.

(ii) The mother-daughter relationship is shown both in its repressive guise and in its more tender erotic dimension for the daughter. The repressive mother quite often works as the spokesperson of class, caste, and religious discourses and forbids her daughter to desire outside such constraints; this is the case in *Kadawuna Poronduwa* (*Broken Promise*, dir. B. A. W. Jayamanne, 1947), *Pitisara Kella* (*Village Lass*, dir. Sirisena Wimalaweera, 1953), and *Deyange Rata* (*God's Country*, dir. L. S. Ramachandran, 1958). But in films such as *Susi* (*Susi*, dir. C. P. Abeyarathna, 1974), *Eya Dan Loku Lamayek* (*Coming of Age*, dir. Dharmasena Pathiraja, 1975), and *Girls*, the daughter derives pleasure from the nurturing, erotic aspects of the maternal.

(iii) The motif of a younger sister or friend protesting the oppressive norms to which the elder sister or friend has to submit occurs in the films *Lasanda* (*Lasanda*, dir. K. A. W. Perera, 1975), *Vasanthaye Samayak* (*A Day in Spring*, dir. T. Arjuna, 1979), *Girls*, and *Opening Flowers*. Such sentiments of resistance to traditional values which regulate desire are important in a context where the feudal virtue of unconditional obedience to one's elders is valorized. That these voices are heard but do not determine the course of the narratives indicates the narratives' commitment to reinforcing feudal ideology concerning women.

A radical rethinking of these subnarratives and their articulation in terms of cinematic codes, especially that of the look, may lead to the production of narratives with a different economy of desire for both men and women. This possibility has implications for conventional notions of realism. The realist argument is conceptualized more in terms of narrative signifieds than in terms of signifiers. It demands that the national cinema become truly national by reflecting the socioeconomic realities which determine life today, that it substitute reality for fantasy. Given the populist myth which informs the Sri Lankan generic cinema, the argument for greater realism has played a progressive role in creating a critical climate favorable to the reception of a cinema which breaks with the generic formula. But the conceptual limitations of the notion of realism are evident in the criticism of the new Sri Lankan cinema. These reviews are for the most part based on the assumption that the characters and the narratives must represent recognizable people and situations, and must create images which are identifiable; this rhetoric poses problems for filmmakers who work not just to reflect what is already there but to make new definitions of the categories "woman," "man," "work," "pleasure," "desire," "politics," and so on.

Three Contemporary Auteurs

Stray dogs should be tied up[10] or they must be shot
—a line from *Dadayama* (*The Hunt*)

The three major auteur-directors of the 1980s, Dharmasiri Bandaranayake, Vasantha Obeyesekere, and Sumithra Peries, have enriched our national cinema by widening its scope both thematically and formally. In their recent films a cinematic sophistication and daring are at work, making considerable demands on the audience by the development of new cinematic idioms, new modes of storytelling, and new themes. I shall focus on one factor they all share, the casting of the actress Swarna Mallawarachchi in leading roles, while also briefly discussing some of the distinctive features in their work.

It has been said that Dharmasena Pathiraja's last two films were ahead of their times, and that if they were to be re-released today they would resonate as they did not in the early 1980s. In *Para Dige* (*Along the Road*, 1979) and *Soldadu Unnahe* (*Old Soldier,* 1981) there is a generic shift away from family melodrama as the dominant mode of narrative cinema. In the latter film, centered on social outcasts, there is no family at all, while in the former the formation of the couple as the basis of the family unit is profoundly problematic. I would like to see these films shown in a retrospective of the Sri Lankan New Wave, so that their achievements and failures could be publicly debated two decades later. The now-familiar idea that the country could be in a state of war, its sovereignty threatened, seemed unthinkable (to everyone except Pathiraja) at the time; directors since then have scarcely attempted to expose the terrible banality of marriage. It is significant that Pathiraja has made no films since these two.

In contrast, Bandaranayake, Obeyesekere, and Peries have tried to re-work the dominant popular genre of the family melodrama, tilting it to-ward a greater realism, rather than renouncing it categorically as Pathiraja did at the cost of his career. In their rewriting of the genre these three auteurs have expanded its formal and thematic possibilities. And a highly significant aspect of some of their major films has been the work of Swarna Mallawarachchi, who returned to the Sinhalese cinema after a long over-seas absence in Europe and Australia.

"I had no desire to be a film star, even in those days. I did not have the physical attributes necessary to be a star. In fact, I am glad that I have not become a star."[11] In Swarna Mallawarachchi's words, in the course of an interview with *Sinesith,* we can read a desire for something different in our national cinema, which is also illustrated by her estimation that one of the great strokes of good fortune in her life was being chosen to play in *Sathsamudura (Seven Seas,* 1967), a relatively low-budget independent film directed by the academic Siri Gunasingha, which aspired to depart from the formulas of the generic cinema. She said that she identified with the desire of the director and a group of others to create a new kind of Sin-halese cinema; she wanted to grow with this cinema. Ironically, her favorite actress was Punya Heendeniya (the "good girl" in *Another Man's Flowers* and *Golden Robes,* analyzed above) and her ideas about acting were influ-enced by Heendeniya, who more than any other has made the image of the good Sinhalese Buddhist girl a most enchanting ideal. This is ironic be-cause Mallawarachchi has appropriated the low-key realism which she found valuable in Heendeniya's performance in order to create a type of femininity that makes the simple opposition of "good girl" and "bad girl" into an untenable myth. There have been appealing bad girls in our cin-ema, notably in Peries's *Golden Robes,* in which Anula Karunatilleke enlists considerable sympathy even while playing alongside Heendeniya's admi-rable good girl. But because of the presence of the good girl, the one des-ignated bad had to pay for her misdeeds. It was to Peries's credit that the bad girl was not simply a foil to the good, as she invariably is in the generic cinema. It is difficult to forget her fresh energy, sensuality, and vigor in *Bakmahadeege (April Wedding,* dir. Dayananda Gunawardana, 1969), *An-other Man's Flowers,* and *Golden Robes.* Swarna Mallawarachchi seems to me to take up this strand in our cinematic history and develop it in a new register. To all these qualities Mallawarachchi, in her recent films, has added others, so that we now have a more complex representation of the often contradictory demands and passions that inform contemporary ideas of femininity. Some of us were tired of the procession of good mothers end-lessly lamenting and good wives who were perfect doormats, and Mal-lawarachchi has given us "woman" as a formidable force.

In Bandaranayake's *Hansavilak* (*Swan Lake,* 1982), Obeyesekere's *Dada-yama* (*The Hunt,* 1987) and *Kadapathaka Chaya* (*Image in a Mirror,* 1989), and Peries's *Sagara Jalaya* (*The Waters of the Ocean,* 1989), the main focus is on the fate of the woman played by Swarna Mallawarachchi. As all these films involve the family, they work within a terrain familiar to the Sin-halese moviegoer, but they depart from traditional expectations in their conception of the female lead. In *Swan Lake* a middle-class woman engages in an extramarital affair with a man who also has a family. The character of Miranda, played by Mallawarachchi, engages our sympathy, and the film involves us in the complexities which follow when desire and what is sanctioned by law and tradition do not coincide. The film does not encour-age simple moral condemnation of adulterous desires (as the two genre films analyzed above do, though in different ways) but rather explores the difficult consequences of the activation of such feelings. It is perhaps one of the first adult films of our cinema, so much of which falls into the category of safe family entertainment. The surrealist techniques deployed by Bandaranayake to represent the complicated emotions generated by such a situation entail the use of ambiguous subjective images and narra-tive repetition to convey obsessive mental states. That a woman with a de-cent husband and a young daughter could fall in love with another man, and risk a great deal for the affair, is credible, harrowing, and forceful in a way that *Floating Flower,* with a similar theme, could not quite achieve. *Swan Lake*'s superiority is due both to its direction and to the realism and poignant dignity that Mallawarachchi brings to the role of Miranda.

There is a similar dignity, in a different register, in her playing of the widowed peasant woman in *The Waters of the Ocean.* Her skill in incarnat-ing a peasant woman without any of the stereotypical traits of the "simple village beauty" is quite remarkable. The romanticism of the stereotype cannot survive in the presence of an actress who expresses her desires and her rage with such directness and force. For Sumithra Peries this film is an important departure, as she has left behind the tender beauties of the good Sinhalese girl and has focused instead on the life of a woman striving to live with her young son in the extremely harsh social and physical envi-ronment of the dry zone. The Mallawarachchi character can be crudely categorized as a shrew, over-quick to take offense, yet it seems better for our cinema to see women assert themselves rather than moan and groan for all eternity.

The two most forceful roles of Mallawarachchi's career to date are those in the two Obeyesekere films, *The Hunt* and *Image in a Mirror*. The roles are similar, but the latter film indicates, more than any other, the seriousness of Mallawarachchi's commitment to acting as a profession. In this film she begins as an appealing schoolgirl who survives rape by her brother-in-law and arranged marriage to reach middle age and a pragmatism which holds wealth and comfort as the supreme good. Her eventual killing of the rapist by throwing acid in his face is a profoundly ambivalent act of vengeance, but the film moves beyond this climactic moment to show her living in great affluence but completely alienated from her family. Mallawarachchi portrays this unappealing character without flinching. In this film, more than in any other, Mallawarachchi seems to figure as a particular incarnation of the fatal woman, the woman fated to destroy man. In the history of western representation the myth of the femme fatale is of Woman as a destructive force, using sexuality as a lure. But *Image in a Mirror* demystifies this myth: this woman was not fated to destroy this man; rather, specific power relationships, familial and social, have transformed an innocent schoolgirl into an avenger, a destroyer.

In *The Hunt*, too, we see the transformation of the innocent village girl, falling in love with a rich man with a red sports car, into a woman demanding her rights from the man who has violated her. This transformation is marked visually through the image. The section dealing with the youthful love affair is marked by a romantic color coding and has a generic feel to it, while the second half of the film, the hunting of the seducer by the seduced, shifts into harsher registers of both sound and image. The girl transformed into an avenging woman is one of the most powerful figures in the Sinhalese cinema, and her final gesture of attacking her lover with a huge pole, while he tries to run her down in his red sports car, is an unparalleled moment in our screen history; for though she is run over repeatedly, the ferocity with which she has hunted him down continues to reverberate. Even in such a situation of unequal power, the woman's assertion of right is only beaten down, not quite silenced, by brute force.

Western feminist writing on the cinema began in the early 1970s with an expression of a desire for strong female characters in film, women who were not heroines but heroes: figures able to determine a course of action, alter a particular narrative trajectory. In response, western filmmakers have produced a complex body of film in the last two decades. In the Sinhalese cinema, too, we now have the figure of a woman who makes things happen in the sense of acting (doing) rather than simply suffering. This is a significant shift in our cinema. Even when the woman's initiatives to transform an oppressive situation end in failure, what remains in memory from this small body of work is the sense of a will to resist and change existing forms of terror and oppression. That her efforts often fail is a measure of the tough realism of these films; they refuse facile resolutions in marriage, which one of the pervasive myths of our cinema has made the great harmonizer of social conflict. To this viewer, the afterimage of Mallawarachchi's work is a desire to further widen the range of what is possible and desirable for women in our national cinema.

8 Sri Lankan Family Melodrama: A Cinema of Primitive Attractions

> I think a truly national cinema will emerge from the much abused form of melodrama when truly serious and considerate artists bring the pressure of their entire intellect upon it.
>
> —Ritwik Ghatak[1]

> I look forward to receiving your completed scenario. I hope it will contain *pathos, thrills*, well-timed and well-calculated *comedy situations*, intermingled with the other emotions, which I am sure every large picture requires.
>
> —William Fox to F. W. Murnau[2]

> If the film industry is destroyed, there can be no "art" cinema. So I say we have to work out a balance between commercial and artistic films. There are hundreds of people who are dependent on the film industry for their survival.
>
> —Anoja Weerasinghe[3]

The much abused form of melodrama is now critically respectable, thanks to the work of scholars and critics who have theoretically and historically explored its centrality in popular culture. Some have argued for its importance even within the tradition of high modernism. Despite this critical valorization of melodrama, there is a hierarchy of the popular—Murnau's *Sunrise*, Sirkean melodramas, and those of Fassbinder and, closer to home, Ghatak are at the top of a critical paradigm. My concern here is with a form of melodrama that is critically thoroughly disreputable, the Sri Lankan melodrama, which has been castigated decade after decade by local film critics and intelligentsia committed to the development of a truly indigenous national cinema.

Underlying virtually all this criticism is the implication that because the generic formula was copied from Indian cinema (Tamil and Hindi) it is alien and, given its mythical formulaic structure, unable to express or represent Sri Lankan reality. I wish to mount a different argument, in the hope of critically salvaging the maligned generic formula of the Sri Lankan melodrama for a different practice.

I have stated before that in the period 1947–1979 there were basically two types of films being made in Sri Lanka: genre films and those that departed from genre toward a social-realist mode; and that, unlike Indian cinema (from which it derives its generic model), Sri Lankan cinema is monogeneric, limited to the family melodrama. Sri Lankan critical discourse refers to this genre as the "formula" film.

The Formula

B. A. W. Jayamanne, whose stage play *Kadawuna Poronduwa* (*Broken Promise*) was made into the first Sinhalese film in 1947 (though it was shot and processed in South India), described the formula as follows:

> [T]he duration of a film had to be two and a half hours. One hour of this had to be given to scenes with dialogue. Half an hour to songs (about ten), another half hour given to silent background scenes, with an interval of fifteen minutes.[4]

His description fails to account for fifteen minutes, but the plan gives some indications of how the structure of the film was conceptualized. His description and William Fox's letter to F. W. Murnau quoted above share the belief that a popular film has to have certain essential ingredients, whether they are "pathos," "thrills," "comic situations," situations that generate "emotions," or songs (always accompanied by dance or movement), and background "scenes" of visual interest. This is a structure developed not from the interiority of character-driven plot but rather from a set of ingredients around which a narrative is generated. This way of working is similar, though not identical, to George Mélies's method of working in cinema's beginning in the early part of the twentieth century:

> As for the scenario, the "fable," the "story," I only worried about it at the very end. I can assert that the scenario so executed was of no importance whatsoever because my sole aim was to use it as a "pretext" for the "staging," for the "tricks" or for picturesque tableaux.[5]

These statements by early practitioners of cinema indicate that this particular approach is not a foolish third-world formal structure but an older filmic economy. Though the earliest Sinhalese films were made well into the era of sound, they are based on an economy that has much in common with a conception of cinema prevalent in the early silent era.

Though the Sri Lankan genre film always tells a story, its great investment in picturesque tableaux and trick effects impels me to think this structure is impervious to value judgments based on taste or nationalist rhetoric. The melodramatic form of the Sinhalese cinema is vital—it continues to attract people in the fourth decade of its existence. Wherein this vitality lies is a question that has fascinated me for well over a decade. Depending on the methodological tools at my disposal, I have come up with different answers, and I am returning now to this genre with a rather different perspective from the one I had twenty years ago when, under the influence of British *Screen* theory, I viewed this melodramatic structure and form with some reservation. This was due to the way in which the twin operations of "narrative" and "spectacle" were conceptualized in the 1970s. The psychoanalytic paradigm made it impossible to think of the genre outside a mode of guilty pleasures.

If one forgets psychoanalysis for the moment and starts with an idea of modernity and modernization, and what they might mean in the context of the genesis of a national cinema and the creation of a new public sphere, then it is possible to develop analytic tools that can salvage the abused genre. The formula film can be divided into its narrative operations and its scenic operations. The narrative economy of this type of cinema is characterized by what I call prodigality—arbitrary rupture of the continuity and causality of the action, and the proliferation of minor plots, characters, and events to such a dizzying degree that one forgets the main action line. The term "prodigality" also indicates the non-parsimonious, uneconomic expenditure of energy so characteristic of these films. Though the plots can be called "episodic," the economy is extravagantly wasteful.

The scenic operations can be thought through with the help of a set of terms coined or revived by Tom Gunning, a historian of silent cinema. In a series of pioneering articles,[6] he has situated the cinema of the period 1895–1906 (the so-called "primitive" era) within the context of modernization and the concomitant transformation of the human sensorium. Gunning calls early cinema a "cinema of attractions," and its effect an aesthetic of shock and astonishment. According to him and other historians, this silent cinema is prior to the hegemony of narrative film. Thus it is characterized more by a desire to "show" something than to "tell" and is an unashamedly exhibitionist cinema, unlike the voyeurism of the later classical mode (in Hollywood). Concomitant with this propensity to display views is an ability to solicit the viewer directly, signified by such devices as frontal composition, the recurring look at the camera, and gratuitous displays of cinematic trick effects. It is a cinema that delights in its visibility and conceives of its impact on the viewer as a series of visual shocks and thrills.

Gunning points out that the term "attraction" refers back both to nineteenth-century popular entertainment, such as fairground amusement parks, magic and variety theatre, and the circus, and to Sergei Eisenstein's radicalization of the concept in his theatrical, filmic, and theoretical work. Gunning reminds us of the enthusiasm of the avant-garde for the emerging mass culture at the turn of the century and of their fascination with the new kinds of stimuli provided for an audience not acculturated to the traditional high arts, an audience created by processes of modernization and urbanization. The conjunction of a new audience (largely working-class) with a new set of perceptions gave a utopian dimension to the creation of a new public sphere. The traditional aesthetic of contemplative absorption necessary for the "consumption" of bourgeois high art was challenged by the new mode of exhibitionist confrontation with the viewer. Film was aligned with this mode of perception both in its structure and in its early exhibition as a vaudeville attraction. The "attraction," then, according to Gunning, is an aggressive and sufficiently autonomous peak moment in a performance that is visually striking.[7]

What is fascinating in Gunning's formulation is his insistence that although the pleasures peculiar to attraction are different from those of storytelling, attraction is not opposed to the narrative impulse.

> In fact, the cinema of attraction does not disappear with the dominance of narrative, but rather goes underground, both into certain avant-garde practices and as part of narrative films, more evident in some genres (musicals) than in others.[8]

The exhibitionist scenography of the cinema of attraction is characterized by a temporal operation fascinated by the instant rather than by the developing situation. It pursues the fleeting, intense moment, whether it be a pleasurable thrill or a thrilling repulsion. The early films are largely one-shot films, in which editing is not significant. A visual economy of this sort is not interested in causality and verisimilitude. But even in the more complex work of Mélies and E. S. Porter, where editing does have a function, the principle of attraction, the series of relatively autonomous thrills, can still be said to operate.[9]

Spectacular Moments, Denigrated Attractions

In this section I will think through the Sri Lankan formula film using the ideas generated by Gunning. Across the forty-odd-year history of the Sri Lankan cinema, certain scenes or attractions recur with absolute predictability:

Love scenes, with songs and dances
Nightclub scenes
Wedding scenes
Lullaby scenes
Crying scenes, with songs
Fight scenes
Rape scenes
Murder scenes
Deathbed scenes

These scenes are so identified with the formula film that on occasion a director proclaims an intention to make a "serious film" (which really means a departure from the formula) by saying that there won't be a single song in it. Though the formula film always tells a story, as I mentioned earlier, its narrative economy is prodigal. It is, in this respect, quite different from the tightly knit narrative economy of classical Hollywood cinema. This feature of the formula film probably derives from the variety-theater format of the *Nurti* plays that were first adapted to the screen.

The mandatory scenes of attraction are what make the local melodramas so "tasteless" to their critics in comparison with the realism of western melodrama, and I don't want to argue that the formula films are great cinema (most of them are very poor both technically and conceptually). But I do think that the formulaic structures, the films' formal properties, are an immensely valuable cultural resource that could be put to better use. The prodigal narrative economy and the mandatory scenes conceived as attractions (the repertoire of which can be changed) can work together in tension, even in a montage of attractions. Audience appreciation of such a flexible structure, which permits arbitrary shifting of visual and narrative registers, is striking, and the formula's ability to effect instant displacement between reality and fantasy could certainly open the social field to cinematic refiguring.

The love scene, with its songs and dances, is a peak "autonomous" moment: the image of fulfilled desires. It is an enchanted space and time created by cinematic magic. The changes of locations and costumes in a single scene, the shots of the lovers driving in motorcars in scenic locations, are equally fantasies of social mobility. In the very early films these scenes were shot in long take; more recent films (influenced by video clips) use a fragmented editing style. But in both the lovers are conscious of performing not only for each other but also for the viewer, presenting themselves frontally.

The frontal address is especially important with the female performer, who looks directly at the viewers, soliciting their gaze. These moments of the pure "visibility" of material and personal felicity are simple allegories of love transcending class, the recurring plot motif in the Sri Lankan cinema. They offer a series of intense scenes (in which the narrative logic of before and after does not operate) that can last as long as two or three minutes. Unlike scenes of kissing and copulation in western cinema, which usually have a narrative trajectory leading to a climax and resolution of tension, these love scenes figure a highly formalized "foreplay" that extends time in a non-climactic duration. They are the felicitous moments in otherwise catastrophic narratives of class-crossed lovers. Several of the new directors of the 1980s have been particularly respectful of this dimension of the popular cinema and have explored their utopian impulse in darker, more dystopian registers—as, for example, Vasantha Obeyesekere has done in *Grasshoppers* and *The Hunt.*

The fight scenes (low-tech karate-type fighting) have a peculiar attraction because the sound is post-dubbed, quite often out of synch, and very loud. These scenes have a visceral intensity in both the audio and visual registers. That they seem incredible is not the point; for the aficionados of this cinema (still largely urban working-class males), such attractions provide moments of corporeal intensity and magical possibility.

The deathbed scene, in which a dying parent extracts a vow from a child to renounce individual desire in favor of duty, is also constructed as a frontal composition, just like the happy endings, where all concerned gather together as though posing for a photograph. The deathbed scene figures a moment of irreversible temporal change in order to render palpable one of the key themes of the family melodrama—the conflict between duty and desire, between loyalty to the family and the expression of individualistic values.

Though such scenes are related to the narrative, they also hold and expand climactic moments to increase their emotional effect. Their duration (they are usually in long take) extends well beyond the needs of the plot. If the death scene provides a shock that fissures the seeming unity of the family, the "family photograph" affirms its wholeness.

Rape scenes are almost always allegories of class and power in Sri Lankan cinema. Usually a rich man rapes a poor woman. She gets raped when she leaves her home, usually looking for employment. Through this figure of the woman, the major schema of the genre's mythical binary structure (which I have mapped out elsewhere) is articulated.

Attractions of Modernity

In this section I will use the concept of attraction as my main analytic tool, to see how it might yield different results from those available to me in psychoanalytic feminist film theory of the 1970s. In *Pitisara Kella* (*Village Lass,* 1953), directed by Sirisena Wimalaweera, a young village girl loves a poor village boy. But the girl's mother orders her to give up her true love and marry a rich man who has city connections. After their marriage he impregnates and abandons her. She accuses her mother of destroying her life. Their house catches fire and the mother dies in the flames, causing the village lass to come to the city. After an initial period of hardship she becomes a famous dancer in the city, taking on westernized habits. This narrative of the pressures of modernization on a woman who cannot depend on marriage as a means of economic survival is elaborated within a moralistic frame. The woman's passage into modernity, signified by the city, is fraught with danger (she is solicited as a prostitute but chooses dancing as a career instead), and she herself becomes urban, rich, westernized, and bad. At the height of her career, in a key attraction, she addresses her own image in her dressing-room mirror, while smoking and striking a pose signifying hardened western sophistication, with "You were once a village girl but now you are a dancing girl."

The shock or thrill of this scene is that it is not a scene of narcissistic rapture but an image which invokes a memory of a difficult process of transformation. It is quite usual in such scenes, as happens here, for the image then to step out of the mirror and address the speaker in a multiplied series of attractions. This spectacle offers the rare attraction of a woman's economic mastery (she is no longer an abject victim), and yet at the narrative level she stands condemned.

The condemnation is achieved once the unfaithful husband desires to return to his wife. The wife, no longer a docile village lass, drives her husband to murder by telling him she will only accept him back if he brings her eight thousand rupees. In his desperation to return to her he kills her manager and attempts to steal the money in his keeping. The modern woman's economic independence is seen as a cynical desire for money, which leads to catastrophe. After her husband is imprisoned she renounces her career and uses her ill-gotten wealth to become a giver of alms to the poor, and while engaging in this culturally valorized activity she meets her true love at the foot of a giant Buddha statue. The film ends, if not with a wedding, at least with a hopeful meeting, affirming the importance of traditional values.

Two scenic attractions prior to the scene with the mirror show the prodigality of the narrative structure. One is a comic routine of a village couple come to town. The comedy is generated by their rustic appearance and response to the city, as well as by a routine of cuckolded husband and shrewish wife. The husband terminates this episode with the line "the village has light, Colombo is dark." The other is a scene of a transvestite performer dancing to a riveted crowd on the street. There is no causal narrative motivation in these extended attractions, but they can be retrospectively read as scenes where consensual assumptions about gender roles are disturbed, given as city attractions to be enjoyed but not condoned. But because the main character is not present in either of these scenes, the sense of their arbitrariness in terms of plot logic may hover in the mind of the viewer unaccustomed to this narrative economy. The modern woman in the film also transforms her gender identity, but in a more somber manner. The absence of the family (or its destruction) is the precondition for the woman's need for independence, and the city figures as an ambivalent locus of woman's independence and loss (of virtue).

The director of this film, Wimalaweera, was the earliest ideologue of an authentically indigenous *Sinhalese* cinema, though his films were entirely dependent on the Indian formula. Thematically, such cinema calls on women to return to traditional virtues and pieties, and yet through its "attractions" it also, perhaps unwittingly, suggests the attraction, however ambivalent, of modernity for women.

My attempt to rethink the aesthetic/signifying viability of the formula (its financial viability seems unquestionable in the early 1990s) has a historical urgency in the context of the current problems in the film industry, which are exacerbated by, among other factors, the introduction of television and video in the early 1980s. Anoja Weerasinghe, one of Sri Lanka's leading actresses and a star in Pakistani cinema, has defended the formula film:

> I would say that the film industry in Sri Lanka today exists as it does only due to the dedication and devotion of those who are involved in it. One of the reasons why I don't like to attack the commercial cinema is because most of these films are produced by persons involved in the film industry themselves. What happened was that the outside producers abandoned the film industry as a bad investment. The film artists stepped in. It is we who have preserved the film industry in this country, it is we who have not allowed it to die, even if it was by making copies of Hindi films. It was a matter of life and death. Nobody asks us why we are making copies of Hindi films. They only attack us for copying them. Today, once more the film industry is beginning to flourish. There can be no "film as art" if the film industry doesn't exist as an industry. If the film industry is destroyed, there can be no "art" cinema. So I say we have to work out a balance between commercial and artistic films. There are hundreds of people who are dependent on the film industry for their survival—from the light boy on the camera crew, to the toilet attendant in the cinema. We have to safeguard their livelihood. While giving people what they want, we can also begin to introduce them to something different.[10]

Anoja Weerasinghe's cogent pragmatism goes against the dominant rhetoric on the Sinhalese cinema, which has declared that its aesthetic advancement depends on its emancipation from Indian generic influence.

My defense of the formula, though, is based on the belief that it is still underexploited as a set of formal and structural possibilities, and could work as a corollary to Weerasinghe's argument. In fact, as I have said elsewhere, the more astute film directors have not moved too far from the formula because of the danger of losing both their audience and their careers. How innovation may be effected in the context of a popular cinema, without completely alienating the audience, remains a pressing question for the Sri Lankan cinema, especially given the competition now from television and video. Within the post-1977 "free-market" economy and culture, which has expanded without any restraint in recent years, the nationalist rhetoric on the Sinhalese cinema has lost its bite: in a national space saturated with slick global media products, it seems futile.

9 An Alternative Cinematic and Critical Practice: *Palama Yata (Under the Bridge)* as Critical Melodrama

Part One

In 1972 the distinguished Sri Lankan film critic Neil I. Perera wrote an article for *Attha* called "Ungrammatical Cinema."[1] In it he talks about a young man's response to seeing Ingmar Bergman's *Wild Strawberries:* "I can see that there is something serious being said in this film, but I cannot grasp it. Can you explain this to me?" In order to solve the problem involved in this question he wrote the article, reflecting on his own viewing, some ten years before, of several major international modernist films, such as *Hiroshima Mon Amour, Last Year at Marienbad, La Dolce Vita, Ashes and Diamonds,* and Sri Lanka's own Lester James Peries's *Nidhanaya (The Treasure).*

The question he asks is a curious one—"What makes some films so fascinating to watch and yet so difficult to understand?" He poses here an important question about cinematic fascination which makes viewers vulnerable—vulnerable because these films seem "ungrammatical," because viewers must learn their grammar and syntax even as they watch them spellbound. In fact, he invokes the image of a child in order to highlight this difficulty. The analogy's point is that children's perceptual capacity outruns their conceptual capacity—a child constantly asks, "What is this?" and yet stares wide-eyed. Perera says that these films make us, as viewers, childlike in this sense and yet do provide deep intellectual and emotional stimulation.

I find this article utterly engaging because a mature Sri Lankan film critic has shown a responsiveness to a young man's intellectual curiosity which then leads him to explore in an open way what films can do to us.

He seems to explore cinematic ontology experientially. This attitude is very different from that of the Sri Lankan "realist" critics who are so sure of what films must do that they go to a film armed with an image of our "reality," unflinchingly measure it in relation to that monolithic construct in their heads, and give it a plus or a minus. This grading practice is what I would call the policing of meaning, fitting the film to one's own preconceptions of what film must do. In this model the film is rarely given an active, productive function. The knowing critic always already knows what reality is and knows what film must do in relation to it.

Neil Perera's approach is far more modest and appealing because of its generosity of spirit, its intellectual and emotional readiness to be transformed by the cinematic experience, and its understanding that cinema is a "language" without a grammar. But it isn't only great European modernist films that address us in a multiplicity of unpredictable ways. And here, following Perera's practice of listening to a young male cinephile, I wish to retell what a friend recently told me about how a group of young Sri Lankan women individually reported their experience and reading of a recent Sinhalese film, *Sthree* (*Woman*, 1991), directed by Malini Fonseka.

This is an ambitious film that I thought would be impossible to make in Sri Lanka because of its subject. Who would want to see the story of an old woman and her bull—even if the woman were played by Malini Fonseka, one of our leading stars? As it turned out, many did: according to my friend, the young women (who rarely see films, because they come from a rural area without cinemas) read it as an allegory of our recent violent history. They read the vengeful killing of the cattle thief by the old woman as an allegory of a mother's fierce and absolutely justifiable anger at the disappearance and brutal murder of her bull/son—she does, after all, caress the bull and address him as "son."

This reading made sense to me on reflection, because there is a sequence in the film which invokes the goddess/demoness Kali, via her statue. This image of the bloodthirsty Kali is, I think, one of the rare cinematic moments in a film that is rather undistinguished formally (in parts barely visible because of poor lighting, poor projection, or both), despite its ambitions. I was therefore quite lukewarm about the film until I heard this particular reading of it. Until then I too, like an urban Sri Lankan Marxist woman, thought, what's all this fuss about a bull when so many human beings are being killed today in Sri Lanka? I find the young women's more inventive reading enthralling. It doesn't make it a good film, but it does show how people do make something out of what is given them in popular culture, however unpromising the material might be. This is a particularly moving example of how a film (whether modernist or not) is actively produced by the viewer. Malini Fonseka's intention in making this film is irrelevant; all that matters in this instance is what sense we make of it here and now.

Part Two

Palama Yata (*Under the Bridge*, 1990), a film by H. D. Premarathna, is most certainly a film of multiple address in its structure, a deft blend of melodrama and realism. The different, often contradictory, ways in which this film was interpreted by both the public and the critics make a study of its reception worthwhile. The fierce critical debate it provoked, its huge box-office success, and its mega-advertising campaign (unprecedented in the history of Sri Lankan cinema) certainly qualify it as a mass-media event. I don't intend to do a detailed analysis of this critical debate here, nor one of the film itself. What I want to do is extend my defense of the formula film, which I laid out in the previous chapter, by making a defense of melodrama within the context not only of the formula film but also of films usually designated "serious" or realistic by Sri Lankan critics.

To this end I want to look at *Under the Bridge* as a hybrid of a certain realism and melodrama. To do this I shall draw on a few of the historical and theoretical insights in the literature on cinematic melodrama, which traces its antecedents to nineteenth-century theatrical melodrama. It is important to remember here that B. A. W. Jayamanne's Minerva players, who created Sri Lanka's earliest films, entered film from the *Nurti* theatrical tradition. *Nurti*, deriving from Indian Parsi theater, was a melodramatic form of variety entertainment which was influenced by nineteenth-century western forms of variety theater. The origins of Sinhalese cinema are thus hybrid.

Christine Gledhill agrees with Peter Brooks that melodramatic staging of highly polarized conflicts is less about the release of individual repression and more about "the public enactment of socially unacknowledged states"—the family is a means to this end.[2] So a staging of the "social unconscious" is essential to the melodramatic impulse, which is why melodrama includes not just tears but terror as well. This imperative to and delight in a spectacular staging of the socially repressed or inexpressible is probably what makes melodrama still so popular in South Asian mass culture.

I want to discuss *Under the Bridge* in terms of both melodrama's capacity to stage the social and psychic unconscious and its relationship to forms of realism. While melodrama may be limited by its will to stage conflict in highly polarized forms, such as good vs. bad, the limitations inherent in polarization may be modified by a realism in the acting and the mise en scène.

The critical debate on *Under the Bridge* anthologized in K. D. Perera's *"Under the Bridge" and its Critics* is itself sharply polarized.[3] There were those critics who thought it a good film and those who thought it bad. This melodramatic polarization of the critical field is a noteworthy phenomenon in the Sri Lankan context. But what is even more striking to me is that critics of neither camp discuss the film as melodrama. Indeed, a concept of genre is absent as a critical tool in the evaluation of this film. So I see my function here as being to reformulate the terms of the debate, not to take sides, though I do in fact like the film.

I would call *Under the Bridge* a maternal melodrama because it spotlights and stages the tensions of the life of a lumpenproletariat mother. It is an iconoclastic representation of the maternal within the national cinema. The icon that is shattered is that of the sexually pure, long-suffering, sacrificial mother. We do have other maternal melodramas in our cinema which represent bad mothers, e.g., *Duhulu Malak* (*Floating Flower*) and *Ihatha Atmaya* (*Previous Birth*). The mothers in these films are middle-class, so in this respect, too, *Under the Bridge* marks a departure from tradition. What is new about the representation of the lumpen mother, Dottie, in this film is that her active sexuality, expressed in adulterous desire, is made appealing. But her desire is polarized, for she is torn between her lover and her love for her son, her desire to give the child a proper future. The love triangle is unusual, because Dottie's husband is absent, in prison. One might say that this triangular configuration is melodramatic, because it polarizes conflict in order to heighten it, stage it. The choice of the actress Geetha Kumarasingha as the unconventional mother is perfect because in her past roles she has always represented sexual desires in the realm of taboo (in *Karumakkarayo* [*The Wretched*] and *Siribo Aiya* [*Brother Siribo*], both dealing with incest). One has only to think of exchanging her for Vasanthi Chaturani (an archetypal good girl) in this maternal role to realize how an actress's body gets coded and overcoded by the roles she has played.

The polarization of economic, sexual, and familial conflicts is carried out through a melodramatic narrative structure. If the imperative of the melodramatic imagination is to stage the unspeakable, the socially repressed, then the narrative structure of melodrama has to be flexible. That is, it cannot work within the logic of linear causality and psychologically motivated action. Linear causality and psychological motivation of action lead to a certain coherence, whereas the melodramatic experience is about the repressed and the attempt to articulate it. Therefore, melodramatic narratives lack convincing cause-and-effect relations and are structured on revelations, loaded moments, sudden reversals, and last-minute rescues. Realist narratives shy away from these structural elements. Melodramas are constructed on these principles because they are concerned with intensity and with staging contradictory desires. Melodrama has been aptly called the art of proper exaggeration, and these structural features show how it is created at the level of the plot. It can also be done in terms of acting and mise en scène. Or, alternatively, one of the elements, such as the plot, can be melodramatic while the acting may be realistic; any of these elements can be structured so that melodramatic devices and realist ones are mixed in uncertain ways. It is in this sense that I see *Under the Bridge* as a hybrid of melodrama and realism.

I would suggest that the film's great popularity has to do with the convergence of a melodramatic aesthetic on a certain realism. While the melodramatic plot allows the "unorthodox" desires of the lumpen mother Dottie to be staged, the realism of the film is to be found in Geetha Kumarasingha's conception and performance of that role. The plot is under-motivated, with weak causal links, in typically melodramatic fashion. Dottie's catastrophic fall into a state of degradation under the influence of her gangster lover is never explained. It is shown as a fait accompli. A simple title saying "ten years later" shows us the changed Dottie addicted to drugs and alcohol, endangering her son's life. The plot transition condenses her emotional experience melodramatically. Dottie has to reach the lower depths of misery; why she got there and the various moments in this journey are of no importance. She has to reach a point of intense degradation before something else can happen.

Here it is worth mentioning H. D. Premarathna's *Sikuruliya* (*Ill-Fated Lass,* 1978), which displays a fine melodramatic sensibility in contriving the marriage of Beauty and the Beast (a midget). The ill-fated one circulates among several men before she is rescued by her true love. But none of her liaisons is judged moralistically, so the woman is not condemned by the melodramatic narrative. This sympathetic representation of woman is central to Premarathna's work and brings a new sophistication in its refusal to punish the woman who breaks the norms of female sexual conduct. Like much of melodramatic cinema, Sri Lankan cinema has thrived on punishing the woman and on a consequent spectacular, often masochistic, display of victimhood. In such a context Premarathna's *Under the Bridge* marks a significant advance, although the refusal to punish the melodramatic woman characterizes Premarathna's earlier work as well.

Under the Bridge is a well-structured narrative and has a tighter formal organization than any of Premarathna's previous work. This formal care strengthens the film's realist effect; there are in fact very few prodigal narrative strands. The realism in Kumarasingha's performance as Dottie is especially evident in certain key scenes, such as the seduction. The manner in which Dottie registers on her face, through a half-smile, her ambivalent desires for the gangster makes the representation of adulterous desire complex, no small achievement for Sri Lankan cinema. It is this nuanced, complicated representation of sexual desire without moralistic condemnation that makes the scene of seduction so powerful.

Even the narrative plotting swerves from full, melodramatically polarized conflict by making the imprisoned husband's return peaceful. It is not unusual, according to the melodramatic conventions of our cinema, for an absent husband to return to punish the adulterous wife by butchering her either in imagination, as in *Floating Flower,* or in reality, as in *Suddilage Katawa* (*Suddhi's Story,* 1988). But in the case of *Under the Bridge* our conventional expectations are left unfulfilled by Dottie's husband, who returns only to see his son and leave quietly again. That the same actor plays similar roles in this film and in *Suddhi's Story* but reacts so differently is, I think, worth noting. It is as though a certain cinematic education in the performance of genre roles is going on among certain films, actors, and the generic roles themselves.

The other aspect of a realist inflection I see in this film is the scenario of the weak son killing the strong gangster villain, which certainly has a melodramatic charge to it. However, I still see a new realism in this: while in *Previous Birth,* for example, the son (unknowingly) kills his adulterous and mad mother, in *Under the Bridge* it is Dottie who fights back against her degradation and attacks her lover. It is after she has initiated this act of self-defense and self-reclamation that the son joins in, inadvertently killing the villain in defense of his mother and himself. Nowhere in this scenario is the mother condemned for the choices she has made. This is a major achievement in the context of the Sri Lankan cinema.

The main slogan used to advertise the film was "The story of a mother courage of the lower depths." This conjunction of the maternal woman with the idea of the illicit (the lower depths) creates an unusual sexual representation of the maternal, which would have contributed to the film's popularity. In Sri Lankan genre cinema this configuration marks a new realism. Conflicting emotions (both sexual and other) are presented without moralizing.

The criticism that found *Under the Bridge* deficient and inadequate was based on its allegedly inaccurate representation of the lumpen milieu under the bridge. This view holds that the film was a look at "under the bridge" from on top of the bridge, i.e., that it romanticized misery. In fact, the film feels strangely depopulated and has been criticized as an unrealistic representation of a milieu where people live in close proximity to each other due to poverty, so that such isolation is improbable. According to this view, if the film is called *Under the Bridge* then it must show a slice of life there, not the erotic life and struggles of one woman. Perhaps it is the title that has led critics to expect more than the film gives; perhaps if it were called "Dottie's Story" much of the adverse criticism might not have arisen. Perhaps the sense of isolation and the foregrounding of Dottie's emotional and economic struggles need not be used to condemn the film if we view the film as melodrama—let us remember Fassbinder's *Angst essen Seele auf* (*Fear Eats the Soul*), where the German city in which the circular drama of ethnic and sexual oppression is enacted seems strangely empty, depopulated. These are melodramatic devices that intensify the emotional experiences of the protagonists and are justified as such. To wish for an "epic presentation" of life under the bridge, as some did, is to wish the film to change its genre. This is not fruitful criticism. At a time when Sri Lankan films are showing signs of widening their range, to melodramatically pose options as an either- or choice between "good" (i.e., realist) and genre films is constricting and debilitating. Such criticism makes it more difficult to develop a critical melodramatic genre cinema, with its own heightened sense of realism. This sense of realism can best be gauged in relation to previous generic work and to a practical sense of realism or believability in the head of the spectator. H. D. Premarathna's *Under the Bridge,* more than any other work of his, approaches these ideals both formally and thematically. Perhaps in this instance the audience was definitely ahead of the critics in endorsing the film.

Postscript from 1999[4]

The polemical arguments made in the late 1980s in favor of the genre cinema by Anoja Weerasinghe, one of the major stars of the Sinhalese cinema, and by myself as a critic in the early 1990s, have by now hit a dead end. With the introduction of video and satellite television the market is flooded with a vast array of audiovisual entertainment with which the Sinhalese genre cinema, with its very low production values due to outdated and poor technical facilities and unimaginative use of generic possibilities, cannot hope to compete. Indian films and film clips with high production values and extraordinary virtuosity in songs and dance numbers are shown on MTV India, which is beamed to Sri Lanka on Rupert Murdoch's Star TV. Indian film, which has always been a threat to the Sinhalese cinema (and whose importation was restricted in the 1970s and early '80s, on the recommendation of the 1964 Royal Commission on the Film Industry) is in the late 1990s freely available on television. Film attendance has fallen, and the industry's productivity is at an all-time low. Film technicians are unemployed, while some of the stars have gone into television and some who have the capital have opened up other businesses. The state of the movie theaters, even the best, is deplorable, in terms of image and sound projection as well as ventilation. Those who can afford it watch film on video or on television. A spate of porn movies has also failed to create a lucrative market. It now seems that only the most dedicated filmmakers will continue to make films in Sri Lanka, against great odds. While cinema as an industry seems nearly dead, a few intransigent and perhaps brilliant films will be made, and the public (cinephiles and critics) will continue to receive them with passion at least for the foreseeable future.

The predicament of reflecting on and thinking with disappearing objects has been a determining condition of intellectual work on culture in the twentieth century. But I can't help thinking that this object, Sri Lankan cinema, might have been made to disappear less quickly if there had been more political will and imagination.

Part Four
Movements of Time

10 Deleuzian Redemption of Bazin: Notes on the Neorealist Moment

Within Anglophone academic film studies André Bazin's work has had a checkered career, at first used as a particular instance of polemical film theory against Eisenstein (i.e., the Montage versus Sequence-Shot Debate) and then deployed as a straw man to mount critiques of realism in the cinema. More recently there have been several attempts to redeem his work from this kind of reductive reading. I am particularly interested in Gilles Deleuze's rereading of Bazin's theory of Italian neorealism, not only for what it yields in an understanding of Bazin's own sensitivity to the emergence of a new cinematic economy in postwar Italy, but also for what it offers methodologically to contemporary film criticism.[1] For Bazin, theorizing and criticism were not separate activities, as they were to become, to a large extent, in 1970s and '80s academic film studies. The overvaluation of theory over criticism has, I believe, impoverished the field. Bazin's film criticism is still rewarding to read because of the way in which theoretical ideas and criticism work together. Concepts generated by Deleuze's Bazin, elaborated below, will be used in examining Hollywood films in the final section.

I will approach Deleuze's Bazin via Sam Rohdie's analysis of Bazin on Italian neorealism in his book *The Passion of Pier Paolo Pasolini*,[2] because he offers a modernist Bazin. Both Deleuze and Rohdie agree that there were two major critical responses to Italian neorealism when it first appeared in postwar Europe. There were, on the one hand, the Italian film critics who defined neorealism in terms of the social content of the films (i.e., the Resistance, the postwar situation, poverty, etc.), and on the other, the French film critics (foremost among whom was Bazin) who recognized that something new had emerged in the field of the image itself in the postwar Italian cinema and formulated this discovery in terms of formal aesthetic criteria. For Bazin there are two cinemas, each with its own history: a "cinema of reality" and a "cinema of the image,"[3] and according to

Rohdie, Bazin "preferred the former, Pasolini belonged with the latter, more with the Soviet silent cinema, with Vertov and Eisenstein, than with Italian neorealist cinema. 'Reality is there, why manipulate it?' Rossellini had said" (*Passion* 3). However, as Rohdie explains via Bazin, Rossellini was no naive realist; he too was a modernist who created a cinematic means to aim at an "ambiguous, to be deciphered real" (*C2* 1). Nor, then, was Bazin a naive realist in his preference for a cinema of reality; he too, like Rossellini, was responding to cinema's capacity to embody and figure a world whose traditional spatio-temporal coordinates had been shattered by the war. This capacity, according to Rohdie,

> involves the sense that the film is being made as you watch it, that film is a process in which it seeks its own shape as it forms itself rather than imposing a shape beforehand: Rossellini's notational spontaneity, his expectant patient waiting for it. This aspect of Italian cinema relates to Bazin's remark on neo-realist films that they had an a posteriori, not a priori, sense, finding the reality they were part of, not constructing reality in order to fill a concept or express an idea from outside reality in some privileged, safe place. (*Passion* 84)

It was this effort to figure from within the ambiguity of an already elusive reality, in all its opacity, which made the neorealist experiment a modernist one, according to Rohdie. Though the particular historical situation of postwar Italy was crucial for this cinema, there is, according to Deleuze, something embryonic in the economy of its image which cannot be limited to the content of these films.

One can better understand the nature of what was embryonic in the new realism by contrasting its spatio-temporal organization with that of the old. In an image space organized according to the traditional rules of perspective, "I see" would also mean "I understand." Vision and cognition work together to orient the viewer and the viewed, as well as the agents in the film, in a harmonious, hierarchical relation of spatial integration. In such an image, unfolding in sequence, time becomes narrativized and thereby subordinated to the logic of action, that is to say, spatialized. This is what Rohdie calls a "temporal narrative perspective" (*Passion* 22) and Deleuze considers the economy of the old realism. The neorealist image, on the other hand, does something quite different. As Rohdie says, "Neorealism loosened the connective logic between shots, favoring a logic within them; its cinema tended to be more spatial than it was temporal with a corresponding reduction of the narrational. Sometimes it was said that neorealism presented facts, not a story" (*Passion* 22). In his assertion that the neorealist cinema "tended to be more spatial than it was temporal" (despite the weakening of the narrative links between shots), Rohdie's reading of Bazin departs from Deleuze's.

Though Rohdie does offer a cogent modernist Bazin, his critical tools do not enable him to make a further move regarding the emergence of a new kind of temporality in the neorealist image, which Deleuze highlights through his reading of Bazin's perceptive description of neorealist duration. Rohdie maintains that despite the weakening of the narrative (temporal) axis of this cinema and the strengthening of the shot via deep focus, and the long take and consequent weight given to time within the shot, it is still a cinema that spatializes time insofar as deep focus is read as a spatial experience. Rohdie's conception of time seems restricted to narrative time. For Deleuze the depth produced by the deep-focus image is not only spatial but can become temporal. Traveling in the depth of the image can become an experience of time.

The neorealist image also introduces duration, both within and between images, by delinking objects, spaces, bodies, and even sound from their narrative determination, so that at moments these become eventful in themselves and may float in the space, unable to fulfil any narrative obligation. The neorealist "action" may seem to float in the situation, and in the aberrant (non-narrative) movement of its components a little bit of time may rise to the surface. A time thus emerges that does not serve a narrative drive, in which movements and gestures, objects and faces, colors and textures, sounds and speech just float; this time produces optical and sound images which oscillate between two poles, banal and limit situations, the latter of which may well erupt within the everyday (*C2* 4).

It is important to distinguish between the sensory-motor situation of the old realism and the optical and auditory situation of the new. Deleuze elaborates the distinction lucidly:

> What led movement-images—that is, the self-moving image—to produce narration, was the sensory-motor schema. That's to say, someone on the screen perceives, feels, reacts. It takes some believing: the hero, in a given situation, reacts; the hero always knows how to react. And it implies a particular conception of cinema. Why did it become American, Hollywoodian? For the simple reason that the schema was American property. This all came to an end with the second World War. Suddenly people no longer really believed it was possible to react to situations.

The postwar situation was beyond them. So we got Italian neorealism presenting people placed in situations that cannot advance through reactions, through actions. No possible reactions—does that mean everything becomes lifeless? No, not at all. We get optical and aural situations, which give rise to completely novel ways of understanding and resisting.[4]

Optical and aural images activate a hearing and seeing function that does not translate directly into actions and reactions.

Deleuze speaks of the neorealist gaze as marked by the loss of traditional spatio-temporal coordinates. It is not a world coordinated by rules of perspective. He calls this kind of space an "any-space-whatever" whose two forms are emptiness and lack of connection between parts (C2 4). Because of these qualities action becomes difficult, if not impossible, in such spaces and mutates into a kind of aberrant movement. What emerges in this impasse is a cinema of the seer and not of the agent. This is because "I see" does not mean "I understand" in this economy.

Deleuze points out the importance of the figure of the child in Italian neorealist cinema and says that even adults are reduced to a childlike state in a delinked world where sensory-motor action is of no avail (C2 3). He further describes this state as one of motor helplessness but sensory alertness. This is not a cinema of action built on sensory-motor situations but rather a cinema that builds up what Deleuze calls "optical and sound situations," which are situations where perceptions and actions are no longer linked or linkable and the "spaces are neither coordinated nor filled" (C2 40–41). In such a cinema both the viewer of the film and the viewers within the film have to learn how to look, listen, and feel, and must link these perceptions to what may be called thinking or imagining without a detour via habitual responses. Here there are no rules learned from previous cinema to coordinate the viewer's responses either. According to Deleuze, what is new in the neorealist image is the influx of sensory data useless for habitual action; "the image becomes invested by the senses before action can take shape in it and use or confront its elements" (C2 4). This surplus of sensory material overwhelms viewers of the film and disorganizes their capacity for coded responses and action. The same thing happens to the viewer within the film:

He shifts, runs and becomes animated in vain, the situation he is in outstrips his motor capacities on all sides, and makes him hear what is no longer subject to the rules of a response or an action. He records

> rather than reacts. He is prey to a vision, pursued by it or pursuing it,
> rather than engaged in an action. (*C2* 3)

It is an image which makes us gasp because we do not know what to do, what to say, or indeed how to look.

Such an image event infused with the senses has the capacity, according to Deleuze, to enable thinking across a gap. To think across a gap is to make linkages across cuts that are "non-rational." This is the creativity of this new form of image. It helps to form links across incommensurable gaps between any sensory image whatever and a virtual image. The new freedom of linkage is one of the powers of this new image. Elsewhere Deleuze speaks of the brain as an interval, operating through gaps. If that is so, then this Bazinian synaptic vision of a lacunary real, mimetically grasped by film, is related to processes of thinking, or is an inducement to thought through the activation of imagination and memory—and the failure of memory as well.

According to Deleuze, despite the different ways in which contemporary Italian critics and Bazin approached neorealism (the first in terms of social content, the other in terms of formal criteria), they both argued a relation with reality, whether in terms of content or in terms of a particular aesthetic formal structure. Deleuze shifts this emphasis by saying that the neorealist image is inventive not because it aims at a lacunary reality but because it links the senses to thought by jettisoning habitual modes of response resulting from the proper coordination of perceptions, actions, and affects of the movement-image. Perception, affection, and action are the three forms of the movement image of the old realism, while the sensory-motor mechanism coordinates these three types of images. The creativity of the neorealist image as seen by Deleuze, then, is a consequence of a relationship to mental processes that are no less lacunary (*C2* 1).

The action drama of the old realism is different from the optical drama of the new image. Because in the latter the transition from a perception to an action is occluded, something like a mimetic act is required to link one image to another for the viewer both within and of the film. Rohdie does say that

> [a]t the centre of Bazin's aesthetics was a return to the mimetic. In
> effect, Bazin argued that classical cinema had written with the signs
> of reality; modern cinema needed to write with things themselves, to
> write, as Pasolini insisted, with reality. It was a call—in the name of
> modernism—to make the cinema once again primarily a mimetic art.

> Paradoxically, this permitted, more than had been the case previously, the introduction into the cinema, and in a direct fashion, of literature, the novel, paintings. (*Passion* 18)

Here, then, Rohdie is noting that Bazin's was not a theory of mimesis as representation (adaptation of a text) but as performance within reality. Rohdie adds that there was no extra-diegetic either for Bazin or for the neorealists, which was why this new image was mimed from within reality. This is also why this image, according to Bazin, can only be aimed at by the filmmaker, and its elements can hit the viewer or the character like a stray bullet. Because this image has contingency as one of its components, chance is not orchestrated within the plot in terms of the dynamics of suspense, for example. The contingency of this image is included in Bazin's formulation of the neorealist "fact image."

Bazin's notion of the neorealist "fact image" helps Deleuze to take Bazin further than any other commentator has been able to. Bazin gives an example of such an image by describing an episode from the final Po Valley sequence of Rossellini's film *Paisan*. This sequence leads up to the massacre of the fisher folk for having fed the partisans. Bazin at first describes it in the following way:

> 1. A small group of partisans and allied soldiers have been given a supply of food by a family of fisher folk living in an isolated farm house in the heart of the marshlands of the Po delta. Having been handed a basket of eels, they take off. Some while later, a German patrol discovers this, and executes the inhabitants of the farm. 2. An American officer and a partisan are wandering at twilight in the marshes. There is a burst of gunfire in the distance. From a highly elliptical conversation we gather that the Germans have shot the fishermen. 3. The dead bodies of the men and women lie stretched out in front of the little farmhouse. In the twilight, a half-naked baby cries endlessly.
>
> Even with such a succinct description, this fragment of the story reveals enormous ellipses—or rather, great holes. A complex train of action is reduced to three or four brief fragments, in themselves already elliptical enough in comparison with the reality they are unfolding. Let us pass over the first purely descriptive fragment. The second event is conveyed to us by something only the partisans can know: distant gunfire. The third is presented to us independently of the presence of the partisans. It is not even certain that there were any witnesses to the

scene. A baby cries besides its dead parents. There is a fact. How did the Germans discover that the parents were guilty? How is it that the child is still alive? That is not the film's concern, and yet a whole train of connected events led to this particular outcome. In any case, the film maker does not ordinarily show us everything. That is impossible, but the things he selects and the things he leaves out tend to form a logical pattern by way of which the mind passes easily from cause to effect. *The technique of Rossellini undoubtedly maintains an intelligible succession of events, but these do not mesh like a chain with the sprockets of a wheel. The mind has to leap from one event to the other as one leaps from stone to stone in crossing a river. It may happen that one's foot hesitates between two rocks, or that one misses one's footing and slips. The mind does likewise. Actually it is not of the essence of a stone to allow people to cross rivers without wetting their feet any more than the division of a melon exists to allow the head of the family to divide it equally.* Facts are facts, our imagination makes use of them, but they do not exist inherently for this purpose. (*WIC2* 34–35; emphasis added)

I love this passage for its humor as much as for its powerful description of *Paisan,* which foregrounds the difficulties of describing it even as the writing delineates the shape of the neorealist "fact image." It is also exemplary of a writing where film criticism and film theory have not yet become separated, as they certainly have since then within academic film studies. Bazin further clarifies the nature of the "fact image" by saying that it does not function as a sign. An image which functions as a sign is for Bazin an abstraction created through classical editing, deriving from D. W. Griffith. He cites a close-up of a doorknob turning, as a man waits in a cell for the executioner to arrive, as an example of an image which works functionally as a sign. This kind of logic is likened to "a tool whose function has predetermined its form" (*WIC2* 36). In contrast, the "fact image" is slippery because it is fragmentary, only partially visible, like the rock over which water flows (which is unlike a brick enveloped by the wall), and our minds move from one rock, or shot, to another, uncertainly, hesitantly. Bazin says that

> the close-up of the door knob is less a fact than a sign brought into arbitrary relief by the camera, and is no more independent semantically than a preposition in a sentence. The opposite is true of the marsh or the death of the peasants. (*WIC2* 37)

So the "fact image" has a certain semantic autonomy within a sequence and can harbor sensory forces that cannot be reduced to the logic of action. For Bazin, the nature of "image facts is not only to maintain with other image facts the relationships invented by the mind. These are in a sense the centrifugal properties of the images—those which make the narrative possible. Each image being on its own, just a fragment of reality existing before any meaning, the entire surface of the scene should manifest an equally concrete density" (*WIC2* 37). The facticity of the "fact image" does not yield information, does not advance plot and narration, but makes its intransigent presence felt in the image.

"In the twilight, a half-naked baby cries endlessly"

The crying child, in the scene from *Paisan,* appears in a medium-long shot, while its wail sounds very close by. We are both too near and too far. When I watch this sequence, which terminates with the orphaned child, no more than a little dot, wandering to and fro in a vast landscape amidst the dead bodies, and hear that cry, I understand with Rohdie that the neorealist image is written from within reality; with Bazin that part of its density (inexhaustibility) is this feeling of being too far and too close at the same time; and with Deleuze that the "fact image" releases a perception of time delinked from action, charged by the senses. This does not make the moment contemplative; it is too harrowing for that. It is more like when one's mouth opens in a silent scream or a cry of wonder; "when everything has been said, when the main scene seems over, there is what comes afterwards" (*C2* 7).

The neorealist moment may hit or graze one like a stray bullet, and its quality is variable in speed, rhythm, and duration (the scene described above, for instance, is very brief indeed), but it can be marked by extreme immobility as well. This may be because it makes one feel that one does not know what to say, one does not know what to think, one does not quite know even what to look at, and yet there is so much to see and hear—the neorealist moment.

"Infinitesimal injections of a temporality" (*C2* 8)

What from the perspective of the action proper to the movement image may seem like immobility is, in neorealism, a new kind of movement, a movement of time, which, according to Deleuze, opens up a hitherto imperceptible sense of duration in bodies, objects, and even the cosmos. In *Humberto D*, Bazin says, one glimpses on a number of occasions what a neorealist cinema of time could be: a cinema of duration rather than of succession, a coexistence of temporalities. Bazin delineates these moments in wonderful descriptive prose while at the same time discussing the problem of describing such a sense of duration in language.

> If I try to recount the film to someone who has not seen it—for example what Humberto D is doing in his room or the little servant Maria in the kitchen, what is there left for me to describe? An impalpable show of gestures without meaning, from which the person I am talking to cannot derive the slightest idea of the emotion that gripped the viewer. The subject here is sacrificed beforehand, like the wax in the casting of the bronze. . . . Have I already said that it is Zavattini's dream to make a whole film out of ninety minutes in the life of a man to whom nothing happens? (*WIC2* 77, 81–82)

Bazin practices here a kind of immanent self-reflexivity in his writing.

Bazin says that neorealist description or duration divides events (gestures, for example, but I think they could just as well be gradations of light) into ever smaller units, taking them to the very limits of our capacity to perceive them in time (*WIC2* 81), thus departing radically from a notion of abstract dramatic duration. He describes this abstract duration as an expressionism in the ordering of time. The maid's early-morning routine embodies this act of dividing time into ever smaller units of gesture.

The Neorealist Encounter of GI Joe and Paisan

I should like to elaborate one final example of my own from *Paisan*, where the idea of an "injection of temporality" is presented in the performance of a speech act. Here the movement is toward, not a division of time into ever smaller units, but an amplification of time into larger circuits of fantasy and memory. The Naples episode, with the African-American GI generically referred to as Joe by the little orphaned boy who is, in turn, generically called Paisan ("peasant") by the GI, brings out the density of temporal amplification and coexistence in an optical and aural image.

The sequence begins with a children's game where street kids, including

Paisan, engage robustly in the black-market auction of the drunken GI Joe, immediately evoking the narrative of African slavery in a marvelously farcical scene where the American victory is inverted by marking the ethnicity of GI Joe. As the street kids bid higher and higher for the "negro" soldier, commenting on the quality of his teeth, his torn jacket, his shoes, an older youth barges in, outbidding them all and terminating the game. The youth takes his "slave" and both move through a crowded street, and Paisan, who is close behind, outwits the older kid by yelling, "Police, beat it!" at which signal the crowd disperses, enabling Paisan to grab hold of the dazed soldier and run with him into a puppet show. Here GI Joe creates a disturbance by rushing onto the stage to keep the black Moor from being vanquished by the white Knight fighting for God, Justice, and Liberty, in one of the great mimetic scenes of cinema (see chapter 3). He and Paisan stumble out of the puppet theater and meander along until GI Joe slumps down on a sidewalk, exclaiming, "I'm tired now, I am tired, that's enough," while Paisan tries to pull him up by his coat. As he does this Paisan's harmonica drops out of his pocket, and he picks it up and plays it. On hearing this music Joe seems to lose his tiredness and reaches out to the child, saying, "Let me try it, please." Paisan then, becoming the Pied Piper, keeps moving as he plays, luring the soldier with his music across a desolate bombed-out cityscape, onto a pile of rubble scattered with tin cans that rattle as they both fall on it. GI Joe snatches the harmonica and blows on the wrong side; Paisan snatches it back. Discouraged, GI Joe turns away, then turns yet again toward the music and suddenly, out of the blue, starts singing a spiritual, "Nobody Knows the Trouble I've Seen," which Paisan listens to quietly. As the song comes to an end Paisan shows evidence of his own trouble, a key, to GI Joe, saying, "It's my key, but the house is not there now, we live outside, I don't like the cave." As they don't know each other's languages, except for a few clichéd words, this cross-cultural neorealist encounter (like most encounters in the film as a whole) proceeds through a mimetic reading of auditory, gestural, and verbal signs. But it is in this episode that both a child and an adult, a hero and the "rescued," enter a playful mode of childlike inventiveness which nevertheless has some extraordinarily somber moments. So instead of responding with pathos to a homeless child, GI Joe takes up the key with "I wonder how much I can get for that, Mr. Young Man?" referring playfully to the world of black-market barter of which he himself has been a victim. Just then a ship's siren blast is heard, to which GI Joe responds with a rhythmic repetition, "Ship, ship, ship." Even as he rocks rhythmically and Paisan yells out, "What are you saying?" GI Joe enacts a little aural and optical drama.

> GI Joe: You like this ship? Paisan, it's wonderful.
> Would you like a little storm for your personal amusement? Yeah, bring it on, Mr. Admiral.
> (He mimics Morse code, to the delight of Paisan.)
> I love that. What shall we do in this storm?
> Admiral says there is a plane ready. Come on, Paisan, let's get on it. (He mimics the movements of a pilot.) Look at the sky, not a cloud, I love this, Paisan. Look at the millions of stars. If I had two ropes I would swing here forever . . . I'm a hero. There's New York City with a thousand lights . . . There's City Hall. Hi, Mr. Mayor. They are throwing ticker tape. Now we will go up Broadway. I own Broadway. We'll go into the Waldorf-Astoria, it's only for the elite. A thousand servants, all for me. Look at the food, caviar, wine . . . I've got enough to eat. Come on, we'll go sleep. (The sound of a train's whistle is heard.) Paisan, come on, the train. We'll have to get ready to go home. It's going to take me home for another celebration. . . .

As GI Joe gets into the act by mimetically receiving auditory signals from the real situation he is in, his body moves wholeheartedly into a child's motion of flying an imaginary plane and the mimicry of its sound. GI Joe is now the "agent of action" in the optical and aural drama of his own making, while Paisan becomes his enthusiastic partner and audience. From one mimetic sound cue to another, a whole train of events linked to the war—fighting bravely, returning home to America as war heroes, being feted on Broadway with ticker tape—is narrated in a marvelous mimetic performance (incorporating Paisan) which gets stuck on the repetition of the word "home," performed as a refrain.

> I'm goin' home, goin' home, goin' home, goin' home, goin' home, goin' home, goin' home, goin' home, goin' home? goin' home? goin' home? I don't want to go home. My home is an old shack, with tin cans for doors, I don't need that key. I don't want to play no more, Paisan. I don't want to go home, I don't want to go home, I don't want to go home.

After this he simply falls asleep on the pile of rubble, to the sound of rattling tin cans, oblivious to Paisan's pleas for him not to fall asleep, because, as he says, "You sleep, I take your shoes."

This sequence, this scene in particular, is, I think, a marvelous contribution to African-American cinema and is unthinkable in Hollywood cinema of that time. *Paisan* is a film that dramatizes a decisive moment of Euro-American cross-cultural exchange at the levels of military, interpersonal, and commodity relations. And Rossellini's ability to include the mimetic fabulation of the personal and cultural history of an African-American GI at the moment of America's greatest victory is entirely dependent on the kind of image he helped to create. For this is no sensory-motor drama of actions and reactions to a perceived situation that we have witnessed, because nothing on that pile of rubble connects with anything else, and it is in that empty, desolate, disconnected, banal place, thin in affect, that an optical and aural drama of a speech act, rich in affective intensity, combining reportage and fantasy, unfolds, creating a connection across decades with some of the formal and thematic concerns of, for instance, Spike Lee in *Do the Right Thing*.

The thematics of home, possession, and dispossession are explored in both works. In the final sequence of the Naples episode GI Joe bumps into Paisan once again by chance and recognizes him (by his harmonica) as the same boy who stole his boots the day before while he was both drunk and sleepy. He demands his boots back and forces Paisan to take him to his home so that he can speak to his father and mother. Paisan says that he has no home, perhaps understanding the English word "home." When Joe is taken to the cave which is Paisan's "home," a swarm of children surround him as he walks into it. Seeing women and children emerging from the misty cave, as though in a vision, he stops and asks Paisan, "Where's your father and mother?" Paisan says, "I don't understand," so GI Joe says, "Your papa and mama?"

"No more mama, papa. Bomb, boom, boom," replies Paisan. These stark, thin words cut to a profile shot of Paisan looking up at GI Joe; then a shot of Joe running to his jeep and driving away concludes this strange, piecemeal, indecisive, neorealist cross-cultural encounter. In the absence of action-movement in these two sequences, an optical and aural image has invented a movement of memory which is not only psychological and cultural. These optical and aural images combine with a power of mimetic fabulation that has made links across cultures, in the most unlikely of places, with the most fragile of means.

Before concluding, we should remember that when Bazin extolled the new image he did not denigrate the art of the old realism, which was built as houses are built, with bricks or cut stones. It is not a matter of calling into question either the utility of these houses or the beauty they may or may not have, or the perfect suitability of bricks to the building of houses. The reality of the brick lies less in its composition than it does in its form and its strength. It would never enter your head to define it as a piece of clay; its peculiar mineral composition matters little. What does count is that it have the right dimensions. A brick is the basic unit of a house. . . . But the big rocks that lie scattered in a ford are now and ever will be no more than mere rocks. Their reality as rocks is not affected when, leaping from one to another, I use them to cross the river. If the service which they have rendered is the same as that of the bridge, it is because I have brought my share of ingenuity to bear on their chance arrangements; I have added the motion which, though it alters neither their nature nor their appearance, gives them a provisional meaning and utility. In the same way, the neorealist film has a meaning, but it is a posteriori, to the extent that it permits our awareness to move from one fact to another, from one fragment of reality to the next, whereas in the classical artistic composition the meaning is established a priori: the house is already there in the brick. (*WIC2* 99)

Bazin the modernist film critic has a fine sense of the value of tradition even as he assists in the comprehension of the new. It is this Bazin, the film critic, whose richness of thought Deleuze celebrates. It is this Bazin who himself says that he is no philosopher and therefore resorts as a film critic to indirection, metaphors of bricks and stones, with which he builds his ideas.

Deleuze was a philosopher who was very attentive to both filmmakers and film critics. Academic film studies can learn a lesson or two from this approach. He has certainly made me reread Bazin more openmindedly than I could more than two decades ago, when I was a student. Deleuze's Bazin is the result of reading the grain of Bazin's thought on cinematic duration as it mutates at the end of the Second World War.

It has been said that Deleuze's ideas on action and time in the cinema are dated in that they refer to classical cinemas or to a certain moment in European modernist cinema, and thus have nothing to offer in understanding current cinema. Given that his work is a taxonomy of cinematic signs, I think the burden is on contemporary writers on cinema to use Deleuze's concepts as tools to develop ideas about contemporary cinema.

If one agrees with Deleuze that a new investment of the image (objects, bodies, setting) with the senses, with duration, is necessary for "action or passion to be born" (*C2* 4), then an understanding of the neorealist moment as formulated by Deleuze's Bazin can be useful in exploring some contemporary American films, as I do in Part Five of this book.[5]

11 Modes of Performance in Chantal Akerman's *Jeanne Dielman, 23 Quai du Commerce, 1080 Bruxelles*

Actors think they have to show an inside. They do, but it's themselves, not another character. It's enough anyway for me, so far. Hardly any women really have confidence enough to carry through on their feelings. Instead the content is the most simple and obvious thing. They deal with that and forget to look for formal ways to express what they are and what they want, their own rhythms, their own ways of looking at things.

—Chantal Akerman[1]

Australian audiences were not able to view four of Chantal Akerman's films until long after European and American audiences.[2] By now, useful conflicting arguments have been elaborated around Akerman's work which help extend the ongoing debate on feminist film production and theory.[3] Her body of work calls for a formulation of some problems connected with the female body in a performance context. How can one perform (i.e., be the object of another's gaze) while acknowledging the mechanisms of narcissism for the performer and voyeurism for the audience? How can one deal with the problem of fiction or acting as a truth that has to do with feigning emotions? These questions concern both the performer as a woman and the audience and are, I think, relevant to any feminist project in theater and film.

The radical ways in which *Jeanne Dielman* constructs space and time through narration and mise en scène have been dealt with lucidly elsewhere. The aspect of the film which has been least theorized is its performance, so I will concentrate on this area. Delphine Seyrig's performance of Jeanne Dielman has been described in disconcertingly conservative and impressionistic terms, using adjectives which do not further understanding but function purely as exclamations. For example, Marsha Kinder says that

> Delphine Seyrig gives a brilliant performance; she is always fascinating to watch even when she is frozen and impassive. Not since Liv Ullman in Bergman's *Persona* or Falconetti in Dreyer's *Passion of Joan of Arc* has an actress had such a difficult role that demands such a range of subtle expressiveness from her face and body. Both Seyrig and Akerman would have delighted Béla Balázs by the forceful way they recover and advance the language of gesture and facial expression.[4]

At one level this response indicates an inability to perceive the cinematic representation of a face and body as a sign. At another level Kinder's statement that Seyrig is "fascinating to watch even when she is frozen and impassive" is naive and dangerous, because she is unaware of the problematic nature of the fascination of the female body in the cinema and unable to see how Akerman and Seyrig consciously work to undercut it. At a time when feminist film theory has been working precisely to problematize that fascination, the use of such terminology is regressive.

Kinder's comparison of Delphine Seyrig's performance as Jeanne Dielman to Ullman's in Bergman's *Persona* and Falconetti's in Dreyer's *Passion of Joan of Arc* obscures the profound differences between these three exemplary "martyrs," differences which are constructed by very different modes of performing, relations of production, and cinematic codes. It is by no means self-evident that qualities such as "range," "subtlety," and "expressiveness" in performing are virtues within *Jeanne Dielman.* They are familiar categories of description of what common sense designates as "good acting." The implication is that the unsubtle, the inexpressive, and the narrow are by definition bad. By attempting to theorize these assumptions I hope to suggest that this is not necessarily so. I do, however, agree with Kinder when she says that Seyrig and Akerman advance the language of gesture, want to show how they do so, and cite the traditions from which it derives energy.

It is necessary at this point to precisely define "action" and "gesture," so as to distinguish them. Following the Concise Oxford Dictionary, we may say that "action" is a process of doing things, movements, ways of using energy, while "gesture" is the movement of any part of the body to indicate an idea or convey a feeling. The definition of "gesture" presupposes a sender and a receiver of a coded message. That of "action" does not necessarily assume their absence, but it includes the possibility of making a movement for one's self which has nothing to do with the intention to communicate. An action can be purely reflexive, in the sense that the action is its own meaning and is not a metaphor or a metonym for something else. This does not preclude the fact that actions also signify and generate information, especially in a performance context, but does suggest that such actions have different implications for the performer, and perhaps, therefore, for the viewer too. The generation of information may not be the main concern of such a mode of doing. This is a distinction which Roland Barthes also makes in his essay on the puppets of Bunraku. There he refers to the movements of the visible animators of the puppets as "transitive action," while the movement of the puppets themselves is called "emotive gesture," e.g., a gesture which signifies weeping.

> In our theatrical art the actor pretends to engage in action, but his actions are never anything but gestures: on stage, nothing but theatre, and yet a theatre that is ashamed. Bunrak . . . separates the act from the gesture: *it exhibits the gesture, it allows the act to be seen;* it exposes at once the art and the work, keeping for each its own particular writing.[5]

It seems to me that Seyrig's performance warrants asking whether gesture and action exist discretely in *Jeanne Dielman.* I will return to this point later. If "performing" can be taken as a more or less generic word to designate the act of placing a body in front of an observer (human or mechanical, i.e., a camera), then a continuum can be established between two extreme modes of doing this:

MATRIXED PERFORMING   NON-MATRIXED PERFORMING

The matrixed end involves acting and "might be defined as the creation of character and/or fictional place: details of 'who' and 'where' the performer is are necessary to the performance."[6] All acting is by definition matrixed but not all matrixing involves acting; e.g., a real drunkard when placed in a performance situation becomes himself a sign signifying drunkenness. He does not have to do anything; the context makes him into a sign. So, as Kirby argues, the concept of matrixed performance is wider than acting, and of course there are many modes of acting. But the dominant contemporary form of matrixed performing is realism. This is a mode of acting which, in this case, would make one believe that Delphine Seyrig is Jeanne Dielman. There is no disjunction between the actress and the role. To quote Dreyer, "In Falconetti, who plays Joan, I found . . . the martyr's reincarnation."[7] Bertolt Brecht criticizes such acting for inducing identification and empathy both in the performer and the viewer: "At no moment must the actor go so far as to be wholly transformed into the character he plays. The verdict: 'He did not act Lear; he was Lear' would be an annihilating blow to him."[8] Here the link which connects character to actor is altered. But a performance, however realistic, can have a non-illusion-producing effect through other formal means, as is the case in Dreyer's *Joan,* which is largely composed of close-ups of faces. The performer who "feels" may be distanced by certain formal devices. Given the various elements across which the matrixed/non-matrixed continuum ranges, it is possible to combine varying degrees of "matrixedness" within one or more formal features. Character is often created through gesture and voice (I leave out narration and mise en scène as contributing factors), and if gesture is matrixed but the voice is not, a disjunction of codes can be created. In the kind of performing which is closer to the non-matrixed end the performer would have to be herself or himself, not an imaginary character; Delphine Seyrig would be herself and not Jeanne Dielman. It seems to me that Seyrig constructs the character of Jeanne Dielman in a mode of performing which is close to the non-matrixed end of the continuum, though it cannot be reduced to non-matrixed acting because we do perceive Seyrig as Jeanne Dielman; she is matrixed. Seyrig's mode of performing can be called non-expressive acting, because, while it operates within a plot and character matrix, these traditional structural categories are subverted by the structure of the film and its mode of performing. I will write "Dielman/Seyrig," with the slash between the names, to signify the wedge which separates and yet links the actress to her role in *Jeanne Dielman.* In the following section I shall show how the performance seems to oscillate between different modes, so that it is not useful to define it simply as, say, Brechtian. In fact, for me its fascination lies in its affinity with notions of performance found in the work of Robert Bresson, Jean-Marie Straub and Danièlle Huillet, Yvonne Rainer, and their respective performers.[9]

Jeanne Dielman shows three days in the life of a middle-class, middle-aged, widowed Belgian housewife who lives with her teenaged son. Her work also includes prostitution every afternoon in her apartment while her son is at school. The film is three hours and twenty minutes long. Some sequences are marked by real duration; e.g., when Dielman/Seyrig bathes after prostitution, screen time is equivalent to real time. This is true of some of the domestic tasks too. But there are radical ellipses as well (e.g., on the first two days, after the client arrives and they go into the bedroom, the camera remains in the corridor, the lights dim, and in the next shot Dielman/Seyrig is seen leading the client to the door). The film is shot almost entirely in medium shot and the length of the takes is emphasized by the static camera. Dielman/Seyrig's performance has an energy which is derived from the concentrated doing of tasks rather than from any attempt to convey feeling. In fact the feeling is irrelevant; what is central is the doing of tasks, the use of energy in actions. I am reminded here of Aristotle's definition of tragedy: "imitation of an *action*."[10] In classical Greek theater there was no question of imitating a feeling via the face, because masks were used. In most films, however, the face has become one of the chief means of emoting, along with the voice. In classical theater the word "actor" can be used to mean "he who performs an action," whereas now the word connotes the ability to express deep and subtle feeling, and a more neutral word, such as "performer," is needed to describe that which one does when one places one's body as an object of sight for another. Seyrig is keenly aware of the distinction between acting as expression of deep feeling and acting as the doing of actions:

> I usually take an interest in the form or style of the films I act in; yet I realise that as an actress, I've been expressing things that are not my own, but others'. I feel a much greater involvement in this film. It's not a coincidence that Chantal asked me to do it. It's not just being an actress, but acting within a context that means something to me personally. This never happened to me before. In the past I was always able to bring something I like to the part I was playing, something between the lines. But now I feel I don't have to hide behind a mask, I can be my own size. It changes *acting* into *action*, what it was meant to be.[11]

Delphine Seyrig's performance is non-expressive for two reasons. Except in two or three scenes, she uses neither her face nor her voice to generate or register emotion. This means that the viewer is not clued to respond in the "appropriate" way. Neither her face nor her voice invite instant identification and empathy, because she is concentrating on the performance of tasks, not the creation or simulation of emotions. Seyrig's performance can be situated in the tradition of Bresson's performers. As Susan Sontag says in her exemplary essay on him, "Bresson also came to reject the species of involvement created in films by the expressiveness of acting." This was what led him to work with non-professional actors, or "models," as he preferred to call them. "His idea is for the actors not to act out the lines, but simply to say them with as little expression as possible. (To get this effect, Bresson rehearses his actors for several months before shooting begins.) Emotional climaxes are rendered very elliptically."[12] Bresson dismisses emotive acting (saying that acting is for the theater, a bastard art) in order to preserve what he thinks of as the purity of the cinematic medium from contamination by emotive acting.

Dielman/Seyrig resembles the Bressonian performer both in the execution of tasks and in speech. The tasks are done with concentration that has to do with doing as opposed to feeling. The dialogue is delivered without inflection, with no attempt to feel the line and pump it with the rise and fall of complex feeling. The voice-made-strange is located in a realistic matrix of amplified real sound and silence: e.g., Dielman/Seyrig's footsteps, the opening and closing of doors, sounds of cutlery and crockery. When the human voice speaks as though reading the character's lines within this matrix, a gap is opened up. Traditional codes of performing are exposed by the discontinuity between body and voice, and within the voice itself when what is said is put against the manner of saying it. The illusion of the subject with harmonious voice and gesture, spirit and body, is disarticulated. The voice does not emanate from the depths of her soul; it comes from some other place. Questions as to its authenticity are immaterial. The image and sound do not fit comfortably, therefore the audience is also decentered. The uninflected delivery indicates the construction of the voice for the viewer/listener but is also a bait to capture something else, something usually rendered inaudible by the expressive voice. Identification is difficult, but what we experience is not necessarily an analytic distance alone. Once again I resort to quoting Sontag's elegant formulations of the complexities involved in this:

> But all claims for intellectual coolness or respect for the mystery of action laid aside—surely Brecht knew, as must Bresson, that such distancing is a source of great emotional power. It is precisely the defect of the naturalistic theatre and cinema that, giving itself too readily, it easily consumes and exhausts its effect. Ultimately, the greatest source of emotional power in art lies not in any particular subject matter, however passionate, however universal. It lies in form. The detachment and retardation of emotions, through the consciousness of form, makes them far stronger and more intense in the end.[13]

The voice as mediator is foregrounded, just as the refusal of the subjective shot distances the spectator from the character and therefore foregrounds the mediation of the camera. In moments of emotional intensity, the tone counterpoints the content; when Dielman/Seyrig talks with her son just before they go to bed, for example, the son initiates a narrative of his Oedipal anxieties in an uninflected tone and Dielman/Seyrig similarly narrates her story to her son. Similarly, Bresson's film about Joan of Arc, aptly called *The Trial of Joan of Arc* (in contrast to Dreyer's *Passion of Joan of Arc*), is entirely characterized by non expressive acting. In Straub and Huillet's *Not Reconciled*, the main female character, Johanna, utters her highly charged rhetorical monologue on everyday life under fascism in an uninflected tone of voice. In Dielman/Seyrig's sequence with the neighbor whose child she baby-sits, we are shown a shot of Dielman/Seyrig listening to the neighbor's long story about shopping, which turns into a narrative of her life. In this shot we hear the neighbor's voice, but she is absent from the image because there is no subjective shot from Dielman/Seyrig's point of view. This piece of "communication" is marked by Dielman/Seyrig's total lack of reaction, either gestural or verbal. Such a mode of performing contrasts markedly with another famous image of "listening": Jane Fonda's listening to the Vietnamese in Godard and Gorin's *Letter to Jane*. The latter film deconstructs the facial grimace signifying compassion that is put on by Hollywood stars and U.S. presidents. According to Godard and Gorin, "It is an expression of an expression. . . . One can right away see that it doesn't reflect anything or rather that it only reflects itself. But a self that is nowhere, lost in the infinite immensity and immortal tendons of the *Pieta* by Michelangelo."[14] Godard and Gorin analyze the ideological implication of that look in the following:

> Godard: It's a working model of Cartesian thought process. I think, therefore I am—the same that inspires the statue of that figure by Rodin. Why not carry this statue around wherever there is a catastrophe in the world to inspire the crowds with a feeling of pity?
> Gorin: The swindle of capitalist art and humanism would be exposed immediately. One must realise that stars are not allowed to think. They are only social functions. They are thought and they make you think.[15]

In contrast, the Bressonian non-expressive performers produce a quite different effect, because they do not try to feel and show emotions. The fact that Seyrig is a professional actress whom we have seen in many different roles makes the analogy between her and Bresson's non-actors problematic. Akerman explains why she chose an actress to play the role:

If I'd used my mother, it would have been just my mother. It was important that it be an actress, because it wasn't just Jeanne Dielman. Otherwise, each gesture would not have had the essence of that gesture, its
truth.[16]

Akerman is here talking about a process of abstraction, about purifying
gesture/action of idiosyncratic phatic detail. I have combined the concepts
"gesture" and "action" with a slash to suggest an answer to the question
asked above: whether it is possible to make a clear distinction between gesture and action within one performer, who is human rather than a puppet.
In *Jeanne Dielman,* Dielman/Seyrig seems to perform actions for herself
and also for the camera. But the actions are never metonymic in the way
realistic acting is. When she makes a meat loaf we see her make it from the
beginning to the end: screen time and real time coincide. Similarly, when
she bathes, a part does not stand for the whole, so the duration of the actions becomes important. Indeed, an action such as the kneading of the
meat loaf does not further the narrative flow; it holds it in suspension. The
traditional linking of action with plot is absent. The action, once started,
is predictable, and therefore one concentrates not on what will happen
next but on the action itself, its rhythm. Akerman quite clearly states that
the performing was "worked out as a schema: she doesn't add her own
madness to these gestures, she doesn't make superfluous movements, she
doesn't huff and puff. It's a work of mise-en-scène: I wanted precise gestures, defined within the space, which she did very well. It isn't necessary
for her to play a character with particular habits or particular ways."[17] This
reads more like a "New Dance" choreographer's instructions to a dancer
than a film director's instructions to an actress on how to perform the role
of a housewife or a woman under the influence. Elements of everyday action are transformed into a system of precise movements, explicable in
terms neither of plot development nor of characterization.

Dielman/Seyrig's silence and non-expressivity is quite different from,
say, Seyrig's enigmatic silence in *Last Year at Marienbad.* There she is the
vehicle of Alain Robbe-Grillet and Alain Resnais's notion of woman as
enigma. In *Jeanne Dielman* there is no mystery (though there is a certain
opacity of motivation), because all is on the surface for us to see through
the duration of each gesture/action and task. Only in the scene where we
are shown Dielman/Seyrig being fucked by her third client does she register feelings such as disgust on her face and through her arms. The scale

and duration of the shot are the same as the average, but the high angle is conspicuously different, even if partly motivated by the horizontal position of the bodies. This scene violently ruptures the mode of performing established throughout the film. It is purely gestural. It is the weight of another body on hers which makes her emit gestural signs. Soon after, she returns to her non-expressive state and murders the client with the same precision and efficiency with which we see her accomplish her domestic tasks. In the last sequence, when she sits quietly at the table for seven minutes, slight shades of expression seem to flicker across her face and expire. Similarly though not identically, in an earlier scene set on the second day, she sits listlessly in a chair when the rhythm of her "ritual" has been disturbed. Here her performance comes close to a low-keyed realism, but she does not in any way put on the signs of "listlessness" familiar to us in most films.

It is important to make the point that the mode of performing worked out by Seyrig and Akerman in *Jeanne Dielman* is not naturalized by the narrative. It is true that Dielman/Seyrig spends most of her time alone, so that the need to react and show emotion, that is to say, use gesture, is less, but as the example of her sequence with the neighbor shows, the mode of performing is not entirely determined by the narrative situation. Also, there is a continuity in Seyrig's mode of performing and Aurore Clement's in Akerman's *Les Rendez-vous d'Anna*. This film is a series of encounters Anna/Clement has with women and men on her way back from Germany to Paris, via Brussels, after attending a screening of her new film. When Anna/Clement listens to a lover narrate his life story (in an uninflected tone), they stand attentively, almost formally, and do not look at each other. When she meets the mother of her ex-fiancé, they sit on a bench on a railway platform, facing the camera in medium shot, and talk about their lives. When the older woman narrates her life story—her total estrangement from her husband—Anna/Clement moves closer to her in one small swift movement so that her body touches and supports the other woman; no looks are exchanged, and the woman continues her narrative in the same non-expressive manner we have come to expect. The concentration is on the gesture/action; any emotions take care of themselves. When Anna/Clement talks to her mother about her work and her lesbian sexual experience, they are both in a hotel bed, facing the camera in medium shot. This absence of eye-line matches is not, however, symbolic of the "distance between characters," as a certain type of film criticism might interpret it. Such a metaphoric interpretation cannot explain why the same mode of non-expressive performing is adhered to when Anna/Clement listens and speaks to her lover and her mother. If she is close to anyone, it is certainly her mother, both physically and emotionally, but in the performance the formal distance is maintained, hence the erotic power of that incestuous scene of mother and daughter in bed.

The effect of non-expressive performing within a mise en scène which counters illusionist space,[18] within a narrative which reintroduces time as duration and film as a temporal form, is that the familiar pleasures of the cinema, especially those related to viewing the female body, are subverted. The voyeurism inherent in the medium is subverted by making the presence of the look's source felt.[19] Undoubtedly those viewers at the National Film Theater screening who began talking and then walked out did so because of this lack of pleasure. But for those who were able to readjust to a new sense of time as duration the film did offer certain kinds of pleasures quite different from those we have been conditioned to expect in most narrative films. One can enjoy the film by tuning into the rhythm of the editing and the rhythm of Dielman/Seyrig's movements. There is, as Akerman says, a loving acknowledgment of the denigrated tasks of women within the domestic sphere. These tasks are lovingly viewed at a distance because they also signify women's absence; they are beautiful and lethal because they help her transcend her situation. It is not only the audience who enter a new kind of rhythm and its attendant pleasures. Seyrig says about her work in *Jeanne Dielman:*

> I have become aware how inhibiting it is to be watched on a set mostly by men. A woman is a foreigner in an all-male world—the film industry. I wanted to be surrounded by women in this part so that I wouldn't behave in any way other than I would as Jeanne Dielman. There is a difference in the way you walk when you are in a room full of men rather than a room full of women, you don't undress the same way, wash the same way, or brush the hair the same way. It is important that I be looked at by women while working.[20]

It could be said that Dreyer manipulated Falconetti to obtain the performance in *Joan* and subsequently idolized it, and that Bergman in *Persona* lived his fantasies through his actress/wife; in contrast, Akerman collaborates with her performer by giving her the space and time she needs to work in a new way. The performer is no longer a function of the male director.[21]

Postscript from 1999

I would like to briefly specify the kind of temporal moves Seyrig and Akerman activate in this film by using some of the Deleuzian concepts elaborated in the previous chapter, which were unavailable to me when this piece was first written, nearly twenty years ago. Dielman/Seyrig's performance of everyday domestic tasks may be thought of as a form of sensory-motor action that is automatic because it is habitual.[22] Saying this does not adequately describe the quality of her performance, but it offers a conceptual tool for understanding the magnitude of what can happen when the sensory-motor mechanism gets jammed and the hand loses its grip in the slightest of "slips,"[23] making a shoe brush slip, a piece of cutlery drop, a dressing-gown button wrongly, or potatoes burn. The rhythm of the young maid's actions in her early-morning routine in De Sica's *Humberto D,* as described by Bazin (referred to in the previous chapter), is qualitatively different from Dielman/Seyrig's performance of the domestic routine, though they are both governed by an automatic sensory-motor mechanism. What they do share is an interruption of the smooth workings of sensory-motor movement and a consequent making visible of a time irreducible to actions and reactions. The slightest slip makes one shudder at the break in the elegant precision and measured beat of Dielman/Seyrig's unvarying routine, which is subject to sensory-motor comfort. This shuddering of time itself becomes perceptible as an ametrical beat or rhythm intruding into the orderly routine. When over the long duration of the film such minute, banal, ametrical beats proliferate unexpectedly, something unravels at the heart of this film's movement. As Melissa McMahon points out, it is a pair of kitchen scissors left in the wrong place (the bedroom) that become the unpremeditated murder of Dielman/Seyrig's client at the end of the film.[24]

The murder leads to one of the longest long takes in this film (or in any I have seen), in which Dielman/Seyrig simply sits at a table and breathes as a neon light beats across the room and her face, giving the interminable duration (three minutes) a pulse, the image a fluctuating tonality, and her face an almost ineffable expressivity, making the image itself breathe. I seem now to come closer to seeing what Marsha Kinder (of whom I was so critical then) saw on Dielman's face two decades ago. After everything is done, there is still, certainly, what comes after it.

In this "after" of sensory-motor collapse nothing much happens in terms of actions and reactions, but simply the passing of time itself; and in that time (so reminiscent of the last shot in *Blue Steel*, discussed in chapter 14), the film returns us to ourselves, leaving me, as a critic, with hardly anything to say, except a sharpened ability to see minute movements on the face which are hard to put into words.

But on the day after seeing this film, and perhaps even for a few days after (after every viewing of the film, for me), it is impossible to walk into the kitchen, turn a light on or off, make a cup of coffee, use a teaspoon, or whatever else one does at home without an acute, almost intolerable, kinetic awareness of every minute gesture and movement of one's own body and the weight, texture, and materiality of objects. This "vital intuition"[25] of time, rather than an intellectual consciousness of it, which has insidiously seeped into one's muscles, helps retard the smooth or impatient motion through everyday banality to get to the heart of one's own action. What actually transpires there where action is halted or delayed, and how one might begin to perceive and conceptualize that which resists conceptualization, are some of the problems I will explore in chapter 14.

The vital intuition of time that *Jeanne Dielman* infuses one's body with may be thought of as a mimetic trace of the film's own duration. This ephemeral mimetic gift or burden does not mimic the film, because it is Dielman/Seyrig's sensory-motor movements that now return on mine as a perception of the weight of time (which is not the same thing as "time weighing on us"). Rather, it sensitizes fingertips to the weight of a teaspoon or the resistance of a light switch. In so doing Dielman/Seyrig is no victim or martyr but an "indirect mediator,"[26] a conductor of time.

12 *Life Is a Dream:* Raul Ruiz Was a Surrealist in Sydney—A Capillary Memory of a Cultural Event[1]

One doesn't decide to make a surrealist film; one is either surrealist or not.
—Robert Benayoun[2]

I am not an ideologue of the baroque. I am simply Latin American. I can't help but be baroque. Allegory for me is much more than a game or an element of a style.
—Raul Ruiz[3]

Presenting Raul Ruiz, the Chilean-born filmmaker based in France, as a surrealist was a canny move on the part of the Australian media. I doubt that billing him as, say, a late-twentieth-century baroque allegorical filmmaker would have been good publicity for the retrospective of his work held as part of the 1993 Carnivale (a Sydney institution celebrating Australian multiculturalism), because "surreal" is now part of our everyday language in a way in which "baroque" and "allegory" are not. And indeed there are many surrealist elements in Ruiz's oeuvre.[4]

But Ruiz says that though he puts things together in a surrealist manner, he does so without conviction, only because of the speed at which he has to work.[5] There are very few readings of his work in the English-language literature on his cinema, which tends more toward enumerating the special effects.[6] When surrealism is used as an exhaustive term it does not enable readings, except perhaps at a literal level.

So in order to understand how Ruiz's cinema works it is necessary to situate surrealism itself within the ambit of the baroque and allegory via the work of Walter Benjamin. Susan Sontag draws out the implications of this nexus in the following:

> Both the baroque and Surrealism, sensibilities with which Benjamin profoundly identified, see reality as things. Benjamin describes the

baroque as a world of things (emblems, ruins) and spatialised ideas. . . .
The genius of Surrealism was to generalise with ebullient candour the
baroque cult of ruins; to perceive that the nihilistic energies of the
modern era make everything a ruin or fragment—and therefore col-
lectible. . . . He drew from the obscure, disdained German baroque
drama elements of the modern sensibility: the taste for allegory,
Surrealist shock effects, discontinuous utterance, the sense of historical catastrophe.[7]

For both Benjamin and Ruiz, what Sontag calls the "taste" for allegory is
really something like an affliction.[8] So Benjamin can say that "the only
pleasure the melancholic permits himself, and it is a powerful one, is allegory."[9] Ruiz corroborates by saying that he tends to see life as a museum,[10]
echoing Benjamin's Baudelaire, who said, "Everything for me becomes Allegory."[11] Sontag clinches the link between baroque allegory and surrealism in saying,

> The melancholic always feels threatened by the dominion of the thing-
> like, but Surrealist taste mocks these terrors. Surrealism's great gift to
> sensibility was to make melancholy cheerful.[12]

When Ruiz spoke of the two baroque diseases, namely melancholy and
enthusiasm, he was no doubt speaking of the Spanish tradition and not
the Germanic.[13] Benjamin is, in fact, explicit about the absence of the ludic
in the German baroque plays. I will take this point up later. But for now I
want to return to "Raul Ruiz the Surrealist," as Adrian Martin calls him,
with a sense of the affinity between the two modes of vision as highlighted
by Sontag. According to Martin, Ruiz's cinema has

> conjured up, as in a feverish dream, the images and obsessions of his-
> toric and eternal surrealism alike. Some caution is necessary, however, in
> any global round up of the properly surreal. Since surrealism does have
> an historic dimension, some of its most familiar gestures and images
> have inexorably become repetitive, congealed, vulgar and empty.[14]

Therefore, Martin goes on to assert the necessity of separating the banal manifestation of surrealism from the profound. To do this he borrows
the phrase "decorative and stereotypical aspects" from Ruiz and inserts it
within his own sentence: "We must separate the purely decorative and
stereotypical aspects of surrealism from the deeper, more fertile surrealist
impulse."[15] Here Martin implies that Ruiz is endorsing the jettisoning of

the "decorative and stereotypical aspects" of surrealism when in fact what he says is quite different. The context is a rhetorical question asked of Ruiz in an interview: "You also cite Bunuel as one of your major film makers. But you aren't a surrealist?" Ruiz replies, "I would have loved to have made *The Exterminating Angel.* But I am not a surrealist. What interests me in surrealism is the slapstick aspects, decorative and stereotypical aspects, everything that was recovered by Dali through advertising. I am not at all convinced by the surrealist metaphysics."[16] In this reply Ruiz is neither endorsing nor rejecting the pop, banal aspects of surrealism; rather, he leaves open the possibility of using them for his own allegorical practice. If and when they do return, then, they will perhaps be recognizable as surrealist stereotypes, that is to say drained of their putative marvelous life, therefore allegorized. By the way, I take the surrealist metaphysic to be André Breton's notion of absolute reality or the marvelous, accessed via dream and the unconscious. As Martin points out, "The medium of cinema was for the surrealists a privileged gateway to the realm of fantasy, the unconscious, dreams and desire,"[17] while for Ruiz cinema is an allegorical system, which is why its figures are ghosts, shadows, zombies, the dead. This is the perverse logic that Ruiz draws out of the ontology of the medium he sees as allegorizing.[18]

Martin concludes his piece with the following:

> Surrealists have always loved the "walking undead" of the cinema, from Boris Karloff to the Zombies of George Romero's films. This is doubtless because the merry undead live out the fine message once delivered by Ado Kyrou that "with everything possible, everything is fundamentally simple."[19]

Looking at a film like *Three Crowns of a Sailor,* one can see that Ruiz draws the opposite conclusion from a similar premise. The cinema is a ghosting medium, its figures are dead; everything is thus made possible, and therefore everything is fundamentally complex.

Speaking at a forum on his films organized by the Australian Film Institute in 1993, Ruiz explained the baroque by saying, "Let's take the point of view of an enemy of the baroque, say any French citizen. A baroque point of view would say why be simple when you can be complex."[20] He went on to say that the baroque is a multiplication of points of view, of an object, a space, a body. One can locate in this baroque possibility all of Ruiz's special effects, which he calls not "special effects" but rather "natural effects." The close-up, for Ruiz, shows that the part is bigger than the whole,[21] while the cinematic instant can be longer than the day. These cinematic capabilities, which have a baroque dimension, form the basis of a method for Ruiz.

He pointed out at the forum that the baroque period in Spain was a time of dictatorship and political repression, in which religious and political simulation arose as forms of resistance and survival. He added that the baroque is fashionable now and has been so a couple of times in the last twenty years. But as distinct from this he maps out his relationship to it in the following way, which is implicit in the quotation that I started with.

For Ruiz, the baroque is not only a European mode of art production but also a contemporary, living, popular folk tradition in Chile, one that is connected to the popular traditions of the baroque in Europe. In this popular tradition baroque modes of construction are related to a system of economy rather than to the opulence and social privilege with which they are usually associated in the high baroque. He explains this in an everyday image: a small restaurant that packs in the maximum number of tables and chairs in order to maximize profit at a particular time of day. The idea is to put the maximum in the minimum.[22] So baroque excess may be understood as a practice of economy.

In an interview, he says that he became aware of this tradition as a result of the Chilean nationalist revival of the 1960s and adds that he had always been reluctant to use the folk traditions of myth and legend as a basis for his films; the discovery that some of these practices were in fact part of an unbroken tradition deriving from the Spanish popular baroque eliminated his reluctance.[23] It is worth remembering here that he was outspoken in his criticism of the valorization of the folk in the nationalist revival and spoke against the Quilapayun culture,[24] a kind of left kitsch which, by the way, is what a section of the Australian left loved to love in the late '70s. The baroque aspect that he found still operative has, according to him, more to do with games, rules for improvisation, and a puzzle-like element in the construction of, say, poetry. He says that this tradition offers a complex way of developing art when one realizes that art has to be a game of making things more and more complex.[25]

He speaks of his initial dissatisfaction with the canonical high Chilean allegorical mode which was mandatory for all schoolchildren, and of the pleasure he finds in the popular baroque allegorical emblematic epigrams, such as "the scattered body," "the siesta of the saints," "the world in reverse," on the basis of which the folk tradition still improvises poetry.[26] The baroque is also important for Ruiz because of its relationship to Arab culture.[27] All of this indicates that the baroque is a complex cultural process and method for Ruiz, not just a set of surrealist special effects. If polyvalence and polyphony are attributes of the baroque, is there not something contradictory in the conjunction of a baroque vision with that of allegory? Most major theoretical texts on allegory speak of it in a somewhat contradictory way, as Ruiz does. Benjamin defined allegory in the following way: "any person, any object, any relationship can mean absolutely anything else" (*Origin* 175). For Ruiz the problem of allegory is that, unlike metaphor, allegory is a "one-way street," requiring a clear idea that "this means that." If metaphor is polyvalent, if it permits many associations and works associatively (i.e., works in a realm of correspondences both sensuous and non-sensuous), then allegory is the severing of any such associative link, and of name and meaning. Therefore a sense of the arbitrary is highlighted in allegorical conjunctions. Because of this logic of construction allegory often seems willed, reductive, and heavy. Ruiz can, however, create an extraordinary experience of lightness when working in such a mode because of the alchemy produced by the embedding of allegory in a baroque visual spatial rhetoric and a correspondingly dense temporality that he draws out from the cinematic apparatus. This is perhaps why he can say, seemingly contradicting himself, that allegorical bodies are both complex and always open in the sense that further arbitrary connections between one thing and another can be deliriously multiplied.[28]

> This connecting aspect of allegory is one of the things that fascinated me. . . . you make an allegory and this allegory touches an element of real life and makes this element become an allegory of something else, of some distant object and when this object is touched it becomes an allegory and so on. . . . it seems to me that in this moment, especially, most of the arts have refused this form of allegory which was such an important element in the history of culture.[29]

Cinema for Ruiz is a way of connecting many kinds of cultural elements that are usually separate; he points out that *bridge* was a very important word in the baroque.[30] Recognizing a construction as allegorical may be quite an achievement for someone like me, but that is only the beginning, for to read it in a way adequate to its complexity is quite another thing. But the allegorical mode is generous to its obtuse reader because it often carries with it an interpretative context; it shows us how it puts itself together more out of a kind of exhaustion of the will to allegory[31] than for any more modernist reason. "A coffin is like a bed, a boat, a toothbrush, a car, a handkerchief . . . a coffin is like a coffin," says the sailor in *Three Crowns of a Sailor*. It is the same in *TV Dante*, when the chocolate sauce is poured over the green apples after a delirious sequence of allegorical images of body parts being cooked like food. I am reminded of that small restaurant packed to capacity: one more table and the whole system will collapse.

The theme of the "Torment of the Flesh" (*Origin* 220), identified by Benjamin, persists across medieval and baroque allegory well into Ruiz's work. According to Benjamin,

> The allegorisation of the physis (nature) can only be carried through in all its vigour in respect of the corpse and the characters of the Trauerspiel die because it is only thus as corpses (ghosts) that they can enter into the homeland of allegory. (*Origin* 217)

In this we can see why Ruiz perceives cinema as an allegorical system. If the cinematic bodies are not already dead and ghostly, then at least they have to be anomalous, like those of the virgin prostitute, the femme fatale with only one orifice, old Dr. Wepayoung in the body of a young child, and the impersonator whose identity is mercurial, to mention a few in *Three Crowns of a Sailor*.

Thinking about allegorical vision and changing allegorical intention, I feel the need as a Sri Lankan Australian to mention an image of the corpse that's past all mourning, past all capacity for mourning, in Ruiz's cinema.[32] This is the recurrent image of a mangled corpse being eaten by dogs, who often stop to scratch themselves. No thoughtful skeleton here (I am thinking of *Darkness at Noon* and *TV Dante*), brooding over this image as skeletons do over piles of skulls in medieval and even early-twentieth-century emblems. But in *TV Dante* the poet does cry out once, in an ostentatious act of lamentation, upon seeing this image beyond grief. Grief is personal, mourning is a public act; it presupposes an audience, thus a certain sense of theater.[33] It follows then that the emblematic allegorical figures come with the injunction "Read me." Allegories and ghosts are temporal phantasms that sustain the act of mourning. Benjamin says that they have an "affinity for mourners, for those who ponder over signs and over the future" (*Origin* 193).

Discussing the disparity and dissonance central to the Spanish baroque aesthetic of Balthasar Gracian, Ruiz comments on the function of death for himself:

I try to remember that disparity exists. And this is done well in remembering death. But as such death becomes a completely other thing than a complaisance of dying, something other than melancholy. On the contrary it becomes an implement for working; a tool. In fact, if there were a general manifestation of death, let us say a kind of annihilation wherein something is wiped out, then death may have other representations such as sleep, forgetting, absence, discontinuities in cinematic montage. . . . Once formalised these forms of death become rhetorical tools for an audio-visual medium.[34]

Ruiz has drawn from the disintegrating power of death a cinematic life; he has been able to read the apparatus in death's shadow and has thereby been able to enrich the affective experience of allegory as well as of film. The ludic element is perhaps a direct result of his ability to draw so much play/life from a putatively dead, i.e., immobile, apparatus. In Ruiz it is the ludic aspect that makes real the reality of eternal passing, which according to Susan Buck-Morss is the temporality of allegory, as distinct from that of the aesthetic symbol.[35] The impersonator in *Three Crowns of a Sailor* who insists that the person who jumped overboard yesterday was not him but "The Other" is a good example of these shadowy beings without qualities who are created according to the logic of the cinematographic instant, which is multiple because it is articulated through multiple moments of "death," every twenty-fourth fraction of a second.[36] Here its useful to mention Ruiz's notion of the unconscious as something that happens between people rather than in dreams, which he offers as a critique of identity. So the psychic apparatus is envisaged as an intersubjective space. The correspondence that may be drawn between the psychic and the cinematic apparatus here suggests a sort of limitless space-time of production.

Since I am talking about the ludic in Ruiz and the thematic of the torment of the flesh, this is a good moment to turn to that great tormentor of flesh, that mythical avatar, the femme fatale in *Three Crowns of a Sailor*. Lisa Lyon, the American bodybuilder and performance artist made famous by Robert Mapplethorpe,[37] gives body to the femme fatale, who in Ruiz's hands becomes an allegory of art. It goes without saying that one can enjoy this segment as well as the whole film at a literal level without seeing its allegorical structure. But I want to try and read it as allegory and see where it goes.

According to Herbert Cysarz, allegorical emblems work in the following way: "Every idea, however abstract, is compressed into an image, and this image, however concrete, is then stamped out in verbal form" (quoted in *Origin* 199). An allegorical construction thus must be both concrete and abstract at the same time. Lisa Lyon, as an allegory of art, conforms to these principles of construction.

The man without a name or qualities, the sailor, is brought into a dance hall by a friend, who sets the allegorical scene by saying, "Here you forget all the cares of the world. The only true heaven is art, beauty." The sailor's narrative voiceover comment about the femme fatale is allegorizing: "Mathilde was nudity made art; the cursed woman made me suffer so much that I forgot all my cares." The sailor, aroused by the femme fatale's deliriously sensual mambo dance, is audibly moved to emit a spoken commentary of a very tentative kind:

> Yes, that's it, or rather you see what I mean . . . yes. I thought that . . . I was feeling good. No, rather . . . You see what I mean. Yes, that's it, or rather . . . you see what I mean . . .

Diegetically this commentary could be read as belonging to the framing story of the sailor's narration to the student of seeing the femme fatale; at the same time it could also be read as an expression of the ineffability of art. The femme fatale, true to form, is unmoved by the sailor's agitation and speaks eloquently, in maxims and "beautiful, interspersed, apophthegms" (*Origin* 196), which are a familiar baroque idiom. For example, her opening gambit, "Nudity is an art, besides art is only nudity," has the generality and finality of a maxim and functions here as a "flash of light" does in baroque painting.[38] The maxim is, according to Benjamin, "a flash of light in the entangling darkness of allegory" (*Origin* 197); it creates a temporal moment in which a constellation can form between unrelated images. In the baroque Trauerspiel these terse and pithy sayings are, according to Benjamin, its very pillars, thus central to its structure. Here too it is through these rhetorical figures that the femme fatale is explicitly and humorously metamorphosed allegorically into an emblem of art. Birken's comment is certainly applicable to how the allegory works in this film: "the spoken word makes no pretence to be dialogue, and is primarily a commentary on the images, spoken by the images" (quoted in *Origin* 195). The conversation between the femme fatale, the sailor, and his friend is structured according to such a logic, though it does work as dialogue too. The wonder of the scene is in the performance which imbues the allegorizing procedures with a delicious ambivalence and consequent lightness.

When the friend tries to break the ice by saying, "He admires you like one admires art," the allegory, Mathilde, replies with "There is no more art, only too much civilization. Art is barbarous." Then she tells the sailor, "I don't know what your opinion is," to which he replies, "Same as yours." And she rejoins, "That's what they all say, but nudity scares them sooner or later." We will very soon see this prophecy fulfilled. The friend mediates again, saying, "My friend would like to stay alone with you," which statement Mathilde, the femme fatale, immediately allegorizes with "He is right, art is loneliness." There is a nice break in the sequence at this point, when she says, "I will see you tomorrow, when and where I choose." The break functions like a sign for suspense without the corresponding affect. When they meet again, the purple prose of the allegorical emblem enunciates a nineteenth-century romantic view of art as transcendence of which allegory is the very ruin:

> This disgusts me. We should have met outdoors in the eye of the storm, far from the prejudices of the world, at the supreme moment lightning would have annihilated us. Nothingness is perfect nudity. I'll render your desires transcendent.

This emblem is highly aware of its immanence, even as it articulates the desire for transcendence in the idiom of high romantic agony proper to a Tristan and Isolde, encoded in the temporality of the symbol, which is that of "fleeting eternity."[39] This is the famous doubleness of allegory in operation. The sailor then responds obtusely, "I want to see you naked"; the allegorical emblem, trying to educate the sailor in how to read her, says, "Tangible nudity is the skin which clothes the being." Unable to follow a line of abstract inquiry to do with, say, intangible nudity and where that might lead, he can only come up with the simple, and in this allegorical context entirely simple-minded, "I want to make love to you," so he has to listen to the devastating maxim "Love can't be made, love is." Not quite devastated, because obsessed with complete revelation, he says, "I have never seen someone completely naked." Then the allegory, naked woman as art, says, "But I am not naked" and proceeds to disrobe by rehearsing a gesture performed by Magritte in his painting *The Rape*. In Magritte the gesture is a metaphoric operation, condensing one orifice into another. In *Three Crowns of a Sailor*, when Lisa Lyon as the femme fatale detaches her nipples and vulva from where they naturally belong and places them on a table ornamented with stars, they do not form a new constellation, as they do in the ambiguously gendered head of Magritte. The body, denuded of its sexual anatomy and thus subject to "the disjunctive atomising principle of allegory" (*Origin* 208), becomes more eloquent than ever. "You see, I have only one orifice. I do everything with my mouth," she says. This is baroque economy (putting the maximum in the minimum) at its ludic best. Because allegory does not work like metaphor, the two things (femme fatale, art) do not perfectly transfer (which is the meaning of the Greek *metapherein,* from which the word *metaphor* derives). Because of the methodological impossibility of a complete fusion, it is impossible to forget the tangible cinematic image of Lisa Lyon's built-up body, her particular form of willed corporeality, even as she verbally enunciates an abstract romantic ontology of art.

Benjamin says that nakedness as an emblem appeared in the middle ages as a radical attempt at the subjugation of flesh in western Christian allegory. This was so because flesh was suspect, tied to the fall from grace, and was also associated with the demonic (*Origin* 222). According to Friedrich von Bezhold, "whenever medieval scholarship came across unclothed figures, it sought to explain this impropriety with reference to a symbolism which was frequently far-fetched, and generally hostile" (quoted in *Origin* 222). But in Ruiz's allegorical presentation of Lisa Lyon's body as an emblem of art the equation is anything but far-fetched; in fact there is something quite familiar in presenting the naked female form as art, thus evoking a whole genre of western painting. I want therefore to call this aspect an inconspicuous practice of allegory, drawing on the distinction that Benjamin makes between conspicuous and inconspicuous allegorical constructs (*Origin* 191). The proscenium theater space within which the elaborate baroque configuration of Lisa Lyon's mambo dance is displayed renders it in a certain way an amalgam of both conspicuous and inconspicuous allegory. While this sequence has the ostentation and hyperbole proper to allegory and the emblem, it simultaneously operates on another register related to the theatricality of the setting itself, which in fact naturalizes the grandiloquent. This stereotype is given the proper illusionist space to play in, to display her virtuosity, so that she returns in a register of the ludic.

I want now to return to Benjamin's comment that German allegory of the Trauerspiel knew nothing of inconspicuous allegory, only the ostentatious, unlike the Spanish allegory of a Calderon. Benjamin says that "because of its obsession with earnestness the German Trauerspiel never mastered the art of using allegory inconspicuously. Only comedy could lighten the gravity of the allegorical will" (*Origin* 191). Ruiz is a master of the inconspicuous use of allegory. One of his contributions to the history of the stereotype in cinema is that he has given us the fatal woman in a ludic register without diminishing her power to fascinate. It is this toxic mixture that gives her allegorical embodiment such a miraculous lightness.

At the very moment when the femme fatale begins to disrobe we are made aware of an everyday image of a man (uncommonly like Ruiz in shape) reading a newspaper and watching television in that same baroque room with no windows, who finally intervenes in the scene to eject the besotted, hence too earnest, sailor from this world of allegorical play governed by the arbitrary rule of dead objects. The breasts and vulva of the femme fatale, simulacra all, have been ceremoniously discarded as exhausted allegorical emblems, while the orifice where nature and history meet, whose emissions are an "eternal passing," is allegorized with all the wonder of a miracle.

That surrealism still finds so much life in these exhausted emblems of female mythic nature suggests that it has lost an awareness of the tension between repetition and change in the problem of returning to the stereotype. Ruiz's cunning allegorical practice, in contrast, offers a form of realism (believability) for the moment, and Lisa Lyon as femme fatale as art is for me its most memorable emblem.

Perhaps the figure of the femme fatale survives as a trickster here because she returns as an allegorical emblem rather than in the more familiar form of a mythic symbol. As a mythic symbol she would of course have to die. But as an emblem she activates a form of demonic agency (neither human nor divine but in between) which is said to be proper to all allegorical heroes.[40] This means, among other things, that agency and image become closely linked, even to the extent of being fixed; femme fatale equals trickster, but this very fixity also permits the ascription of a certain kind of action to allegorical images.

What then is the emblematic action or trick that this allegory of art performs? She is an allegory simulating an aesthetic symbol in order to lure the sailor and ruin his impossible desire. This simulation is achieved partly via her commentary, which espouses a romantic notion of art consonant with the valorization of the aesthetic symbol. This then is also the famed stereotypic duplicity of the femme fatale mirroring the doubleness of allegory.

In staging an antique battle (here I assume that the nineteenth century is our antiquity) between the claims of the symbol and those of allegory through the late-twentieth-century body of Lisa Lyon, is Ruiz giving us in a ludic register (play, enthusiasm, frenzy)[41] what was first staged as melodrama in the nineteenth-century romantic debates where the symbol killed the taste for allegory? Perhaps he is. But I don't think this is simply an instance of reversal and play with genre. For in staging this reversal, both in a nineteenth-century dance hall with a proscenium stage and in a baroque boudoir that seems to recede into infinity, Ruiz and Lyon have been able to allegorically metamorphose the mythic symbol "Woman" and the spaces and temporality that have traditionally defined that symbol.

The placement of this scene is an index of its centrality to the film as a commentary on Ruiz's own allegorical practice. As such it may be read as an allegory of allegorical efficacy.[42] It is, I think, important that this whole scene is placed between two scenes of the loss of the maternal, two spacetimes charged with fantasy. First, the sailor learning of the death of his real mother in numerous fictional accounts stumbles into the dance hall seeking forgetfulness. Then, soon after the scene with the femme fatale, the sailor finds the rented mother on board the ghost ship, a substitute for the real one, but really an allegory of memory.[43]

The Maternal as Emblematic Memory

Historical surrealism brings a willed and enabling break with tradition which is one of the meanings of the avant-garde, in its desire to create the new. In the case of Ruiz and Baudelaire, the break with tradition was anything but willed. Baudelaire's allegorical work was a response to the shock of modernity, while for Ruiz the loss of tradition is marked by the Chilean diaspora. From a position of loss of country, language, and identity, Ruiz begins to recover by allegorizing the moment of rupture in a film such as *Three Crowns of a Sailor*. But for the allegorist there is really no return to a moment of plenitude, as Ruiz expresses in the following anecdote. When asked how he felt on returning to Chile after ten years of exile, he said,

> The first time was a shock. I felt like one of the living dead. It wasn't a feeling of nostalgia, it was more like—*saudade*—you could call that nostalgia for something that was never there. It's a mixed feeling— you're also glad it was never there.[44]

This paradoxical mixture of remembering and forgetting, this peculiar non-retentive multiple temporality, seems to create an affective register for turning toward tradition, toward a cultural memory, as a precondition for invention. As there seems to be a correspondence between *saudade* and Proust's involuntary memory, I want to read the former via Benjamin's commentary on the latter. "An experienced event is finite, at any rate confined to one sphere of experience; a remembered event is infinite, because it is only a key to everything that happened before it and after it."[45] But if what evokes *saudade* was never there, either in experience or memory, then does this not transform the past into a pure virtuality and thereby make it inexhaustible? Then memory's work would not be retention or recovery but invention across a temporal abyss.

The rented mother as an allegory of memory is reminiscent of Benjamin's angel of history, who according to Irving Wohlfarth is also an allegory of memory, i.e., remembrance (*Eingedenken*).[46] Therefore, I will frame my reading of this sequence on a hunch—namely, that the rented mother as an allegory of memory may be to Ruiz's film what the corpse was to baroque allegory and what the whore was to Baudelaire's. She is something like an allegory of allegory, its very matrix.[47]

Two letters are read out in *Three Crowns of a Sailor*. One is written by the sailor to his mother as he departs on the ghost ship, with haunting lines like "I forgive you for not giving me a name, I forgive you the nights without electricity, I forgive you Valparaiso." The other is from the rented mother to her sons on the ghost ship, after she has been made to disembark for having inadvertently caused a fatal fight over access to her. The spaces in which these two letters are heard echo each other in subliminal ways that are partly a function of mise en scène, the tonality of the images and of the music. Both letters are heard over images of the ocean and sky, but at all times these images are intersected by human constructs such as steel bridges and parts of the ship itself. So we see nature through a grid of delicate steel decorative motifs, as it were. The film plays with the similarity of the French words for sea and mother (*la mer, la mère*) and yet does not succumb in an oceanic surrender to the maternal as mythic symbol.

The doubling of the absolutely singular is, according to Benjamin, a sign of the tenacity and fanaticism of the allegorical will (*Origin* 193). The doubles, the real mother and the rented mother, are a testimony to such a will. This doubling is different from a splitting. The splitting of the mythic symbol "Mother" usually produces the good and the bad mother of both myth (Pattini and Kali) and psychoanalysis. The doubling here produces instead a delicious sense of non-sense, which is perhaps an affective precondition for allegory to begin its work of signification, while the humor in it certainly enhances our receptivity to this anomalous figure.

What function does this rented mother perform in this film, which has been described as an allegory of contemporary exile? Why does she pop up in a ship of the dead, a place where memory would have no function at all? The essential question to ask here, under Benjamin's tutelage, is "What kind of memory does she emblematize?" for Benjamin has shown us how memory itself has mutated under certain historico-technological pressures and that therefore is not unitary. He maps out this process of the fragmentation of memory in his essay "The Storyteller," which may be summarized thus: Since the disintegration of the epic, *Mnemosyne* has been separated into *Gedächtnis* and *Eingedenken,* the memory of the many and the remembrance of the one. Benjamin explains this in detail in the following:

> Mnemosyne, the rememberer, was the Muse of the epic art of the Greeks because memory is the epic faculty par excellence. . . . Memory creates the chain of tradition which passes a happening on from genera- tion to generation. It is the muse-derived element of the epic art and encompasses its varieties. In the first place among these is the one prac- ticed by the storyteller. It starts the web which all stories together form in the end. One ties on to the next, as the great storytellers, particularly the oriental ones, have always readily shown. In each of them there is a Scheherezade who thinks of a fresh story whenever her tale comes to a stop. This is epic memory (Gedächtnis) and the storyteller's muse.[48]

Gilbert Adair has aptly called the Ruiz of *Three Crowns of a Sailor* She- heruizade,[49] for he has drawn both Chilean and European seafaring tales into a mise en abîme structure that seems truly inexhaustible, thus hap- pily contradicting Benjamin's melancholy reflection on the demise of oral storytelling in an era dominated by information and the loss of a capacity for experience, and yet in a sense confirming a certain Benjaminian con- viction about cinema's double-edged capacity for destruction and creation of experience.[50]

Benjamin further describes the mutation and fragmentation of memory in the following passage:

> Against it (the storyteller) is to be set another principle, the Muse of the novel, which initially—that is to say in the epic—lies concealed, not yet differentiated from that of the story. In epics it can at most be occasion- ally divined, particularly at such solemn Homeric moments as the initial invocations of the Muse. What these passages prefigure is the perpetuat-

ing memory of the novelist as opposed to the short-lived reminiscences of the storyteller. The former is dedicated to the one hero, the one odyssey or the one struggle; the latter to the many scattered occurrences. It is in other words, remembrance (*Eingedenken*) that, as the novelist's muse, joins memory (*Gedächtnis*), the storyteller's, their original unity having come apart with the disintegration of the epic.[51]

With this theory of memory and its vicissitudes in mind I want to analyze the sequence of the rented mother. The first captain who rents the mother introduces her by saying, "There are two types of contamination, contamination of solids like furniture and this ship, and the contamination of the gaseous, air, the wind," and adds that "only one thing is pure, our lady the sea and alcohol," thus drawing our lady the sea and oblivion into some sort of equivalence. The gestures of cutting an image from a magazine and of choosing an uncontaminated cigarette from a contaminated pack introduce this sequence. The fiction is now well and truly in the realm of the inflation and contamination of solids and the gaseous that circulate from the exterior to the interior and it is to assuage such a state of things that the rented mother is hired.[52] Following this preliminary introduction the sailor muses, "I thought I had met a person able to explain the meaning of life." Here it is worth noting Wolhfarth's observation that Benjamin echoes Georg Lukacs in saying that "the notion of the meaning of life is the center around which the novel revolves."[53]

In their actual encounter in private, the sailor and the rented mother address each other in a shot-reverse-shot sequence during which the image rocks from side to side in a gentle movement while the rented mother asks a series of questions: "Who are you?" "Where are you from?" "What do your parents do?" "What did you do in Valparaiso?" The sailor does not respond to "Who are you?" "Nowhere" is his initial answer to the question "Where are you from?" and silence his reply to the further inquiry "From Valparaiso?" So when reminded, "You must come from somewhere. From the north? From the south?" he finally responds, "Yes, south" and, in answer to the question "What did you do there?" adds that he was doing nothing, just drinking, in Valparaiso. This elicits a smile of recognition, and the rented mother christens the nameless sailor "lumpenproletariat." This is the rented mother as remembrance (*Eingedenken*) offering the amnesiac sailor a rudimentary sense of personal memory, a sense of spatio-temporal coordination. So it is also the moment of the birth of desire: "I wanted to see her every day," he says.

But there is a problem of access to the maternal as memory. As a result the sailor fights and kills the first captain and narrates the fatality of the act in the following way: "Maybe I already told you, but to get on the boat you had to kill on land and sea. It was the secret rule and I obeyed it unknowingly. I spent two weeks in chains. When I was set free my mother had been made to leave the boat. She had written us a letter." Access to the maternal as memory is costly. In fact she can now be accessed only indirectly and at the price of death, via the letter she leaves for the sailors, read by the man without qualities par excellence, the impersonator.

In her letter she no longer speaks in the form of memory as remembrance of the one (*Eingedenken*), but as epic memory or a variant thereof (*Gedächtnis*): "You will follow her precepts," says the impersonator, before he reads her letter. "Develop the memory which belongs to everyone. If someone remembers something forgotten by the others, let him forget it too. You will honor her with understanding: Let everyone understand the same thing. If someone seems to understand something the others do not, let him admit his ignorance. You will honor her with feelings: you will love and hate at the same time. You will honor her with imagination: invent new ways of being and acting together. Never forget that memory, feeling, imagination, and understanding must be used for an honest and productive life."

The impersonator's enunciation of memory as a series of techniques or practices is important, because the precepts, which have the ring of something sacred and perhaps even pious at the very end, cannot be taken at their face value as truths. The rented mother speaks with a forked tongue. She is both epic memory (*Gedächtnis*), memory of the many and of the storyteller, and memory of the one (*Eingedenken*), remembrance, novelistic memory. Memory itself has now been allegorically marked by a destructive, fragmenting power.

If there is a desire here, it is the wish to remember dismembered and forgotten memory itself. In emblematizing memory as a contradictory, ambiguous, and difficult practice via the allegory of the rented mother, Ruiz is not only redeeming the wish for memory in all its fragmented, irreconcilable complexity; he also offers something to a maternal imaginary as well, which is why I've pursued this analysis. Though at first she did remind me of Benjamin's angel of history, it is now clear to me that she is no angel. If anything, she is rather more like the medieval devil, saying one thing and meaning something else, which is of course one way of defining allegory.

What of my hunch that this maternal allegory of memory is central to Ruiz's own allegorical practice? I will confirm my hunch via what Benjamin says about the structure of creativity he sees active in Baudelaire's allegorical practice, which I think is applicable to Ruiz as well. "If it is fantasy which presents the correspondences to memory, it is thinking which dedicates allegories to it. Memory brings the two together."[54] "The two" might be either fantasy and thinking or allegories and correspondences, this is not very clear; but what is clear is the centrality given to the function of memory itself, memory as technique and method and also as governed by chance, i.e., memory in both its voluntary and involuntary aspects. From the point of view of voluntary memory (*Erinnerung*), involuntary memory (a variant of *Eingedenken*) may be more like a forgetting for Benjamin.[55] This makes intelligible the power attributed to forgetting in Ruiz's allegorical practice.

Her forked tongue and her discourse on memory (performed by the impersonator, the improviser in extremis, wielding a hammer like an arrhythmic baton) suggest that the solace this avatar of the maternal offers is not that of braiding the two types of estranged memory into an organic totality. This maternal allegory of memory, therefore of time and of experience (*Erfahrung*), exhorts her sons via her letter to invent a provisional collectivity across the figure of death itself, this death who is now an ally both of forgetting and of the will to remember.

The victory of allegory over symbol, whether staged via the emblem of the naked woman as art or that of the rented mother as emblematic memory, thus clarifies a facet of allegorical will and intuition: its methodological capacity to create memory and forgetting. Would surrealism ever be able to even dream of emblematizing the mythic symbol "Mother" as an allegory of memory, in close proximity to the other myth, the femme fatale, as Ruiz does? I think not, because eternal surrealism is still enthralled by what Patricia Mellencamp calls the "McGuffin [red herring] of female sexuality."[56]

The maternal as emblematic memory is an image of time, a time image in the Deleuzian sense.[57] Ruiz has extracted a sonic time image from the mythic symbol "mother" via allegorical doubling and the device of the letter performed by the impersonator. Hence the mother is no longer the dark continent, the silent body, or the guardian of tradition. This mater, matter as memory, effects "incorporeal transformations"[58] of those who listen to her speech, the ghosts on the ghost ship. She does not lull; she speaks of the conditions that might make a possible future.

The fiction of the maternal body as "semiotic chora"[59] has sustained a formidable modernist history of male creativity. For women that fiction may not be particularly generative.[60] But Ruiz's allegory of the maternal as a speech act (hence a pure cinematographic utterance in Deleuzian terms)[61] is certainly more enabling. This speech act, which has detached itself not only from its sender but also from its receiver, passes into a seascape. This floating utterance touches the image formed of sea, sky, and steel. I too am touched by the corrosive allegorical impulse. So all I can see in the final image (of this sequence) of the rusty ghost ship cutting a passage through the sea is an image of memory as a writing on water.

Part Five
Convulsive Knowing

13 A Slapstick Time: Mimetic Convulsion, Convulsive Knowing

Psychoanalysis attempts to relate the figure of the clown to reactions in the earliest period of childhood prior to the ego having taken a definite shape. Whatever the case, we will certainly learn more about the figure of the clown from children, who communicate as mysteriously with the image he creates as they do with animals, than we will by searching for a meaning in his actions, which are designed precisely to negate meaning. Only if we knew this language shared by clown and child alike, a language which does not aspire to the generation of meaning, would we understand this figure in which nature bids farewell in shock-like fashion.

—Theodor Adorno[1]

This is space before action, always haunted by a child, or by a clown, or by both at once.

—Gilles Deleuze[2]

Part One

Introduction: Time Framing Chaplin

If modernity is cinematic (characterized by speed, shock, fragmentation, dominance of the visual, power of objects over subjects, mechanical temporality, mobility of vision, spatio-temporal dislocation, etc.), then the silent slapstick bodies of American film comedy certainly have a privileged relationship to modernity, not simply as an expression of it but as a force that complicates the temporality of this very modernity.[3] In this sense the slapstick bodies of American cinema may be taken as allegorical of film's relationship to modernity. By what ploy then does the slapstick body, this fragile, flip-flopping, slipping, falling, pratfalling, frenzied, silly, childlike, and clownlike body challenge the mighty power of modernity itself? The ploy deployed (according to Adorno's rather enigmatic statement that frames this essay and makes it possible) is mimetic. The clues to this reading lie in the notion of "a language which does not aspire to the generation of meaning" and in the link between the figures of child and clown. That which links a "natural" being (a child) with a creature of pure artifice (a clown) is a particular conception of play, which within the tradition of Frankfurt School thought is understood to be mimetic. Indeed, Walter Benjamin and Theodore Adorno elevate mimesis (the archaic traces of which are found in performative acts of human self-preservation against a hostile nature, in sympathetic magic, and in the shaman's imitation of nature) to the status of a human faculty which has undergone the vicissitudes of time and history, so much so that not only does it take different forms in different periods of human history, but the crucial "question is whether we are concerned with the decay of this faculty or with its transformation."[4] Adorno and Max Horkheimer imply a distinction between mimesis and mimicry. Mimicry, for instance, can be identified in acts of adaptation to the environment by plants and animals, acts of self-preservation which, when successful, seem to obliterate all difference.[5] The human performance of mimesis, on the other hand, involves a certain difference, a difference located in a constitutive agon between an emerging sense of "self" and the other, posited as nature. These distinctions between mimesis and mimicry and the idea of adaptation to the other (as either obliteration of difference or the very condition of its emergence), will be taken up later in thinking about slapstick as a mimetic performance. According to Gunter Gebauer and Christoph Wulf, "mimesis originally denoted a *physical action* and developed first in oral cultures. It has an indicative character, with attention turning repeatedly to the gestural over the history of the concept." They argue that because the concept of mimesis refers to a sensory, bodily, gestural dynamic which engages the external world it "necessarily loses its intellectual centrality with the rise of rational thought."[6]

If western modernity marks the triumph of instrumental reason, then the human mimetic faculty, which consists of an impulse structure open to the world, enters a crisis which involves a collision between technology (a second nature) and the human sensorium. In this collision the mimetic faculty either reinvents itself or dies. It is this collision that Adorno sees Chaplin dramatizing when he refers to him as that figure in whom "nature bids farewell in shock-like fashion." Walter Benjamin, Siegfried Kracauer, and Theodor Adorno have all written on Chaplin's performance as a mimetic mode staged at that haunted, bewitched crossroads where modernity and mimesis fatally collide.[7] This chapter will take up the Frankfurt School's bio-anthropological, vitalistic formulations of mimesis by using the figure of Chaplin as a preeminent emblematic figure of cine-mimesis who performs the crisis of mimesis in modernity in an exemplary fashion.

I wish to pursue this mimetically charged twentieth-century Everyman so as to find out how it is that such a body can wrest from a situation of absolute terror or absolute meanness something other than terror or meanness, how it can draw from an object unforeseen affects and rhythms and movements, how the mimetically charged body can disorganize space and time so as to invent an image of happiness for Chaplin himself and for his global audience, which included people in the colonies. Chaplin galvanized a global audience (in a way that Buster Keaton, say, did not), perhaps because he offered a glimpse of an alternative modernity to the peoples of the world who would come to western modernity always already a little too late, almost as though always already a little retarded. To such an audience (of which I am a descendant), Chaplin's famous walk (the lateral, duck-like move while going forward) would offer something like a mimetic cipher of differential rhythms and movements in the very heart of the infamous "homogeneous empty time" of the capitalist-industrial everyday.

Chaplin's well-recognized anachronism, his nature as a figure from another time and tradition (a clown) entering the cinematic space of modernity (the real subject of his 1925 film *The Circus*), enables him to be both too soon and too late: he is a utopian figure interrupting modern temporality.[8] The historical belatedness of this figure, the anachronism that fouls up the mechanical temporality of the modern, is supplemented by that which is too soon: his mimetic ability to transform the oppressive thing— object, person, structure—better than can anyone else around. The hope for mimesis therefore hinges on this cinematic figure, far more than on any other. Through this figure the cinematic apparatus itself takes on the mimetic prowess said to be waning in other spheres where it was previously alive and well. In this sense Chaplin is an avatar of mimesis rising up in the very place where it is destroyed.

Framing Chaplin in relation to ideas pertaining to the historical experience of modern temporality (ideas derived from critical theory) provides a point of entry into thinking the temporal aspects of his performance. But in themselves these are not sufficient for analyzing what exactly happens in a certain performance of time, because they are primarily sociological in conception. This is where some of Gilles Deleuze's concepts will provide a more performative conception of time with which to apprehend and conceptualize a certain slapstick temporality.

The hauntingly suggestive two-faceted image of child-clown also recurs enigmatically in the work of Gilles Deleuze, when he discusses a cinema of the body which is not about slapstick in the generic sense.[9] In fact, in his classification of American film comedy into the four stages of the burlesque, slapstick comedy is placed in the realm of the movement image.[10] He sees both its manic sensory-motor birth in the work of Mack Sennett and its subsequent affective charging in the second period by the work of Chaplin, Keaton, and others as the first two phases of a burlesque cinema of sensory-motor acceleration.[11] The difference between the first and second period hinges on the introduction of affect into slapstick, via the use of the face in close-up. Deleuze's evocation of the child-clown figure links up with Adorno's perception because this figure operates in "space before action," implying both the undoing of the spatio-temporal coordinates of a scene or object, and knowledge of how to perform in uncoordinated space. My descriptive and theoretical effort in this paper is in part to learn how to perceive mimetically the slapstick bodies that move too fast or, as the case might be, too slow (as discussed in Part Two), and in part to map out the temporalities invented by them. Through this exploration, I hope that a way of apprehending mimetic transformation as a particular mode of performance of time will emerge. Gilles Deleuze's work on Chaplin, especially his concepts of sensory-motor-driven action, and the formulation of the temporality of the cinematic image and of other forms of time will provide analytic tools with which to elaborate the temporality of mimetic slapstick.

Prompted by these ideas, I will ask of the slapstick gag, "What's your time?" To be able to get an answer we must run through a rather bumpy theoretical terrain, risking the collision of concepts that don't belong together, not unlike the way in which in early slapstick films motorcars crash into the homely space of bedrooms, flinging beds into streets and making them run like motorcars as sleeping couples wake up screaming. I anticipate such theoretical collisions because within the homely and at times stifling space of academic film theory itself there are not that many ready-made temporal concepts to draw from.

This paper will show how a mimetic conception of play is central to a certain tradition of slapstick performance in the silent cinema of Hollywood. This showing (rather than telling), largely executed by striving toward a mimetic rather than a purely cognitive description of slapstick gags, is itself my ploy for apprehending and mapping out a particular slapstick temporality. Chaplin will also provide a point of departure for glancing at mimetic performance in American cinema as it pertains to the gendered body. While there were female slapstick performers in the silent era, such as Mabel Normand and Charlotte Greenwood, the focus of the first part of this paper is on Chaplin's mimetically charged male slapstick body. The issue of gender will be touched on as it relates to an understanding of the historical decay of male slapstick energy in Part Two, the coda to this paper.

Since the legendary "Slapstick Symposium" of 1985, the genre has received some sustained attention from Anglophone film scholars.[12] I situate my work within this tradition by contributing to a temporal inquiry into slapstick, which I think has not been the main focus of much of that work. Donald Crafton's influential essay "Pie and Chase: Gag, Spectacle, and Narrative in Slapstick Comedy," first delivered at this symposium (and which has drawn a polemical reply from Tom Gunning), exemplifies my point:

> One way to look at narrative is to see it as a system for providing the spectator with sufficient knowledge to make causal links between represented events. According to this view, the gag's status as an irreconcilable difference becomes clear. Rather than provide knowledge, slapstick misdirects the viewer's attention, and obfuscates the linearity of cause-effect relations. Gags provide the opposite of epistemological comprehension by the spectator. They are atemporal bursts of violence and/or hedonism that are as ephemeral and as gratifying as the sight of someone's pie-smitten face.[13]

In this standard opposition between narrative and gag the former is seen as a temporal operation while the latter is seen as atemporal. The distinction between narrative and gag on industrial grounds is certainly important in the development of early American film comedy. But to move on from this to a description of the gag as "atemporal" is inadequate. If one's focus is on temporality then one needs concepts with which to specify the nature of the "ephemeral" in the gag and in slapstick—as a nonnarrative, temporal operation.

While the Anglophone scholarship on slapstick as a genre is relatively recent, the Euro-American scholarship on Chaplin (not restricted to slapstick) is of course voluminous, with a long history. As I have indicated above, it is the Frankfurt School's understanding of Chaplin as a mimetic performer that I find most enabling in trying to develop notions of slapstick temporality. The Anglophone tradition of criticism and scholarship works very well in thematic and contextual analysis of Chaplin,[14] but when it comes to describing his mode of performance the lack of temporal performative concepts limits some of this work to cognitive description (as in Noel Carroll's taxonomy of sight gags in silent cinema)[15] or thematic readings. In his essay Carroll invites others to add to his "informal cartography of the sight gag,"[16] and I hope my work contributes to the understanding of some (by no means all) slapstick gags as temporal operations (not something Carroll focuses on). In the course of my analysis of a selection of gags from Chaplin's films I will engage with an aspect of Carroll's work, and also of Garrett Stewart's, to demonstrate the methodological distinctions between cognitive and mimetic description and between thematic and time-based readings of performance.[17]

Child-Clown as Crystal Image

The composite image of child-clown found in both Adorno's and Deleuze's writing can be read as a temporal image via the latter's concept of the crystal image, composed of a small circuit between the two terms. Deleuze's crystal image is in its smallest circuit an exchange between an actual and a virtual image to the point where the difference between the two becomes indiscernible.[18] There is a marvelous instance of such a crystal image in Chaplin's *The Circus*. Chaplin as the Tramp is hungry, as usual; as he tries to steal a hot dog from a little child a thief plants a stolen purse in Chaplin's pocket so as to evade a suspicious cop. Through a series of plot complications pivoting on a play between the notions of the actual thief and the virtual thief, Chaplin is found with the stolen purse and is pursued by a cop, creating the inevitable chase, which culminates in an amusement park attraction—a hall of mirrors. The actual-virtual circuit is emphasized when Chaplin drops his hat and can't tell the difference between the actual and the virtual hats, just as the cop can't tell the difference between the two Chaplins because there are tens of Chaplins multiplied by the crystalline formation of the faceted mirrors, and there are just as many cops. The point is the continuous movement between the actual and the virtual, which makes their difference indiscernible. The child-clown figure is a crystal image in this sense.

It is necessary to say here, following Deleuze and Bergson, that this is also a certain image of time, or time image. The crystal image in its smallest circuit offers a formulation of time and memory as a paradox. According to this formulation of time, "the past and the present do not denote two successive moments, but two elements which coexist: One is the present, which does not cease to pass, and the other is the past, which does not cease to be but through which all presents pass."[19] This coexistence of the past and the present, rather than their succession, enables a conception of time as the duration of a past that is and of a present that was. In this paradoxical formulation of time and memory the past is the virtual and the present (as the most contracted moment of the past) is the actual.

Here I have attempted to mobilize the composite, atemporal, pictorial figure of the child-clown as a crystal (time) image, with the image of the child as the virtual to the actuality of the clown. Through this temporalizing a link can be made between this figure, who is now a composite of two modalities of time (an actual present and a virtual past), and two modalities of the mimetic faculty, namely its ontogenetic and phylogenetic aspects. Ontogenetic mimesis, pertaining to the life of the individual organism, here refers to the figure of the child in whom the mimetic faculty is still alive; while phylogenetic mimesis is the memory of the race from its "primitive" beginnings, where the mimetic faculty was thought to be integral to survival in a hostile environment, through performative modes such as sympathetic magic, shamanism, and similar mimetic practices. The slippage between these two temporal axes of the mimetic faculty, the phylogenetic and the ontogenetic, can now be conceptually activated in relationship to the temporalized image of Chaplin as child-clown who runs a circuit between the virtual (past) and the actual (present). This is why Chaplin has popped up recently to emblematize the emerging new technologies—as a video-store logo and, in the early days, to sell computers too: not because he is for all times (universal), but because he signals, across several generations, as a memory image: the very forking of time, time as both virtual and actual. His anachronistic iconicity (derby hat, baggy pants, tight-fitting coat, cane, and oversized shoes), combined with his gestural work, enables Chaplin to embody time in its eternal aspect, as a past that is preserved (the virtual) and a present that passes (the actual).

Sensory-Motor Gesture vs. Mimetic Gesture

By making a distinction between sensory-motor and mimetic gestures I hope to draw out some characteristics of mimetic play relevant to Chaplin's performance. To do this it might be useful first to map out the similarities and differences between the child and the clown. According to Susan Buck-Morss, Walter Benjamin considered the repression of child-

hood and its cognitive modes a problem of the utmost political signifi-
cance.[20] He shows how child's play is permeated by mimetic modes of behavior when he says that "the child plays at being not only a shopkeeper
or teacher but also a windmill and a train."[21] What is at stake in the child's
mimetic ability is a form of bodily knowing, a relationship to action which
has not lost its sensory links. The loss of this capacity desiccates rationality
and turns it into instrumental reason, which dominates the human body,
nature, and the other.

There are obvious similarities and differences between the child and the
clown. They are similar in their motor incapacity (total in infancy, then
steadily diminishing to the toddler's monstrous motion) and sensory alertness, their lack of language, and their work with the body and the sensorium to signal an impulsive vitalism, a mimetic relationship to objects
and spontaneity. The differences are that the clown's body is trained; his
motor incapacity (slipping, falling, pratfalls) is simulated, and is in fact a
sign of virtuosity. The cinematic clown always lives under the threat of
imminent danger of one kind or another (subject to relations of power)
and also may have a certain cunning, the opposite of spontaneous behavior. Despite this, the clown seems to feel a "compulsion to become and behave like something else"[22]—a child. For Benjamin this compulsion is an
essential attribute of the mimetic impulse and one worth keeping in mind
when observing Chaplin play not only with objects but also with subject-
object relations of power.

Not only does the clown feel compelled to become and behave like a
child, but according to a western myth children have a special affinity with
clowns as well. That this affinity has nothing to do with cuteness was
brought home to me through an incident at the movies. After Chaplin's
death, my father and I took my nephews to a retrospective of his early
shorts in Colombo. One of the boys spent most of the time hiding behind
a seat, too afraid to look. This memory of a child shuddering, terrified
by the clown, comes to mind as a reminder of the violence and cruelty
so integral to the slapstick dynamic, as integral as laughter. The relationship between children's affinity with clowns and my nephew's shuddering, I imagine, lies in the life of bodily impulse that governs both child
and clown, a reservoir of their violence. This impulsive vitalism is crucial
to mimetic performance, of which speed and rhythm are components—
distilling the violence of impulse. What is violated are familiar coordinates of space, objects as well as subject-object relations. The differential

rhythms and speeds at which these are performed, rather than themes as such, are what make us convulse with laughter or shudder in terror.

In *The Circus*, the Tramp tries to watch the circus performance through a hole in the big top which is a little too high for him. Seeing a man slumped down after being knocked out by a baddie, he simply tips him over with his cane and uses him as a stool to stand on so he can watch the show comfortably. This mimetic diverting of a subject into an object is, of course, both cruel and funny and points to the characteristic amorality of slapstick's impulsive (unsocialized) energy as well as to a rudimentary aspect of mimetic transformation, where a subject is made into an object. It is rudimentary because this transformative slapstick act (a simple reversal) does not work with speed and rhythm so as to derail stable subject-object relations, which happens in the more complex sequences discussed later.

What is at issue in mimetic behavior that draws from figures of nature (animal or child) is an unsevered link between a perception and a possible action. This unsevered link or capacity is what Adorno, following Benjamin, calls the mimetic impulse. This is not stimulus-response in the behaviorists' sense, nor is it the behavior proper to a cinema governed by a sensory-motor mechanism.[23] Rather, it is, according to Benjamin's formulation, the capacity to make correspondences, the perception of non-sensuous similarities across incommensurables—like eating an old shoe as if it were a gourmet meal, as Chaplin does in *The Gold Rush* (1925).

This is the very example Noel Carroll gives as an instance of a sight gag as mimed metaphor, in his taxonomy of sight gags. In fact, since a metaphor entails the perception of similarity between dissimilar things, why do I need to mobilize Benjamin's notion of mimesis as "the compulsion to become and behave like something else" in order to apprehend Chaplin's performance? The doctrine of similarity for Benjamin is not about sameness, but about a capacity or faculty by which humans can make correspondences between dissimilar things.[24] Thus, it is about an encounter with otherness and the production of difference. Benjamin speaks of non-sensuous correspondences made in a flash or on the run: "like a flash, similarity appears. For its production by man—like its perception by him—is in many cases, and particularly the most important, limited to flashes. It flits past."[25] This ability to make correspondences by means of spontaneous fantasy is a form of inventive reception attuned to an instant—a fundamental aspect of mimetic behavior. The gag from *The Gold Rush* does draw an analogy between two dissimilar things through the art of miming (Carroll's mimed metaphor), but not all miming is mimetic, and the feature that makes this mimed gag an example of mimetic performance is not so much the continual metamorphosis of the shoe into different kinds of food, both fish and fowl (fish bones, wish bone), but crucially the thing-like resignation of the subject's (Chaplin's) visage (animated only by involuntary hiccups), as opposed to the vitality of the object (the old shoe). Thus we may understand something of the complexity of the "compulsion to become and behave like something else" which characterizes the mimetic impulse.

While Carroll's category of the "mimed metaphor" does produce conceptual knowledge of Chaplin's work in this famous gag, insofar as it demarcates stable subject-object relations (the Tramp transforms the shoe into a gourmet meal), it remains at a level of conscious rationality. By proceeding differently, by pursuing a mimetic lead, one can, I believe, begin to see what happens to the libidinalized (hunger-driven) body in its encounter with the drive for gold (incarnating the power of the object in this film). By using the concept of mimesis one can chart impulsive moves and the vicissitudes of the impulse itself in the transference of energy from subject to object and beyond. Perceiving the shoe–gourmet meal as a mimed metaphor is a relatively stabilizing operation of a far more volatile process. This cognitive drive can be viewed as sensory-motor evasion of the thing, whereas to perceive mimetically entails a running between the putative subject and object, not knowing who is what.

When Chaplin as a stage hand in *Behind the Screen* (1916) is ordered by his big fat boss to set up the scene and add the "finishing touches" to it, he takes a bear rug and diverts the object by doing a barber-shop routine with the bear's head, becoming a fastidious and impassioned barber. The diverting of an object to another "function" via intricate, tactile, gestural work is a mimetic mode of operation in the sense that it makes us see non-sensuous similarity between dissimilar things. The way Chaplin gets carried away with massaging the bear's scalp, parting its hair and combing it, wiping its face, and so on has no perceptible function in the rudimentary narrative of the film. It is a gag or a slapstick routine that mimetically draws a series of correspondences between the human and the animal and that "does not aspire to the generation of meaning" and in this is more akin to child's play. To read this gag as a mimed metaphor wouldn't be wrong, of course, but the libidinalized mimetic gestures (a kind of tactile frenzy animating Chaplin's fingertips, which do not seem to want to finish touching and by continuing to touch undo the order) will escape cognitive description severed from its mimetic core.

The clown's mode of performance under various forms of duress (a donkey or a cop chasing him, or hunger, or the desire to get the girl) is mimetic. Mimetic performance exceeds the economy of sensory-motor action. Indeed, if sensory motor action is an organization of action in a circuit of habitual behavior, then the clown disorganizes the coordinates that make such behavior possible. In *The Circus* Chaplin is shown a series of funny routines, including the "William Tell Act," by the other clowns as a training exercise. He is incapable of mastering a simple comic routine, precisely because it has become a routine, a cliché. He does everything either too soon or too late, provoking audience laughter at his spontaneous, unintentional moves. The routines of the professional clowns, having become clichés, fail to convulse the audience in laughter.

Deleuze defines a cliché as a sensory-motor image of the thing, that is, a habitual or automatic reaction to a perception.[26] So a mimetic move or gesture would draw out something other than the same from the cliché. The banal technology of a revolving door in *The Cure* (1917) may be seen, in its everyday function of smoothly taking people in and out, as a sensory-motor operation. But the instant Chaplin enters it, it behaves in an aberrant fashion, at first going much too slow and getting the big baddie's gouty foot caught in it, then going much too fast so that people just spin inside it at high speed without being able to get out. After many such repetitions of different rhythms, speeds, and movements have been drawn from the revolving door, a drunken Chaplin with a spinning head goes into it and gets spun around and flung out like a top, careening up a flight of stairs and across the whole performance area of the sanatorium, knocking people over in the process. Through the accelerated repetition of the same movement the cliché, or the sensory-motor image of the object, is transformed into a mimetic image, where at first Chaplin gets caught in the door, then becomes like the door, and finally takes flight as a mobile spinning top. This is an example of the wild trajectories and moves that mimetic gesture-action is capable of inventing by engaging with the sensory motor move as a first step, so to speak.

Sensory-motor moves are more like mimicry of the thing, a form of total adaptation or enslavement to the object, which in flight (through variations or modulations of speed and rhythm) become mimetic. In a complicated sequence such as the one described above, subject-object relations are set adrift through the creation of different speeds and rhythms.

Therefore it makes no sense to speak of "Chaplin's use of objects" here, as though there were stable subject-object relations, with Chaplin the subject transforming the object. Rather, in mimetic transformation stable subject-object relations are undone and in their place, so to speak, there is a performance of time.

An analysis of the assembly-line sequence in *Modern Times* (1936) helps to make clear the slippery, volatile, ambivalent nature of subject-object relations in mimetic performance: in the encounter between the fragile, helpless slapstick body and the gigantic machine of modernity. Chaplin as the Tramp has at last found work on an assembly line, tightening nuts and bolts. The Taylorized repetition of the one gesture at a regulated speed does not accommodate such contingencies as a bodily itch or a wanton fly, which, when responded to, creates havoc with the homogenized rhythmic relations between the Tramp, his fellow workers, and the assembly line. Through a series of comic routines the unitary power of the assembly line's homogeneous mechanical rhythm is asserted repeatedly, so that when the lunch break comes the Tramp is not able to stop his body from obeying this rhythm—his arms continue to move in an involuntary mimetic spasm, still obeying the laws of the assembly line, which lands him in the soup because he is unable to hold a bowl steady and spills it all over. The Tramp's body now can only mimic (involuntarily) the power of the object, which subjects him even in his free time. When he resumes work this process of subjugation of subject by object reaches a crisis point as he gets sucked in by the machine as fodder. Once he is inside the machine we are given a cross-section of it which looks like the side view of a film projector with the Tramp gliding through it, transforming his body into a film strip (as read, marvelously, by Garrett Stewart), which of course is what "Charlie Chaplin" is.[27]

I will use Stewart's essay to demonstrate the difference between a thematic reading of performance and a mimetic reading. Stewart reads this film as Chaplin's self-reflexive enactment of his own demise as a silent artist in the era of sound cinema, and this particular scene as enacting "the myth of descent, the archetype of the dying and rising god in a moment of incontestable meditation of the cinema upon its own means."[28] This is a cognitive reading in arguing that Chaplin shows us the process by which he becomes an image, and it thematizes via a mythical reference. While I do draw from aspects of the cognitive reading, I depart from it by observing how Chaplin performs gesturally. His mimetic performance progresses from an involuntary mimicry of the object to a taking-

on of its power, converting and diverting its oppressive energy into something else by drawing from it multiple rhythms, movements, and flour-
ishes. Through this mimetic performance the Tramp draws out gestures
and movements that were previously unavailable both to him and to the
machine as well. So when the machine spits him out he has become mimetically charged to such an extent that he begins to see wild correspondences between widely different things that have a circular shape and tries
to tighten each of them, whether it be a nose, a button on a woman's
bosom, or a fire hydrant. He has to be hospitalized, but only after he has
reached a peak of mimetic frenzy, taking us through the various movements of mimetic activation: from mimicry (both voluntary and involuntary) to mimetic fantasy, to mimetic frenzy or convulsion (the last of
which the narrative sees as a form of madness). If in all of this there is a
polemic against the machine, it is unequivocally so only in relation to its
univocal rhythm. There is no doubt that for Chaplin the condition of
mimesis in modernity is inseparable from the technology of cinematic
mass reproduction. It is the machine which subjugates that also provides
the mimetic means to blur subject-object relations and draw out unforeseen rhythms, correspondences, and modulations of time—truly modern
times.

Unlimited Divisibility of Time in Mimetic Play

Let me begin by drawing a crude analogy between a banal, contemporary, "spatial" practice and Chaplin's performance of time, as a way of
grasping it in a homely way before developing it conceptually. When I endlessly modify a word or sentence in writing this essay on the computer, say
by clicking to create a space between the letters of a word, this process of
cutting into and opening space by dividing words is, theoretically, endless.
Similarly, Chaplin divides time "endlessly." As I said, the analogy is crude
because the speed and rhythm at which I click makes no difference to the
structure of what I write, nor to myself, whereas in Chaplin's case speed,
rhythm, modulations of movement, and inflections of gesture do transform the thing, as well as subject-object relations and chronological time.
Chaplin's mimetic capacity to endlessly divide time may then be formulated as the answer to the question of the temporality of a mimetic slapstick act—unlimited divisibility of time. This time can be conceptually
mapped out and clarified further via Deleuze's two conceptions of time,
Chronos and Aion.[29]

Chronos vs. Aion

These two conceptions of time encoded in Greek will help map out the distinction between a spatially grounded, ritualized, temporal practice and a temporal operation which works with repetition that makes a difference. This model presents two correlated and yet opposed temporal operations. According to Deleuze, Chronos and Aion are two different images of the eternal return which offer two opposed readings of time (*Logic* 61–64). The two different readings are obtained by delinking past, present, and future from any idea of a single temporality or continuum. Through the philosophy of the Stoics, Deleuze makes a distinction between, on the one hand, a limited and yet infinite cyclical present and, on the other, an unlimited past and future (61):

> It will be said that only the present exists; that it absorbs or contracts in itself the past and the future, and that from contraction to contraction, with ever greater depth, it reaches the limits of the entire Universe and becomes a living cosmic present. It suffices in this case to proceed according to the order of the decontractions, in order that the Universe begin again and that all its presents be restored. Thus the time of the present is always a limited but infinite time; infinite because cyclical, animating a physical eternal return as the return of the Same. . . . Sometimes, on the other hand, it will be said that only the past and future subsist, that they subdivide each present, ad infinitum, however small it may be. . . . The complementarity of past and future appears then clearly: each present is divided into past and future, ad infinitum. Or rather such time is not infinite, since it never comes back upon itself; it is unlimited, a pure straight line the extremes of which endlessly distance themselves from each other and become deferred into the past and the future. (62)

Deleuze places the generic figure of the actor, dancer, or mime as the non-thick body which treads lightly on the present (the instant present of Aion, rather than the thick present of Chronos) while facing both the past and the future (68). Deleuze summarizes their differences tersely: "There are two times, one of which is composed only of interlocking presents; the other is constantly decomposed into elongated pasts and future" (62). I think Chaplin has a particularly privileged relationship to this non-Chronic present in that he ceaselessly divides and subdivides the present instant (by milking the gag, as they say in the trade) so as to delay and elude its endless pressure on the gossamer wings of the past and the future (168). He continually sidesteps the present, delays its imperative through a repetition that makes a difference. In so doing he operates in a temporality that Deleuze calls Aion—time as unlimitedly divisible. The routine of delaying paying for his meal, because he has no money, while the big waiter is waiting to bash him up in *The Immigrant* (1917) is a good example of his evasion and sidestepping of the present. Chaplin's mimetic performance at its peak takes the linguistic form of the infinitive—to delay, to spin, to groom, to eat, to slide, to roll, to run, etc. What Chaplin shows us is "the present without thickness, the present of the actor, dancer, or mime —the pure perverse 'moment.' It is the present of the pure operation, not of incorporation" (168). Only a performative act can draw out this kind of temporality from the relentless pressure of Chronos, here embodied by the weighty presence of the waiter.

This particular gag, involving a certain power play, may also be viewed via Michel de Certeau's much-used concepts of strategy and tactic, the distinction between which invokes the struggle of the powerless against the mighty—"we are concerned with battles or games between the strong and the weak, and with the 'actions' which remain possible for the latter."[30] The male cinematic slapstick body certainly has a mighty assailant to combat, whether it be a revolving door, a gigantic machine, or a manhole in the road, an advanced feeding machine or the big fat bully. In the absence of spatial power all that it can deploy is the power of mimesis, which can enable a tactical deployment of timing.

Strategy vs. Tactic

De Certeau's distinction between strategy and tactic offers another amplification of the temporal operation of the child-clown. The command of place as institutional power is necessary to plan and execute a strategic action, whereas tactics have no access to a place that is legitimized for them to act in:

> Tactics are procedures that gain validity in relation to the pertinence
> they lend to time—to the circumstances which the precise instant of an
> intervention transforms into a favourable situation, to the rapidity of
> the movements that change the organisation of a space, to the relations
> among successive moments in an action, to the possible intersections of
> durations and heterogeneous rhythms, etc. . . . Strategies pin their hopes

on the resistance that the establishment of a place offers to the erosion of time; tactics on a clever utilisation of time, of the opportunities it presents and also of the play that it introduces into the foundations of power.[31]

The emphasis on the tactical value of the instant, and of rhythm in particular, makes it seem that this passage has been written with Chaplin's body in mind. The gag as performed by the clown may also be viewed as a tactical mimetic operation, as in the case of the play with the counterfeit coin in the routine of delaying payment for the meal in *The Immigrant*. So the tactician has to raid a strategized place and convert it into an "any-space-whatever"[32] with the only weapon he has—the capacity to divide time, so as to delay being bashed up. Deleuze's concept of any-space-whatever is, in his terminology, deterritorialized space, space whose coordinates are delinked. He describes how this might be achieved either through the close-up or via color, but in the case of Chaplin, certainly, mimetic gestural performance has the power to create any-space-whatevers, which is a way of disorganizing spatialized arrangements of power. In this way the tactician is a mimetic operator of time, eluding the incorporation of Chronos. As stated, the child-clown deploys mimesis, which implies a certain cunning in his fight for survival. It is this cunning aspect of mimesis that is highlighted by de Certeau's concepts.

So far I have mapped out two conceptions of time, one of which, Chronos, depends on a ritualized, structured repetition for its authority, power, and efficacy. Aion is the other, the very opposite of Chronic performance of time, interrupting and disrupting the brute force of Chronos, a playing with time.

Rite vs. Play

The opposition between a ritualized (cyclical) relationship to time and a playing with time can be elaborated through the distinctions Giorgio Agamben makes between ritual and play, and between ritual object and the toy.[33] I will take up Agamben's formulation to clarify mimetic play as a game with time. Ritual may be taken in both its anthropological sense and its use to refer to routinized ritual behavior necessary to the operations of modern institutions: factories, prisons, hospitals, restaurants. Ritual eliminates chance and controls outcomes. Therefore the temporality of strategic action may be thought of as pulsed chronometric, chronological time, which is an objective duration, a measurable and continuous quantity of time. Play or games are governed by contingency and chance: another aspect of time as Aion, a floating, non-pulsed time of the infinitive. This temporality may be likened to Deleuze's idea of the event, which is a becoming, as a non-circular (that is, non-Chronic) eternal return (*Logic* 176).

What is needed in order to convert structured ritual into eventful play is not a technician of the sacred but a tactician of the instant. The clown has the skill to deal with chance bearing down like destiny in the shape of Mack Swain or Eric Campbell as the big bully, or as a revolving door, as in *The Cure*, or as a hole in his pocket through which his last coin drops, leaving him no money to pay the giant waiter who is waiting to bash him up. Mack Swain, the weight and the thickness of the present—by another name, Chronos—is Chaplin's mortal enemy; Aion is that aspect of time whose eternal movement Chaplin keeps showing us even as we enter the electronic and digital era. In releasing the object from the determinations of its structural (ritualized) coordinates Chaplin performs gesturally, as Deleuze might say, like certain modern musicians, expanding and contracting micro intervals within coded intervals, through an individuation of a crystal image in the heart of the commodity form of comedy, where laughter itself is measured, pulsed, and given a monetary value. To alight on an instant, to link it in a flash to a past and a future, is the work of the clown and child playing and signaling to us as though from a great distance, on the disappearing ground of the moment. Like ghosts, they are (in a particular cluster) also the very signal of time.

Ritual Object vs. Play Object (Toy)

For Benjamin, children convert almost anything into a toy. They put together things that don't usually go together, diverting objects from their familiar, ritualized, strategized functions. Ritual needs ritual objects whose use is determined by the rite and is usually fixed. Ritual behavior, in the anthropological sense, is cyclical and carries with it a sense of continuity; it refers to a ritual calendar that bears witness to a community and memorializes it through repetition of the same. The child-clown who stumbles and falls into the space-time of modernity often has to convert ritual objects into toys. What does this mean? According to Agamben, the toy encodes a dual temporality: 1. "Once upon a time," offering a promise and fulfillment of a wish; and 2. "No longer," the ruined discarded novelty which makes the outdated toy akin to the fated commodity.[34] The toy is both promise and obsolescence. In play activity, a child drops out of chronological time by creating two temporalities (at least). Baudelaire and Benjamin have discussed the miniaturized nature of the toy, which marks its commodity form. Agamben says that archaeology has a hard time separating toys from ritual objects—dolls, for instance. The obsolescence of the toy is accelerated by the way the child explores it, tears it, opens it, bangs it, eats it—in short, child's play! Adults don't usually do this to the commodities they buy, and when they do it is not because of some mimetic curiosity but rather in some frustration. Because of their curiosity about things, Benjamin says that children recycle the waste of a ruined world. This aspect of the child's play must be linked with the clown's, which courts danger and suffering.

According to Kracauer, "the leitmotif of slapstick comedy is the play with danger, with catastrophe, and its prevention in the nick of time." And commenting on Kracauer's understanding of the play of the child-clown, Miriam Hansen says, "The games slapstick comedy performs take place 'on the brink of the abyss'; the genre engages, in a ludic form, the threat of annihilation." Chance (which, as Hansen explains, is for Kracauer a historical category) plays a crucial role in this dangerous play in offering "a tiny window, at once hope and obligation, of survival, of continuing life after the grand metaphysical stakes have been lost."[35]

The body most equipped to seize the "tiny" or brief instant chance proffers is the mimetically activated body of the child-clown, because he is able to transform ritually structured time into mimetic play and tactically deploy ritualized objects as toys. Agamben says that "Levi-Strauss drew the opposition between ritual and play into an exemplary formula: while rites transform events into structures, play transforms structures into events."[36]

Structure vs. Event

In elaborating this final pair of concepts I will put Agamben's formulation into collision with Deleuze's,[37] not only for the thrill of playing with concepts (ritual object or toy, which will it be?), but also because through this I can signal in passing the damage done (sensory blindness, paralysis of motion) by a linguistically grounded rather than temporal reading of film.

In Agamben's formulation, the rite converts events into structure by abolishing the interval separating mythic past and present, collapsing both into synchronic time. Play opposes this by tending "to break the connection between past and present, and to break down and crumble the whole structure into events. If ritual is therefore a machine for transforming diachrony into synchrony, play, conversely, is a machine for transforming synchrony into diachrony."[38] This notion of diachrony (with its structural linguistic derivations) is too coarse to be able to specify what a temporal figure like Chaplin does in converting structured ritual into eventful play. And besides, in Agamben's conception of the Chronos/Aion pair Chronos is allied to diachrony, while Aion, as an image of eternity, is allied to synchrony. In contrast, in Deleuze's model of time the notions of diachrony and synchrony are not mapped onto Chronos and Aion, perhaps because they do not have the performative capacity to differentiate sufficiently, or perhaps they cannot be mapped onto concepts that seek to create a philosophy of Becoming rather than of Being. In Agamben's schema Aion is a category of Being, while for Deleuze it is the temporality of Becoming. Agamben ties time back to a structural linguistic framework which cuts out movement and the movement of time.

In juxtaposing Deleuze's conceptualization of Aion to Agamben's I have tried to specify how the slapstick body draws out an Aionic instant through the division of time. Through this specification I have attempted to show how the severing of the link between the past and the present is the trauma that the mimetic body of Chaplin tries to simultaneously embody and heal through the mediation of mimetic memory.[39]

Here then is a schematic presentation of the dualistic cluster of concepts with which I have staged a collision between two operations of time to arrive at an understanding of the mimetically charged slapstick time of the child-clown.

i. Chronos vs. Aion
ii. Strategy vs. Tactic
iii. Rite vs. Play
iv. Ritual Object vs. Play Object, Toy
v. Structure vs. Event

Deleuze has said that Chaplin converts a large machine by tactically using it as a tool, by tinkering with it, prising it open, while Keaton miniaturized the gigantic to accommodate the individual.[40] If this is so, then certainly both of them in their own ways convert threatening objects into toys so as to avert threat. So ritual objects and ritualized behavior are transformed into processes of play. Play here has to be understood as mimetic behavior. But in contrast to children at play, the clown courts danger, suffering, and death, suggesting that mimetic skills and their retooling and reschooling may be necessary for survival within the pressures of the modern everyday. However, they signal not only survival but also the possibility of wresting that promise of happiness from modernity via a mimetically recharged body.

Part Two

Controlled Performance of Mimesis, or Mimesis unto Death

In this final section I trace the exhaustion of the kind of slapstick energy examined above through two films of Preston Sturges's, *The Lady Eve* (1941) and *Unfaithfully Yours* (1948). In these films mimetic slapstick is not yet dead but neither is it quite alive; rather, it does not live any longer.[41] This curious afterlife of the slapstick of the male body may sound like the melancholy or depressive moment of slapstick in American cinema, but there is still so much noise and energy in these films, generated either by gender trouble between heterosexual couples or by a piece of mechanical technology, that the tone of the films is certainly not melancholic. The truly melancholy moment of slapstick must surely be in that final, (knowingly) unfunny, slow-paced farewell slapstick duet performed by two has-been clowns, Buster Keaton and Charlie Chaplin, in *Limelight* (1952).

The Lady Eve is a classic screwball comedy belonging to the genre of the comedy of remarriage as defined by Stanley Cavell in his book *Pursuits of Happiness*.[42] *Unfaithfully Yours* has a remarriage plot structure but moves in and out of a melodramatic-noir register which colors, darkly, the extended slapstick scene at the end of the film as well as the motif of remarriage itself. It is noteworthy that Preston Sturges used actors unable to perform slapstick (Henry Fonda, Rex Harrison, Joel McCrea) in situations which required the agility of a slapstick body. Even when he used the great silent slapstick comedian Harold Lloyd in his *The Sin of Harold Diddlebock* (or *Mad Wednesday*, 1947) and incorporated a famous scene from one of his silent films, the aged Lloyd as a clerk looks like a degraded copy of his original self, all slapstick energy drained from his body.

The Lady Eve and *Unfaithfully Yours* enact rituals of degradation and punishment on male characters who cannot move except in their own narrow spheres, expertise in snakes in the case of the Henry Fonda character Hopsy/Charles in *The Lady Eve,* and expertise in music in the case of the Rex Harrison character Sir Alfred in *Unfaithfully Yours*. In contrast a woman and a machine (the tape recorder in *Unfaithfully Yours*), both mimetic bodies, propel the action and make the men slip, fall, and get into a terrible mess. Hopsy refuses to believe that Barbara Stanwyck, as Lady Eve, is the same as the cardsharp Jean because—this is his reason—"they look too much alike." This is strange reasoning indeed, and yet it seems that his body mimetically apprehends that she is the same, because he falls for her just as he did on the ocean liner when she made him trip over her extended foot and thus engineered their first meeting and love affair. She masterminds all the slapstick in this film, or quite simply her presence is enough to make Hopsy trip and fall and get into a mess repetitively, as in the series of mishaps at the dinner party given by his father, reducing him to the state of an uncoordinated little boy, smiling dopily and leaving the room repeatedly to change his soiled clothes.

Men have lost it, but a tape recorder and a woman can perform mimetically and control the performance of mimesis as well, and it is the business of women (in screwball comedy), if they so wish, to awaken this waning impulse, either as a gift or as a lethal weapon. This is why some of these comedies create combat zones where the estranged couples fight sometimes unto death, as in *The War of the Roses* (dir. Danny DeVito, 1989). This film is so harsh not because of the wonderful slapstick war about real estate and property but because of one final gesture whose identity and agency are indeterminable. When the couple lie dying in the midst of the wreckage they have caused, Oliver Rose (the husband, played by Michael Douglas) places his hand gently on his wife's arm as a sign of final reconciliation, and Barbara (Kathleen Turner) quietly reciprocates by touching it. On contact, Oliver's arm gets violently pushed or pulled away (we can't quite tell which), thus deactivating the vicious mimetic circuit of brilliantly inventive revenge. The violent electrified energy generated by this touch, unattributable to a human agency (either husband's or wife's), feels magnified because it is both small and of short duration in comparison with the hyperbole of the long action sequences. What is this energy which is generated by the contact of bodies but is not controlled by them? It is the apparatus's own magically (mimetically) charged response to the soppy humanism of a weak gesture of reconciliation, signaling in a flash (fast-motion) the impossibility of a "happy ending" after the generation of such violent energy. There can be no mimetic awakening here, as in, say, *Bringing Up Baby* (dir. Howard Hawks, 1938), only mimesis unto death, told as a parabolic comic tale of divorce by Danny DeVito as the divorce lawyer. Through these films it becomes clear that the controlled performance of mimesis is a perversion of the mimetic impulse, taking the fun, play, and unpredictability out of the encounter with the other and thus deactivating the mimetic impulse. Even as objects loom larger and larger in *The War of the Roses,* the couple's gigantic compulsion to mirror each other in mimetic revenge obliterates difference and leads to their demise. Their compulsive repetition returns the mimetic impulse to mere mimicry. But the apparatus, in activating an unrepeatable gesture, demonstrates in a flash the intransigence of mimetically activated energy.

Mimetic Doubling

Mistaken identity as a comic gag leading to slapstick is as old as Greek new comedy (Menander), but the way it returns with a twist, in for example Chaplin's *The Great Dictator* (1940) and in *The Lady Eve,* enables this gag to develop an image of identity as constituted in difference. In *The Great Dictator* Hynkel and the little Jewish barber, both played by Chaplin wearing the same moustache, bring the image of the Jew (as the absolute other) right into the very heart of the constitution of the fascist leader's image. As Adorno and Horkheimer say, the fascist "cannot stand the Jews, yet imitates them."[43] The Jew is thus constructed as a phantasmic projection of the fascist in an attempt to fortify the ego and make it impermeable. The irresistible compulsion to imitate the Jew is seen as the return of the repressed, the non-rational mimetic aspects of subjectivity itself, of which the Jew is made an emblem. This mimetic doubling and the ensuing comic device of mistaken identity make apparent the unconscious dynamic of mimetic performance.

In contrast, Hynkel's slapstick address to a mass rally, conceived as an extended gag, with sound amplification via microphones, exemplifies the fascist ritual itself as a perversion of mimesis or as a consciously controlled performance of mimesis—they are the same thing. The performance aims at absolute control (essential to fascist ritual where play is proscribed) of every gesture, movement, and sound of both body and voice via the technologies of mass reproduction and amplification of sound. The slapstick performance with the microphones dramatizes this proscription of mimesis and its return as controlled and yet uncontrollable performance. Chaplin as Hynkel inserts slapstick fragmentation into the very structure of the utterance—a nonsense language with recognizable German and English words. German with its composite words and gutturality lends itself to this slapstick fragmentation, but what's stunning is the way Chaplin lines and punctures the fragmented torrent of masterful words with bodily convulsions like coughing and choking on them, so that this fascist performance of language, which seeks to transcend the body (through absolute control of its gestural and impulsive vitalism) in order to create a body politic through a mass media simulation, is undone by the body itself. Even as Hynkel's body emits coughs that undermine the image of mastery he creates, his rhetorical flurry makes the microphones themselves behave mimetically, bending away from him, flip-flopping, shuddering under the spell of his perverted mimetic prowess. Here the megalomania of the subject in control is undermined by the involuntary slapstick gestures of the body and voice.

In contrast to this slapstick performance, the last speech, on democracy, peace, and human brotherhood, delivered (with no slapstick at all) by Chaplin as the Jewish barber mistaken for Hynkel, is a poor performance because there is not a trace of the mimetic in it, perverted or otherwise. In this last speech Chaplin speaks earnestly, almost as himself (on the eve of America's involvement in World War II), in direct address "attraction," looking straight into our eyes; and the message, at this distance, fails because the performance is weak (even contemporary critics registered it as a problem with the film).

In the case of *Lady Eve*, the role of mimetic double is abandoned by Jean after she has avenged herself by marrying the man who rejected her for being a cardsharp. Once she has got what she wants by calling all the shots, she abandons her playacting role as both "director" and "actor," realizing that all the fun has gone out of this controlled performance of mimesis. She knows, as we do now, that part of the fun and madness of mimetic play lies in making subject-object relations run after each other so fast that they get blurred into varying movements, rhythms, and speeds, rather than consolidated.

Mimesis Degree Zero

The final slapstick scene in *Unfaithfully Yours* is excruciatingly unfunny and long. For these reasons many think that Sturges really lost his comic sense entirely in this scene, if not in this film as a whole.[44] There is, I think, another way to look at this scene. As a suave, urbane, brilliant English orchestral conductor, Sir Alfred charms and overwhelms everyone he encounters until he imagines his wife to be having an affair with his secretary. While conducting his orchestra in this scene he fantasizes three intricate scenarios of revenge on his wife and her imagined lover, in three different genres, each in keeping with the mood of the music he conducts. The problems begin when he tries to actualize his fantasies of revenge.

The very slow slapstick occurs when he tries to actualize his fantasy with objects that resist his every move. A sharp contrast is made between Sir Alfred's performative ease in everyday life (such as the fluency of his repartee, the elegant sweep of his walk through a hotel) or as a conductor, drawing magical sound out of instruments played by a group of (mostly) men who look like clerks, on the one hand, and his subjugation by objects in the slapstick scene on the other. The object that offers the most inventive resistance is the tape recorder, which displays its mimetic prowess by converting Sir Alfred's voice into different tones, registers, and timbres, even managing to make him sound like a cow.[45] As each object repeatedly offers its own unique resistance to him, such as the chair through which he falls, the flowers that make him sneeze convulsively, and the telephone he gets entangled in, Sir Alfred slowly, methodically, and doggedly keeps on keeping on. This extreme slowness, to the point of slow-wittedness, is really a performance where all mimetic impulses, the capacity to play (to divide time endlessly), have reached degree zero.[46] Here repetition only brings more of the same, while the mimetically capacious tape recorder "copies" sounds and transposes them into wildly different registers. The mimetic machine refuses to be "his master's voice," and thereby undoes Sir Alfred's mastery. This scene is not funny, because it is about the death of mimesis or mimetic deactivation. Or rather, it is funny in a painful, non-ha-ha way. If one expects it to be funny because it moves wholeheartedly into slapstick and starts laughing in anticipation, the laughter will soon dry out and hurt the muscles of the mouth. It is advisable, therefore, to keep a straight face when observing this scene of the mimetic degradation of a supremely elegant and masterful man who knows that he is, so as to get the most out of it—enjoy this spectacle of Chronic fatigue, the exhaustion of the energy to play with time.

Mimetic Convulsions

As a fragile and yet insistent, action-oriented performative energy/impulse/faculty, with libidinal and cognitive aspects, mimesis found, in the slapstick bodies of early American cinema, avatars for its renewal. In pursuing a slapstick time of the mimetically charged male body we have also glanced at its decay in American cinema. Through this rather bumpy, lengthy, and circuitous chase I have also tried to satisfy my own curiosity about why I (perhaps we) convulse in laughter or shudder at particular gags, a technical rather than a metaphysical curiosity. This inquiry into bodily convulsion (registering violations of normative temporality, of the distinctions between the organic or human and the non-organic or mechanical, and of stable subject-object relations) has been guided by strange bedfellows, Adorno and Deleuze, and a few others as well.

The thrilling and scary image of screaming couples waking up in motorized beds on freeways, from a slapstick short I saw when I was just a little girl, makes me want to conclude with the Adorno of *Aesthetic Theory*, because he expresses the process of wresting happiness (which drives the child-clown) with a visceral exactitude in the link he makes between "mimetic comportment" and "aesthetic comportment":

> Aesthetic comportment, however, is neither immediately mimesis nor its repression but rather the process that mimesis sets in motion and in which, modified, mimesis is preserved.

> Ultimately, aesthetic comportment is to be defined as the capacity to shudder, as if goose bumps were the first aesthetic image. What later came to be called subjectivity, freeing itself from the blind anxiety of the shudder, is at the same time the shudder's own development; life in the subject is nothing but what shudders, the reaction to the total spell that transcends the spell. Consciousness without shudder is reified consciousness. That shudder in which subjectivity stirs without yet being subjectivity is the act of being touched by the other. Aesthetic comportment assimilates itself to that other rather than subordinating it. Such a constitutive relation of the subject to objectivity in aesthetic comportment joins eros and knowledge.[47]

This is the image of happiness that Chaplin offers through his mimetic convulsions, common to both the shudder and laughter. There is a warning here for film scholars and critics—cognitive work such as ours can't, I fear, be immune to this shudder (because there is a mimetic core to rationality too, intimates the *untimely* Adorno of the *Aesthetic Theory*).[48] And as for laughter—?

14 "Eyes in the Back of Your Head": Erotics of Learning in *Blue Steel* and *The Silence of the Lambs*

"In the field you gotta have eyes in the back of your head."[1]

As a film critic I take this admonition to heart; it is not only cops who need this impossible vision to stay alive. To be alive as a film critic in the field of cinema studies one must, I believe, try to develop perception akin to this, which is not unlike the register of "vision" Mrs. Stephens (Helen's blind mother) has in *Peeping Tom* (see chapter 6). Otherwise one risks becoming blind to the image in the drive to narrativize what is seen rather than letting the image guide and sensitize one to its own movements, rhythms, and durations. For a certain kind of cultural studies narrativization probably works very well, enabling large claims about general trends in culture (to do with "race," "gender," "class," and "ethnicity") to be made. But as a film critic I must confess that I cannot make a single move without an involvement in an aural or visual image. While this may well be a personal idiosyncrasy, I would also like to make one large claim (a truism, really) for cinema and film studies, "my field." Its coherence as a discipline must depend on, at least, an attentiveness to the object, film: on, dare I say, the primacy even of the object. While reception, context, and so on are no doubt crucial in understanding what films do and what we do with films, the object's own mode of existence, its aesthetic qualities, are crucial to its power of invention, an invention that implicates the human senses through their recharging by technology. For decades, formalist film studies have certainly asserted the importance of studying film as text; more recent work, especially in Australia, has begun to focus on that which is not text-like in film, the image (both aural and visual) and its materiality of movement, rhythm, color, light, sound, and duration.[2] I do believe that paying attention to the filmic yields a different kind of knowledge from that offered by reading the narrative line alone. The affects of an image, its rhythm, and its duration can halt the movement of narrative action, creating temporal moments that are different from narrative time. A film criticism that believes in film as our collective "archive of memory" or our common "time place" must, I think, address such moments and attempt to describe, testify to, what happens there.[3] For an academic film critic such as myself, filmic knowledge of this kind is nothing short of a store of mimetic capital, the surplus yield of my intellectual labor on a film. This capital is of value because it often shows, among other things, how rational knowledge (my formal academic brief) itself atrophies without an encounter with its mimetic core, which the filmic activates in surprising ways.

The two films analyzed in this chapter, *Blue Steel* (dir. Kathryn Bigelow, 1989) and *The Silence of the Lambs* (dir. Jonathan Demme, 1991), are a fertile training ground for the activation of mimetic perception both for the female agents in the films and by implication for the viewers, and, in activating it, they also question and complicate the taken-for-granted terms of professional knowledge by introducing an affective vitalism to the acquisition of this knowledge. As a female academic investigator, I shall simultaneously follow the various moves of the two agents in these films (Clarice Starling, an FBI trainee, and Megan Turner, a rookie cop, both learning unofficially how to see out the back of their heads) and the movements of the image, so as to get a methodological grip on the affective conditions of professional knowledge for (generic) women—and for myself as well. I want to learn from these films how rationality and mimetic sensitivity collude in and occlude the process of acquiring knowledge, creating knowledge itself as an action problem. In this chapter I pursue the elusive processes of learning from film (learning to discard the straitjacket of the "knowing critic" [see chapter 2] through a mimetically activated perceptual training under the specific generic imperative of, in these cases, action under duress). I shall work out in some detail how these two films recharge perception and action, not by a pedagogy of telling, but by a kind of mimetic showing and knowing.[4] I am hoping that this kind of pedagogy will be instructive for the academic in the field.

The Female Hero and Unraveling Action

The most striking mark of difference in these films' reworking of familiar generic terrain (variations on the thriller) is that the heroes are women. And this does make a difference to the nature of the action, because these films do not simply replace a male with a female hero while maintaining an efficient coordination of perceptions and actions through the mediation of affect that usually governs films with a male action hero. In these films such 100-percent sensory-motor efficiency is fundamentally disturbed. The manner in which the sensory-motor action unravels in these films creates what might be called a neorealist moment, as delineated in chapter 10. Also, this unraveling of what may be called the protocols of generic habit seems to be a precondition for mimetic learning to occur. The kind of temporality that emerges from this process enables a cluster of familiar terms ("gender," "knowledge," "action," "affect," "memory," and "violence") to be reconfigured in unusual ways not evident in films which simply reverse gender and maintain a uniform logic of efficient sensory-motor action. In trying to specify the quality of unraveling action-time in each of the films, I will use a theory of memory and duration developed by Deleuze from Henri Bergson.[5] I will use their concepts to explore how and to what end the flashback as a form of recollection images appears in these films to do "memory-work"[6] when action reaches an impasse.

Unraveling Everyday and Spectacular Violence

In *Blue Steel* everyday and spectacular violent actions brush against each other to create a kind of abrasion. While Megan Turner, the rookie cop, tries to disarm a man holding up a supermarket, the buildup to the shoot-out is excruciatingly long and slow, as though the entire action is in slow motion. "It is as if the action floats in the situation,"[7] in much the same way that, when Turner shoots at the hold-up man, his gun floats up in the air in genuine slow motion before landing near the psychopath Eugene Hunt, who is lying on the floor of the supermarket with several of the other customers. As Turner makes her way from one long supermarket aisle to another to get into a line of fire her body brushes against some frying pans, making them rattle. Because of the slowness of the scene and its long duration, this brush with domestic utensils not only adds to the suspense: the minute sound feels amplified, leaving a residue. Later in the film Turner hugs her mother, who winces because of a bruise on her arm; this tells Turner that her father has once again beaten her sweet and placid mother.

Domestic violence has already figured in the very first sequence, after just two credit titles; in a fascinating twist, the scene turns out to be a police training session for Turner. In it Turner interrupts a scene of domestic violence where a man is about to shoot a woman. As she disarms the man the victim pulls out a gun from a purse and shoots Turner. This elicits the following admonition from the superior officer (her mentor) directing the scene: "You shot the husband but the wife killed you, Turner. In the field you gotta have eyes in the back of your head." As is clear by now, I have used this statement to frame this chapter instead of the category of gender because I think the latter is itself made shifty, and an oblique approach, with few certitudes, may yield an insight or two as to how to think gender in such a treacherous field; there is no sisterhood here. Hard-won feminist certitudes vis-à-vis domestic violence are of no avail in this treacherous space. We seem to be cautioned against expecting a narrative of rescue with easy victory (both physical and ideological) for the female action hero fighting male violence; the film's refusal to neatly gender violence is itself a noteworthy move. The problem of the blind spot at the back of the head can no longer be tackled by developing technical skill (in coordinating body, gun, and space) alone. The blind spot is also psychic, the forces that occlude are affective, for almost no one, least of all Turner, would have expected the female victim to shoot the person who came to her rescue. I have recounted the action and a bit of dialogue, but it is important to note that this action transpires in a strange color field constructed largely out of autonomous strips of the primary colors, red, yellow, and blue. Because this first scene is staged, its theatrical lighting may be justified, but the image on which the credits appear soon after the mock-up is neither dramatic nor narrative; its color and lighting are neither narratively or dramatically motivated. Rather, it is as if the narrative itself is generated from the qualities and powers of this image.

Charging Action with Affect

The image in question is that of a gun, shot in extreme close-up, over which the credits appear. At first it is not yet a gun but a series of abstract shapes in shades of translucent blue light. The large, abstract close-ups create surfaces, depths, contours. It could be a camera lens that we see, or is it a part of a gun? The continually varying blue light disarms the gun. It is not a sensory-motor image of the gun but rather a gun raised to affective power, a pure quality of blue. In action films guns are functional tools, and therefore what is usually foregrounded is what the guns do, rather than the gun as object. If and when the gun becomes an emotional object it may interact with the action in numerous perverse ways to develop an explosive sensory-motor situation and action. But in *Blue Steel* the long opening credit sequence in close-up offers a different face of the gun from either tool of action or emotional object readied for sensory-motor action. What might the blue steel of the gun, bathed in a translucent, continually varying blue light and dissolves, defaced by a tight close-up, signal about the ensuing action in this thriller/horror film? We are invited to follow not only the movement of the action, which might lead to dead ends (as in the pre-credits training session), but also the adventure of light with color, or color as light, which has the power to trace virtual conjunctions that might open up possible actions. The narrative is about a rookie cop suspended from the police force after her very first job, for having used excessive force to stop a supermarket hold-up. Eugene Hunt, a stockbroker who happens to be shopping there, watches Turner blow off the head of the hold-up man, and grabs the criminal's gun as it lands near him. Inspired by Turner, Hunt uses this gun to kill people randomly with bullets carved with Turner's name. The suspended Turner is therefore reinstated, though in name only, so that she can help crack the case. In the meantime Turner and Hunt meet and fall in love, so that the man she is in love with is also the man she must hunt. Steven Shaviro, in his analysis of *Blue Steel*, offers a superb analytic description of the work of color in this film:

> The film is awash in a delicate and continually varying blue light, sometimes muted to night-time black, at other times crossed by bars of sunlight and shadow. Bigelow's subtle tonalities and use of chiaroscuro are the updated equivalent, for color film, of the black-and-white images of the 1940s film noir.

Despite the historical point about the link between the German expressionist cycle of films, Hollywood film noir, and this work of Bigelow's, he adds that there is no expressionist struggle between light and dark, as a "projection of an intense subjectivity violently at war with itself," to be found in this film. This is because, as Shaviro says, the work of color in this film is one of pure

> modulations of light . . . there is no clear-cut opposition between night and day, or shadow and light, but rather an uncanny sense of luminous darkness. Tonal variations are diffused throughout visual space and not projected upon it. Lighting no longer expresses subjectivity; it is instead

almost as if subjectivity were an effect of atmosphere, or of variations in light.[8]

Conceiving and composing the cinematic image in this way as pure modulation, through a pulsation and oscillation of color, is a way of making forms, bodies, spaces, and boundaries unstable, permeable; the agency of light, color, and movement becomes as important as human agency. Further, if one can make a distinction between light and color then it would be more exact to say that what is modulated in this film is color rather than light; it is color that creates light, shadow, volatile forms. For example, a shot of the police station lobby is figured in a blue light with two or three beams of sunlight crossing it; the sunlight is shaded blue. This is space and light conceived as gradations of fluctuating color. Blue steel: the steel is blue and so are the eyes of the hero, Megan Turner. But this adjectival quality common to several different things (gun, eyes, police uniforms, cars, institutional space, city exteriors) is not metaphorical, it's not saying her gaze is as hard and cold as steel, for instance, or rather, even if it does, this is not the most interesting way to look at how color works in this film. It is not only the gun and the hero's eyes that share similar qualities; even certain spaces and scenes are bathed in a blue translucent light, graded into a range of shades of blue that go to black at one end and to a nearly bleached-out white at the other.

Bigelow came to filmmaking after a training in painting. Her color palette consists of at least three different tonalities: 1. translucent modulations of blue light; 2. the intermittent recurrence of the primary colors red and yellow; and 3. a "normal" everyday light and colors that are slightly yellowish in tone. Within this schema blue is certainly the privileged color, because it is the medium chosen to charge action with affect. What does it mean to charge action with affect? In this film, as in *The Silence of the Lambs,* it means, among other things, running the risk of immobilizing or unraveling action to the point of paralysis from which it must struggle to reactivate itself, as two scenes, one of Turner arresting her father and the other of Turner arresting her lover, show. The film itself seems to emerge from a blue matrix of light just as, on several occasions, the hero and villain do. The blue is not used symbolically but more in the way a modern painter might use it, in its varied hues, as a means of composition as well as decomposition of image-object-space. The other primaries, red and yellow, appear as city signs in a highly formalized manner. When Eugene and

Turner get out of the cab they are sharing at their first meeting because of a traffic jam, a high-angle shot of the jammed cars reveals about eight to be bluish in tone while just two are different in color, one red and the other yellow. Later a prostitute walks the streets clad in a bright yellow dress with a bright red belt. Eugene, on the prowl, emerges from a color field of a bluish hue and is propositioned by the prostitute. The very next shot, a pan across a red and yellow Hitachi sign, picks up Eugene undressing, emitting animal-like grunts and groans while rubbing his body with the blood-drenched yellow dress of the prostitute in an orgy of blood lust. The large blue close-up credit sequence of the gun may be read as a combination of three different kinds of images. At first, because it is difficult to read the image, we can say, following Deleuze, that the shot effects an absolute de-territorialization of the image. We can't identify it as a particular thing; it is pure modulation of color, shape, light, and texture, achieved through the micro movements of the rhythmic overlapping dissolves and the smooth panning movements of the camera, as well as the movement of the surface-object itself and the varying shades of the blue light. Halfway through this abstract image a few decisive signs begin to emerge, identifying it as a Smith & Wesson gun made in the U.S.A. We now hear the gun being loaded (along with the pure sonic modulation of the accompanying music), its barrel being turned, and at the end of the sequence this self-animated object falls into a holster, but in slow motion. It is then that we know that it belongs to Megan Turner, the rookie cop, dressing for her graduation. In this brief opening credit sequence Bigelow has presented the hero's gun first as pure quality (affection image), then as fetish or part object (impulse image), and finally as professional tool (action image).[9] In this way the images animate registers of affect, impulse, and action in the one sequence without making a single narrative move. The birth of the gun as impulse nestles between, on the one hand, the affective abstract close-ups of what turns out to be a gun, and on the other the gun's falling into its casing, ready for action, at the end of the sequence. The impulse image, according to Deleuze, nestles between the affection image and the action image, embodying a degenerate affect and an embryonic action (*C1* 123). He says that "What makes the impulse image so difficult to reach and even to define or identify, is that it is somehow 'stuck' between the affection image and the action image" (*C1* 134). I think the gun as pure impulse comes into visibility as we hear the sounds of the bullets dropping voluptuously into place and as they push forward ineluctably toward the viewer, in a blue light that bleaches out into an almost white heat in the dead center of the bullet.

This is gun as pulsive force, pure violence, what Eugene will later call "my brightness, my radiance," referring not to the gun but to Turner, who is for him indistinguishable from it, incarnating as she does an impulse to violence.

The Violence of Impulse[10]

The comfortable opposition of good violence and bad violence is undone by the emblematic sign of Megan Turner's name carved on the bullets found in the bodies of the psychopath Hunt's victims. Despite Turner's statement to the contrary, she does seem to be "the kind of girl who gets her name carved on a bullet." In fact an impulse to violence encodes Turner's very first professional act. She empties a whole clip of bullets (when one would have done) into the head of the man who holds up a supermarket. Her colleague and superiors (not all of them unsympathetic) are shocked by this sign of excess. The only one who exults in it is Eugene, who witnesses it as he lies sprawled on the floor. He sees it not as excessive but as the manifestation of an unswerving impulse to violence: as he tells her later, "You shot him without blinking an eye." And in an instantaneous transference he becomes her double and she his unwitting mentor. As we shall see this is not a mutually (or consciously) sanctioned arrangement, and there is a struggle around doubling in this film which will entail an involvement of memory as a key player. Now we are in a messy psychic space rather like late John Ford territory, as in *The Searchers* (1956), where John Wayne's violent impulses are barely tempered by ethical and professional considerations. The hero and the villain (the Indian chief) are two sides of the same dark coin; they are doubles. The point of this comparison is not only that the violent impulse to revenge is central to both films (and that John Wayne also made a Western called *Blue Steel* for Monogram in 1934, directed by Robert Bradbury, in which he saves both a town and a girl from the baddies), but also that it took Ford something like three decades of working within the genre of the Western to arrive at a moment (both cinematic and social) where the Western hero could be reconfigured in such an ethically compromised state, making him similar to the villain. Bigelow has no equivalent rich generic history of female agency in high cinematic action to draw from. She does have, in Jamie Lee Curtis, "the last girl," an invaluable actor with an impeccable slasher- and horror-film past to draw on as instant recall, as for instance when she challenges Eugene with "[I'll] blow your lousy head into the next state."[11] Bigelow makes *Blue Steel* a horror/thriller film so as to be able to work in several registers at the same time and complicate and muddy the emotional registers at the risk of losing credibility. Quite often viewers say that the film is badly made because of an unconvincing plot and characterization, especially Eugene's. This is because the film plunges from psychological thriller to horror, recalling expressionist conventions of character and action (doppelgänger, characters who are impulse incarnate, magical appearances with weak causal links in the action) so as to give full reign to affective intensity and impulse-driven violence while maintaining the semblance of an action-thriller logic (as, say, a melodic line) at the same time. Some scenes are especially expressionist/horror or magical, in the sense of having weak causal motivation: 1. Eugene popping up at Turner's parents' house and sitting talking to her mother, having introduced himself as her fiancé, after having killed her best friend Tracey, and immediately after Turner has arrested her own father for domestic violence; 2. Eugene breaking into Turner's apartment and hiding in her bathroom after being shot in the arm by her, and staying on there right through Turner and Nick Mann's lovemaking; 3. Eugene appearing behind Turner on the crowded railway platform and Turner swinging round to shoot as though now she has "eyes in the back of her head." If we need more signs of a gesturing toward expressionist doubling, there are the bullet wounds to the arm that each inflicts on the other at different moments. And when yet again someone, in this instance Nick Mann (seated with Turner in a police car, waiting endlessly in the park for Eugene to appear looking for his buried gun), asks Turner why she became a cop, she turns her head, which is in profile, to face Mann only to plunge half of it into darkness as she answers, "Him." Turner is shot by Bigelow to maximize her androgynous appearance and strengths. If one accepts the register of horror cinema in which this film moves then none of these scenes will be judged by the criteria of realist credibility proper to action thrillers alone. The pathological impulse to violence is now an enabling affect, without which the hero would seem to have no libidinal energy at all for professional action. This film is intent on pushing its female hero hard against a stone wall, creating impasses. My favorite, most unbearable scene is that of Turner pushing her father against a kitchen cupboard to handcuff him, pulling his hands behind his back. She is arresting her father for having yet again beaten up her mother; it is both shocking and thrilling. Turner for her part creates an interesting difficulty for herself as both daughter and cop, which can be formulated thus: a girl cop can't arrest her father—she can't not arrest her father—stone wall. Criminal and cop are also father and daughter, she is now an agent of the law, sanctioned to deploy violence when necessary. The ensuing dialogue between father and daughter in the cop car resolves the impasse for the moment: "I am your father"; "I am ashamed of it." She then stops the car and asks her father why he beats up her mother and in answer he mumbles, "I don't know, I just feel bad and then I do it" and starts crying, reducing himself to a situation of childlike helplessness. Daughter turned mentor warns her father never to hit her mother again and drives him home to find Eugene triumphantly sitting in their living room. There is an expressionist propriety about his magically appearing in the very place that perhaps first inducted Turner into violence, helplessness, and her own growing impulse toward violence. Another excruciating impasse occurs when Turner realizes that Eugene, the man she has fallen in love with and is just about to make love to, is also the psychopathic killer she is professionally engaged in hunting down. Just at this moment he declares his love for her:

> I have found my brightness. I have seen that brightness in you . . . You
> shot him without blinking an eye. You are the only one capable of
> understanding . . . My radiance. The two of us, we could share . . . We
> are one person, you and I, you would do what I do if you knew yourself
> better, you will in time, it is just starting between you and me . . . you
> have no reason to worry, you have everything to live for. I mean death,
> the greatest kick of all.

Turner has unwittingly ignited his impulse to violence. When Eugene walks the rain-drenched streets, soon after he has witnessed Turner's violent act, and stumbles and falls, his stolen gun falls out of his jacket. An elderly man comes over to assist him. Picking up the gun, almost like a child learning to use a new toy, Eugene looks hesitantly at the gun and then at the man—with a dawning look of diabolical glee he fires his first shot and then another and yet another, as the punctured body spits out blood and falls down backward in spectacular slow motion. It is a consummation in blood of Eugene's perception of Turner as his mentor (his radiance) and double. The scene of Eugene's arrest echoes back to the very first sounds of the film, a violent shouting match between a woman and a man, first heard (not seen) over the very first credit title on a black background:

Woman: No! Stop!
Man: I love you.

Woman: No, help!
Man: I'll kill you.
Woman: Help! No.

What is of interest in this staged scene of domestic violence, which functions as a training session for Turner, is the almost instantaneous conversion from "I love you" to "I'll kill you." This is what happens to Turner when she realizes that her would-be lover is also the killer she has been hunting for. Yet in this scene Turner occupies an impossible combination of positions, that of the man who yells "I love you" and "I'll kill you" and that of the woman who says no and calls for help. Turner does not cry out verbally but her body enacts its equivalent by sliding down into a squatting position against the wall, unable to hold itself up, and yet with her gun held in outstretched hands, tears welling up and trickling down, even as she arrests him with exemplary rationality: "You have the right to remain silent . . . anything you say can and will be used . . . you have a right to an attorney. . . . " In charging action with affect in this way *Blue Steel* is similar to the psychological thriller/horror *The Silence of the Lambs*. But in the latter film it is the evocation of the Gothic that really makes a shift from action to affect and back to recharged action possible. The double registers in which these films operate create double trouble for the female action heroes. How to move on two fronts simultaneously becomes a question that needs answers on the run; the two fronts, the logics of rational action and those of affect, seem to get in each other's way. It is at this critical juncture of collusion and occlusion of forces that memory comes riding, riding slowly, sometimes oh-so-slowly, to the rescue.

Memory to the Rescue in the Nick of Time

Eugene and Turner each have one flashback which replays earlier images and scenes from the film. Both occur at moments of difficulty with action. Eugene is being hunted by Turner while he is hunting, digging like a dog on all fours, for the gun he has buried in the park. She comes up to him and tempts him with the following acid taunt:

Looking for something? It's okay, I have one (she unzips her jacket revealing in a tight close-up her gun resting snugly under her arm, against a white linen blouse). Come on, Eugene, grab mine, you never know, you, you might be able to grab it before I get to it and blow your lousy head into the next state.

As he stands up from his crouch, the camera starts moving and so does Eugene, almost in a trance state, mesmerized, transfixed by the challenge. A series of flashback images appear in the gap or hesitation created by the camera's moving toward Turner more quickly than he can, showing his first encounter with Turner in the supermarket: 1. The gun flying down in a slow motion long shot; 2. A tight close-up of it falling near Eugene as he huddles on the floor; 3. A close shot of Turner holding it with outstretched arms, yelling to the hold-up guy to drop his gun. At this point the sequence is interrupted by a tight shot-reverse-shot series of Eugene looking at Turner and then a close-up of Turner's gun strapped to her body, to a close-up of Turner's face, ending with a return shot to Eugene. Then the flashback resumes: 4. Three close-ups of Eugene on the supermarket floor, pulling the criminal's gun toward him. These shots are taken from two different angles, creating a jump-cut effect. The scene cuts again, to a close-up shot-reverse-shot schema of Eugene, Turner, Eugene, Eugene's hand reaching out, and finally Turner's gun, which is grabbed by Mann, who arrives in the nick of time and averts a premature confrontation between hero and villain.

Turner's flashback occurs when she is trapped in the hospital after being raped by Eugene. She can't get out, because a cop is guarding her, and she is emotionally distraught not only because of having been raped but also because Nick Mann, her lover (and superior officer), is lying unconscious in the same hospital after having been shot by Eugene. All the while Eugene, whose victims already include Turner's best and only friend, Tracey, is on the hunt for the next one. Turner's flashback occurs at this moment of extreme personal and professional anguish. She is given her medicine by a nurse who, when asked what time it is, says, "It's almost five, the sun will be up soon," which explains the soft light that illuminates the blue tone of the hospital-room wall. The nurse draws a screen across the bluish space, casting Turner into a shadow in which she turns her head to look, presumably, out of the window. An external shot shows the city bathed in a soft pastel dawn light from which the film cuts to an establishing long shot of Turner sitting quietly at the window, lit by a warm yellowish sunlight reflected from the outside. The rest of the image is plunged in darkness. As the camera travels slowly and steadily toward her the flashback begins: 1. Eugene as she first saw him, drenched in rain and looking appealing. There is a cut back to the establishing shot of Turner at the window, with a moving camera bringing her closer, and then the flashback resumes: 2. Eugene, with gun held out, imitating Turner and mimicking the sound of her gun, "Pow"; 3. A dead body with a bleeding gunshot wound; 4. A bullet casing with Turner's name carved on it. Here the traveling shot of Turner at the window intervenes again, now nearly in close-up, the dark area almost obliterated. Then the flashback continues: 5. Eugene gripping Turner from behind, on the staircase of her apartment; 6. Turner being raped by him and kicking him away; 7. Tracey turning round screaming on the staircase; 8. Eugene, still holding Turner from behind (so she can't see him), shooting Tracey. Then we see Turner in her own bed waking up from a nightmare, and this shot cuts to the cop who is guarding her stubbing out a cigarette.

The rhythmic and tonal differences between Turner's and Eugene's flashbacks illustrate how memory works in relation to action in this film. Memory fuels Eugene's obsession, the jump-cut repetition of the shots of the gun creating a circuit with no exit. His actual-virtual circuit (memory-work)[12] is caught in a loop which casts a trancelike spell on him, whereas Turner's actual-virtual circuits are supple and improvisatory, igniting action. She tricks the cop guarding her into giving her a cigarette, and as he lights it she punches him unconscious. The ignited lighter is picked up by the camera as it falls onto the reflecting surface of the next shot in a small close-up, making it look like a gun on fire. The cigarette lighter as action object has assisted the hero, and once that function is fulfilled the image returns it to its other function, as an affection image tracing virtual conjunctions, imaging the pulsive force—the violence—of the impulse itself. Virtualized objects and memory (which according to Bergson's theory is virtual, not actual, but real), color, light, and camera movements in this sequence activate the female hero, who is seated at a window gazing out (in that most feminine of painterly poses), bathed in an early morning light. Turner extinguishes the flame of the virtual gun and dresses in the uniform of the cop she has knocked out, all fired up to activate what her memory, actualized in the flashback, intimated by jumbling up the sequence of the past violent events.

Falsifying Memory[13]

Both sets of flashbacks falsify the actual sequence of events. In Turner's flashback, shots five, seven, and eight of the flashback form a continuous sequence of Tracey's murder by Eugene. Shot six (of her being raped and kicking Eugene off her body) is cut into the sequence of Tracey's murder, interrupting its temporal coherence, and thereby kindling an impulse to transform an impossible situation. Eugene's flashback also falsifies its actual temporal sequence: the first shot of the virtual sequence is in fact the second shot of the actual sequence, the second shot of the virtual sequence the third in the actual, the third in the virtual the first in the actual. In his flashback the gun becomes a magical object that he is trying to grasp, aided by the cinematic magic of the jump cut. In his memory-work the virtual, as it interacts with his actual situation, creates a trance-like quality such that the camera moves faster than the character, who seems to be in a dream. During her recollection, in contrast, Turner is completely still, while the camera, light, and falsifying memory-work draw a virtual line of action whose affective power Turner will go on to actualize. Because she doesn't have "eyes in the back of her head," the tactile, not to mention olfactory, evidence she has about the killer who gripped her from behind has no value in the eyes of the law. And yet the affective power of Turner's flashback lies in the way it enables her to "see," through the power of recollection-images, her link with Eugene literalized by his grip on her, thereby creating a composite body of hero and villain which will shoot the fatal bullet, branded with her name, into her friend's body. Even as the similarity between hero and villain is made visible to Turner through the flashback recollection, the insertion into this sequence of an anachronistic image of her kicking Eugene off her body as he rapes her loosens the identificatory grip. Once acknowledged or confronted in the temporal mode of recollection, the violence of the impulse animating the hero has a chance of returning with a difference: modulated, channeled, perhaps. Turner, now disguised in the stolen police uniform, checks on her lover and partner Nick Mann in intensive care and then walks out of the hospital in a slow-motion silhouette into a blue gaseous light with transparent white smoke rising from the ground. This blue has reached a peak of crystallization by now so that it feels like the air the hero breathes, her element. While it looks like liquid nitrogen (cold), it feels warm: perhaps because of the slow-motion walk through it and because of the white smoke that rises from the ground? Here too there is really an optical drama of color that takes on rhythmic value (both hot and cold) before the final sensory-motor showdown between hero and villain begins. Turner's slow-motion walk into and within a pulsating blue field of light is intercut with a series of reverse shots of the awakening city in quite a different register: yellowish tones. She takes a long time to emerge out of the blue space (which is flattened by the telephoto lens and made dense by a pulsating blue, with the slow motion stretching time), as though it is now a limitless time zone[14] rather than a definable space, insofar as it is marked rhythmically by a pulsation of blue.[15] And when she finally does enter the space of the city's actual streets and subway it is as though the affective rhythmic qualities of the color have saturated her through and through, giving her "eyes in the back of the head," so that when Eugene stalks her on the subway platform she senses his presence, swinging round to shoot him. But he shoots her first, in the arm (mirroring the wound she inflicted on him earlier on), which only highlights their growing separation despite this final rite of passage by blood which links them. In this affectively complicated (and therefore empowered) way the wounded hero moves into the final duel.

An Optical Drama of Color: Translucent Blue vs. Opaque White

The optical drama of modulated, translucent blue in *Blue Steel* is, at one terrifying moment of the film, highlighted by returning the image to its absolute other, a pure opaque white surface. Eugene, who has escaped Turner's effort to kill him, is nevertheless wounded by her as he tries to kill Nick Mann. On the run, he breaks into her apartment, hides in her bathroom, and extracts the bullet lodged in his arm. Turner and Mann, both exhausted and traumatized by the latter's near brush with death (unwittingly caused by Turner), return to her apartment. As they make love the shots are punctuated or punctured by shots of Eugene in the bathroom, loading his gun with bloodied fingers. In semi-darkness Eugene pulls down a white towel and wraps the gun; this action is shown in an extreme close shot that nearly covers the whole image in an opaque pure white surface that stills the movement of colored light. The shot cuts to Turner in the next room putting on a white shirt, which also nearly covers the whole image, blocking the pulsating blue tones visible there before. This opaque pure white surface blocks the movement of color and it is at that very moment that Eugene shoots down Mann and rapes Turner. White, "radiance," and "brightness" in this film are linked to Eugene's psychopathology. The film does not offer a counter-force to it in darkness or blackness, which would have simply reversed the light/dark opposition of the expressionist image and of film noir. The luminous blue, which could be both day and night, inside and outside, institutional space and city street, does not partake of a dualistic struggle, because it creates a fluctuating space which doesn't really feel like a space at all any more but more like a pulsation; it makes space temporal by infusing color with a rhythm, a throbbing. This rhythmic use of color creates a pulsating zone, hospitable to the expression of the volatile pulsive force of the impulse, impervious to good and evil.

Sensory-Motor Duel or Surrender to the Impulse?

In the final showdown on Wall Street between hero and villain, Turner commandeers a car and runs over Eugene, who rises up repeatedly like a monster refusing to die. Despite this, Turner fires only three shots to make Eugene's punctured body slump down. The hero's newly acquired restraint is noteworthy (a contrast to early excesses), just as is the villain's final surrender to an ineluctable impulse incarnated (for him) in the steel-blue gaze of the hero as she rears her head (framed by the car window) to kill him. It seems to me that while this climactic scene has some of the main elements of a sensory-motor duel, there is something in Eugene's final gesture of simply standing (without any readable expression on his face) and facing the bullets after his have run out that intimates that he is still enthralled by the impulse. His posture and facial expression (reflecting his violence) "cease to be a reaction linked to a situation" (i.e., sensory-motor), and instead "they become internal and natural to the character, innate" (C1 135). It could be said, following the logic of the impulse, that Eugene has, in that final instant, "chosen" to surrender himself to the death impulse he sees incarnated in Turner as though it were his destiny. This mid-long-shot image of Eugene seen by Turner is oddly reminiscent of the shot (also repeated in her recollection image) in which she first saw him standing in the rain, looking appealingly drenched and vulnerable. It is odd because there is an absolute difference in his countenance and posture now, which eroticizes his presence in a manner unseen before. The eroticism one senses, is, I think, a consequence of his absolute, even voluptuous, surrender to the ineluctable violence of the impulse. But Turner, refusing to mirror his desire, has been able here (as she wasn't in the supermarket) to transpose her impulse to violence into the service of a decisively rational sensory-motor action, signaled by the focus-pull on the series of shots coordinating eye, hand, and gun. One might say that Turner has reached that critical instant—when time hurtling down as destiny swerves from its course—through a repetition that saves, and thus breaks with the "order of impulse(s)."[16] So after Turner kills Eugene her gun becomes almost playful, bouncing gently onto the seat of the car in a slow-motion small close-up, while her hand also comes down softly to rest on the seat, separated from the gun, thereby not only delinking the sensory-motor circuit between gun, hand, and eye but also exhausting or exorcising the violent impulsive force that has been given full vent.

The Hero's Face: A Turning Away and a Turning Around[17]

Thus disarmed, all action spent, there is yet what comes after, a still, averted face in a slow-motion close-up. Turner's face is in profile, ever so slightly at an angle, with her murderous steel-blue gaze laid to rest, eyes looking down but open, blinking in slow motion, framed by the blue steel of the car window. This shot is held for about thirty seconds (excessive within the Hollywood economy), even as more blue frames within frames proliferate, as do shades of blue, as several police cars draw up. We may ask this face, following Deleuze, "What are you thinking?" for it is reflective; while of Turner's full frontal close-up smile (presumably at herself in the mirror) at the very beginning of the film, as she dresses up for her graduation, we can ask, "What are you feeling?" When asked whether it was difficult for her to shoot in New York City, Bigelow is reported to have said that it wasn't, because she made the face into a landscape.[18] Certainly, through this turning around and turning away of Turner's face Bigelow has created, out of Jamie Lee Curtis's face, a transparent surface, reflecting resemblances to her famous parents Janet Leigh and Tony Curtis, but also an opaque surface, activating an uncanny resemblance between male and female, hero and villain, simply by a micro movement, a change of angle, or a play of light on or tilt of this face. Both her face and the cityscape have been used as matters of expression, subjecting them to micro movements or movement of color, evoking a pulsating oscillation of qualities of hot and cold, hard and soft.

The use of slow motion not only for action scenes shot with a telephoto lens (reducing depth) but also for a close-up of a face in profile held for an unusually long duration makes visible, and attunes one to sensing, oscillations and micro fissures, leakages between polarized categories. One can therefore say that the two prime modulators in this film are color and slow motion.[19] The final scene is an unusually quiet and slow ending for a violent action thriller, but, as has been noted, this is not the only quiet moment in this film. What are at first police sirens on the sound track, when electronically modulated, begin to sound like seagulls, and I am instantly reminded of the rhythmic qualities of the very long last shot of Chantal Akerman's *News from Home,* which leaves Manhattan from this same Wall Street area, on the Staten Island ferry, with seagulls on the sound track. The end of *Blue Steel* also has an uncanny correspondence to the end of Akerman's *Jeanne Dielman* (see chapter 11) because of the long duration of the shot of Jeanne seated at a table (with a neon streetlight beating on her face) after having killed a man. These rhythmic memory triggers make me ask, is our hero at a dead end professionally or has she just begun, having completed her true rite of passage, marked by blood? The (un-heroic) restful posture of the wounded hero, her slightly tilted head mul-tiply framed by the shaded blue steel of police cars, the rhythmic modu-lations on the sound track, the way in which two (male) fellow cops gently encircle and hold her body at the waist and arm as they help her out of the car in slow motion, and finally the empty frames of the modulated blue steel create a feeling of movement in this static shot. It is difficult to pin down why, but certainly the shot does not feel like a dead end. I do realize that to say this is to relinquish argument (a cop-out?) in favor of simply, and as precisely as possible, registering the emergence of something that can certainly be pointed out in the qualities of the image and sound but that can't quite be narrativized or conceptualized. It is this kind of expe-rience of an image, not ineffable, but eluding conceptualization and cer-tainly narrativization, that Deleuze, following Peirce, calls "firstness": the emergence of something new.[20] This is an unusual way to think of the old idea of "the new": as the emergence of a quality and of our capacity to sense it. If we concede this experience then we must say that there is a gap between the seeable and the sayable. To acknowledge this gap is, for those of us in the field of cinema studies, a way of conceding the role of mimetic mentorship to film.

"You don't want Hannibal Lecter inside your head"

Mentorship is, happily, an explicit theme in *The Silence of the Lambs,* which Bruce Robbins, in his "Murder and Mentorship: Advance-ment in *The Silence of the Lambs,*" has usefully foregrounded, widening the terms of the critical debate on this film.[21] I am here less interested in the eroticizing of the transmission of knowledge from mentor to student and in the defused eroticism and seduction that mark the entry into profes-sional life, which concern Robbins. Rather, taking up his central insight on the importance of mentorship in the film, I want to focus on the mimetic acquisition of knowledge by the female hero. This focus entails engaging with how the senses are trained to perceive, know, and act and how the female hero rewires herself mimetically, on the run, as she straddles the impossibility of being both agent and victim at once. FBI trainee Clarice Starling, played by Jodie Foster, is enlisted, even before she has graduated, to solve the mystery of the serial killer known as Buffalo Bill because the case has reached a dead end. Dr. Crawford, who has nominally given her the status of FBI agent, feels that such an unconventional move is necessary if any progress is to be made in gaining access to the professional knowledge held by the imprisoned former psychiatrist Dr. Hannibal Lecter, a cannibalistic psychopathic killer. Dr. Crawford believes that Starling might succeed with Lecter where other efforts have failed (perhaps presuming a conventional seduction scenario between male teacher and female pupil), but he withholds information from her and uses her as bait to gain knowledge of Buffalo Bill from Dr. Lecter.

Orality, Animality, and Cognition

Starling's professional drive and will to move up from her white-trash background are immediately noted by Hannibal Lecter. But beyond his ability to read social signs, he, like the other imprisoned psychopaths, is marked by an untrammeled use of the senses. We register his ferocious orality, as well as a heightened olfactory sense whereby he names the kind of cream Agent Starling uses and also knows that she has stopped bleeding from a scratch to the inside of her thigh that he couldn't possibly have seen, while his neighbor Miggs yells at her, "I can smell your cunt." In these traits the psychopaths have a link with the world of animals where smell has, among other things, a "cognitive" function. As Adorno and Horkheimer have shown us, it is the most animal of our senses, and it does not respect boundaries, making them permeable.[22] It is noteworthy that in the book on which the film is based, Starling locates Jamie Gum in total darkness in the climactic scene by smelling his presence; she knows the smell of schizophrenic sweat, which gives her an olfactory spatial cue. In the film, for obvious reasons, the sense that comes to the rescue when vision is occluded is not smell but hearing. This capacity to shift senses and make one do the work of the other (echoing *The Piano*) is a skill that Lecter has inducted Starling into, one might say, unwittingly. Though Lecter is a classical pedagogue when he quotes Marcus Aurelius and presses Starling to get at first principles, in his pathology he abandons the hierarchical training of the senses implicit in such an education. It is this pathology of the senses that is most instructive for Starling. If one finds the sight of Lecter sniffing the air like an animal and the manner in which his mouth is libidinalized in his conversations with Starling fascinating, then his talk of first principles, of which he insists that simplicity is one, feels like a real let-down, though it does give a valuable narrative clue. It is a let-down because, in an affective and action space made intelligible by mimetic modes of knowing, the injunction to get down to first principles feels like an admonition to stop thinking on the run. It's obvious that Starling doesn't resort to first principles when she is in mortal danger in the monster's dungeon. Instead she overcomes her blind spot by shifting from vision to smell (in the book) or hearing (in the film). Deduction from first principles is only possible in the safety of a discussion with her girl friend about the psychopathology of serial killers.

Movement of Memory

The work of memory is just as important to this film as it is to *Blue Steel*. In fact, the title *The Silence of the Lambs* encapsulates the germinal memory image animating the film's quest. There are three recollection images in the film from Starling's point of view, two of which occur at moments when there are difficulties with action. They are both childhood memories, one an image of life, the other of death. The primal scene of a fantasy of rescue (of lambs) which Dr. Lecter elicits from Starling is also a childhood memory, but it is embodied in language rather than in images, unlike the two recollections actualized in the two flashbacks. The first flashback occurs after Starling's first interview with Dr. Lecter, in which he dismisses her and tells her to "fly back to school" and Miggs throws semen at her as she leaves. In response to Miggs's indecent act Lecter recalls Starling and gives her some advice, including the words "Look deep within YOUR-self . . . ," which Starling works out is the name of a storage facility. All of this happens in an escalating rhythm which leaves Starling overwhelmed as she stumbles out of the maximum security prison into the parking lot. At this moment she has her first flashback: herself as a little girl running to greet and hug her father as he returns home from his work as the town marshal. This scene cuts back to the present, where Starling is practicing target shooting. The second flashback occurs when Starling goes to West Virginia for the autopsy of Buffalo Bill's latest victim. At the funeral parlor she has to face a professionally awkward situation in dealing with the local cops (all male) who have found the dead girl's body and are hanging around. At that moment of a hesitation in the action Starling, hearing organ music, goes toward a door and enters a room in a close-up which cuts to a coffin with her father in it. She enters this shot of the coffin as a little girl who kisses her dead father, shot in action, farewell. The film then cuts back to the cops standing around drinking coffee in the autopsy room. Starling returns to this room and gently and very tactfully, but firmly, takes professional control of the scene by thanking the men for the important work they have done in salvaging the body and asking them to leave so that the autopsy can take place. These two flashbacks or recollection images are simple in their before-and-after structure and in offering narrative information about Starling's past, but they also have an affective quality that recharges action for the hero. They occur at moments when action reaches a hiatus, thereby signaling the importance of the movement of memory for action. In both instances the affective matrix of the recollection charges the professional action of the hero, and both are memories of a father who was a cop, killed in action. Such a matrix is essential for the female action hero who has no tradition to call on for sustenance and guidance; she has to make one up for herself. The return to the present from a zone of affectively charged recollection gives a temporal depth to the action. Both here and in *Blue Steel,* memories are what come to the rescue when the hero hits a stone wall. With the recollection images Starling's "subjectivity . . . takes on a new sense, which is no longer motor or material, but temporal and spiritual" (*C2* 47). This sense or quality reaches its peak of crystallization in the final interview between Starling and Lecter.

Face as Close-up as Affect

Agent Starling interviews Hannibal Lecter four times: three times in a maximum security prison, where they are separated by a glass wall, and once in a courthouse, where they are separated by iron bars. Robbins finds this image of the caged mentor the most compelling image of mentorship in the film, but does not describe in any detail the filmic construction of these scenes. They have an interesting visual progression, which I will analyze below. Because the privileged shot scale in these interviews is the close-up we can, following Deleuze, say that what emerges in these conversations is the rise of affect, which halts Agent Starling's elicitation of information; it is almost as though no information or knowledge can be given and received without traversing an affective register. In the first and second interviews we are sensitized to the wild olfactory impulses of the psychopaths that make barriers permeable; through this process protocol is abandoned and a form of communication is invented, as in Lecter's giving Starling a towel to dry herself with when she comes to see him drenched after the visit to the "Your Self Storage" facility. At this second meeting Lecter asks her how she felt when she discovered the severed head, and she replies, "Scared at first and then exhilarated." It is noteworthy that in contrast Dr. Crawford, Starling's official mentor, censors the affective dimension in her: when she tells him that she doesn't know how she feels about the death of Miggs (induced by Lecter), he replies, "You don't have to feel anything about it." But it is in the third interview that Lecter actually gets into Starling's head, by eliciting a childhood memory, the first circuit of the third recollection image. He asks her, "What is your worst memory of childhood?" to which she replies, "The death of my father." This exchange marks a change of the shot scale to extreme close-ups, and with each question and answer they seem to get closer, visually, to each other even as the answers go deeper into the affective lives of the psychopath Buffalo Bill and Agent Starling. As each quid-pro-quo question and answer traces deeper circuits of memory and experience, Lecter's face appears in close-up beside and just a little behind Starling's by means of the reflection of his face on the glass which in fact separates them. It is Starling's affective vulnerability that enables this strange encounter between mentor and pupil. In the fourth and final interview Lecter is reading a book inside a barred cage when Starling enters the space. Though his back is turned, he senses her presence, as though he has "eyes in the back of his head," and greets her urbanely: "Good evening, Clarice. People will say we're in love." Despite this mimetic, kinetic apperception of her presence it is here that he gives Starling his lecture on "first principles." But at the same time he draws out her childhood memory or primal scene (the deepest circuit of the third recollection image), which, as many have pointed out, is not a sexual fantasy but one of rescue, of action and agency. As Lecter elicits this story his face appears in an extreme close-up, lit by a radiant warm white light emanating from within the image, which seems to dissolve the iron bars. Starling pushes for information, but Lecter suspends this movement so that a movement of expression may happen between two people separated by iron bars. Such is the power of the close-up as affect that it can deterritorialize the image, virtualize the actual. In being able to delink the image from its proper coordinates, the close-up has the power to facilitate virtual conjunctions, like that occurring between Lecter and Starling (see *C1*, chapter 7). The real space is virtualized through light, framing, and shot scale even as the deepest circuit of memory, the fantasy of rescuing the lambs, is drawn out by Lecter and traced by Starling. As Starling narrates her ordeal of hearing the slaughter of the lambs, and her attempted rescue of one, her face too is drawn into an extreme close-up which obliterates the iron bars, so that we are left with two faces exchanging a gift of memory. It is intriguing that Lecter thanks Starling for recounting her childhood trauma, and in exchange he returns the Buffalo Bill case file (which she has forgetfully left behind) to her, having previously assured her that all she needs to crack the case is there. He also adds, "Let me know if the lambs stop screaming": an exemplary demonstration of concern by an interested mentor who believes in the link between affective rewiring and effective action.

Parallel Editing Reaches a Dead End

The two final action sequences of the film, in their very juxtaposition, also highlight the crucial relationship of action to affect drawn by this film. Agent Starling is able to surmise what Buffalo Bill is doing in skinning his victims when she sees Frederica Billmore's wardrobe with a dress that has the exact design (stitched in lace) that Buffalo Bill has cut out in the flesh of his most recent victim. Agent Starling calls Dr. Crawford to tell him this and to her disappointment is told that he has already identified the killer, one Jamie Gum, and is on his way to get him. He thanks Starling for what she has done but makes clear that from now on the action is his. From here the film cuts to a high action scene in a military airbase in Illinois, where armed men and Dr. Crawford run across a tarmac on their way to get Jamie Gum/Buffalo Bill, while Agent Starling is simply sitting talking to Frederica's friend Tracy in a girly, chatty mode. From now on the film cuts between Clarice, who is following clues gathered from this conversation and observation, and Jack Crawford and his men, who are moving in high action mode. With a mordant sense of humor, the film plays a nice joke at the expense of parallel editing—one of the great inventions of American cinema, dating from the silent era of D. W. Griffith. The film cunningly cuts between Dr. Crawford's line of action (as he raids the house he believes Jamie Gum/Buffalo Bill occupies) and the line of movement followed by Agent Starling as she follows a clue derived from talking to Tracy about sewing, which she said was Frederica's life. As Agent Starling goes to the home of Mrs. Litman, for whom the two girls had last sewn, Dr. Crawford and his men surround the house they think Jamie Gum lives in and wait for a decoy flower-delivery man to ring the doorbell. He does so, at a nod from Dr. Crawford, and we are given a close shot of a doorbell ringing inside a house and Buffalo Bill getting ready to answer it. The trick this editing plays is that the ringing doorbell we see in close-up is not the one we saw being rung by the delivery man (but we do not know this for a while). As there is no answer to the ring, Dr. Crawford signals to his men to raid the house. After breaking into the house and quickly searching it, a black cop says, "There's no one here, Jack"; Dr. Crawford, realizing what has happened, blurts out "Clarice!" in terror. Meanwhile Agent Starling has rung the doorbell of Mrs. Litman's house. Buffalo Bill opens the door while Agent Starling, still in a conversational mode, introduces herself as FBI. Buffalo Bill, whom we have seen several times before, both outside and inside his house, and whom we know to be the serial killer, invites her in and closes the door, while the camera takes an ominous high-angle shot of the scene. Then the camera does something quite unusual by going outside the house to establish the scene, to orient us after its disorienting editing trick and to underline the punch line by panning across three railway tracks to focus on the house that Agent Starling has just gone into. Clearly, parallel editing (that resilient rhetorical figure of American action cinema) has led to a dead end in terms of action, and the three railway tracks outside Buffalo Bill's house, which the camera pans across in a sweeping curve to the accompaniment of the ominous theme music, suggest that the film is entering a register where action alone is powerless to effect change. Because the parallel tracks fail to converge and resolve the action, the dualistic structure of American action cinema has to give way to the deadly play of a third track, so to speak. This is the optical drama of the affect.

Gothic House

The establishing shot of Buffalo Bill's house, brought into visibility through the pan across the railway tracks, creates a somber mood and colors the landscape with foreboding. Once inside the house Starling discreetly looks around as Gum, who has offered to find Mrs. Litman's phone number, asks her if the FBI has any clues, to which she replies, "No, no, no" (her voice trembling) while her glance rests on spools of colored thread with moths fluttering around and resting on them. She realizes that she is in mortal danger and catches her breath as she readies her gun for shooting. I wish she would run out of the house, but heroes don't do that; instead she orders Gum to surrender. Gum, like the supermarket hold-up man in *Blue Steel,* scorns the female hero's command with a mock campy gesture of surrender and slips out of the room, making it necessary for Starling to follow him into the entrails of the Gothic house, where she is more victim than hero. The trappings of the Gothic house or castle, well or dungeon—a trapped princess or senator's daughter; putrefying body parts; walls, objects, and patches of color that exude the intensity of the "non-organic life of things"—are all there. The camera permeated by the Gothic milieu also takes on a function different from its omniscient narrative one. Earlier the camera showed us Buffalo Bill's gun lying in the adjacent room while he spoke to Starling, then it went out to establish the scene, but now it draws attention to itself differently by mysteriously gliding ahead, almost luring Starling into the depths of the house. At this moment the non-organic life of the suburban Gothic house animates the camera with a Gothic energy. The camera seems to take on the function of affective mentorship in the final climactic scene: unreliable though this mentor is, it enables a pedagogy of the image (for the viewer) and action, agency, and victory for the female hero. In the climactic scene Agent Starling is lured into the depths of the house by the camera; the house is plunged into darkness by Buffalo Bill, who then brings her into visibility by putting on his infrared glasses. The exact coincidence between the viewer's and Buffalo Bill's points of view, in framing Starling with the hard-edged frame-within-frame of the infrared glasses, makes us complicit with the characters' terror and pleasure. The tinted image shows Starling flailing around with her gun as she stumbles, falls, and desperately tries to find her coordinates while the steady frame enframes and traps both her and the space around and beyond her. Insofar as the framing is emphatic, drawing attention to itself, it has the properties of the perception image, which is an encoding of the act of framing while revealing space in depth. In showing Starling breathlessly flailing around with her gun, the infrared vision (which is also that of the camera) gives us the mid-shot proper to the action image as well. Starling wants to convert the space into a sensory-motor one so that she can act, while the close-up of Gum moving in slow motion indicates that he is after something other than a duel. With the extreme close-up of Starling's head we leave both the perception image and the action image and enter the realm of the affection image.

Phantom Hand

As a slow-motion image of Starling's head appears in close up, with her hair moving sensuously from side to side, a white, disembodied, phantom hand floats in from frame left and tries to touch or caress her hair and face. At this moment music suddenly wells up, signaling an act of cinematic transubstantiation, both horror and fascination at the same time. Starling's heavy panting, the most prominent sound up to now, is drowned out by the music. The moment of the floating hand (of the killer) is very brief, but memory seems to stretch it out because of the horrible fascination of the image itself. Though we know that it is Buffalo Bill's hand that is in the frame, what we in fact see is a hand that is as weightless as light itself, floating, trying to caress her hair and face. This is a moment I would gladly prolong. Such is the pedagogy of this metacinematic moment that even as I am in terror for Starling's plight, I also savor the sensation at the tip of those fingers and the texture of that hair. But Demme swiftly cuts this image to show Buffalo Bill's right hand cocking the gun in a masterly, leisurely fashion and it is this sound that cues Starling to shoot to kill. All of this happens fast, while memory (certainly mine) prolongs this moment of affective intensity, returning to the fascinating and terrifying moment of the disembodied cinematic touch to savor it again and yet again. In that tension between the desire for a prolongation of the affect (at the expense of the female hero) and the urgency of action for her (and for me), this feminist critic finds herself somewhat convulsed, her politics compromised, wanting both to eat her cake and have it. But then these two films and their female heroes have also, in different ways, demonstrated a complicity with the villains: can I as an academic investigator be immune when writing about them, especially as the reason is learning?

15   *Do the Right Thing:* Blocking and Unblocking the Block

> The block where the bulk of the film takes place should be a character in its own right. I need to remember my early years for this.
>
> —Spike Lee[1]

> Neither origin nor destination, "home" is an effort to organise a "limited space" that is never sealed in, and so it is not an enclosure but a way of going outside.
>
> —Meaghan Morris[2]

> Colours do not move a people. Flags can do nothing without trumpets.
>
> —Gilles Deleuze and Felix Guattari[3]

The Block

An Australian student once told me that she thought *Do the Right Thing* (1989) looked a bit like *Sesame Street,* and when I first saw the film I too felt as if it had been shot on a set, maybe because I've never seen it on the big screen, or maybe because its opening credit sequence, shot on a sound stage, colors the rest of the film.[4] Anyway, both these images conjure up for me the memory of the endless summers on Sixth Street between Avenues A and B of New York's East Village, where I lived when Francis Ford Coppola shot *The Godfather: Part II* in 1973 on our block, with Italian-looking extras drawn from our very mixed neighborhood. Our block, which was not bright and cheerful to begin with and was made more somber by the period set, is, post–*Godfather II,* densely tree-lined, a result of the deal made for its use.

The actual coordinates of his chosen block are clearly vital for Lee's work, as they are not for Coppola. At the time the rumor was that Coppola couldn't film in Little Italy because of the Mafia, so our block agreed to stand in for it in exchange for the trees, a rarity in the East Village. Spike Lee's journal of *Do the Right Thing* records that the film was shot on

Stuyvesant Avenue between Lexington and Quincy, in Brooklyn, and that despite the economically sensible suggestions from Universal Studios to shoot it on their back lot or in D. C. or Baltimore, with a non-union crew, Lee insisted on the real location in Bedford-Stuyvesant, a Brooklyn ghetto.[5] This seemingly traditional neorealist imperative is especially intriguing because Lee then converted the real location to make it look like a set. It is well known that he hired Minister Farrakhan's security men, the Fruit of Islam, to rid the block of its two crack houses, that he painted the facades in vibrant Afro-Caribbean color, and that the sidewalks and stoops were scrubbed clean of garbage and drug debris. Why did he take an actual location and make it look so clean and artificial that some critics thought he was being evasive, not dealing with real matters like drugs and crime? This chapter will try to come at this question obliquely, looking at the aesthetics of *Do the Right Thing* to try to understand what Spike Lee's cinematic project is.

Nearly ten years after its controversial U.S. reception as a violent film inciting violence, or a polemical film that stages the debates on violence, one of the things that strikes me as a teacher of cross-cultural perspectives on cinema is the way in which it unfailingly engages Australian students, who are largely though by no means exclusively Anglo-Celtic.[6] It is usual for polemical films, such as Jean-Luc Godard's 1960s Dziga Vertov films, to be poignantly dated when viewed after their moment has passed. This is not so with *Do the Right Thing*. It does stand up beyond its moment of reception, and I shall argue that this is because of the way in which Lee marks and reinvests the block with aesthetic value.

Marking the Block

Toni Morrison, in a recent interview, said that she was not really interested in polemics, that what she was trying to do in her writing was something else.[7] Instead of this something else, Jana Wendt, the interviewer, diligently pursued the theme of race relations and asked a naive question about when Morrison might include white characters in her books. Lee, at least until he made *Clockers*, was plagued with the equivalent question: "When are you going to deal with drugs?" Morrison's reply, delivered softly, slowly, and very gently and politely, was "You can't imagine what a racist question that is." Wendt was visibly shaken by this response, which in its semantics was an accusation but in its delivery was more an exhilarating cross-cultural encounter. Morrison's reply to a naively ethnocentric and (unwittingly) violent question was not in a tit-for-tat mode. It was not "You are racist!" but rather "You can't imagine how racist . . . ," delivered at a speed and in a tone, pitch, and timbre which unwound the rhythm of the urbane question-and-answer mode of the interview itself. What I saw was a transformation of the violence of white innocence into something else. I feel I learned more about interracial exchange, and about the relativization of whiteness from its normative status, through this change of rhythm and the ensuing brief pause than through all of the information generated through the relaxed punctual rhythm of the questions and answers.

Spike Lee's films engage with polemics. He is himself a savvy polemicist and publicist and a good actor of a very particular deadpan kind. How else could one walk up to the podium (with John Singleton), address the glittering Oscar audience, read out the names of the nominees for a prize, and announce the winner without smiling, even once—completely deadpan, vocally and facially—and then just leave without really acknowledging the Hollywood audience? (I wanna be him.) *Do the Right Thing* does, of course, have strongly polemical moments. According to some, it was not nominated for the best-picture Oscar because of its putative violence, and the fact that Bruce Beresford's film *Driving Miss Daisy,* about the heartwarming friendship between a Southern Jewish woman and her African-American chauffeur, won the award instead certainly confirms the limits of Hollywood liberalism. But I don't think that either *Do the Right Thing* or Lee's cinematic project can be entirely subsumed within an adversarial mode. He, like Morrison, is after something else, something less ephemeral than polemics, in his own fashion. As Lee himself says, "I'm looking for a place, a home, where I can make the films I want to make without outside or inside interference."[8]

There is evident in *Do the Right Thing* a preoccupation with aesthetics that tends to be overlooked in critical writing about the film (though not, I think, in the film's enthusiastic public reception), in the quick move to deal with its violence. When I first saw the film, after everyone else had seen it and after having read about its volatile public reception in the U.S., I remember waiting for the infamous violence, which was a long time coming. What I experienced for long periods of the film was a leisurely pace, more like a stroll with the camera up and down a block which every now and then was punctured by sharper fragmented aural or visual rhythms. The camera is at times in tune with Mookie, one of the main characters (played by Lee), who works to the rhythm of a stroll, a to-ing and fro-ing, a dillying and a dallying. Critics tend to move quickly to the violent moments (that is to say, to narrativize the film) and forget to register the non-eventful, leisurely moments. There are many of these moments, and they are rich in neorealist detail: Jade simply combing Mother Sister's hair; Mother Sister hanging out the window, casting her acerbic gaze at life passing by while Da Mayor serenades her; the children playing in the water of the fire hydrant, drawing pictures on the asphalt, buying ice blocks from the vendor; the chorus of three men drinking, laughing, peeing, yarning away their time; the posse of youth hanging around; Radio Raheem walking down the block and being greeted by them and by Mister Señor Love Daddy at the local storefront radio station; Love Daddy's roll call of African-American artists; Mookie and Teena playing with an ice cube instead of doing "the nasty." These scenes introduce a variety of tones, moods, and rhythms to the film. I am drawn to the film by its intricate banal (summertime) rhythms rather than its narrative, perhaps because once upon a time, on Sixth Street between Avenues A and B, I too, like Mother Sister, simply watched life pass by for what felt like an eternity.

The moments cited above, and many more, create a kind of drifting and do not, I think, have cumulative narrative drive. Attempting to narrativize them always makes one move too fast, much too fast, to the burning of the pizzeria as the main narrative event. Because of the day-in-the-life-of-a-block structure of the film, much of what happens does not line up in a cause-and-effect sequence obeying the rules of sensory-motor action. As the film's rhythmic modulations draw me in, I feel an affinity between them and Toni Morrison's vocal modulations, which make her speaking sound like singing; before I saw her on television, I had never heard anything like her speech. This affinity tempts me to think of Lee's film as a sort of opera of the everyday, in which everyday speech, movements, gestures, and color are made rhythmic and expressive.

One example is the hilarious Keystone Cops slapstick rhythm injected into the firemen's movements, making them tumble and fall as the fire hose swells with rushing water, in the climactic scene of the burning of the pizzeria. I am not the only one to see this bit of slapstick in an unlikely place, in the middle of a terrible event: Mister Señor Love Daddy also responds to it, yelling as the out-of-control fire hose sprays his store's front window, pretending that this necessitates a change of shirts. This surprising slapstick moment is one of many ametrical rhythms, transforming this climactic event from a sensory-motor action to something closer to an optical drama.[9] A gesture of Mookie's stands out in this regard for its enigmatic quality. Just before he empties the garbage can and throws it though the pizzeria window, thus instigating the riot, he holds his hands together, palm to palm, and slowly slides them down his face, pulling his closed eyes open. The gesture itself is a familiar one—I do it when I am tired—but it is enigmatic in that heated context, marking the moment when Mookie changes from an observer to a catalyst. But the gesture itself breaks any sense of sensory-motor rhythm that might coordinate the scene and actions, because it is too slow, too quiet, too . . . difficult to name. This rhythmic variation is not the familiar technique of building tempo and suspense by varying speed (slow then fast); rather, it injects durations that can't be homogenized in a sweeping movement. That odd gesture converts Mookie into a mediator between a perception and a possible action; he embodies an affect which is difficult to name but can be felt in the movement of his hands and the opening of his eyes.

Another example is the delicious rhythmic verbal and gestural give-and-take at the film's beginning between Sal of Sal's Famous Pizzeria and his racist son Pino, at the end of which, exasperated by his son's racist attitude, Sal exclaims, "I'm going to kill someone today." What does impel Sal to "kill" Radio Raheem's boom box at the end of the film is the rhythm and volume of Public Enemy's "Fight the Power," blaring out once too often. We would lose something if we thought that, as in a well-made play, a gun (or baseball bat) seen in the first act must be used by the third. There is no causal link between the impulse to kill someone, incited by his own son's bigotry and intransigence, and the "killing" of the radio and of Radio Raheem; the violence is not inevitable. The terrible act occurs fortuitously (like the infamous stray bullets in neorealist cinema) because, despite protestations from Mookie at the end of a long hot day's work, Sal decides to let the last customers come in (call it good will or wanting to make a few more dollars) after they have closed shop.

Lee's obsession with the block is not realist like Coppola's, whose East Sixth Street set for *Godfather II* was created as a meticulous image of Little Italy once upon a time, with every little bottle in every storefront authentically labeled for historical verisimilitude, for perhaps only five minutes of screen time—in street scenes, where such detail was invisible. If anything, Lee is a neorealist in the Deleuzian sense of loosening the sensory-motor rhythm of the movements that constitute the film.

Under the pressure of intense heat, color, close-up shots, and rhythmic gestures and speech acts, Spike Lee's block floats in the situation, just as the action (such as it is) floats in the situation: this is another way of saying that the set and action are not organized according to a sensory-motor logic. For a long stretch of its two-hour duration nothing much happens, except people just hangin' around, going up and down the block, looking, talking, looking for trouble, just listening to music, drinking, combing hair, just passing the time. Saying that the set floats in the situation implies that it has an autonomous existence, and saying that the action floats in the situation means that the action and situation do not mesh so tightly that you only see the foreground of action and not the background on which it is performed. But more importantly, when the fit between the situation and the action is not tight or sensory-motor-driven, the action itself has a certain freedom, which I'd want to call a rhythmic freedom from the necessity of the situation.

I want to trace this rhythmic (aesthetic) freedom by focusing on the role of "Fight the Power" as *Do the Right Thing's* refrain, so as to understand how and with what Lee rolls his joint, demarcates his territory, and constructs a dwelling of his own. To do this I now need to call up a cluster of concepts from Deleuze and Guattari's chapter "1837: Of the Refrain" in *A Thousand Plateaus: Capitalism and Schizophrenia:*

> The role of the refrain has often been emphasized: it is territorial. . . . Bird songs: the bird sings to mark a territory. The Greek modes and Hindu rhythms are themselves territorial, provincial and regional. The refrain may assume other functions, amorous, professional or social, liturgical or cosmic: it always carries earth with it; it has a land (sometimes a spiritual land) as its concomitant; it has an essential relation to the Natal, a Native. A musical "nome" is a little tune, a melodic formula that seeks recognition and remains the bedrock or ground of polyphony (cantus firmus). (*TP* 312)

The concepts of refrain, milieu, territory, territorialization and deterritorialization, and the interval or in-between are essential to understanding the complex process of making a dwelling by expressive markings. Ronald Bogue, in his "Rhizomusicosmology," offers a lucid exposition of this chapter: "Using studies of birdsong as their guiding inspiration, Deleuze and Guattari treat the refrain as any kind of rhythmic pattern that stakes out a territory."[10] A territory thus marked is characterized by three aspects: a point of stability, which could be a *pacing* or rhythm, like a child singing in the dark to calm himself; a *circle of property,* like a cat spraying the corners of a space around it to claim possession; and an *opening* to the outside, like a bird's song at dawn which opens its territory to other milieus and the cosmos at large. Meaghan Morris, in "Crazy Talk is Not Enough," offers an unusual entry point into understanding this process of "home making" as a temporal act, by focusing repeatedly, but at varying speeds, on the Deleuzian-Guattarian image of the child in the dark, gripped with fear, singing to calm herself. The three aspects of territorialization, a point of stability, a circle of property, and an opening to the outside, she points out, are not sequential but simultaneous spatio-temporal operations of every territory that a refrain demarcates.[11]

The distinction between milieu and territory is important in understanding the process of territorialization and deterritorialization.

> The elements from which territories are formed are milieus and rhythms which themselves are created out of chaos. A milieu is a coded block of space-time, a code being defined by "periodic repetition." . . . The repetitive vibrations of a milieu are measured, but they are not rhythmic, for rhythm takes place between two milieus or between milieu and chaos. Measure may be regular, but rhythm "is the Unequal or Incommensurable." (*TP* 384–85)

Bogue quotes this passage and adds that rhythm operates "not in a homogeneous space-time, but with heterogeneous blocks" ("Rhizo" 88). This makes clear that an interval or the in-between is needed for rhythm to arise, and it may be more apparent by now that I have chosen the vocabulary of block, blocking and unblocking (because they are terms immanent to the film itself), instead of Deleuze and Guattari's terms, territorializing and deterritorializing.

So if one takes hip-hop as the enabling milieu of *Do the Right Thing,* then one could say that "Fight the Power"'s own vibrations are interfered with and used by Lee as a milieu component with which to stake out a filmic territory.[12] Its sonic markings create the filmic territory; the territory does not preexist the marking. This territorializing marking is characterized by the increasing expressivity of rhythm and the emergence of expressive qualities: color, odor, sound silhouette. "A territory borrows from all the milieus; it bites into them, seizes them bodily (although it remains vulnerable to intrusions). It is built from aspects or portions of milieus" (*TP* 315). A component torn off a milieu acquires a power to mark or express only when it becomes independent of prior functions and "acquires a temporal constancy and a spatial range that make it a territorial, or rather territorialising, mark: a signature" (*TP* 315). Bogue says that "autonomy is evident as well in the shifting relations that link various qualities within the territory" ("Rhizo" 90). I will pursue sound as expressive quality here because it has an unparalleled power in this film as a transformative force, both creative and destructive. Deleuze and Guattari speak eloquently of its ambiguity:

> Sound invades us, impels us, drags us, transpierces us. It takes leave of the earth, as much in order to drop us into a black hole as to open us up to a cosmos. It makes us want to die. Since its force of deterritorialisation is the strongest, it also effects the most massive of reterritorialisations, the most numbing, the most redundant. Ecstasy and hypnosis. Colours do not move a people. Flags can do nothing without trumpets. . . . The potential fascism of music. (*TP* 348)

Some Sonic Blocks

The DJ, Mister Señor Love Daddy, is also the observer-narrator-voiceover within the film, intervening in its actions through his control of the sonic waves of the radio station, I Love Radio. The block's temporal coherence is marked and varied by Love Daddy's intermittent interruptions of the day-in-the-life-of-the-block. His rapping begins the film after the credit sequence, in a tight close-up of an alarm clock, a microphone, and lips yelling out "Waaaake up! wake up! wake up! wake up! up ya wake! up ya wake! up ya wake! . . . I have today's forecast: *hot.*" He also ends the twenty-four hours of the film with a farewell song to the dead Radio Raheem and signs off the film with "We love you, brother." He cuts in and out of the day in hip-hop style, editing his speech—inverting phrases and repeating them to create reversible relations (nonsense), a non-uniform time, "a time of flux, of multiple speeds and reversible relations" ("Rhizo" 93). His long roll call of African-American artists stretches time and layers it with the sounds that the proper names invoke and evoke. In these ways Love Daddy plays with rhythm and time, and his structural centrality helps to create the fluidity, layering, and cutting up of time in the film. According to Tricia Rose, fluidity, layering, and cutting are the three main formal techniques common to all three forms of hip-hop expression: graffiti, break dance, and rap.[13]

When Radio Raheem walks into Sal's Famous Pizzeria for the first time on the hottest day of that summer, with his ghetto blaster blaring out Public Enemy's "Fight the Power," Sal intones rhythmically, "No music, no rap, no music, no music, no music." It's not that he doesn't like music, he just doesn't like rap, for he says, "What happened to nice music with words you could understand?" And it's also not that he doesn't have rhythm, because his banning of Radio Raheem's music in his pizzeria is done with gestural and rhythmic flair: "No music, no music, no music." So it's not a black-white thing; everyone on the block is given over to a speaking which is marked by a rhythmic contagion.

Even the Korean shopkeepers, a husband-and-wife team, catch the spirit under duress, learning to say "motherfucker" rhythmically, thus eliciting a smile of bemused appreciation from Radio Raheem himself when he berates them for not knowing the date on the batteries he purchases from them and for not speaking English properly. It is at such moments that a character such as Radio Raheem gets individuated beyond a familiar type, a delicious moment of cross-race learning the lingo on the job, which makes Radio Raheem go from "Don't you speak English, motherfucker?" to "You all right, motherfucker." By then the Korean man has begun to chant "motherfucker" as a little refrain. And perhaps it is this informal learning of street lingo that helps him to come up with another crucial refrain, as the black mob turns to his shop after having set fire to Sal's Pizzeria. The Korean, with a broom in hand, attempts to shoo away the black mob with "I no white, I no white, I black, I black, you me same." Which makes the black mob leader, the crusty ML, retort, "Same! me black, open your eyes, motherfucker!" At this point Sweet Dick Willy and Coconut Sid intervene and one of them says, "Leave the Korean alone, he's all right," as they crack up laughing, and even ML sees the black humor in this instant construction of racialized identity under duress and decides that "he's all right." In a previous scene, in which ML grumbles about the Koreans' enterprise in setting up a business as soon as they get off the boat, Sweet Dick Willy remarks bitingly that the blacks also got off a boat many years ago, trying to dampen the impulse to find racialized scapegoats for the apathy of one's own ethnic group.

Toward the end of the film this Korean shopkeeper is prominent among the black youth who run after the police car carrying away Radio Raheem's dead body, banging on it in anger at his murder by a cop. This scene is so brief that it was only after watching the film ten times or more that I noticed that the baton pushing the Korean man away from the speeding police car is held by a black cop; and on further viewing it became clear that it is an African-American female cop, along with her white mate, who are clearing the way for the police car. There is a brief instant when the white male cop on the left and the black female cop on the right frame with their outstretched batons an African-American youth and the Korean as the police car speeds away into the night. What can I say? Say what I can, like Mister Señor Love Daddy, I say, "I saw it, it I saw, and my mouth was opened." And I might add that I saw it at the correct speed, not by looking at it frame by frame, though I must confess that I did slow the film down to check the gender of the black cop. And now I wonder, how come no one else wrote about this micro-moment in everything written about the violence of this film? Surely it is evidence that the film is no simple tract inciting black people to riot, as some white critics tried to claim. This hidden moment is also perfectly consistent with the complicated, unpredictable ways in which intraracial and interracial relations are blocked out in the film. So it's not a unique moment tucked away so that the perceptive critic can feel good about deciphering it. It is, perhaps, a harrowing example of the clouded complexities of African-American experience which Lee's "Forty Acres and a Mule Filmworks" enterprise sets out to make audible, visible, and legible. America's racist history and Hollywood's complicity with it is firmly memorialized in the branding of Lee's production company "Forty Acres and a Mule," the sum of wealth promised (though not always given) to the emancipated slaves.

While Lee's project is thus under the sign of history, it seeks a certain relief from the burden of history and the weight of memory via his logo, "A Spike Lee Joint," which signals the weightless and memoryless floating realm of commodity and sign production of late-twentieth-century America. Phrases of an emergent "Black" identity that derive from the civil rights movement—"My people, my people," "Brother, brother brother," "Brothers and sisters," "Power to the people," "Black power"—are now deployed through hip-hop in such a way that their semantic inadequacy is assumed, even as their phatic performative value for those who choose to recycle clichés with style is abundantly clear. Lee populates his sonic block with a collection of African-American types (the elderly Mother Sister, with echoes of a Southern familial past; the old Da Mayor, a gentleman alcoholic; Mookie, the irresponsible young black father who sponges off his sister Jade, the responsible sister and voice of reason; Radio Raheem, inseparable from his boom box; Buggin' Out, always looking for some trouble; the posse of youth; the eloquent chorus of black men just hanging out at the corner; the black mother beating the shit out of her son, who just escaped being run over by an ice-cream van, and furiously defending her right to bring up her son as she thinks fit) so as to explore their lack of commonality and their erratic communality. In setting intraracial differences within a wider series of interracial differences, Lee humorously highlights how bigotry is not the prerogative of any one ethnic group, as in the hilarious racial slur sequence constructed as a rap session, where a member of each ethnic community characterizes another through stereotypes of habit, food, and taste. And as the scene is directly addressed to the viewers, they too are implicated in this robust, rhythmic display of racist venom.[14]

A Sonic Brick: "Fight the Power" as Refrain and Signature Tune

Unlike all other music in the film, Public Enemy's "Fight the Power" works as repetitively as the poor mule would have had to if it ploughed the forty acres. Both the title of the film and the title of this song (*Do the Right Thing*, "Fight the Power") are imperatives with a habitual familiar quality to the point of being clichés. This is why, when Da Mayor stops Mookie on one of his delivery rounds to say, "Doctor, always try to do the right thing!" Mookie asks "That's it?" to which Da Mayor replies, "That's it," and Mookie says, "I got it, I'm gone." This is Lee's way of telling us (and it's true that some needed to be told), "Don't waste your time looking for the 'right thing'; it's the red herring in the picture, the film's not that simplistic; c'mon, c'mon, let's get this mule movin', mmmmm, damn!"

The film begins and ends with "Fight the Power." It is heard twelve times in all, *twelve times,* within the course of the film; at the beginning and the end, as non-diegetic sound, and ten times in the body of the film, always as the only sound blasting out from Radio Raheem's boom box. Each person or group hearing this refrain has a reaction to it, which in each instance is different from Radio Raheem's absolute identification with the song and the radio. Together these form a mobile sonic block, his abode, territory, and signature tune. So this song as recurrent refrain constructs two poles in the film, its intrinsic non-diegetic quality as it works with or against the image and the response or force of the diegetic listener. This variability of functions, and the multiple repetitions of the song as refrain, effect qualitative transformations of the film. I now wish to explore the temporal (aesthetic) power of this refrain, by first sketching out its repeated appearance on the block.

1. After the long opening credit sequence in an MTV-style rendition of "Fight the Power" with Rosie Perez's b-boy dance, it is first heard intradiegetically when the hip-hop posse greet Radio Raheem. After the usual

phatic rap greetings Ella and two of the boys do an unusual routine, turning themselves into "onlookers" commenting on Radio Raheem's appearance and laughing like cartoon characters while he looks on in an enigmatic close-up. This is a strangely difficult scene to read because of this instant transformation of participants into observers and commentators, a transformation one becomes more accustomed to as the film proceeds. This instant switching of functions, evident in other scenes as well, further slackens the already loose sensory-motor mechanisms of the film.

2. From this scene Radio Raheem moves further down the block and is greeted by the other agent of hip-hop, Mister Señor Love Daddy, so hip-hop's MTV image is acknowledged, used, and returned (in a complicated move) to the block, its place of origin.

3. When we next hear Radio Raheem, the fire hydrant is flowing in full force and members of the posse stop the flow of the water so that he and his radio can pass by undrenched. We now enter a rhythm marked by an impeding of flows, in this instance of water, later of the song.

4. When the refrain next emerges in the ghetto-blaster sound skirmish between "Fight the Power" and the Puerto Rican boys' salsa rhythms, the two musics vie with each other without any clear victory. This stalemate seems to be a result of the sensory-motor slackening of tension through the mixing of different musical rhythms.

5. In Radio Raheem's fifth appearance on the block he greets Mookie, reduces the volume of his refrain, puts the radio down, and tells the story of the two hands, with "LOVE" and "HATE" engraved on his knuckle-dusters.

6. The refrain's flow is impeded on each of the five next times it is heard, because people hate its sound, or the sheer volume, or its endless repetition. Radio Raheem goes to Sal's with it on full blast and gets the "no music" rap from Sal, which makes him reluctantly turn off the sound.

7. The refrain gets distorted when the batteries run down, leading Radio Raheem into the "Don't you speak English, motherfucker" routine with the Korean shopkeepers.

8. When the refrain has been recharged by twenty batteries, the chorus of men cover their ears and curse the music in unison as Radio Raheem goes past them at full blast.

9. Radio Raheem and Buggin' Out discuss boycotting Sal's pizzeria late into the night with the song blaring out, which elicits an abusive "Cut out that rap music, I've been trying to get some motherfucking . . . " from a neighboring apartment. Even Buggin' Out asks Radio Raheem why he

Do the Right Thing   243

plays only one song, and he replies "I like nothing else" and agrees to boy-cott Sal. He adds movingly, "Tellin' me, Radio Raheem, to turn down my box and he didn't even say please." (That "please" kills me.)

10. Radio Raheem and Buggin' Out go into Sal's with the refrain at full blast on the hottest night of that summer, demanding that Sal put up some brothers on the wall of fame, and Sal yells out to shut off the "jungle mu-sic," the "nigger radio," then smashes the radio with a baseball bat, adding, "I just killed your fucking radio," thus setting off a riot which ends in the murder of Radio Raheem by the cops and the burning of the pizzeria by its clients. The refrain is heard one last time, as non-diegetic sound, when the camera scans the debris of the pizzeria, which includes Radio Raheem's smashed boom box. This second non-diegetic appearance, so different in affect from its empowered opening MTV rendition, offers a powerful and lucid montage critique, if one cares to take note of it. It leaves me with a question: what power has been fought in this act of destruction?

Ten Times

The repeated sonic markings of the block by Radio Raheem's ten appearances with "Fight the Power" transform him into a "territorial mo-tif" in Deleuze and Guattari's terms, or a "rhythmic character" in Olivier Messiaen's terms, as Bogue points out, where it is not the character who has rhythm but rather the rhythm itself which becomes a character. To understand this notion of "rhythmic character" one must know that for Messiaen, as well as Deleuze and Guattari, there is a fundamental differ-ence between meter and rhythm: "metre presupposes an even division of a uniform time, rhythm presupposes a time of flux, of multiple speeds and reversible relations." One of Messiaen's chief techniques for gener-ating ametrical rhythms is what he calls "added values": "short values added to any rhythm whatever, whether by a note, or by a rest, or by the dot." And his notion of "rhythmic characters" is an extension of this idea ("Rhizo" 93).

> By progressively modifying a figure through the addition or subtraction of rhythmic values, the composer can develop rhythmic characters whose dynamic relationships are like those of characters on the stage. . . .
> Let's imagine a scene in a play between three characters: the first acts in a brutal manner by hitting the second; the second character suffers this act, since his actions are dominated by those of the first; lastly, the

third character is present at the conflict but remains inactive. If we transpose this parable into the field of rhythm, we have three rhythmic groups; the first, whose note-values are always increasing, is the character who attacks; the second, whose note-values decrease, is the character who is attacked; and the third, whose note-values never change, is the character who remains immobile. ("Rhizo" 94)

In music, with its very solid mathematical base, one can unambiguously speak of increased or diminished value—but in this film the register is not mathematics but emotions, so the concept of *varied* value is more appropriate.[15] I suggest that we read "Fight the Power" as the beat and the different reactions to it as the "varied values," which make it a rhythmic rather than metrical character. It is now necessary to ask, what can a "rhythmic character" of this kind do? This necessity is provoked by the power that a rhythmic character or motif has to connect the territory with forces both within and without. These forces, according to Deleuze and Guattari, are those of inner impulses or drives as well as external circumstance. Every territory has a center of intensity where its forces come together; this center is both within and without the territory, embodied, for instance, in the idea of an imagined or lost homeland, or the natal, always at hand yet difficult to reach. In this film we reach this burning hearth on the sound waves transmitted by Radio Raheem, as rhythmic character ("Rhizo" 90–91).

A Hesitant, Faint Refrain

"One ventures from home on the thread of a tune that is always in danger of breaking."[16]
Spike Lee negotiates or straddles three impossibilities in developing his cinema and the terms of his independence.

1. Spike Lee can't not make films,
2. Spike Lee can't make Hollywood films,
3. Spike Lee can't not make films with Hollywood.
Stone-WAAAAAAAAAAAAAAAAAAAAAAAAAAAAAAAAAAAAAAAALL![17]

As the pizzeria burns, the fire brigade arrives and a cop calls out on a loudspeaker for the mob to "please go home," to which Mookie, standing on the shattered block, replies, "This is our home." This barely audible retort brings home to me pointedly and poignantly what Deleuze and Guattari call the ambiguity of the natal, the lost or unknown homeland. The two elders on the block, Da Mayor and Mother Sister, seem to know this only too well when they say to each other on the morning after, "Hope the block's still standing." "We're still standin'." This is the ambiguity of the natal as it appears to an African American; the lost homeland, the promised land, and its embodied memory in a song or a name, Mother Sister.

Raymond Bellour said, at the 1982 Australian Screen Studies Association conference in Melbourne, that Hollywood cinema is a machine for the manufacture of the couple. So Lee too gives us his odd romantic couple (Ossie Davis and Ruby Dee, two African-American actors who have in fact been husband and wife for forty years), two figures who seem anachronistic in a hip-hop space. Mother Sister is always watchin' an' waitin', while Da Mayor sweeps the sidewalk for a dollar from Sal, buys beer with it, and sweet-talks Mother Sister, who spurns him. When the riot begins Mother Sister is the first to shout "burn it down, burn it down," and when it burns, it is she who screams "no, no, no, no," with the same hysteria, while it is Da Mayor's embrace that calms and comforts her. When they wake up the morning after in Mother Sister's apartment, finally reconciled, Lee is re-working, in his own way, the Hollywood (American) dream of the couple and at the same time paying tribute to two fine African-American actors of an older generation who could never have been a cinematic romantic couple within the terms of that cinema.[18] So two of the key means of symbolically marking and creating community, death and "marriage," have come to pass, though in an untimely way, with elders remarrying and a youth dying. Such events hold the territory together only precariously; they can't be foundational events as in classical cinema, especially when the strongest image of community is a riot that destroys something as basic as a business that feeds the block. "Fight the Power" as refrain has marked a block; created territorial motifs and counterpoints to it; and gathered a rhythmic force of hatred and absolute devotion, LOVE and HATE, shattering the block, plunging it into a black hole called "race riot" by the white media and politics.

Lee's film does not conclude with the "riot" but rather on the morning after. Lee revisits the site of the riot, a pervasive media-saturated image of contemporary African-American–Anglo-American relations hitting a stone wall. How then does Lee revisit the burned-down pizzeria? On the lines of a hesitant, unpredictable, rhythmic movement, both vocal and gestural. Sal scrunches up five hundred dollars (Mookie's salary and more) into little pellets, throwing them at Mookie, one at a time, with excessive force. Mookie throws back two hundred at Sal, because, as he says, his salary is only two hundred and fifty. Then they improvise a little rhyme to accompany the gestural refrain of throwing paper pellets, not unlike children playing on Sesame Street:

> Sal: Keep it.
> Mookie. You keep it.
> Sal: You keep it.
> Mookie: You keep it.
> Sal: You keep it.
> Mookie: You keep it.

You will hear a metrical beat if you only hear the repetition of the same phrase, a mimicry, not much else. But if what you hear are differences, i.e., minutely "varied values" of gesture, inflection, pitch, timbre, and emphases that are trying to establish some equilibrium, call it a pacing, in the midst of terrible chaos, then you may at the same time see a shifting line of property and an emerging thin, fragile line leading to an outside, opening a channel. If we can see these, we may be able to hear a halting, hesitant, not-quite-yet refrain, but a refrain nevertheless, that's trying to invent a small gesture of sociability in a black hole. For this kind of cross-cultural move a little mimetic play seems useful.[19]

Notes

Introduction

1. This phrase is Theodor Adorno's. See "The Actuality of Philosophy," *Telos* 31 (spring 1977), 120–33. This is his inaugural lecture to the Philosophy Faculty of the University of Frankfurt. I took courage to borrow and use the phrase in a non-philosophical, film context, thanks to Susan Buck-Morss's fine commentary on Adorno's dialectical idea in *The Origin of Negative Dialectics: Theodor W. Adorno, Walter Benjamin, and the Frankfurt Institute* (Sussex: The Harvester Press, 1977), 85–88.

2. Several Australian writers on film have recently—and, it would seem, somewhat independently—come up with different ideas about the importance of description to film analysis. See Adrian Martin, *Once upon a Time in America* (London: British Film Institute, 1998); Meaghan Morris's review of the above book, "On Going to Bed Early: *Once upon a Time in America*," in *The Best Australian Essays 1999*, ed. Peter Craven (Melbourne: Bookman Press, 1999), 341–53; Lesley Stern and George Kouvaros, eds., *Falling for You: Essays on Cinema and Performance* (Sydney: Power Publications, 1999), especially "Descriptive Acts: Introduction," 1–35.

3. Theodor Adorno, *Aesthetic Theory*, trans. Robert Hullot-Kentor (London: Athlone Press, 1997).

4. Michael Taussig, *Mimesis and Alterity: A Particular History of the Senses* (New York and London: Routledge, 1993).

5. Adorno, "The Actuality of Philosophy," 131.

6. Buck-Morss, *Origin*, 87–88.

7. Gilles Deleuze, *Cinema 1: The Movement Image*, trans. Hugh Tomlinson and Barbara Habberjam (Minneapolis: University of Minnesota Press, 1986), and *Cinema 2: The Time Image*, trans. Hugh Tomlinson and Robert Galeta (Minneapolis: University of Minnesota Press, 1989).

8. Walter Benjamin, "On the Mimetic Faculty," in *Reflections: Essays, Aphorisms, Autobiographical Writing*, trans. Edmund Jephcott (New York: Schocken, 1978), 333–36.

1. "Love me tender, love me true, never let me go"

This chapter was presented at the Australian Cultural Studies Conference, Murdoch University, Western Australia, 24 June 1991. A shorter version of it was first published in *Feminism and the Politics of Difference*, ed. Sneja Gunew

and Anna Yeatman (Sydney: Allen and Unwin, 1993). I wish to thank
Meaghan Morris for suggesting that I do a Sri Lankan reading of *Night Cries*.

1. T. Minh-ha Trinh, "Why a Fish Pond? Fiction at the Heart of Documentation," interview by L. Jayamanne and Anne Rutherford, *Film News* 20 (10
November 1990), 10.

2. Kumar Shahani, "Interrogating Internationalism," *Journal of Arts and Ideas*
19 (May 1990), 12.

3. Raoul Ruiz, "Between Institutions: Interview with Raul Ruiz," interview by
Ian Christie and Malcolm Coad, *Afterimage* 10 (fall 1981), 113. I wish to add
a personal anecdote here for its methodological implications. About three
years into my stay in the U.S., a friend who had bought a tape recorder
asked me to speak into it to test it. When the sound was replayed, I failed to
recognize my voice. About ten years later, after coming to Australia, I was
able to use that sense of displacement and loss as a method for organizing
the sound track of a film I made there called *A Song of Ceylon* (1985).

4. Though some of the early publicity for *Night Cries* drew a connection between it and Charles Chauvel's 1955 film *Jedda*, in 1991 I did not take my cue
from it. My feeling then was that to address the problematic of *Jedda* as
Night Cries intertext was perhaps to take on a "white man's burden," and as
such no concern of mine, and that it had been discharged as far as seemed
rewarding by Ingrid Perez's article "*Night Cries:* Cries from the Heart" (*Film
News* 20.7 [August 1990], 16). However, I have changed my mind in the late
1990s. I bring this up here because my failure to discuss this putative relationship aroused considerable discontent when I first presented this essay in
1991. For my part, I was discontented with Perez's article because it did not
mention, let alone discuss, the function of Jimmy Little in *Night Cries*. This
chapter is in a way a response to that omission.

5. Adrian Martin, "Indefinite Objects: Independent Film and Video," in *The
Australian Screen,* ed. Albert Moran and Tom O'Regan (Ringwood: Penguin,
1989), 184.

6. From the late 1930s to the mid-1960s, the Australian government enforced
the adoption of Aboriginal children into white families with the intention
of assimilating them, both culturally and biologically, into white "civilization." Moffatt's film about this policy was made several years before the
publication of "Bringing Them Home: Report of the National Inquiry into
the Separation of Aboriginal and Torres Strait Islander Children from Their
Families" (Human Rights and Equal Opportunity Commission: Sydney,
1997). The publication of this report spurred major media attention to
public memory, public mourning, reparation, and reconciliation.

7. Ross Gibson, "Camera Natura: Landscape in Australian Feature Films,"
Framework 22–23 (fall 1983), 49.

8. Ian Burn and Ann Stephen, "Traditional Painter: The Transfiguration of
Albert Namatjira," *Age Monthly Review* 6 (7 November 1986), 13.

9. Geoff Batchen, "Complicities," in *ARTFUL,* College of Fine Arts, Student Association, University of New South Wales (October 1990), unpaginated.

10. "A Black Void" is a response to a discussion of the film at a Power Institute public education forum with Homi Bhabha and myself. I wish to thank Homi Bhabha, Geoff Batchen, Bette Mifsud, and Eloise Lindsay in particular for their contributions, which have helped me rethink aspects of the film.

11. Bhabha used these terms in referring to *Night Cries.* I use them here because they are appropriate to the work this film does to reclaim cultural memory. See chapter 13 for my elaboration of the idea of anachronism in relation to Chaplin.

12. See chapter 3 for an elaboration of Walter Benjamin's concept of non-sensuous similarity.

13. Meaghan Morris, "Beyond Assimilation: Aboriginality, Media History, and Public Memory," *Aedon, Melbourne University Literary Arts Review* 4.1 (1996), 15.

14. Colin Johnson, "Chauvel and the Centering of the Aboriginal Male in Australian Film," *Continuum* 1.1 (1987), 47–56.

15. Bette Mifsud asked me what I meant by an "aesthetic of assimilation" at the Power Institute forum. I coined the term heuristically. I could not use "appropriation" as it has been theorized in current postmodern debates because of the specific history being dealt with in this film. "Assimilation" felt right because it denotes a violent history but also has enabling connotations. It suggests ways of turning horrific situations and making them do something other than horrify. This ambivalence, I thought, was appropriate to what the film was doing. I don't think it would be productive to describe "assimilation" as a set of aesthetic devices in the way the political modernism of the 1970s did. This would severely delimit what can happen in processes of assimilation, and one would want to be surprised, at the very least, by such processes. Also, the ideas of assimilation work very differently from the earlier notions of cultural decolonization, in which forms of indigenous practices and institutions that prevailed before conquest are restored as dominant cultural practices. An aesthetic of assimilation acknowledges the modern and tries with a certain cunning to continually redefine its terms so as to prevent the erasure of memory and of our capacity to remember.

16. See chapter 11, note 26, for an elaboration of Gilles Deleuze's concept of the indirect mediator.

17. See chapter 3 for an elaboration of Michael Taussig's idea of mimetic capital.

2. Reception, Genre, and the Knowing Critic

This chapter was presented at the Conference on Asian Cinema, New York University, 10 June 1992. It was first published in *The Filmmaker and the Prostitute: Dennis O'Rourke's* The Good Woman of Bangkok, ed. Chris

Berry, Annette Hamilton, and Laleen Jayamanne (Sydney: Power Publications, 1997).

1. As I discuss in chapter 9, the knowing critic is one who always already knows what a film is about and what it can do, even before seeing it.

2. Meaghan Morris, "Tooth and Claw: Tales of Survival and Crocodile Dundee," in *The Pirate's Fiancée: Feminism, Reading, Postmodernism* (London and New York: Verso, 1988), 244.

3. See Miriam Hansen's "Early Cinema: Whose Public Sphere?" in *Early Cinema: Space, Frame, Narrative,* ed. Thomas Elsaesser (London: British Film Institute, 1990), 238.

4. Adrian Martin, "The Street Angel and the Badman: *The Good Woman of Bangkok,*" *Photofile* 35 (May 1992), 15.

5. Laura Mulvey, "Visual Pleasure and Narrative Cinema," *Movies and Methods,* vol. 2, ed. Bill Nichols (Berkeley: University of California Press, 1985), 307–15.

6. Jeannie Martin, "Missionary Positions," in *The Filmmaker and the Prostitute,* ed. Chris Berry, Annette Hamilton, and Laleen Jayamanne (Sydney: Power Publications, 1997), 17.

7. *Coming Out Show,* Radio National, Australian Broadcasting Corporation, 14 March 1992.

8. Adrian Martin, "The Street Angel," 12.

9. *Screen,* Australian Broadcasting Corporation, 5 May 1992. My views on the film changed a great deal after my discussion with O'Rourke.

10. Meaghan Morris, "Postmodernity and Lyotard's Sublime," in *The Pirate's Fiancée,* 218. The formulation in this essay helped me figure out how to respond to this critical dilemma. Morris says that judging without criteria, judging without the underpinnings of a general model of justice, is a form of Aristotelian prudence.

11. Martha Ansara, "A Man's World," in *The Filmmaker and the Prostitute: Dennis O'Rourke's* The Good Woman of Bangkok, ed. Chris Berry, Annette Hamilton, and Laleen Jayamanne (Sydney: Power Publications, 1997), 21.

12. Adrian Martin, "The Street Angel," 13.

13. On D. W. Griffith's rescue fantasies and their implication for film form, see Miriam Hansen, *Babel and Babylon: Spectatorship in American Silent Film* (Cambridge: Harvard University Press, 1991), chapter 10, "Crisis of Femininity, Fantasies of Rescue."

14. Sylvia Lawson, "Skin Trade Stories," in *The Filmmaker and the Prostitute: Dennis O'Rourke's* The Good Woman of Bangkok, ed. Chris Berry, Annette Hamilton, and Laleen Jayamanne (Sydney: Power Publications, 1997), 14.

15. 2BL, Australian Broadcasting Corporation, 26 March 1992.

16. *The 7:30 Report,* Australian Broadcasting Corporation, 24 March 1992.

17. *Late Night Live,* Australian Broadcasting Corporation, 22 March 1992.

18. Meaghan Morris, "Personal Relationships and Sexuality in the Australian Cinema," in *The New Australian Cinema,* ed. Scott Murray (Melbourne: Thomas Nelson, 1981), 142.

19. Lawson, "Skin Trade Stories." At the time, the prime minister of Australia was Paul Keating.

20. *The Sentimental Bloke* is a famous Australian silent film directed by Raymond Longford, based on the well-known C. J. Dennis poem "Songs of a Sentimental Bloke."

21. Karen Shimakawa, " 'Fake Intimacy': Locating National Identity in Dennis O'Rourke's *The Good Woman of Bangkok,*" *Discourse* 17.3 (spring 1995), 126–50.

22. Shimakawa, "Fake Intimacy," 149.

23. All my information on this matter is taken from John Tulloch, *Legends on the Screen* (Melbourne: Currency Press and the Australian Film Institute, 1981), 44–63.

3. Postcolonial Gothic

This chapter was commissioned by "Under Capricorn: A Conference on Art, Politics, and Culture," Wellington, New Zealand, and was read there on 5 March 1994. *The Piano* (1993, Australia) was written and directed by Jane Campion, a New Zealand–born resident of Australia, who shot the film in New Zealand with international stars Holly Hunter, Harvey Keitel, and Sam Neill.

1. Leslie Fiedler, "On Terror for Love," in *The Gothic Novel: A Casebook,* ed. Victor Sage (London: Macmillan, 1990), 134. Fiedler's use of "he" is noteworthy, considering the large number of women who wrote Gothic fiction. David B. Morris, in his article "Gothic Sublimity" (*New Literary History* 16.2 [winter 1985], 299–319), disagrees with this definition in that he sees the relation between love and terror as one not of substitution but of interpenetration. Because of the centrality of terror to Gothic fiction, the sublime is, according to him, a "vital, integral part of the Gothic novel, not merely an incidental, ornamental, scenic prop" (300).

2. "Who's Going to Win—and Why," *Who* 108 (21 March 1994), 84. "Masterpiece Theater effect" is a category invented by this magazine to describe art cinema. This particular quotation is taken from a section describing the films nominated for the Oscars in 1994.

3. This paper was written after *The Piano* won the Palme d'Or at the Cannes Film Festival of 1993 but before it won three Oscars (for best original screenplay, best actress, and best supporting actress) at the 1993 Academy Awards, held in March 1994. *The Piano* was distributed in the U.S. by Miramax, the Disney-owned producer and distributor known for its art-house films. In

Sydney it was exhibited at the Pitt Centre, a cinema complex owned by a major distributor, where art-house films meet mainstream ones. The publication and novelization of its script and Grant Matthews's exhibition in Australia of stills from the film fit within a discourse of art cinema and its product tie-ins. Miro Bilbrough's piece "Crafting *The Piano*" (*Object* 12 [summer 1994], 36–38) also fits into this context, with its examination of artisans' influence on the crafting of the costumes in the film. According to figures given to me by the Australian Film Commission, *The Piano* was the ninth largest box-office success in 1993 and the highest-grossing Australian film. The other eight were all Hollywood films, one of them *Schindler's List.*

4. Jane Campion, *The Piano* (London: Bloomsbury, 1993), 149.

5. Stuart Dryburgh said this in answer to a question about the Gothic aesthetic of the film at "Frame by Frame," the Sydney Film Festival forum on *The Piano*, 21 June 1994. When asked how the notion of the Gothic formed the film, he spoke mostly in terms of the color of the film and added that the filmmakers had not worked with any antecedent visual style. The production designer, Andrew McAlpine, speaks of "this green cathedral of *nikau* and *punga* . . . a very gothic landscape" in the interview accompanying the published script (Campion, *The Piano,* 140).

6. Peter Brooks, *The Melodramatic Imagination: Balzac, Henry James, Melodrama, and the Mode of Excess* (New Haven: Yale University Press, 1976), 20.

7. MaryBeth Inverso, *The Gothic Impulse in Contemporary Drama* (Ann Arbor and London: UMI Research Press, 1990), 9.

8. On first viewing I was not fascinated by the film, and it was only by pursuing younger women's fascination with it that I was able to respond to and write about it. This "fascination with fascination," I soon discovered (I thank Kathryn Bird for the phrase), was an integral part of what this film was about.

9. This phrase appears in Wilhelm Worringer's *Form in Gothic,* trans. Sir Herbert Read (London: Alec Tiranti, 1957), 39. It is interesting that the term "will" is used by several characters in *The Piano* to describe the Gothic woman, Ada, including herself. It is crucial to my argument to maintain her generic attributes and not conflate them with categories of social gender. By doing this I can bypass dead-end questions like "Why is Ada like a man?" It is a dead-end question because it leaves no room for film to be productive on its own terms, genre being one term among many.

10. What is made into a commodity and sold in this film is something that could be called (following the history of feminist film theory) "female desire." Melodrama as genre instituted a successful commodification and marketing of affect in numerous national cinemas, including of course Hollywood, and also Indian and Sri Lankan. That the promise of happiness intrinsic to melodrama is often not delivered by films in this genre may speak to a certain sense of historical realism which imbues each culture. Per-

haps the history of feminism and its wide dissemination makes it possible for a film such as this to resolve hitherto irreconcilable conflicts. This is a claim that also has to be argued for in terms of the film's own workings, which I hope to do in this paper.

11. Jane Campion, interview by Miro Bilbrough, *Cinema Papers* 93 (May 1993), 8.

12. Mary Colbert, "Jane Campion on Her Gothic Film *The Piano*," *Sight and Sound* 3.10 (October 1993), 6, emphasis added.

13. Ibid.

14. See Peter Cochrane, "Seduction and Consent," *24 Hours* 214 (November 1993), 44–48; Kerryn Goldsworthy, "What Music Is," *Arena* 7 (October–November 1993), 46–48; Valerie Hazel, "Strains of Silence," *Photofile* 40 (November 1993), 39–41. The short piece by Graham Fuller, "The Wuthering Heights of Jane Campion's *The Piano*" (*Interview* 7 [November 1993], 46), is the only one I have seen that tries to elaborate a little on the Gothic form of the film. See also Joan Kirkby, " 'Big My Secret': Emily Dickinson and *The Piano*," *EDIS Bulletin* 8 (May–June 1994), 6–7.

15. Susan Dermody and Elizabeth Jacka, *The Screening of Australia: Anatomy of a National Cinema*, vol. 2 (Melbourne: Currency Press, 1988), 239.

16. Campion, interview by Bilbrough, 8, 6.

17. Freud, as quoted by J. Laplanche and J. B. Pontalis, *The Language of Psychoanalysis*, trans. D. Nicholson-Smith (London: Hogarth Press, 1983), 274.

18. My thanks to Carmel Raffel, a pianist herself, for hearing this and sharing it with me, and also for describing Ada's playing as like a soliloquy.

19. Gilles Deleuze, *Cinema 1: The Movement Image*, trans. Hugh Tomlinson and Barbara Habberjam (Minneapolis: University of Minnesota Press, 1986), 50.

20. Stella Bruzzi, "Bodyscape," *Sight and Sound* 3.10 (October 1993), 7–8.

21. The Australian Broadcasting Corporation's Radio National discussion of *The Piano* in its religious program, 27 March 1994, was largely (though not wholly) a new-age reading of the film as being about Ada finding herself deep down within herself and how this discovery links up with something greater in the wider world. I was struck by the tone of reverence, awe, and solemnity with which the film was discussed. I found this rather annoying because the violence and mordant Gothic humor of the film is anything but solemn.

22. Worringer, *Form*, 65.

23. Campion, *The Piano*, 49.

24. Sigmund Freud, "On Narcissism: An Introduction" (1914), in *The Standard Edition of the Psychological Works of Sigmund Freud*, trans. James Strachey, vol. 14 (London: Hogarth Press, 1986), 73–102. See also *Feminism and Psychoanalysis, A Critical Dictionary*, ed. Elizabeth Wright (Oxford, England, and Cambridge, Mass.: Blackwell, 1992), entries on "Narcissism," "Object," "Maternal Voice."

25. I want to remember here what Jodie Foster said when she received the Oscar for best actress for her performance as Clarice Starling, the FBI agent who kills the serial killer in Jonathan Demy's *Silence of the Lambs*. She said (I quote from memory) that it was great that the academy was recognizing a "feminist hero," i.e., the role and function of Clarice.

26. The narrator is interior in the sense that the narration is itself part of the story; the story is told by a character internal to the story. The presence of several interior narrators can create a Chinese-box effect, as in Mary Shelley's *Frankenstein* or Emily Bronte's *Wuthering Heights*. George E. Haggerty refers to the internal narrator as a "Gothic gesture" which attempts to "explore the subjective and the personal and to give coherent expression to much that is incoherent and beyond understanding as well as interpretation" (*Gothic Fiction/Gothic Form* [University Park and London: Pennsylvania State University Press, 1989], 66).

27. Italo Calvino, *Six Memos for the Next Millennium* (Cambridge: Harvard University Press, 1988), 18. My thanks to Jodi Brooks for introducing me to this book.

28. Julia Kristeva, *Black Sun: Depression and Melancholia*, trans. Leon S. Roudiez (New York: Columbia University Press, 1989), 21–22.

29. Ibid., 9.

30. Sigmund Freud, "Mourning and Melancholia" (1914–1916), in *The Standard Edition of the Psychological Works of Sigmund Freud*, trans. James Strachey, vol. 14 (London: Hogarth Press, 1986), 245.

31. My thanks to Carmel Raffel for explaining what musical transposition is and helping me thereby to use it here. A piece of music is usually transposed from the original key to another so as to enable a singer to sing. Similarly, melancholy is the unperformability of sadness until it is transposed into another affective register.

32. Here I am indebted to Sarah Kofman's reading of Freud's "On Narcissism" in her *The Enigma of Woman: Woman in Freud's Writings*, trans. Catherine Porter (Ithaca: Cornell University Press, 1985), 50–58. Kofman makes the point that it is no accident that Freud wrote this text, which has "Nietzschean overtones[,] . . . during a period when Freud was particularly attracted to Lou Andreas-Salome."

33. Kristeva, *Black Sun*, 128. Kristeva uses this formulation to describe the work of Holbein in chapter 5, "Holbein's Dead Christ."

34. Freud, "Mourning," 243–60.

35. Kristeva, *Black Sun*, 40–42.

36. Campion discusses this film in her interview by Bilbrough.

37. In German Expressionist cinema the double is always a source of fear and often kills its other, as in *The Student of Prague*.

38. At the Sydney Film Festival forum, Dryburgh said that Ada wrote the sentence because Baines could get someone else to read it. As it happens, the script includes a scene in which he does; the scene was filmed but edited out. This was also reported in the *Sydney Morning Herald*, 23 June 1994.

39. Emily Bronte, *Wuthering Heights* (Edinburgh: Thornton, 1911), 121.

40. See Theodore Adorno, *Aesthetic Theory*, trans. Robert Hullot-Kentor (London: Athlone Press, 1997), 96. This is only one place in this book where he demonstrates this link.

41. Walter Benjamin, "On the Mimetic Faculty," in *Reflections: Essays, Aphorisms, Autobiographical Writings,* trans. Edmund Jephcott (New York: Schocken, 1978), 336.

42. Walter Benjamin, "The Doctrine of the Similar" (1933), *New German Critique* 17 (1979), 65–69.

43. See note 77 for a brief reading of this scene enacting the death drive as an encounter with Gothic sublimity.

44. See Patricia Yaeger, "Toward a Female Sublime," in *Gender and Theory: Dialogues on Feminist Criticism.,* ed. Linda Kauffman (Oxford: Blackwell, 1989), 191–221. Here she says, "The Romantic sublime is a genre that is, historically and psychologically, a masculine mode of writing and relationship. It is also a genre that is—in the present age—of questionable use; it is old-fashioned, outmoded, concerned with self-centered imperialism, with a 'pursuit of the infinitude of the private self' that we, in the twentieth century, regard with some embarrassment. . . . Nevertheless, as a pre-fabricated structure, as a literary genre or moment concerned with empowerment, transport, and the self's strong sense of authority, the sublime is a genre the woman writer needs" (192). See Anthony Vidler's *The Architectural Uncanny: Essays in the Modern Unhomely* (Cambridge: MIT Press, 1992), 20–21, for an account of what he calls "the subgenres of the sublime—the grotesque, the caricature, the fairy story, the melodrama, the ghostly romance, and the horror story." He adds that these pop-cultural spin-offs "were considered to be subversive of its [the sublime's] overarching premises and its transcendent ambitions."

45. My thanks to Myra Katz for bringing this to my notice, and also for discussing the film with me while I was writing this piece.

46. Edmund Burke, *The Sublime and the Beautiful* (New York: P. F. Collier & Son, 1969), 102. Morris, "Gothic Sublimity," includes an account of how Burke's theorizing of the sublime enabled the "poeticizing" of the British novel. Also see Vijay Mishra, *The Gothic Sublime* (Albany: State University of New York Press, 1994), especially chapter 1, for the distinctions between the Burkean sublime and the Gothic sublime. What is useful here for my purpose is the notion of "the unspeakable" as a Gothic cliché. Thinking with such a generic notion would stop one from asking futile questions like

"Why is Ada silent?" and expecting a secret answer. In fear and trembling I have just touched a tip of the formidable scholarship on the sublime only to be able to work out how a particular version of it is useful for the Gothic woman, Ada McGrath. I wish to thank Meaghan Morris for her generous and invaluable assistance in introducing me to the literature on the Gothic sublime and for discussing several versions of this chapter.

47. Gary Lee Stonum, *Dickinson Sublime* (Madison: University of Wisconsin Press, 1990), 69.

48. Kirkby, "Big My Secret." The Dickinson poems are nos. 1737 ("Rearrange a 'Wife's' affection!") and 536 ("The Heart asks Pleasure—first—").

49. Interviewed by Bilbrough, Campion said, "I admire Dickinson and Bronte, the sensibility they bring to their work and to the world. . . . I use and put their labour into a more popular and acceptable form and sometimes I feel guilty as I think it's a corrupted use of their pure wisdom" (7). Campion is talking here about the commodification of what may be called female desire.

50. Stonum, *Dickinson Sublime*, 69. The Dickinson sublime and the Gothic sublimity of *The Piano* are different despite the numerous links between the film and the poet. It seems to me that according to Stonum's analysis the Dickinson sublime is a variant of the Romantic sublime. Campion has drawn an analogy between Emily Dickinson herself and Ada McGrath: "In a way, Dickinson led such a secret life, and my main character, Ada, does as well" (interview by Bilbrough, 6).

51. See Anne McClintock, "The Return of Female Fetishism and the Fiction of the Phallus," *New Formations* 19, special issue on perversity (spring 1993), 1–21; this is an excellent article for theorizing female fetishism outside a psychoanalytic framework, within which it is an impossibility.

52. As I understand it, to think with a cluster of images (constellations) is to read correspondences (non-sensuous similarities) across discontinuities.

53. There is a montage between this sentence and the one immediately before it. But it is a connection that may best be thought of (in Deleuze's terms) as an "irrational cut," i.e., the joining of two or more things on a discontinuity. This discontinuous movement has been made possible by feminism and the forms of knowledge and desire it has made possible for women. Within such a history Gothic romance may be temporalized, so that Cathy's terrifying knowledge of the loss of self in love appears to us late-twentieth-century feminists as the antiquity of our affective lives. I use the collective "our" here because these intimate private knowledges which were writ large, perhaps for the first time, by the historical Gothic genre's theatricality are now also worked on in other interdisciplinary feminist knowledges.

54. Fiedler, "On Terror," 136.

55. I wish to thank Toni Ross for helping me construct and clarify my argument here.

56. Jane Campion, interview by Bilbrough, 8.

57. Michael Taussig, *Mimesis and Alterity: A Particular History of the Senses* (New York and London: Routledge, 1993), 247–48.

58. Benjamin, "On the Mimetic Faculty," 332.

59. For Benjamin and Adorno, mimicry is the bio-anthropological dimension of mimesis, which has many other determinations.

60. Taussig, *Mimesis and Alterity*, 19–20.

61. Theodor Adorno and Max Horkheimer, "Elements of Anti-Semitism," in *Dialectic of Enlightenment*, trans. John Cumming (London: Verso, 1994). In this essay they examine the link between modernity and the repression of mimesis, as well as the controlled performance of mimesis within German fascism and its integral relationship to anti-Semitism. In *Aesthetic Theory*, Adorno says, "Art is a refuge for mimetic comportment" (53). This clearly implies that mimesis is under threat and it is within this state of danger that the idea was theorized, with the hope of redeeming it for a particular modernity. Adorno says that Plato's theorem that enthusiasm is a precondition for philosophy, or for thought in the emphatic sense, hints that mimesis contains rationality. This implies that Plato was working with two notions of mimesis: the pre-Platonic notion of mimesis as Dionysian performance or enthusiasm, and the Platonic polemic against this very notion, which proposed mimesis as mere copy of copy. The complex history of mimesis in western thought is mapped out in *Mimesis in Contemporary Theory: An Interdisciplinary Approach*, vol. 1, *The Literary and Philosophical Debate*, ed. Mihai Spariosu (Philadelphia and Amsterdam: John Benjamins, 1984), especially Spariosu's introduction, i–xxiv. See also Spariosu's "Plato's *Ion*: Mimesis, Poetry, and Power," in *Mimesis in Contemporary Theory: An Interdisciplinary Approach*, vol. 2: *Mimesis, Semiosis, and Power*, ed. Ronald Bogue (Philadelphia and Amsterdam: John Benjamins, 1991), 13–26.

62. My thanks to Alexander Garcia Duttman for these marvelous insights into mimesis in a private conversation in Sydney, 1984.

63. Taussig, *Mimesis and Alterity*, 200–203. The account Taussig quotes of the reaction of the first Eskimo audience to the film footage of Nanook catching the walrus is similar to that of the Maori man in *The Piano*: "The projector light shone out. There was complete silence in the hut. They saw Nanook. But Nanook was there in the hut with them, and they couldn't understand. Then they saw the walrus, and then, said Bob (Flaherty), pandemonium broke loose. "Hold him!" they screamed. "Hold him!" and they scrambled over chairs and each other to get to the screen and help Nanook hold that walrus!" See Frances Hubbard Flaherty, *The Odyssey of a Film-Maker: Robert Flaherty's Story* (Putney, Vt.: Threshold Books, 1984), 18.

64. Godard's scene is a pure time image in the sense that one can read it as an allegorical memory image embodying three stages of spectatorship in the history of cinema. The contemporary viewer is also drawn into this allegory in a far more complex way than in *The Piano*. However, my point in citing them together is to suggest the importance of mimesis as a mode of appre-

hending the image which makes subject-object relations volatile. I want not to essentialize mimesis but to see what happens when it is figured as a mythical moment. When Benjamin posits the primitive body and that of the child as the figures of phylogenetic and ontogenetic mimesis, respectively, some form of essence seems to be invoked which links these two bodies with nature. Taussig calls this the nature that culture uses to create second nature.

65. I wish to thank Jodi Brooks for this phrase.

66. I wish to thank Chris Caines for discussing with me the work of Harvey Keitel in this and other films, and also Andrew Plain for introducing me to a way of thinking about Keitel's importance in American and other cinemas.

67. David Thompson, "Harvey Keitel, Staying Power," *Sight and Sound* 3.1 (January 1993), 22–25.

68. Ibid.

69. The mimetic contagion between bodies noted earlier is rarely operative in a purely cinematic register in this film. The only time that the camera itself is propelled by such an energy is the scene where Baines takes Ada and Flora to the beached piano. The camera's encircling movement is the nearest it comes to a mimetic gesture. So it seems that the mimetic exists in this film more as a theme, a dynamic between characters rather than between all the filmic elements. I wish to thank George Kouvaros for his question about mimetic contagion and the filmic in this film, to which this is an answer.

70. Kathryn Bird made an interesting point in reminding me that Keitel was considered for the role of Willard in Francis Ford Coppola's *Apocalypse Now*. Martin Sheen, who finally got the role, goes through the film with a catatonic stare. Keitel, as Bird suggested, could not have acted as a frozen screen on which the great American public could live out its Vietnam trauma. Keitel would bollix up the sense of clear separation needed for that role; besides, he doesn't have blue eyes.

71. I have taken the ideas of man, woman, and child as primordial bodies, and the notion of a differential time between them, from Gilles Deleuze's *Cinema 2: The Time Image,* trans. Hugh Tomlinson and Robert Galeta (Minneapolis: University of Minnesota Press, 1989), chapter 8. I think a differential temporality between these figures is made possible by the entanglement of melodrama and the Gothic. The figures who are mother, daughter, husband-villain, and lover in the melodramatic narrative become hero-heroine (Ada), messenger (Flora), and helpers (Stewart and Baines) in the Gothic romance.

72. The bracketed words are in the script but not the film.

73. Peter Otto, "Forgetting Colonialism," *Meanjin* 52.3 (1993), 545–59.

74. Terry Heller, *The Delights of Terror: An Aesthetic of the Tale of Terror* (Urbana: University of Illinois Press, 1987), 201.

75. How might one describe Ada's Gothic gesture of opening her eyes to repulse

her rapist husband? Is it a gaze, a glance, or a look? Because of the Gothic density of the gesture I use all these terms interchangeably.

76. Heller, *Delights,* 206.

77. I think it is possible to read Ada's encounter with death as also a version of the Gothic sublime. But in this instance it is she who is the agent of the sublime, whereas in the rape scene the agent is Stewart. The long shot of Ada suspended underwater may be viewed as a voluptuous, hesitant, suspended moment of encounter with death. It is not quite an attraction-revulsion dynamic (which is said to be a fundamental law of Gothic emotion) but more a luxurious encounter with an oceanic sublime. She certainly seems to be "[having her] elixir and drinking it too," which is what Gothic melodrama promises (Inverso, *Gothic Impulse,* 9) but does not often deliver quite as convincingly as in this moment of great lucidity and voluptuous transport. The erotic dimension of this sublime encounter, enhanced by (Gothic) special effects such as slow-motion photography, makes it quite different from the second movement of the romantic sublime, namely, the terror of disintegration, as it has been described. Here there is a movement of voluptuous surrender. Ada as agent of the sublime gains mileage in this vertiginous plunging, which seems qualitatively different from the affective register of the romantic sublime. I wish to thank Melissa McMahon and Paul Willemen for having discussed these aspects of the film with me.

78. Walter Benjamin, *The Origin of German Tragic Drama,* trans. John Osborne (London: New Left Books, 1977). According to Benjamin, the privileged emblems of Baroque allegory are the ruin, the corpse, and the ghost. This is so because in these forms the operations of time, as incessant flow and decay, are made perceptible. So modern allegorical constructs are temporal forms imagined and willed in order to perceive, make tangible, time as eternal passing. In Benjamin's work on Baudelaire he develops the idea of the industrial commodity as allegory. Gothic allegory, as distinct from Baroque, pertains to the psychic life of the self, its temporal layers.

79. It is this mnemonic relinking with the piano, after a catastrophe, that makes this film an allegory for women intellectuals, no matter what their sexual preference.

4. Speaking of *Ceylon*

This chapter was presented at the 1986 Edinburgh Film Festival's "Third Cinema Conference" on 20 August. It was first published in *Questions of Third Cinema,* ed. Jim Pines and Paul Willemen (London: British Film Institute, 1989). The title is a composite of two comments made by two Australians in relation to *A Song of Ceylon.* To Rex Butler I owe the first part ("Speaking of *Ceylon,*" *Frogger* 19 [November 1985], 1–9), and a speaker at a Sydney Film Festival Forum in 1985 referred to the film as being about "a clash of cultures." My appropriation of their words is an attempt to work out a structure for this chapter that is partially isomorphic with that of the film. This chapter has three parts: 1. some problems in the field of feminist film theory; 2. aspects of the work of conceptualizing the film; 3. modes of performing and readings of the film.

Part three consists of extensive quotations from Rex Butler's interview of me for *Frogger*. As you will see, this interview, which is more like a reading, in turn uses bits from a fictional interview I wrote between a woman named Anna Rodrigo and myself as author (Laleen Jayamanne, "To Render the Body Ecstatic: Anna Rodrigo Interviews Laleen Jayamanne," in *Fade to Black* [Sydney: Sydney College of the Arts Film Group, 1985], 6–9). The present chapter is structured by quotations from this fictional interview, which you will read at irregular intervals.

This work comes out of, among other things, an engagement with a specific history of feminism and film, and is an attempt to work through one or two major problems in the field.

1. Jayamanne, "To Render," 6.

2. Laleen Jayamanne, "Puppets and Puppeteers, Actors and Lovers," *Cantrills Film Notes* 47–48 (1985), 2.

3. Jayamanne, "To Render," 6.

4. Ibid.

5. I would like to thank Homi Bhabha for one of the most interesting questions asked of me in relation to my film (at the Third Cinema Conference, held in conjunction with the Edinburgh Film Festival in 1986). He asked (I paraphrase from memory), "What was it that resisted, at the time of conceptualizing the film, at the time of making it, the very theories that you were using?" I said then that the film had taken a cue from the verbal text, which said, "He shakes, he shivers, he chants *gathas*," and had tried to develop the implications of this description in terms of the images. Insofar as this is a description of the male priest in extremis, it shifts the burden of the hysterical body to the male figure of authority. If psychoanalysis as a discourse and profession owes a debt to the hystericized body of woman, this film attempts to spread that contagion beyond strict gender divisions.

6. Jayamanne, "To Render," 7.

7. Ibid.

8. Jayamanne, "Puppets," 3.

9. Roland Barthes, "Diderot, Brecht, Eisenstein," in *Image, Music Text*, trans. Stephen Heath (Glasgow: Fontana, Collins, 1977), 70.

10. Butler, "Speaking," 2–4.

11. Jayamanne, "To Render," 8.

12. Jayamanne, "Puppets," 4.

13. Jayamanne, "To Render," 9.

14. Ibid.

5. Anna Rodrigo Interviews Laleen Jayamanne on *A Song of Ceylon*

This is a revised version of "Do You Think I Am a Woman, Ha! Do You?" *Discourse* 11.2 (spring–summer 1989).

6. Anna Rodrigo Interviews Laleen Jayamanne on *Row Row Row Your Boat*

This is a revised version of "Anna Rodrigo Talks with Laleen Jayamanne," in *Dissonance: Feminism and the Arts, 1970–90*, ed. Catriona Moore (Sydney: Allen and Unwin, 1994). *Row Row Row Your Boat* (1992), a fourteen-minute video by Laleen Jayamanne, was funded by the New Image Research fund of the Australian Film Commission. The texts inserted into this interview are contained in this video and are from *The Thief of Baghdad* (1940), directed by Ludwig Berger, Michael Powell, and Tim Whelan.

1. Lesley Thornton, "If upon Leaving, What We Have to Say, We Speak: A Conversation Piece," in *Discourses: Conversations in Postmodern Art and Culture*, ed. Russell Ferguson et al. (New York: New Museum of Contemporary Art and Cambridge: MIT Press, 1990), 54.

2. Kaja Silverman, *The Acoustic Mirror: The Female Voice in Psychoanalysis and Cinema* (Bloomington: Indiana University Press, 1988), 32, 40. Further references to this book will be given in parentheses in the text.

7. Myths of Femininity in the Sri Lankan Cinema, 1947–1989

A version of this chapter was presented at "Sri Lanka in Crisis," a conference sponsored by the International Centre for Ethnic Studies, Colombo, 15 August 1989. This is a revised version of "Hunger for Images: Myths of Femininity in the Sri Lankan Cinema, 1947–1989," *South Asian Bulletin* 12.1 (1992), edited by Reggie Siriwardana.

1. Adrian Martin, "No Flowers for the Cinephile: The Fates of Cultural Populism, 1960–1970," in *Island in the Stream: Myths of Place in Australian Culture*, ed. Paul Foss (Sydney: Pluto Press, 1988), 137.

2. John Flaus, "The Western Myth: *Ride Lonesome* and *Guns in the afternoon*," *SUFG Bulletin* (Sydney University Film Group), Term 1 (1970), 44.

3. Laleen Jayamanne, "Positions of Women in the Sri Lankan Cinema, 1947–1979," Ph.D. dissertation, University of New South Wales (1981), 1.

4. Paul Willemen, "Regional Cinema," in *Indian Cinema: British Film Institute Dossier 5*, ed. Behrose Ghandy and Paul Willemen (London: British Film Institute, 1980), 29.

5. Ashoka Mammen, "Notes on Production, 1945–72," in *Indian Cinema: British Film Institute Dossier 5*, ed. Behrose Ghandy and Paul Willemen (London: British Film Institute, 1980), 25.

6. The Sinhalese word *himi* means both "husband" and "owner."

7. Kumudu Kusum Kumara, "Duhulu Malak," *Sithuvili* 5 (1976), 4. This and other translations from non-English sources are my own.

8. K. W. Perera, "Duhulu Malak," *Cinemanurupa* 10–12 (1976), 2.

9. Philip Cooray, The *Lonely Artist: A Critical Introduction to the Films of Lester James Peries* (Colombo: Lake House, 1970), 40.

10. The Sinhalese word for marriage, *bandinawa,* also means "to tie." This line is uttered by Swarna Mallawarachchi's character, discussed in the text.

11. Swarna Mallawarachchi, interview by Ashley Rathnavibhushana, *Sinesith* 15 (1989), 25.

8. Sri Lankan Family Melodrama

This chapter was first published in *Screen* 33.2 (summer 1992). By the late 1990s, the Sri Lankan film industry had almost ceased to exist.

1. Quoted in K. Aiyer, "On Melodrama," in K. Aiyer, ed., *Filmfare* (Bombay, Vikas: 1967), 11.

2. Quoted in Lotte H. Eisner, *Murnau* (London: Secker & Warburg, 1965), 183, emphasis added.

3. Anoja Weerasinghe, "Anoja Weerasinghe, The Star and the Actress: An Interview," unnamed interviewer, *Framework* 37, special issue on the Sri Lankan cinema (1989), 98.

4. Quoted in H. Perera, "Early Sinhala Cinema," *Cinemanurupa* 6 (1962), 3.

5. Quoted in Georges Sadoul, *George Mélies* (Paris: Éditions Seghers, 1970), 118.

6. Tom Gunning, "An Aesthetic of Astonishment: Early Film and the (In)credulous Spectator," *Art & Text* 34 (1989), 31–45; "The Cinema of Attraction: Early Film, Its Spectator, and the Avant-Garde," *Wide Angle* 8.3–4 (1986), 63–70; " 'Primitive' Cinema: A Frame-up? Or, The Trick's on Us," *Cinema Journal* 28.2 (1988), 3–12.

7. Gunning, "Aesthetic of Astonishment."

8. Gunning, "Cinema of Attraction," 64.

9. Gunning, " 'Primitive' Cinema."

10. Weerasinghe, "Anoja Weerasinghe," 98.

9. An Alternative Cinematic and Critical Practice

This chapter is a shorter version of the Neil I. Perera Memorial Lecture I delivered in Colombo, 25 January 1992. In writing it I was guided by the question of how one can produce alternative readings of films without constructing some monolithic Big Bad Thing, be it Hollywood or our own formula films. I concluded that the field of Sri Lankan film criticism, as I found it while researching the national cinema, must be changed. Certainly our best critics have striven toward this ideal since the early 1950s. I was, however, criticized by some for trying to undo the work that had been done in the past.

1. Neil I. Perera, "Ungrammatical Cinema," *Attha* (Sri Lanka), 12 March 1972.

2. Christine Gledhill, ed., *Home Is Where the Heart Is: Studies in Melodrama and the Woman's Film* (London: British Film Institute, 1987), 31. See also Peter Brooks, *The Melodramatic Imagination: Balzac, Henry James, Melodrama, and the Mode of Excess* (New Haven: Yale University Press, 1976).

3. K. D. Perera, ed., *"Under the Bridge" and Its Critics* (Colombo: Lanka Kala Kendra, 1990).

4. My information on the current state of the industry is derived from private conversations with directors and critics in late 1998.

10. Deleuzian Redemption of Bazin

1. Gilles Deleuze, *Cinema 2: The Time Image*, trans. Hugh Tomlinson and Robert Galeta (Minneapolis: University of Minnesota Press, 1989), 1–24. Further references to this book (abbreviated to *C2*) will be given in parentheses in the text.

2. Sam Rohdie, *The Passion of Pier Paolo Pasolini* (London: British Film Institute and Bloomington: Indiana University Press, 1995). Further references to this book (abbreviated to *Passion*) will be given in parentheses in the text.

3. André Bazin, "The Ontology of the Photographic Image" and "The Evolution of the Language of Cinema," in *What Is Cinema?* vol. 1, trans. Hugh Gray (Berkeley: University of California Press, 1967), 9–16 and 23–40. Bazin's major essays on neorealism are in *What Is Cinema?* vol. 2, trans. Hugh Gray (Berkeley: University of California Press, 1971). Further references to volume 2 (abbreviated to *WIC2*) will be given in parentheses in the text.

4. Gilles Deleuze, *Negotiations, 1972–1990/Gilles Deleuze*, trans. Martin Joughin (New York: Columbia University Press, 1995), 123.

5. See Miriam Hansen, "The Future of Cinema Studies in the Age of Global Media: Aesthetics, Spectatorship, and Public Spheres—Interview with Miriam Hansen," interview by Laleen Jayamanne and Anne Rutherford, *UTS Review* 5.1 (1999), 94–110, for her views on cinema as our common repository of time and archive of memory.

11. Modes of Performance in Chantal Akerman's *Jeanne Dielman, 23 Quai du Commerce, 1080 Bruxelles*

This is a revised version of an article first published in the *Australian Journal of Screen Theory* 8 (1980).

1. Quoted in a handout distributed at the screenings by the National Film Theater of Australia.

2. *Hôtel Monterey* (1972), *Le 15/8* (1973, co-directed with S. Szlingerbaum), *Jeanne Dielman* (1975), and *Les Rendez-vous d'Anna* (1978).

3. See Angela Martin, "Chantal Akerman's Films: A Dossier," *Feminist Review* 3 (1979), 24–47.

4. Marsha Kinder, "Reflections on *Jeanne Dielman*," *Film Quarterly* 30.4 (summer 1977), 6.

5. Roland Barthes, "Lesson in Writing," in *Image, Music, Text,* trans. Stephen Heath (Glasgow: Fontana, Collins, 1977), 176, emphasis added.

6. Michael Kirby, "On Acting and Not-Acting," *The Drama Review* 16.1 (1972), 5. I am indebted to Kirby for his formulation of this distinction between matrixed and non-matrixed performing. I also thank Douglas Dunn, Meredith Monk, Peter Schuman, and Robert Wilson for the opportunities they offered me to work with them in their theater, dance, and opera while I was a graduate student in drama at New York University in the early 1970s. This work has predisposed me kinetically to develop an interest in film performance, because these practitioners were all especially concerned with duration as a key element of experimentation.

7. Carl Theodor Dreyer, *Dreyer in Double Reflection: Translation of Carl Th. Dreyer's Writings about the Film (Om Filmen),* ed. Donald Skoller (New York: E. P. Dutton, 1973), 50.

8. Bertolt Brecht, "A Short Organum for the Theatre" (1949), in *Brecht on Theatre,* ed. John Willett (New York: Hill and Wang and London: Eyre Methuen, 1964), 193.

9. These connections need to be worked on elsewhere. While Straub and Huillet's work directly acknowledges the influence of Brecht's, in the case of Bresson such influence is not clear. Their conceptions of art seem, in fact, quite opposed to each other. Rainer's first film, *Lives of Performers,* draws from the "New Dance" of which she was a pioneer in the sixties. This mode of dancing eschewed the use of dance for emotional expression and turned it into a task-oriented activity, influenced by developments in sculpture and the other visual arts which were breaking up the boundaries of previously hermetic fields. The performers in her film brought to it modes of performing which were cool and non-emotional. The tension in the film is between this mode of performing and the highly charged, melodramatic discourse of the voiceover and of the performers.

10. Aristotle, "Poetics," trans. Ingram Bywater, in *The Basic Works of Aristotle,* ed. Richard McKeon (New York: Random House, 1941), 1460, emphasis added. In order to appropriate the terminology and conceptions of performance implicit in Aristotle's formulation (which referred to the fortunes of great men) to a mundane, non-apocalyptic situation, as in *Jeanne Dielman,* one would have to talk of tasks rather than action. The sphere, after all, is domestic and the focus is on the female body, not the body politic. The

action in the film is certainly not of the magnitude which would satisfy Aristotle's definition of tragedy.

11. Quoted in Kinder, "Reflections," 8, emphasis added.

12. Susan Sontag, "Spiritual Style in the Films of Robert Bresson," in *Against Interpretation* (New York: Delta, 1966), 184.

13. Ibid., 181. This formulation problematizes Brecht's polemical formulations in his notes to the opera "The Rise and Fall of the City of Mahagonny." There he opposes "Feeling" to "Reason." Of course, Brecht himself modifies this opposition in his later "A Short Organum for the Theatre."

14. Jean-Luc Godard and Jean-Pierre Gorin, script of *Letter to Jane*, in *Women and Film*, 1.3–4 (1973), 50. On 10 August 1980, as I was writing this article, the Australian Broadcasting Corporation's TV program *Four Corners* telecast an interview with Paul Reutershan, a U.S. Vietnam war veteran. He was dying of cancer caused by Agent Orange, and perhaps because of heavy morphine sedation his face, seen in close-up, showed no pain as he narrated his involvement in the war, the way in which he and so many others came into contact with Agent Orange in the process of defoliating parts of Vietnam. It was as though he were quoting or cataloguing that pain which was both personal and historical. His voice, too, was non-expressive. The audience could understand the magnitude of that genocidal war because Paul Reutershan, unlike Jane Fonda, did not attempt to "distract" us with coded emotions which could not have spoken the crimes anyway. When we were shown a brief shot of Reutershan's coffin it said more, and said it more precisely, than Jane Fonda's profound look of compassion.

15. Godard and Gorin, script of *Letter to Jane*, 50.

16. Angela Martin, "Chantal Akerman's Films," 41.

17. Ibid.

18. A visual joke which fascinated me was the intermittent disappearance and appearance of one of the two white chairs in Jeanne's kitchen. This happened within the same sequence of shots as well as outside the sequence. The pleasure of noticing this reflexive joke (or bad continuity, according to the codes of Hollywood) took my attention away from Dielman/Seyrig's actions and also served to denaturalize the naturalistic mise en scène. It is interesting that Babette Mangolte was the cinematographer for both *Jeanne Dielman* and Yvonne Rainer's *Lives of Performers*. The way in which objects like chairs and tables are photographed in both films, within the overall structure, makes one attentive to these mundane objects which are usually devoured by the realist text.

19. *Hotel Monterey* is the most formal of Akerman's films I've seen. Here the performer is the camera, as it explores the numerous corridors and rooms of the hotel. There is a witty sequence where the camera goes up and down an elevator. When the door opens all we see are people moving hastily or uncer-

tainly out of sight of the "strange" presence (the camera's) in the elevator. The film drove many people out of the cinema and also elicited fascinating responses from the audience. Akerman seems to be interested in limiting herself to a few rhetorical devices, such as forward and back tracks, lateral tracks, and panning, in order to work with duration. The effect is to resensitize one's visual perception.

20. Kinder, "Reflections," 8. I think that here Seyrig is talking about a certain "performance of narcissism" (see chapter 3). My own theoretical interest in narcissism is relatively recent, and was preceded by a much earlier exploration of narcissism in a performance register. My performance piece with Jacob Burckhardt, *Work in Regress,* and the film version of it, *Works in Regress* (New York City, 1975, 16 mm, 15 min.), are about narcissistic self-reconstitution, among other things. Once I completed these works I had no desire to perform again in a formal sense, because they constituted something like a rite of passage.

21. Godard and Gorin refer to Fonda as a "function" of Hollywood in the script of *Letter to Jane,* 51.

22. See chapter 10 for an elaboration of sensory-motor action and what happens when it breaks down. Also see D. N. Rodowick, *Gilles Deleuze's Time Machine* (Durham and London: Duke University Press, 1997), 74–78, for a useful explication of the sensory-motor schema.

23. "Slip" here should be given the full psychoanalytic force of an unconscious pressure.

24. Melissa McMahon, "Fourth Person Singular: Becoming Ordinary and the Void in the Critical Body Filmic," in *Kiss Me Deadly: Feminism and Cinema for the Moment,* ed. Laleen Jayamanne (Sydney: Power Publications, 1995), 143.

25. Gilles Deleuze, *Cinema 2: The Time Image,* trans. Hugh Tomlinson and Robert Galeta (Minneapolis: University of Minnesota Press, 1989), 22. In montaging two of Bergson's concepts, vitalism and intuition, as "vital intuition," Deleuze highlights several processes by which the time image can capture forces and add dimensions to itself and thereby move beyond a simple formalist exercise of severing the sensory-motor mechanism and remaining at the level of cliché. I wish to thank Melissa McMahon for clarifying the Bergsonian concepts for me.

26. Gilles Deleuze, *Negotiations, 1972–1990/Gilles Deleuze,* trans. Martin Joughin (New York: Columbia University Press, 1995), 128. He uses this phrase while describing the political left's lack of access to information regarding institutional structures in New Caledonia. He says that the right had direct mediators working for them but the left needed parallel, supplementary channels —a different style of obtaining knowledge and thinking. I use the phrase here to highlight the doubled enunciation of time made possible by Dielman/ Seyrig.

12. *Life Is a Dream*

This chapter was written for the "Breath of Balsam: Reorienting Surrealism" conference convened by the Sydney Museum of Contemporary Art and the Humanities Research Centre, Canberra, June 1993. It was first published in *Kiss Me Deadly: Feminism and Cinema for the Moment,* ed. Laleen Jayamanne (Sydney: Power Publications, 1995).

1. In this paper I give a reading of two sequences in Raoul Ruiz's *Three Crowns of the Sailor* (1983). *Life Is a Dream* is a play by Calderon which Ruiz adapted in his 1986 film *Memory of Appearances.* He has said that "there is a way of using dreams and one of using memory. They are not the same, even though they are often confused. . . . Memory is a method/technique, machinery/mechanism. The mnemotechniques are linked completely by chance" (quoted in Christine Buci-Glucksman and Fabrice Revault d'Allonnes, *Raoul Ruiz* [Paris: Editions Dis Voir, Sarl, 1987], 103; unpublished translation by Marie Ramslands). Ruiz structured *Memory of Appearances* on the basis of this mnemotechnique, which was derived from Frances Yates's book *The Art of Memory.* Given the surrealist celebration of dreams, I want here to foreground Ruiz's concern with making a distinction between working with dream and with memory.

2. Quoted by Adrian Martin in "The Artificial Night: Surrealism and Cinema," in *Surrealism: Revolution by Night,* catalogue for an exhibition curated by Michel Lloyd et al. (Canberra: National Gallery of Australia, 1993), 190.

3. Raul Ruiz forum, Australian Film Institute, Sydney, 1993. The text of the forum was published as "Raoul Ruiz," *Agenda* 30–31 (May 1993); however, all quotations in this chapter are taken from a recording of it.

4. See "Who Is Raul Ruiz?" *Sydney Morning Herald,* 29 January 1993. The Australian Broadcasting Corporation's Radio National program *Screen* included an interview with Ruiz in its January 14th discussion of "Surrealism and Cinema." And a flier from the Australian Film Institute advertised a Ruiz retrospective with the line "The Films of Raul Ruiz: A Surreal Journey."

5. *Screen,* "Surrealism and Cinema."

6. The only exceptions I know of are Suzana M. Pick's "The Dialectical Wanderings of Exile," *Screen* 30.4 (fall 1989), 48–64; and Libby Ostinga's "Exile and Metamorphosis: The Magical Cinematic Practice of Raul Ruiz," B.A. honours thesis, Department of Art History and Theory, University of Sydney, 1992.

7. Susan Sontag, introduction to Walter Benjamin's *One-Way Street and Other Writings,* trans. Edmond Jephcott and Kingsley Shorter (London: New Left Books, 1979), 16–17.

8. It is curious that when modern allegory is theorized it is most often accom-

panied by an affect, namely melancholy. The conjoining of melancholy and allegory introduces a pathological dimension to this mode of signification. The pathology of melancholy is analyzed by Freud in his essay "Mourning and Melancholia" (1914–1916, in *The Standard Edition of the Psychological Works of Sigmund Freud,* trans. James Strachey, vol. 14 [London: Hogarth Press, 1986]), 243–60. As Strachey points out in his editor's note to the essay (239), Freud suggests that "there was a connection between melancholia and the oral stage of libidinal development" (249–50).

9. Walter Benjamin, *The Origin of German Tragic Drama,* trans. John Osborne (London: New Left Books, 1977), 185. Further references to this book (abbreviated to *Origin*) will be given in parentheses in the text.

10. Raul Ruiz forum.

11. Quoted in Sontag, introduction to *One-Way Street,* 20.

12. Ibid.

13. Raul Ruiz forum. Ruiz said that "enthusiasm" and the "ludic" are synonymous, much to my surprise. Interestingly, Freud in "Mourning and Melancholia" makes a connection between melancholy and mania (joy, exultation, triumph) (253–54). Perhaps something Italo Calvino has said in his essay "Lightness" may clarify the link that seemed so obvious to Ruiz. Calvino refers to "the special connection between melancholy and humor studied by Raymond Klibansky, Erwin Panofsky, and Fritz Saxl in *Saturn and Melancholy* (1964)" (*Six Memos for the Next Millennium* [Cambridge: Harvard University Press, 1988], 18). He clarifies this in the following: "As melancholy is sadness that has taken on lightness, so humour is comedy that has lost its bodily weight." The ludic as a species of the comic then is inextricably intermingled with melancholy. "Enthusiasm," which the ancients called "poetic inspiration," is here reinvented as a compound, "a veil of minute particles of humours and sensations, a fine dust of atoms" (20). The idea of melancholy humor feels right in relation to the kind of ludic register in which *Three Crowns of a Sailor* operates. This notion may also be useful in thinking the work of some of the great silent comedians, such as Buster Keaton.

14. Adrian Martin, "Artificial Night," 191.

15. Ibid.

16. Buci-Glucksman and Revault d'Allonnes, *Raoul Ruiz,* 103.

17. Adrian Martin, "Artificial Night," 193.

18. Raul Ruiz forum.

19. Adrian Martin, "Artificial Night," 195.

20. Raul Ruiz forum.

21. If allegorical bodies are fragmentary in structure then an allegorical figure is a part which is greater than the whole. I want to thank Jodi Brooks for pointing out this analogy between the fragmenting power of allegory and

the close-up and for reminding me of how this connects with Balazs's and Eisenstein's notions of the close-up.

22. Raoul Ruiz, "Interview with Raoul Ruiz," interview by Pascal Bonitzer and Serge Toubiana, *Cahiers du Cinema* 345 (March 1983), 9.

23. Raoul Ruiz, unpublished interview by Libby Ostinga, Sydney, 1993.

24. Michael Chanan, *Chilean Cinema* (London: British Film Institute, 1976), 32.

25. Ruiz, interview by Ostinga.

26. Buci-Glucksman and Revault d'Allonnes, *Raoul Ruiz*, 96–98.

27. Ruiz, interview by Ostinga.

28. Raul Ruiz forum.

29. Raul Ruiz, "The Cinema of Raul Ruiz," interview by Adrian Martin, *Cinema Papers* 91 (January 1993), 61. I am greatly indebted to Martin for having raised, in this interview, the issues of the baroque and allegorical aspects of Ruiz's cinema, perhaps for the first time in English.

30. Ibid., 35.

31. The notions of "exhaustion of the will to allegory" and the "affliction" of allegory or the compulsion to allegorize are related. They may be understood via the comparison Freud makes between mourning and melancholy, which I discussed in chapter 3. A mourner consciously knows what is lost, but the melancholic subject grieves at the loss of an object without knowing what is lost. According to Freud, "it is an object loss withdrawn from consciousness" ("Mourning," 245). Freud suggests that this loss causes a narcissistic disorder because the loss of the object also means a loss in regard to the ego because of the attendant amnesia; it is a double loss. The internal work of the melancholic, which Freud says is akin to that of the mourner, consumes the ego (243). This may be a reason for the "exhaustion" that marks the tenacious will to allegorize. There is here a correspondence (somewhat difficult to grasp) between the absent, forgotten object of the melancholic's grief and the positive power attributed to forgetting in the construction of allegory in Ruiz's film. Could this form of forgetting be called sublimation?

32. Recent Sri Lankan history is littered with such corpses, burnt on tires as emblems for the living to see and smell.

33. Freud, "Mourning." Strachey says, "The German 'Trauer,' like the English 'mourning,' can mean both the affect of grief and its outward manifestation" (243). In this section I am more interested in the theatrical dimension of public mourning, which no doubt has its own necessity and efficacy.

34. Buci-Glucksman and Revault d'Allonnes, *Raoul Ruiz*, 95.

35. Susan Buck-Morss, *The Dialectics of Seeing: Walter Benjamin and the Arcades Project* (Cambridge: MIT Press, 1991), 167.

36. Raul Ruiz, "Cinema, Prosthetics, and a Short History of Latin America,"

unpublished interview by Paul Garcia, David Bolliger, and Nick O'Sullivan, Sydney, 1993. Ruiz said in passing that the cinematic apparatus necessitates a critique of Bergson's idea of duration, because in every twenty-fourth fraction of a second there is a black space, a death, an instant of forgetting. This suggests the possibility of multiple beginnings. Benjamin's critique of Bergsonian duration could function here as an elaboration for Ruiz. See Walter Benjamin, "On Some Motifs in Baudelaire," in *Illuminations,* trans. Harry Zohn, ed. Hannah Arendt (Glasgow: Fontana, Collins, 1977), 187.

37.   Robert Mapplethorpe, *Lady, Lisa Lyon* (New York: Viking Press, 1983).

38.   The maxim as a rhetorical device is marked by an economy that can be linked to Ruiz's understanding of baroque visual economy. The idea of a "flash of light," as Jodi Brooks has pointed out to me, is a complex one in Benjamin's writing. Irving Wohlfarth relates this mode of involuntary perception to what Benjamin calls "presence of mind": "But presence of mind, as Benjamin conceives it, both collects itself and recollects the past in a flash too instantaneous to be called self-reflexive" (Irving Wohlfarth, "On the Messianic Structure of Walter Benjamin's Last Reflections," *GLYPH, Johns Hopkins Textual Studies 3,* ed. Samuel Weber and Henry Sussman [Baltimore: Johns Hopkins University Press, 1978], 164). So "the flash of light" seems to be a modality of involuntary memory.

39.   Buck-Morss, *Dialectics of Seeing,* 166.

40.   Angus Fletcher, *Allegory: The Theory of a Symbolic Mode* (Ithaca: Cornell University Press, 1982), 50.

41.   Raul Ruiz forum. Ruiz's description matches Erwin Panofsky's account of melancholy both as pathology and as a form of creativity (Raymond Klibansky, Erwin Panofsky, and Fritz Saxl, *Saturn and Melancholy* [London: Thomas Nelson, 1964], 17, 40, 41).

42.   It is necessary to sketch out what I understand by allegorical efficacy. Allegorical efficacy means that the melancholic temperament perceives transience, the flux of time and things, in a heightened way. It means that allegorical constructs are temporal forms imagined and willed in order to perceive, make tangible, the operations of time as incessant flow and decay, hence the privileged emblems of modern allegory are the corpse, the ruin, and the ghost. Perhaps an allegory is efficacious if it can provide an emblem that can make one play with time, wrest an "instant" to reflect on its inexorable movement. It is also efficacious if it can create a process whereby involuntary memory can be generated. In such a dynamic remembrance and forgetting would necessarily be related.

43.   It amazes me that the allegory of the femme fatale has been placed between two figures of the maternal and that by pursuing my fascination with this figure I inadvertently stumbled on the figure of the rented mother. There is a logic of fantasy here that is generative, seemingly inexhaustible. If the propensity to melancholy is connected with a disturbance of the oral function (as Freud says), then the maternal and the loss of the maternal must surely

figure prominently in this pathology. Ruiz has been able to sublimate (not repress) this loss via the melancholy humor of his film. Perhaps this is why there is no logic of a secret to be revealed in this film, despite its mystery and enchantment.

44. Ruiz, interview by Ostinga.

45. Benjamin, "The Image of Proust," in *Illuminations*, 204.

46. Wohlfarth, "Messianic Structure," 154.

47. The matrix of allegory, unlike that of the human embryo, would have to be a temporal form that can sustain incommensurable temporalities. Memory as imagined by both Benjamin and Ruiz is such an entity. Unlike Benjamin, however, Ruiz is able to imagine the maternal in a manner that is untouched by the oedipal.

48. Benjamin, "The Storyteller," in *Illuminations*, 97. See also Wohlfarth, "Messianic Structure," 150.

49. Gilbert Adair, "Raùl Sheheruizade, or 1001 Films," *Sight and Sound* 53.3 (summer 1984), 162.

50. Benjamin, "The Work of Art in the Age of Mechanical Reproduction," in *Illuminations*, 240.

51. Benjamin, "The Storyteller," in *Illuminations*, 98.

52. Gilles Deleuze, *Cinema 1: The Movement Image*, trans. Hugh Tomlinson and Barbara Habberjam (Minneapolis: University of Minnesota Press, 1986), 206. I read Ruiz's notion of "contamination of the gaseous" as equivalent to what Deleuze calls the "inflation of images both in the external world and in people's minds."

53. Wohlfarth, "Messianic Structure," 169. It is the center because the "isolated bourgeois subject is haunted by the loss of objective meaning."

54. Walter Benjamin, "Central Park," *New German Critique* 34 (1985), 40.

55. Wohlfarth, "Messianic Structure," 199. Wohlfarth also draws the analogy between voluntary and involuntary memory and the Freudian distinction between the conscious and the unconscious, where the latter is more like a forgetting from the perspective of the former.

56. Patricia Mellencamp, "Fairy Tales and Feminism: What Rapunzel, Cinderella, Snow White, et al. Forgot to Tell Thelma and Louise," in *Kiss Me Deadly: Feminism and Cinema for the Moment*, ed. Laleen Jayamanne (Sydney: Power Publications, 1995), 25.

57. Gilles Deleuze, *Cinema 2: The Time Image*, trans. Hugh Tomlinson and Robert Galeta (Minneapolis: University of Minnesota Press, 1989). Though Deleuze does not theorize allegorical or baroque temporality in his books on the cinema, one could combine his ideas about the time image with what Ruiz says about allegory to come up with a particular time image deriving from allegorical forms (i.e., temporal constructs), which is I think what I have done in this chapter. Ruiz also spoke about the importance of the

distinction between allegory and montage at the Sydney forum, saying that the movement of the former was centrifugal, while that of the latter was centripetal, but added that he had to think about it further. I have hardly touched on the mise en scène of the femme fatale sequence, but if I did, it would be necessary to work out how allegory relates to the structure of montage, which would also be a question about time. If according to Deleuze the time image is a sensory event before action takes hold of it, then allegories are endlessly open sensory events that seem to go on forever. This is, however, not the logic of interminable analysis familiar from psychoanalysis. I have a feeling that I can spend the rest of my professional life analyzing this film and yet not exhaust it.

58. Ronald Bogue explains Deleuze's idea of "incorporeal transformations" as deriving from both the Stoic idea of incorporeals and from Austin's speech-act theory (*Deleuze and Guattari* [London: Routledge, 1989], 137). According to Bogue, saying something is a way of doing something. The Stoics "recognise two simultaneous and coextensive readings of the universe, one in terms of bodies, causes and a perpetual present, the other in terms of incorporeals, surface effects, and a perpetually contracting and expanding past and future" (68). While words are bodies they have an incorporeal dimension, that of sense/meaning, that can haunt bodies, partly because of the peculiar temporal dimension within which they operate. It is the temporality encoded within the utterance that effects the incorporeal transformation in the sailor.

59. Julia Kristeva, *Desire in Language: A Semiotic Approach to Literature and Art*, ed. Leon S. Roudiez, trans. Thomas Gora, Alice Jardine, and Leon S. Roudiez (New York: Columbia University Press, 1980), 133, 174, 284, 286–87.

60. Women cannot experience difference through such a fiction, and without difference it would be impossible to begin the work of signification.

61. For Deleuze a "pure" sonic image is one that is separate from the visual image but reaches it at some moment in a manner to be deciphered.

13. A Slapstick Time

A version of this chapter was first delivered at "Caught in the Act," a conference on cinema and performance, University of New South Wales, 26 September 1996. A shorter version of it was published in *Falling for You: Essays on Cinema and Performance*, ed. Lesley Stern and George Kouvaros (Sydney: Power Publications, 1999). I wish to thank Miriam Hansen and Jodi Brooks for crucial conceptual assistance, and Lesley Stern and George Kouvaros for their excellent editorial work.

1. Theodor Adorno, "Twice Chaplin," quoted by Gertrude Koch in "Mimesis and Bilderverbot," *Screen* 34.3 (fall 1993), 214. While I have preferred to use Koch's translation, a complete translation of Adorno's essay by John MacKay

was published as "Chaplin Times Two," *Yale Journal of Criticism* 9.1 (1996), 57–61. Adorno, unlike Siegfried Kracauer and Walter Benjamin, had reservations about Chaplin's work as mass art, which he expressed in a letter to Walter Benjamin in 1936 (Ernst Bloch et al., *Aesthetics and Politics: Debates between Bloch, Lukacs, Brecht, Benjamin, and Adorno,* ed. and trans. Ronald Taylor [London: Verso, 1980], 123–24). But John MacKay says, "Like his associates Walter Benjamin and Siegfried Kracauer, Adorno was a great admirer of the screen's most celebrated comedian: Charlie Chaplin" ("Chaplin Times Two," 57). Perhaps he has not taken account of Adorno's views while in Germany. Certainly in Adorno's essay "Chaplin in Malibu" (written during his exile in California, 1941–49, after meeting Chaplin at a dinner party in Malibu) there is a most wonderful kinetic perception of the violent mimetic energy animating Chaplin. Adorno wrote the essay to celebrate Chaplin's seventy-fifth birthday and also to remember Chaplin's instant mimetic replay of a gaffe of Adorno's, which he felt privileged to observe and account for thus: "All the laughter he brings about is so near to cruelty; solely in such proximity to cruelty does it find its legitimation and its element of the salvational" ("Chaplin Times Two," 60–61).

2. Gilles Deleuze, *Cinema 2: The Time Image,* trans. Hugh Tomlinson and Robert Galeta (Minneapolis: University of Minnesota Press, 1989), 203.

3. Several of the articles in *Cinema and the Invention of Modern Life,* ed. Leo Charney and Vanessa R. Schwartz (Berkeley: University of California Press, 1995), help to formulate the relationship of cinema to modernity in this way. Leo Charney's "In a Moment: Film and the Philosophy of Modernity" (279–94) and Ben Singer's "Modernity, Hyperstimulus, and the Rise of Popular Sensationalism" (72–99) have been particularly helpful to me.

4. Walter Benjamin, "On the Mimetic Faculty," in *Reflections: Essays, Aphorisms, Autobiographical Writing,* trans. Edmund Jephcott (New York: Schocken, 1978), 333–34. My essay also uses fragments of Siegfried Kracauer's early writing on American slapstick as found in Miriam Hansen's introduction to *Theory of Film: The Redemption of Physical Reality,* by Siegfried Kracauer (Princeton: Princeton University Press, 1997); and Theodor Adorno, *Aesthetic Theory,* trans. Robert Hullot-Kentor (London: Athlone Press, 1997); Theodor Adorno and Max Horkheimer, *Dialectic of Enlightenment,* trans. John Cumming (London and New York: Verso, 1986).

5. Adorno and Horkheimer, *Dialectic,* 31.

6. Gunter Gebauer and Christoph Wulf, *Mimesis: Culture, Art, Society,* trans. Don Reneau (Berkeley: University of California Press, 1992), 5, 3. This book provides an excellent analytic history of this concept across divergent western traditions of thought and practice.

7. Susan Buck-Morss, *The Dialectics of Seeing: Walter Benjamin and the Arcades Project* (Cambridge: MIT Press, 1989), 269; Adorno, *Aesthetic Theory;* Kracauer, *Theory of Film.*

8. Chaplin's bad timing in *The Circus*, i.e., doing the gags either too soon or too late (the source of his marketability within the narrative), is linked to his anachronism, which makes him a utopian figure.

9. Deleuze, *Cinema 2*, 203.

10. Gilles Deleuze, *Cinema 1: The Movement Image*, trans. Hugh Tomlinson and Barbara Habberjam (Minneapolis: University of Minnesota Press, 1986).

11. See Deleuze, *Cinema 2*, 64–67, for his periodization of American slapstick comedy into four stages.

12. This symposium was convened by Eileen Bowser at the Museum of Modern Art, New York, 1985, and she edited its proceedings as *The Slapstick Symposium* (Brussels: Federation International des Archives du Film, 1988). See Peter Kramer's report on another major event on slapstick, the 1987 Pordenone Festival of Silent Film: "Vitagraph, Slapstick, and Early Cinema," *Screen* 29.2 (spring 1988), 98–104.

13. Donald Crafton, "Pie and Chase: Gag, Spectacle, and Narrative in Slapstick Comedy," in *Classical Hollywood Comedy*, ed. Kristine Brunovska Karnick and Henry Jenkins (New York and London: Routledge, 1995), 119. I have had access to only the English-language writing on slapstick.

14. A recent book on Chaplin's American reception that I find very informative is Charles J. Maland, *Chaplin and American Culture: The Evolution of a Star Image* (Princeton: Princeton University Press, 1989).

15. Noel Carroll, "Notes on Sight Gag," in *Comedy/Cinema/Theory*, ed. Andrew S. Horton (Berkeley: University of California Press, 1991), 25–42.

16. Ibid., 38.

17. Carroll's and Stewart's are but two examples from a vast field of scholarship which, as this is not a polemical paper, I am not engaging with explicitly. In this note I will cite and very briefly comment on a small selection of major texts on silent slapstick comedy that work more or less within the terms outlined above and have helped me to define my own project here. Chapter 8 of Walter Kerr's *The Silent Clowns* (New York: Da Capo Press, 1980) is called "Chaplin: Playfulness Unleashed." This chapter has some nice descriptions of the dynamic of movement in some gags and thematic plot summaries but does not explore the idea of playfulness, merely taking the sense of the term for granted. Gerald Mast's *The Comic Mind: Comedy and the Movies*, 2nd ed. (Chicago: University of Chicago Press, 1979), 112, has a paragraph on the famous assembly-line gag from *Modern Times* (which I discuss later on in this essay) in which he maintains the distinction between the mechanical and the human in Chaplin's performance, whereas in my descriptive analysis this very distinction is shown being obliterated through mimetic play. I further go on to work out what is at stake in such an obliteration. Chapter 4 of William Paul's *Laughing, Screaming: Modern Hollywood Horror and Comedy* (New York: Columbia University Press, 1994) deals with the vulgarity in

Chaplin's *City Lights* and links it to the great Aristophanic tradition of obscenity central to robust comedy. While this is a refreshing change from the way Chaplin is often distinguished from the so-called crude tradition of earlier slapstick comedy (such as Sennett's) by being designated a dancer, I am more interested in the violence of rhythm and speed in his performance of slapstick gags than in either the dance or the vulgar aspects, because of their power to metamorphose. "The Dancer" is the title of chapter 7, on Chaplin, in Dan Kamin's *Charlie Chaplin's One-Man Show*, 2nd ed. (Carbondale and Edwardsville: Southern Illinois University Press, 1991). Here Kamin (who is a professional mime artist himself) constructs an intricate map of the rhythmic modulations of Chaplin's performance, drawing an analogy between Chaplin and the ballet dancer. The chapter concludes, "To view life in all its aspects as dance is more than childish play—it is divine play." My paper is interested in the more mundane image of childish play understood as mimetic. It is not that I am against thematic readings, but that they have to be arrived at by apprehending the multiplicity of movements of a film, not just those of the narrative.

18. Deleuze, *Cinema 2*, chapter 4.

19. Gilles Deleuze, *Bergsonism*, trans. Hugh Tomlinson and Barbara Habberjam (New York: Zone Books, 1988), 59.

20. Buck-Morss, *Dialectics of Seeing*, 263. See 260–65 for an extended discussion of the manifestation of mimesis in child's play. Benjamin's work (both practical and theoretical) on child's play as a mimetic activity is extensive, but I have had access only to the few scattered fragments translated in Buck-Morss.

21. Benjamin, "On the Mimetic Faculty," 333.

22. Ibid.

23. According to Deleuze, the sensory-motor link is that by which the three varieties of the movement image—perception image, affection image, and action image—are coordinated in a smooth operation (*Cinema 1*, 155). It is of interest that Deleuze uses terms from neurophysiology to conceptualize the operations of cinematic images. In fact, he suggests that it may be more productive to think cinematic relations in conjunction with the current research into brain function than with linguistics. There is a link here between the interest of early theorists of modernity in developing a neurological theory of modernity and Deleuze's passing comment.

24. Benjamin, "On the Mimetic Faculty." Also see his "The Doctrine of the Similar," *New German Critique* 17 (spring 1979), 65–69, which was the earlier of the two articles.

25. Benjamin, "On the Mimetic Faculty," 335. It is interesting that Benjamin says that the "rapidity" of writing and reading enables or heightens "the fusion of the semiotic and the mimetic in the sphere of language" ("On the

Mimetic Faculty," 335–36). The differential speeds of the child-clown are, I think, essential to the mimetic performance of an object.

26. Deleuze, *Cinema 2*, 20.

27. This marvelous reading of the image is offered by Garrett Stewart, "Modern Hard Times: Chaplin and the Cinema of Self-Reflection," *Critical Inquiry* 3.2 (winter 1976), 295–314.

28. Ibid., 313.

29. Gilles Deleuze, *The Logic of Sense*, trans. Mark Lester with Charles Stivale (New York: Columbia University Press, 1990), 61–62. Further references to this book (abbreviated to *Logic*) will be given in parentheses in the text. When quotations are sufficiently located only a page number will be given.

30. Michel de Certeau, *The Practice of Everyday Life*, trans. Steven Rendall (Berkeley: University of California Press, 1984), 34.

31. Ibid., 38.

32. Deleuze, *Cinema 2*, 102–22.

33. Giorgio Agamben, "In Playland: Reflections on History and Play," in *Infancy and History: Essays on the Destruction of Experience*, trans. Liz Heron (London and New York: Verso, 1993), 67–87.

34. Ibid., 71.

35. Hansen, introduction to Kracauer's *Theory*, xxii.

36. Agamben, "In Playland," 73–74.

37. Agamben says, "It does not then seem irrelevant that in a fragment of Heraclitus—that is to say, at the origin of European thought—*aion*, time in its original sense, should figure as a 'child playing with dice,' and that 'domain of the baby' should define the scope of this play. . . . Along with *aion*, to indicate time the Greek language also conceives the term *chronos*. . . . In a famous passage in the *Timaeus*, Plato presents the relationship between *chronos* and *aion* as a relationship of copy and model, of cyclical time measured by the movements of the stars and motionless, synchronic temporality. What interests us here is not so much that in the process of a still living translation *aion* should be identified with eternity and *chronos* with diachronic time as that our culture should conceive from its origins a split between two different, correlated and opposed notions of time" ("In Playland," 73). The particular way in which Deleuze theorizes this split is most useful for thinking the temporality of the mimetically activated slapstick body. Agamben simply refers the concept to Greek philosophy without making a distinction between the pre-Socratic Heraclitus and Plato. In doing so he makes Aion a category of Being, whereas for Deleuze, who is concerned with the development of concepts by which to formulate a philosophy of Becoming, Aion is reformulated as the temporal embodiment of this process.

38. Ibid., 74.

39. The capacity to make correspondences in a Benjaminian "flash" is the kind

of mimetic memory at issue here. It would therefore have to be an operation of involuntary memory.

40. Deleuze, *Cinema 1*, 169–77.

41. One might ask why this tradition of slapstick came to an end. One obvious answer is the diminishing popularity of vaudeville, which was the training school for the slapstick comedians. Once this theatrical form died out, the mime and acrobatic skills it deployed also died. The coming of sound is the other reason. One may also speculate about a historically conditioned form of male subjectivity that the male slapstick tradition brought into being. Even as I say this, the mimetic image of Chaplin pops up in a way that makes gender not a foundational category at least for him, in his mimetic rather than narrative moments. I wish to thank Jodi Brooks for the phrase "the melancholy of slapstick," which has helped me formulate this section of the paper, and also for helping to clarify the issue of gender and slapstick.

I have briefly traced how the exhausted American slapstick tradition has been resurrected in and translated into the Hong Kong slapstick-kung fu cinema of Jackie Chan in "Above and beyond One's 'Cultural Heritage': Jackie Chan and His *Drunken Master*," in *ABOVE AND BEYOND: Austral/Asian Interactions,* Australian Centre for Contemporary Art, Melbourne and Institute of Modern Art, Brisbane, 1996, 12–16. I wish to thank Meaghan Morris for asking me, "What happened to silent slapstick?" and for introducing me to the work of Jackie Chan. Now, with the digital special effects of a film like *Matrix* (1999) available, one might indeed ask what is happening to the Jackie Chan tradition of kung fu; its days seem numbered, when actors can "do" kung fu (thanks to technology) without a lifetime of training.

42. Stanley Cavell, *Pursuits of Happiness: The Hollywood Comedy of Remarriage* (Cambridge: Harvard University Press, 1981), chapter 1.

43. Adorno and Horkheimer, *Dialectic*, 183.

44. See Henry Jenkins, "The Laughing Stock of the City: Performance Anxiety, Male Dread, and *Unfaithfully Yours,*" in *Classical Hollywood Comedy* (New York and London: Routledge, 1995), ed. Kristine Brunovska Karnick and Henry Jenkins, 238–61, for an encapsulation of this criticism. In this essay Jenkins reads the predicament of Sir Alfred as an instance of "male dread" but does not deal with the temporal aspects of the slapstick scene.

45. Michael Taussig has eloquently shown how the technologies of mass reproduction are mimetically capacious machines by relocating them within the colonial encounter, in his *Mimesis and Alterity: A Particular History of the Senses* (New York and London: Routledge, 1993). In chapter 14, "The Talking Machine," Taussig demonstrates to us the intimate relationship of the phonograph to the history of colonialism and the link between primitivism and the magic of recorded sound. He reminds us that the major early sound-recording companies had animals as their mascots: the dog of "His Master's Voice" and the cock of the brothers Pathé. This link made between the

animal (first nature) and the technological (second nature) is, according to Taussig, mimetic (magical), exemplifying imitation and sensuous contact as two integral components of mimetic behavior.

46. This phrase "degree zero" is mine, but it accords with Adorno and Horkheimer's description of mimicry as a defense against fear: "the reflexes of stiffening and numbness in humans are archaic schemata of the urge to survive: by adaptation to death, life plays the toll of its continued existence" (Adorno and Horkheimer, *Dialectic*, 180). There is a scene in *The Circus* where Chaplin, escaping from the hall of mirrors pursued by the cop, is confronted by another just outside. Swiftly, he freezes, becoming an inanimate, human-sized, mechanized puppet who moves his limbs to a stiff mechanical rhythm and emits a mechanized series of laughs. Just then the real thief runs out and joins Chaplin, at his instigation, to avoid arrest. The two thieves, the actual and the virtual, now perform a duet as mechanized puppets while the cops scratch their heads, wondering how the thieves got away. The routine consists of Chaplin rhythmically beating the real thief's head with a baton and then laughing in a measured, mechanical manner at the action. This is an exemplary performance of the mimetic assimilation of the organic into the non-organic so as to survive, except that the real thief can only take so many knocks on his head before he falls down, at which sign of life the cops realize what has happened and the chase resumes.

47. Adorno, *Aesthetic Theory*, 331.

48. Adorno, *Aesthetic Theory*, xx. Robert Hullot-Kentor, the translator of the 1997 edition, says in his introduction that leftist students who at first embraced Adorno's work rioted in his seminars because of his refusal to lead them to the barricades in 1969. Instead, in the brief time left to him, he worked on *Aesthetic Theory*, which was published posthumously.

14. "Eyes in the Back of Your Head"

Meaghan Morris helped me to emerge from the thickets of theory and formulate my problem precisely; I am most grateful for her reliable mentorship.

1. This admonition is addressed to Megan Turner (the rookie cop played by Jamie Lee Curtis in Kathryn Bigelow's *Blue Steel*) by her superior officer when she screws up a training session and is "shot dead."

2. See the work of Australian writers such as Jodi Brooks, "Consumed by Cinematic Monstrosity," *Art and Text* 34 (1989), 79–94; Lesley Stern, *The Scorsese Connection* (Bloomington: Indiana University Press and London: British Film Institute, 1995); Adrian Martin, *Once upon a Time in America* (London: British Film Institute, 1998); Lesley Stern and George Kouvaros, eds., *Falling for You: Essays on Cinema and Performance* (Sydney: Power Publications, 1999). For me this move has been made possible by Gilles Deleuze's *Cinema 1: The Movement Image*, trans. Hugh Tomlinson and Barbara Habberjam

(Minneapolis: University of Minnesota Press, 1986), and *Cinema 2: The Time Image,* trans. Hugh Tomlinson and Robert Galeta (Minneapolis: University of Minnesota Press, 1989). Further references to the latter two books (abbreviated to *C1* and *C2*) will be given in parentheses in the text.

3. See Miriam Hansen, "The Future of Cinema Studies in the Age of Global Media: Aesthetics, Spectatorship, and Public Spheres—Interview with Miriam Hansen," interview by Laleen Jayamanne and Anne Rutherford, *UTS Review* 5.1 (May 1999), 94–110.

4. *Blue Steel* has been approached in several different ways by critics. Anna Powell's "Blood on the Borders: *Near Dark* and *Blue Steel*" (*Screen* 35.2 [summer 1994], 136–56) is a narrative analysis of *Blue Steel* in terms of positive versus negative themes but does not consider the color field in which they transpire. Needeya Islam's "'I Wanted to Shoot People': Genre, Gender, and Action in the Films of Kathryn Bigelow," in *Kiss Me Deadly: Feminism and Cinema for the Moment,* ed. Laleen Jayamanne (Sydney: Power Publications, 1995), 91–125, also offers a reading of the narrative but foregrounds questions of female authorship, agency, and genre as well as questions of rhythm. I am grateful to Islam for introducing me to the work of Bigelow and for her enthusiasm for it. Steven Shaviro, in his book *The Cinematic Body* (Minneapolis: University of Minnesota Press, 1993), offers a description and analysis of the work of color and light in this film and how they relate to a masochistic scenario. I use his description as a point of departure for my reading of the film. Yvonne Tasker's *Spectacular Bodies: Gender, Genre, and the Action Cinema* (London and New York: Routledge, 1993) devotes its final chapter to Bigelow's work. While some of my insights, such as the doubling of the hero and villain, are similar to hers, our critical methods are different in that I am interested in the temporality of the image and come at the category of gender via the filmic. While Tasker refers to the female agent of action as a heroine, I prefer to use the phrase *female hero* because the structural connotations of the term *heroine* make the woman named by it a figure in need of rescue, while agency is synonymous with the hero function. Also, the coupling *female hero* feels more "muscular" than *heroine,* reminding us of the work required to bring the two terms into conjunction.

5. Henri Bergson, *Matter and Memory,* trans. Nancy Margaret Paul and W. Scott Palmer (New York: Zone Books, 1991); Gilles Deleuze, *Bergsonism,* trans. Hugh Tomlinson and Barbara Habberjam (New York: Zone Books, 1988).

6. "Memory-work," like Freud's dream-work, is efficacious, and part of my task is to specify how memory works in these films and to what end.

7. Deleuze, *Cinema 2,* 4. The context is a description of Italian neorealism and the full sentence is "It is as if the action floats in the situation, rather than bringing it to a conclusion or strengthening it."

8. Shaviro, *Cinematic Body*, 2, 3.

9. I derive this reading of the sequence by using concepts from chapters 4 to 9 of Deleuze, *Cinema 1*.

10. Deleuze, *Cinema 1*, chapter 8, on the impulse image, has helped generate this analysis. Pursuing the logic of the impulse seems more generative with regard to this film than starting with the category of gender. I wish to thank Karen Hurley for her reading of the sequence in *Thelma and Louise* of Louise's shooting Harlan, the rapist, as an impulse image rather than an action image. Such a reading complicates the understanding of gender and violence, for the violence of the impulse is different from the violence of sensory-motor action. It seems to me that there is an affinity between Turner and Louise in that both are animated by impulse at first, though the protocols of professional conduct frame and constrain Turner's behavior.

11. Carol J. Clover, *Men, Women, and Chain Saws: Gender in the Modern Horror Film* (Princeton: Princeton University Press, 1992), 35–41. Clover coins the phrase "last girl" and discusses her agency as the killer of the monster and survivor of horror.

12. See Bergson, *Matter*, chapter 3: "Of The Survival of Images: Memory and Mind." Bergson shows via his image of the memory cone how the past is preserved in duration or memory in a virtual state and how it can be activated or actualized in the present, for the present, through processes of translation and rotation. This image of the cone of time and its modalities of operation is certainly very cinematic, and Deleuze draws these modalities out in relation to the cinematic flashback as a recollection-image and also more modernist disjunctions of time in cinema.

13. I use the concept of the recollection image as flashback from chapter 3 and the idea of the falsifying power of memory from chapter 6 of Deleuze, *Cinema 2*. In *Bergsonism*, Deleuze makes the point that for Bergson "[d]uration is essentially memory, consciousness and freedom" (51). Memory is freedom because it has the power to play with chronological time, which is subservient to movement. Non-chronological time "produces movements necessarily 'abnormal', essentially 'false'" (Deleuze, *Cinema 2*, 129). For Deleuze the recollection-image is a rather feeble mechanism for activating non-chronological time (optical and sound images), because it feeds into the sensory-motor schema, but I am interested in it as a mechanism of charging action with affect.

14. A definition of "zone" in the Shorter Oxford English Dictionary works well here for my purpose of seeing how space may be temporalized: "A limited area distinguished from those adjacent by some quality or condition."

15. I have used insights from Gilles Deleuze, *Francis Bacon: The Logic of Sensation*, trans. Daniel Smith (unpublished), in trying to think of color as an expression of a duration through rhythm. A fragment from *Francis Bacon* is in Deleuze's "Painting and Sensation," in *The Deleuze Reader*, ed.

Constantin V. Boundas (New York: Columbia University Press, 1993), 187–92. Dana Polan's "Francis Bacon: The Logic of Sensation," in *Gilles Deleuze and the Theater of Philosophy*, ed. Constantin V. Boundas and Dorothy Olkowski (New York: Routledge, 1994), 229–54, has been very useful for understanding Deleuze's thoughts on color.

16. Deleuze, *Cinema 1*, 132–33, "The order of impulses" is time as destiny. Deleuze makes an important distinction between an "open repetition" and a "closed repetition," which is useful in thinking the two flashback sequences as well.

17. Deleuze, *Cinema 1*, chapter 6: "The Affection Image: Face and Close-Up" has been useful in thinking the face of the hero in close-up.

18. An American student told me this anecdote, which he had heard or read.

19. So it is fitting that the very first credits are "Lightning Pictures in association with Precision Films."

20. "Peirce does not conceal the fact that firstness is difficult to define, because it is felt, rather than conceived: it concerns what is new in experience, what is fresh, fleeting and nevertheless eternal" (Deleuze, *Cinema 1*, 98).

21. Bruce Robbins, "Murder and Mentorship: Advancement in *The Silence of the Lambs*," *UTS Review* 1.1 (1995), 30–49. Most of the work on this film within cinema studies has focused on the problematic of female sexuality, and in this context Robbins's refocusing on the film from a cultural studies perspective is, I think, hugely enabling.

22. "The multifarious nuances of the sense of smell embody the archetypal longing for the lower forms of existence, for direct unification with circumambient nature, with the earth and mud. Of all the senses, that of smell— which is attracted without objectifying—bears clearest witness to the urge to lose oneself in and become the "other." . . . When we see we remain what we are; but when we smell we are taken over by otherness. Hence the sense of smell is considered a disgrace in civilization, the sign of lower social strata, lesser races and base animals" (Theodor Adorno and Max Horkheimer, *Dialectic of Enlightenment*, trans. John Cumming [London and New York: Verso, 1986], 184).

While both Lecter and Miggs do manage to objectify Starling (in both sexual and class terms) through a display of their olfactory prowess, there is a sense in which smell demonstrates that knowledge is mimetically acquired through all the senses, even the most mediated.

15. *Do the Right Thing*

This chapter was presented at "Cinema and the Senses: Visual Culture and Spectatorship," a conference at the University of New South Wales, 15 November 1989. It is about to appear as "Forty Acres and a Mule Filmworks"— *Do the Right Thing*—"A Spike Lee Joint": Blocking and Unblocking the

Block" in *Micropolitics of Media Culture: Reading the Rhizomes of Deleuze and Guattari,* ed. Patricia Pisters (Amsterdam: Amsterdam University Press, 2001).

1. Spike Lee, with Lisa Jones, *Do the Right Thing: A Spike Lee Joint* (New York: Fireside, 1989), 29.

2. Meaghan Morris, "Crazy Talk Is Not Enough," *Planning D: Society and Space* 14.4, special issue on Deleuze and Dwelling (1996), 386.

3. Gilles Deleuze and Felix Guattari, *A Thousand Plateaus: Capitalism and Schizophrenia,* trans. Brian Massumi (Minneapolis: University of Minnesota Press, 1988), 348. Further references to this book (abbreviated to *TP*) will be given in parentheses in the text.

4. My thanks to Melissa McMahon for sharing her perception with me.

5. Lee and Jones, *Right Thing,* 55–56.

6. A favorable article on the film is W. J. T. Mitchell's "The Violence of Public Art: *Do The Right Thing,*" *Critical Inquiry* 16 (summer 1990), 880–99, and a hostile one is a response to it by Jerome Christensen, "Spike Lee, Corporate Populist," *Critical Inquiry* 17 (fall 1991), 582–95. Mitchell cites several of the most significant hostile reviews and discusses the way the film moved from its commercial public sphere into that of culture-debating public art as a result of its controversial public reception. See *Spike Lee's* Do The Right Thing, ed. Mark A. Reid (Cambridge: Cambridge University Press, 1997), a collection of essays on the film.

7. Toni Morrison, interview by Jana Wendt, *Uncensored,* Australian Broadcasting Corporation, 16 September 1998.

8. Lee and Jones, *Right Thing,* 31. Lee is discussing his difficulties with the Hollywood studios, but the remark can also be read as expressing his desire to construct a dwelling with aesthetic means.

9. It is rare to find critical writing that deals with Spike Lee's cinematic antecedents, which must surely include Mack Sennett and Godard, among others. Sharon Willis says that white liberals tend to see Lee as a "delegate speaking for a whole population" (*High Contrast: Race and Gender in Contemporary Hollywood Film* [Durham: Duke University Press, 1998], 167). What this tendency occludes is precisely aesthetic play, which does not obey the rules of discursive polemics.

10. Ronald Bogue, "Rhizomusicosmology," *Substance* 66 (1991), 88. Further references to this article (abbreviated to "Rhizo") will be given in parentheses in the text.

11. Morris, "Crazy Talk." I have found this article also indispensable in understanding how "1837: Of the Refrain" relates to other plateaus in the book and how it might contribute to feminist work on temporality and action.

12. Tricia Rose, *Black Noise: Rap Music and Black Culture in Contemporary America* (Hanover and London: Wesleyan University Press, 1994). I have

found the cultural history of hip-hop in this book indispensable to understanding *Do the Right Thing*. According to Rose, "Rap music is a black cultural expression that prioritized black voices from the margins of urban America. Rap music is a form of rhymed storytelling accompanied by highly rhythmic, electronically based music. It began in the mid-1970s in the South Bronx, in New York City, as part of hip-hop, an African-American and Afro-Caribbean youth culture composed of graffiti, break dancing and rap music. Rappers speak with the voice of personal experience, taking on the identity of the observer or narrator" (4).

13.   Ibid.

14.   See Barbara Jean Field's "Slavery, Race, and Ideology in the United States," *New Left Review* 181 (1990), 95–119, for an account of the history and ideology of American racism. In such a sociological and historical context Lee's cross-cultural efforts are, I think, exemplary in their imaginative daring and generosity and their biting, disarming humor.

15.   I wish to thank Brian Rutnam for this formulation and for helping me understand two things about Messiaen's musical theory at around three o'clock in the morning on 15 November 1998.

16.   Morris, "Crazy Talk," 387. She comments perceptively on the importance of the moments of impeded flows and the fragility of the movement outward by also discussing P. J. Hogan's *Muriel's Wedding*.

17.   These are the terms of Kafka's impossibility, though under different circumstances, as spelled out by Deleuze and Guattari in *Kafka: Towards a Minor Literature*, trans. Dana Polan (Minneapolis: University of Minnesota Press, 1986), 16.

18.   Hepburn and Tracy, a prickly couple on screen and lovers off, come to mind as I think of African-American exclusion and Hollywood.

19.   According to Lee, "Universal's main concern . . . was the ending. Was it too open-ended? How would audiences feel leaving the theater? Will Blacks want to go on a rampage? Will whites feel uncomfortable?" (Lee and Jones, *Right Thing*, 281). See *Rush Hour* (dir. Brett Ratner, 1998), with Jackie Chan and Chris Tucker, for more elaborate, virtuoso, mimetic, cross-cultural moves, starring the Mandarin kung fu tradition infused with American slapstick, on the one hand, and contemporary African-American dance moves with hip-hop street origins, on the other.

Works Cited

Adair, Gilbert. "Raùl Sheheruizade, or 10001 Films." *Sight and Sound* 53.3 (summer 1984), 162–64.

Adorno, Theodor. "The Actuality of Philosophy." *Telos* 31 (spring 1977), 120–33.

———. *Aesthetic Theory.* Trans. Robert Hullot-Kentor. London: Athlone Press, 1997.

———. "Chaplin Times Two." Trans. John MacKay. *Yale Journal of Criticism* 9.1 (1996), 57–61.

Adorno, Theodor, and Max Horkheimer. *Dialectic of Enlightenment.* Trans. John Cumming. London and New York: Verso, 1986.

Agamben, Giorgio. "In Playland: Reflections on History and Play." In *Infancy and History: Essays on the Destruction of Experience,* trans. Liz Heron, 67–87. London and New York: Verso, 1993.

Aiyer, K. "On Melodrama." In *Filmfare,* ed. K. Aiyer, 9–15. Bombay: Vikas, 1967.

Ansara, Martha. "A Man's World." In *The Filmmaker and the Prostitute: Dennis O'Rourke's* The Good Woman of Bangkok, ed. Chris Berry, Annette Hamilton, and Laleen Jayamanne, 21–24. Sydney: Power Publications, 1997.

Aristotle. *Poetics.* Trans. Ingram Bywater. In Richard McKeon, ed., *The Basic Works of Aristotle.* New York: Random House, 1941.

Barthes, Roland. *Image, Music, Text.* Trans. Stephen Heath. Glasgow: Fontana, Collins, 1977.

Batchen, Geoff. "Complicities." In *ARTFUL,* published by the Student Association of the College of Fine Arts, University of New South Wales (October 1990), unpaginated.

Bazin, André. "The Evolution of the Language of Cinema." In *What Is Cinema?* vol. 1, trans. Hugh Gray, 23–40. Berkeley: University of California Press, 1967.

———. "The Ontology of the Photographic Image." In *What Is Cinema?* vol. 1, trans. Hugh Gray, 9–16. Berkeley: University of California Press, 1967.

———. *What Is Cinema?* Vol. 2. Trans. Hugh Gray. Berkeley: University of California Press, 1971.

Benjamin, Walter. "Central Park." *New German Critique* 34 (1985), 32–58.

———. "The Doctrine of the Similar." *New German Critique* 17 (spring 1979), 65–69.

———. *Illuminations.* Trans. Harry Zohn. Ed. Hannah Arendt. Glasgow: Fontana, Collins, 1977.

———. "On the Mimetic Faculty." In *Reflections: Essays, Aphorisms, Autobiographical Writing,* trans. Edmund Jephcott, 333–36. New York: Schocken, 1978.

———. *The Origin of German Tragic Drama.* Trans. John Osborne. London: New Left Books, 1977.

Bergson, Henri. *Matter and Memory.* Trans. Nancy Margaret Paul and W. Scott Palmer. New York: Zone Books, 1991.

Bilbrough, Miro. "Crafting *The Piano.*" *Object* 12 (summer 1994), 36–38.

Bloch, Ernst, et al. *Aesthetics and Politics: Debates between Bloch, Lukacs, Brecht, Benjamin, and Adorno.* Ed. and trans. Ronald Taylor. London: Verso, 1980.

Bogue, Ronald. *Deleuze and Guattari.* London: Routledge, 1989.

———. "Rhizomusicosmology." *Substance* 66 (1991), 85–101.

———, ed. *Mimesis in Contemporary Theory: An Interdisciplinary Approach.* Vol. 2, *Mimesis, Semiosis, and Power.* Philadelphia and Amsterdam: John Benjamins, 1991.

Bowser, Eileen. *The Slapstick Symposium.* Brussels: Federation International des Archives du Film, 1988.

Brecht, Bertolt. "A Short Organum for the Theatre." 1949. In *Brecht on Theatre,* ed. John Willett, 179–205. New York: Hill and Wang and London: Eyre Methuen, 1964.

Bronte, Emily. *Wuthering Heights.* Edinburgh: Thornton, 1911.

Brooks, Jodi. "Consumed by Cinematic Monstrosity." *Art and Text* 34 (1989), 79–94.

Brooks, Peter. *The Melodramatic Imagination: Balzac, Henry James, Melodrama, and the Mode of Excess.* New Haven: Yale University Press, 1976.

Bruzzi, Stella. "Bodyscape." *Sight and Sound* 3.10 (October 1993), 7–8.

Buci-Glucksman, Christine, and Fabrice Revault d'Allonnes. *Raoul Ruiz.* Paris: Editions Dis Voir, Sarl, 1987, unpublished translation by Marie Ramslands.

Buck-Morss, Susan. *The Dialectics of Seeing: Walter Benjamin and the Arcades Project.* Cambridge: MIT Press, 1989.

———. *The Origin of Negative Dialectics: Theodor W. Adorno, Walter Benjamin, and the Frankfurt Institute.* Sussex: The Harvester Press, 1977.

Burke, Edmund. *The Sublime and the Beautiful.* New York: P. F. Collier and Son, 1969.

Burn, Ian, and Ann Stephen. "Traditional Painter: The Transfiguration of Albert Namatjira." *Age Monthly Review* 6 (7 November 1986), 11–14.

Butler, Rex. "Speaking of *Ceylon.*" *Frogger* 19 (November 1985), 1–9.

Calvino, Italo. *Six Memos for the Next Millennium.* Cambridge: Harvard University Press, 1988.

Campion, Jane. *The Piano.* Script. London: Bloomsbury, 1993.

———. Interview by Miro Bilbrough. *Cinema Papers* 93 (May 1993), 4–11.

Carroll, Noel. "Notes on Sight Gag." In *Comedy/Cinema/Theory,* ed. Andrew S. Horton, 25–42. Berkeley: University of California Press, 1991.

Cavell, Stanley. *Pursuits of Happiness: The Hollywood Comedy of Remarriage.* Cambridge: Harvard University Press, 1981.

Chanan, Michael. *Chilean Cinema.* London: British Film Institute, 1976.

Charney, Leo. "In a Moment: Film and the Philosophy of Modernity." In *Cinema and the Invention of Modern Life,* ed. Leo Charney and Vanessa R. Schwartz, 279–94. Berkeley: University of California Press, 1995.

Christensen, Jerome. "Spike Lee, Corporate Populist." *Critical Inquiry* 17 (fall 1991), 582–95.

Clover, Carol J. *Men, Women, and Chain Saws: Gender in the Modern Horror Film.* Princeton: Princeton University Press, 1992.

Cochrane, Peter. "Seduction and Consent." *24 Hours* 214 (November 1993), 44–48.

Colbert, Mary. "Jane Campion on Her Gothic Film *The Piano*." *Sight and Sound* 3.10 (October 1993), 6–8.

Cooray, Philip. *The Lonely Artist: A Critical Introduction to the Films of Lester James Peries*. Colombo: Lake House, 1970.

Crafton, Donald. "Pie and Chase: Gag, Spectacle, and Narrative in Slapstick Comedy." In *Classical Hollywood Comedy*, ed. Kristine Brunovska Karnick and Henry Jenkins (New York and London: Routledge, 1995).

De Certeau, Michel. *The Practice of Everyday Life*. Trans. Steven Rendall. Berkeley: University of California Press, 1984.

Deleuze, Gilles. *Bergsonism*. Trans. Hugh Tomlinson and Barbara Habberjam. New York: Zone Books, 1988.

———. *Cinema 1: The Movement Image*. Trans. Hugh Tomlinson and Barbara Habberjam. Minneapolis: University of Minnesota Press, 1986.

———. *Cinema 2: The Time Image*. Trans. Hugh Tomlinson and Robert Galeta. Minneapolis: University of Minnesota Press, 1989.

———. *Francis Bacon: Logique de la Sensation*. Paris: Editions de la différence, 1981, unpublished translation by Daniel Smith.

———. *The Logic of Sense*. Trans. Mark Lester with Charles Stivale. New York: Columbia University Press, 1990.

———. *Negotiations, 1972–1990/Gilles Deleuze*. Trans. Martin Joughin. New York: Columbia University Press, 1995.

———. "Painting and Sensation." In *The Deleuze Reader*, ed. Constantin V. Boundas, 187–92. New York: Columbia University Press, 1993.

Deleuze, Gilles, and Felix Guattari. *Kafka: Towards a Minor Literature*. Trans. Dana Polan. Minneapolis: University of Minnesota Press, 1986.

———. *A Thousand Plateaus: Capitalism and Schizophrenia*. Trans. Brian Massumi. Minneapolis: University of Minnesota Press, 1988.

Dermody, Susan, and Elizabeth Jacka. *The Screening of Australia: Anatomy of a National Cinema*. Vol. 2. Melbourne: Currency Press, 1988.

Dreyer, Carl Theodor. *Dreyer in Double Reflection: Translation of Carl Th. Dreyer's Writings about the Film (Om Filmen)*. Ed. Donald Skoller. New York: E. P. Dutton, 1973.

Eisner, Lotte H. *Murnau*. London: Secker and Warburg, 1965.

Fiedler, Leslie. "On Terror for Love." In *The Gothic Novel: A Casebook*, ed. Victor Sage, 130–38. London: Macmillan, 1990.

Field, Barbara Jean. "Slavery, Race, and Ideology in the United States." *New Left Review* 181 (1990), 95–119.

Flaherty, Frances Hubbard. *The Odyssey of a Film-Maker: Robert Flaherty's Story*. Putney, Vt.: Threshold Books, 1984.

Flaus, John. "The Western Myth: *Ride Lonesome* and *Guns in the Afternoon*." *SUFG Bulletin* (Sydney University Film Group), Term 1 (1970), 44–45.

Fletcher, Angus. *Allegory: The Theory of a Symbolic Mode*. Ithaca: Cornell University Press, 1982.

Freud, Sigmund. "Mourning and Melancholia." 1914–1916. In *The Standard Edition of the Psychological Works of Sigmund Freud*, trans. James Strachey, vol. 14, 243–60. London: Hogarth Press, 1986.

———. "On Narcissism: An Introduction." 1914. In *The Standard Edition of the Psychological Works of Sigmund Freud,* trans. James Strachey, vol. 14, 73–102. London: Hogarth Press, 1986.

Fuller, Graham. "The Wuthering Heights of Jane Campion's *The Piano.*" *Interview* 7 (November 1993), 46–47.

Gebauer, Gunter, and Christoph Wulf. *Mimesis: Culture, Art, Society.* Trans. Don Reneau. Berkeley: University of California Press, 1992.

Gibson, Ross. "Camera Natura: Landscape in Australian Feature Films." *Framework* 22–23 (fall 1983), 48–53.

Gledhill, Christine, ed. *Home Is Where the Heart Is: Studies in Melodrama and the Woman's Film.* London: British Film Institute, 1987.

Godard, Jean-Luc, and Jean-Pierre Gorin. Script of *Letter to Jane. Women and Film* 1.3–4 (1973), 45–52.

Goldsworthy, Kerryn. "What Music Is." *Arena* 7 (October–November 1993), 46–48.

Gunning, Tom. "An Aesthetic of Astonishment: Early Film and the (In)credulous Spectator." *Art & Text* 34 (1989), 31–45.

———. "The Cinema of Attraction: Early Film, Its Spectator, and the Avant-Garde." *Wide Angle* 8.3–4 (1986), 63–70.

———. " 'Primitive' Cinema: A Frame-up? Or, The Trick's on Us." *Cinema Journal* 28.2 (1988), 3–12.

Haggerty, George E. *Gothic Fiction/Gothic Form.* University Park and London: Pennsylvania State University Press, 1989.

Hansen, Miriam. *Babel and Babylon: Spectatorship in American Silent Film.* Cambridge: Harvard University Press, 1991.

———. "Early Cinema: Whose Public Sphere?" In *Early Cinema: Space, Frame, Narrative,* ed. Thomas Elsaesser, 228–46. London: British Film Institute,1990.

———. "The Future of Cinema Studies in the Age of Global Media: Aesthetics, Spectatorship, and Public Spheres—Interview with Miriam Hansen." Interview by Laleen Jayamanne and Anne Rutherford. *UTS Review* 5.1 (May 1999), 94–110.

Hazel, Valerie. "Strains of Silence." *Photofile* 40 (November 1993), 39–41.

Heller, Terry. *The Delights of Terror: An Aesthetic of the Tale of Terror.* Urbana: University of Illinois Press, 1987.

Inverso, MaryBeth. *The Gothic Impulse in Contemporary Drama.* Ann Arbor and London: UMI Research Press, 1990.

Islam, Needeya. " 'I Wanted to Shoot People': Genre, Gender, and Action in the Films of Kathryn Bigelow." In *Kiss Me Deadly: Feminism and Cinema for the Moment,* ed. Laleen Jayamanne, 91–125. Sydney: Power Publications, 1995.

Jayamanne, Laleen. "Above and beyond One's 'Cultural Heritage': Jackie Chan and His *Drunken Master.*" In *ABOVE AND BEYOND: Austral/Asian Interactions,* catalogue for an exhibition curated by Michael Snelling, 12–16. Australian Centre for Contemporary Art, Melbourne, and Institute of Modern Art, Brisbane, 1996.

———. "Positions of Women in the Sri Lankan Cinema, 1947–1979." Ph.D. dissertation, University of New South Wales, 1981.

———. "Puppets and Puppeteers, Actors and Lovers." *Cantrills Film Notes* 47–48 (August 1985), 2–6.

———. "To Render the Body Ecstatic: Anna Rodrigo Interviews Laleen Jayamanne." In *Fade to Black,* 6–9. Sydney: Sydney College of the Arts Film Group, 1985.

Jayamanne, Laleen, Geeta Kapur, and Yvonne Rainer. "Discussing Modernity, 'Third World,' and *The Man Who Envied Women." Art and Text* 23–24 (March–May 1987), 41–51.

Jenkins, Henry. "The Laughing Stock of the City: Performance Anxiety, Male Dread, and *Unfaithfully Yours." In Classical Hollywood Comedy,* ed. Kristine Brunovska Karnick and Henry Jenkins, 238–61. New York and London: Routledge, 1995.

Johnson, Colin. "Chauvel and the Centering of the Aboriginal Male in Australian Film." *Continuum* 1.1 (1987), 47–56.

Kamin, Dan. *Charlie Chaplin's One-Man Show.* 2nd ed. Carbondale and Edwardsville: Southern Illinois University Press, 1991.

Karnick, Kristine Brunovska, and Henry Jenkins, eds. *Classical Hollywood Comedy.* New York and London: Routledge, 1995.

Kerr, Walter. *The Silent Clowns.* New York: Da Capo Press, 1980.

Kinder, Marsha. "Reflections on *Jeanne Dielman." Film Quarterly* 30.4 (summer 1977), 2–8.

Kirby, Michael. "On Acting and Not-Acting." *The Drama Review* 16.1 (1972), 2–11.

Kirkby, Joan. "'Big My Secret': Emily Dickinson and *The Piano." EDIS Bulletin* 8 (May–June 1994), 6–7.

Klibansky, Raymond, Erwin Panofsky, and Fritz Saxl. *Saturn and Melancholy: Studies in the History of Natural Philosophy, Religion, and Art.* London: Thomas Nelson, 1964.

Koch, Gertrude. "Mimesis and Bilderverbot." *Screen* 34.3 (fall 1993), 211–22.

Kofman, Sarah. *The Enigma of Woman: Woman in Freud's Writings.* Trans. Catherine Porter. Ithaca: Cornell University Press, 1985.

Kracauer, Siegfried. *Theory of Film: The Redemption of Physical Reality.* Introduction by Miriam Hansen. Princeton: Princeton University Press, 1997.

Kramer, Peter. "Vitagraph, Slapstick, and Early Cinema." *Screen* 29.2 (spring 1988), 98–104.

Kristeva, Julia. *Black Sun: Depression and Melancholia.* Trans. Leon S. Roudiez. New York: Columbia University Press, 1989.

———. *Desire in Language: A Semiotic Approach to Literature and Art.* Ed. Leon S. Roudiez. Trans. Thomas Gora, Alice Jardine, and Leon S. Roudiez. New York: Columbia University Press, 1980.

Kuleshov, Lev. *Kuleshov on Film: Writings of Lev Kuleshov.* Ed. Ronald Levaco. Berkeley: University of California Press, 1974.

Kumara, Kumudu Kusum. "Duhulu Malak." *Sithuvili* 5 (1976), 4–5.

Laplanche, J., and J.-B. Pontalis. *The Language of Psycho-analysis.* Trans. D. Nicholson-Smith. London: Hogarth Press, 1983.

Lawson, Sylvia. "Skin Trade Stories." In *The Filmmaker and the Prostitute: Dennis O'Rourke's* The Good Woman of Bangkok, ed. Chris Berry, Annette Hamilton, and Laleen Jayamanne, 13–15. Sydney: Power Publications, 1997.

Lee, Spike, with Lisa Jones. *Do the Right Thing: A Spike Lee Joint.* New York: Fireside, 1989.

Maland, Charles J. *Chaplin and American Culture: The Evolution of a Star Image.* Princeton: Princeton University Press, 1989.

Mallawarachchi, Swarna. Interview by Ashley Rathnavibhushana. *Sinesith* 15 (1989), 9–11.

Mammen, Ashoka. "Notes on Production, 1945–72." In *Indian Cinema: British Film Institute Dossier 5,* ed. Behrose Ghandy and Paul Willemen, 20–25. London: British Film Institute, 1980.

Mapplethorpe, Robert. *Lady, Lisa Lyon.* New York: Viking Press, 1983.

Martin, Adrian. "The Artificial Night: Surrealism and Cinema." In *Surrealism: Revolution by Night,* catalogue for an exhibition curated by Michel Lloyd et al., 188–90. Canberra: National Gallery of Australia, 1993.

———. "Indefinite Objects: Independent Film and Video." In *The Australian Screen,* ed. Albert Moran and Tom O'Regan, 172–90. Ringwood: Penguin, 1989.

———. "No Flowers for the Cinephile: The Fates of Cultural Populism, 1960–1970." In *Island in the Stream: Myths of Place in Australian Culture,* ed. Paul Foss, 117–38. Sydney: Pluto Press, 1988.

———. *Once upon a Time in America.* London: British Film Institute, 1998.

———. "The Street Angel and the Badman: *The Good Woman of Bangkok.*" *Photofile* 35 (May 1992), 15–16.

Martin, Angela. "Chantal Akerman's Films: A Dossier." *Feminist Review* 3 (1979), 24–47.

Martin, Jeannie. "Missionary Positions." In *The Filmmaker and the Prostitute: Dennis O'Rourke's* The Good Woman of Bangkok, ed. Chris Berry, Annette Hamilton, and Laleen Jayamanne, 17–19. Sydney: Power Publications, 1997.

Mast, Gerald. *The Comic Mind: Comedy and the Movies.* 2nd ed. Chicago: University of Chicago Press, 1979.

McClintock, Anne. "The Return of Female Fetishism and the Fiction of the Phallus." *New Formations* 19, special issue on perversity (spring 1993), 1–21.

McMahon, Melissa. "Fourth Person Singular: Becoming Ordinary and the Void in the Critical Body Filmic." In *Kiss Me Deadly: Feminism and Cinema for the Moment,* ed. Laleen Jayamanne, 126–46. Sydney: Power Publications, 1995.

Mellencamp, Patricia. "Fairy Tales and Feminism: What Rapunzel, Cinderella, Snow White, et al. Forgot to Tell Thelma and Louise." In *Kiss Me Deadly: Feminism and Cinema for the Moment,* ed. Laleen Jayamanne, 18–76. Sydney: Power Publications, 1995.

Mishra, Vijay. *The Gothic Sublime.* Albany: State University of New York Press, 1994.

Mitchell, W. J. T. "The Violence of Public Art: *Do The Right Thing.*" *Critical Inquiry* 16 (summer 1990), 880–99.

Morris, David B. "Gothic Sublimity." *New Literary History* 16.2 (winter 1985), 299–319.

Morris, Meaghan. "Beyond Assimilation: Aboriginality, Media History, and Public Memory." *Aedon: Melbourne University Literary Arts Review* 4.1 (1996), 12–26.

———. "Crazy Talk Is Not Enough." *Environment and Planning D: Society and Space* 14.4, special issue on Deleuze and dwelling (1996), 384–94.

———. "On Going to Bed Early: Once upon a Time in America." In *The Best Australian Essays 1999,* ed. Peter Craven, 341–53. Melbourne: Bookman Press, 1999.

———. "Personal Relationships and Sexuality in the Australian Cinema." In *The New Australian Cinema,* ed. Scott Murray, 133–51. Melbourne: Thomas Nelson, 1981.

———. *The Pirate's Fiancée: Feminism, Reading, Postmodernism.* London and New York: Verso, 1988.

Morrison, Toni. Interview by Jana Wendt, *Uncensored.* Australian Broadcasting Corporation, 16 September 1998.

Mulvey, Laura. "Visual Pleasure and Narrative Cinema." In *Movies and Methods,* vol. 2, ed. Bill Nichols, 307–15. Berkeley: University of California Press, 1985.

Obeyesekere, Gananath. "Psycho-cultural Exegesis of a Case of Spirit Possession from Sri Lanka." In *Contributions to Asian Studies,* ed. K. Ishwaran, 41–89. Leiden: E. J. Brill, 1975.

Ostinga, Libby. "Exile and Metamorphosis: The Magical Cinematic Practice of Raul Ruiz." B.A. honours thesis, Department of Art History and Theory, University of Sydney, 1992.

Otto, Peter. "Forgetting Colonialism." *Meanjin* 52.3 (1993), 545–59.

Paul, William. *Laughing, Screaming: Modern Hollywood Horror and Comedy.* New York: Columbia University Press, 1994.

Perera, H. "Early Sinhala Cinema." *Cinemanurupa* 6 (1962), 3–5.

Perera, K. D., ed. *"Under the Bridge" and Its Critics.* Colombo: Lanka Kala Kendra, 1990.

Perera, K. W. "Duhulu Malak." *Cinemanurupa* 10–12 (1976), 2–3.

Perera, Neil I. "Ungrammatical Cinema." *Attha* (Sri Lanka), 12 March 1972.

Perez, Ingrid. "*Night Cries:* Cries from the Heart." *Film News* 20.7 (August 1990), 16.

Pick, Suzana M. "The Dialectical Wanderings of Exile." *Screen* 30.4 (fall 1989), 48–64.

Polan, Dana. "Francis Bacon: The Logic of Sensation." In *Gilles Deleuze and the Theater of Philosophy,* ed. Constantin V. Boundas and Dorothy Olkowski, 229–54. New York: Routledge, 1994.

Powell, Anna. "Blood on the Borders: *Near Dark* and *Blue Steel.*" *Screen* 35.2 (summer 1994), 136–56.

Reid, Mark A., ed. *Spike Lee's* Do The Right Thing. New York: Cambridge University Press, 1997.

Robbins, Bruce. "Murder and Mentorship: Advancement in *The Silence of the Lambs.*" *UTS Review* 1.1 (1995), 30–49.

Rodowick, D. N. *Gilles Deleuze's Time Machine.* Durham and London: Duke University Press, 1997.

Rohdie, Sam. *The Passion of Pier Paolo Pasolini.* London: British Film Institute and Bloomington: Indiana University Press, 1995.

Rose, Tricia. *Black Noise: Rap Music and Black Culture in Contemporary America.* Hanover and London: Wesleyan University Press, 1994.

Rubin Suleiman, Susan. *The Female Body in Western Culture: Contemporary Perspectives.* Cambridge: Harvard University Press, 1986.

Ruiz, Raoul. "Between Institutions: Interview with Raul Ruiz." Interview by Ian Christie and Malcolm Coad. *Afterimage* 10 (fall 1981), 113–16.

———. "The Cinema of Raul Ruiz." Interview by Adrian Martin. *Cinema Papers* 91 (January 1993), 61–63.

——. "Cinema, Prosthetics, and a Short History of Latin America." Unpublished interview by Paul Garcia, David Bolliger, and Nick O'Sullivan. Sydney, 1993.

——. "Interview with Raoul Ruiz." Interview by Pascal Bonitzer and Serge Toubiana. *Cahiers du Cinema* 345 (March 1983), 7–11, 74–82.

——. "Raoul Ruiz." *Agenda* 30–31 (May 1993), 50–53.

Sadoul, Georges. *George Mélies.* Paris: Éditions Seghers, 1970.

Schor, Naomi. "Female Fetishism: The Case of George Sand." In *The Female Body in Western Culture: Contemporary Perspectives,* ed. Susan Rubin Suleiman, 363–72. Cambridge: Harvard University Press, 1986.

Shahani, Kumar. "Interrogating Internationalism." *Journal of Arts and Ideas* 19 (May 1990), 12–15.

Shaviro, Steven. *The Cinematic Body.* Minneapolis: University of Minnesota Press, 1993.

Shimakawa, Karen. "'Fake Intimacy': Locating National Identity in Dennis O'Rourke's *The Good Woman of Bangkok.*" *Discourse* 17.3 (spring 1995), 126–50.

Silverman, Kaja. *The Acoustic Mirror: The Female Voice in Psychoanalysis and Cinema.* Bloomington: Indiana University Press, 1988.

Singer, Ben. "Modernity, Hyperstimulus, and the Rise of Popular Sensationalism." In *Cinema and the Invention of Modern Life,* ed. Leo Charney and Vanessa R. Schwartz, 72–99. Berkeley: University of California Press, 1995.

Sontag, Susan. Introduction to *One-Way Street and Other Writings,* by Walter Benjamin, 7–28. Trans. Edmond Jephcott and Kingsley Shorter. London: New Left Books, 1979.

——. "Spiritual Style in the Films of Robert Bresson." In *Against Interpretation,* 177–95. New York: Delta, 1966.

Spariosu, Mihai. "Plato's *Ion:* Mimesis, Poetry, and Power." In *Mimesis in Contemporary Theory: An Interdisciplinary Approach.* Vol. 2, *Mimesis, Semiosis, and Power,* ed. Ronald Bogue, 13–26. Philadelphia and Amsterdam: John Benjamins, 1991.

——, ed. *Mimesis in Contemporary Theory: An Interdisciplinary Approach.* Vol. 1, *The Literary and Philosophical Debate.* Philadelphia and Amsterdam: John Benjamins, 1984.

Stern, Lesley. *The Scorsese Connection.* Bloomington: Indiana University Press and London: British Film Institute, 1995.

Stern, Lesley, and George Kouvaros, eds. *Falling for You: Essays on Cinema and Performance.* Sydney: Power Publications, 1999.

Stewart, Garrett. "Modern Hard Times: Chaplin and the Cinema of Self-Reflection." *Critical Inquiry* 3.2 (winter 1976), 295–314.

Stonum, Gary Lee. *Dickinson Sublime.* Madison: University of Wisconsin Press, 1990.

Tasker, Yvonne. *Spectacular Bodies: Gender, Genre, and the Action Cinema.* London and New York: Routledge, 1993.

Taussig, Michael. *Mimesis and Alterity: A Particular History of the Senses.* New York and London: Routledge, 1993.

Thompson, David. "Harvey Keitel, Staying Power." *Sight and Sound* 3.1 (January 1993), 22–25.

Thornton, Lesley. "If upon Leaving, What We Have to Say, We Speak: A Conversa-
tion Piece." In *Discourses: Conversations in Postmodern Art and Culture,* ed.
Russell Ferguson et al., 44–64. New York: New Museum of Contemporary
Art and Cambridge: MIT Press, 1990.

Trinh, T. Minh-ha. "Why a Fish Pond? Fiction at the Heart of Documentation." Interview by L. Jayamanne and Anne Rutherford. *Film News* 20 (10 November
1990), 10–12.

Tulloch, John. *Legends on the Screen.* Melbourne: Currency Press and the Australian
Film Institute, 1981.

Valerie, Hazel. "Strains of Silence." *Photofile* 40 (November 1993), 39–41.

Vidler, Anthony. *The Architectural Uncanny: Essays in the Modern Unhomely.* Cambridge: MIT Press, 1992.

Weerasinghe, Anoja. "Anoja Weerasinghe, The Star and the Actress: An Interview."
Unnamed interviewer. *Framework* 37, special issue on the Sri Lankan cinema
(1989), 93–102.

"Who's Going to Win—and Why." *Who* 108 (21 March 1994), 80–84.

"Who Is Raul Ruiz?" *Sydney Morning Herald,* 29 January 1993.

Willemen, Paul. "Regional Cinema." In *Indian Cinema: British Film Institute Dossier*
5, ed. Behrose Ghandy and Paul Willemen, 26–37. London: British Film Institute, 1980.

Willis, Sharon. *High Contrast: Race and Gender in Contemporary Hollywood Film.*
Durham: Duke University Press, 1998.

Wohlfarth, Irving. "On the Messianic Structure of Walter Benjamin's Last Reflections." In *GLYPH: Johns Hopkins Textual Studies* 3, ed. Samuel Weber and
Henry Sussman, 148–212. Baltimore: Johns Hopkins University Press, 1978.

Worringer, Wilhelm. *Form in Gothic.* Trans. Sir Herbert Read. London: Alec Tiranti,
1957.

Wright, Elizabeth, ed. *Feminism and Psychoanalysis: A Critical Dictionary.* Oxford,
England, and Cambridge, Mass.: Blackwell, 1992.

Yaeger, Patricia. "Toward a Female Sublime." In *Gender and Theory: Dialogues on
Feminist Criticism,* ed. Linda Kauffman, 191–221. Oxford: Blackwell, 1989.

Index

fight scenes, 120, 121

"Fight the Power," 236, 237–39, 242–45, 246

film criticism, xii–xiii, 13–14, 205, 206–207; American, 233–35, 284n4; Bazin and, 135, 141; British, 82, 118; feminist, 14–23, 71, 82, 114, 160, 231; French, 135, 147; Italian, 135, 139; Sinhalese, 93; Sri Lankan, 4, 93, 96, 98–99, 110, 125–28, 131, 249–50(1), 264–65(9)

film noir, 210

film stills, 56, 57–58, 60, 66

film strip, 192, 278n27

film studies. *See* cinema studies

film theory: Anglophone, 53, 135, 184–86; Bazin and, 135, 141; feminist, 53–54, 67, 122, 149–50, 254n10, 261–62(4)

filmic knowledge, 57–59, 117–18, 206, 226, 260n69, 280n2

Filmmaker and the Prostitute, The (Berry, Hamilton, and Jayamanne), 251–52(2)

filmmakers, 18–19, 140, 147, 161; women, 4, 25, 149, 158

"Films of Raul Ruiz, The: A Surreal Journey," 269n4

film-within-a-film, 82

Fingers, 44, 45

Finnane, Gabrielle, 64

fire hydrant, 243

fire scene, 235, 240, 244, 245–46

"first contact," 39, 41–43

first principles, 224–25, 227

"firstness," 223, 283n20

Flaherty, Robert, 41, 259n63

"flash of light," 168, 189, 272n38, 278–79n39

flashback, 208, 216–20, 225–26, 282n13

Flaus, John, 91

Floating Flower, 98–100, 113, 128, 130

Flora (*The Piano*), 33–35, 40, 45–47, 260nn69,71

folk traditions, 164

Fonda, Henry, 200

Fonda, Jane, 155, 267n14, 268n21

Fonseka, Gamini, 100, 102

Fonseka, Malini, 126–27

Ford, John, 213

forgetting, 172, 177, 271n31, 272nn36,42

Form in Gothic (Worringer), 254n9

formula films, Sri Lankan. *See* family melodrama

"Forty Acres and a Mule Filmworks," 241

Foster, Jodie, 224, 256n25

Four Corners, 267n14

Fox, William, 116, 117

fragmentation, 85, 162, 174, 202–203, 270–71n21

"Frame by Frame," 254n5

framing, 6, 9; *The Silence of the Lambs,* 230; *A Song of Ceylon,* 57, 59–61, 73

Frankenstein (Shelley), 256n26

Frankfurt School, xii, 40, 182, 185

French film criticism, 135, 147

frenzy, 193

Freud, Sigmund, 27, 31–32, 67, 256n32, 269–70nn8,13, 271n31, 272n43, 273n55; dreamwork, 281n6

friendship between women, 109–10

Frogger, 261–62(4)

frontal composition, 106, 119, 121

Fruit of Islam, 233

fundamentalism, feminist, 16

gags, 185, 186, 189–90, 194–96, 202, 205, 276nn8,17

Gahanu Lamai, 109

games, 197

gap, 139

Garcia, Paul, 271–72n36

gaze, 47, 52–53, 121, 261n75; in neorealism, 138

Gebauer, Gunter, 182

Gedächtnis, 174–76

gender identity, 71, 73, 123; in *Blue Steel,* 209, 282n10

gendered body, 185, 279n41

gendered subject in extremis, 27, 29, 52, 66–67, 82–83

gendered subjectivity, 25, 53

genre film, 117–18

German baroque, 162, 170

gesture: in *Do the Right Thing,* 236; in *Humberto D,* 143; in *Jeanne Dielman,* 150–52, 154–57, 160; in slapstick, 187–93, 196–97, 201, 202–203; in *A Song of Ceylon,* 61, 62, 63, 66; in *Three Crowns of a Sailor,* 175

Ghatak, Ritwik, 116

ghost ship, 173, 177–78

ghost train, 14

ghosts, 163, 166, 177, 197, 272n42

GI Joe, 143–46

Gibson, Ross, 5

Hunt, Eugene (*Blue Steel*), 208, 210–21
Hunter, Holly, 24, 28, 253(3)
Hurley, Karen, 282n10
Husband Is the Wife's God, The, 95–98
"husband/owner" (*himi*), 95, 264n6
Hynkel (*The Great Dictator*), 202–203
hysteria, 53, 63, 65, 67, 70, 72, 262n5

I Love Radio, 239
" 'I Wanted to Shoot People': Genre, Gender, and Action in the Films of Kathryn Bigelow" (Islam), 281n4
"I-You relationship," 19
icons, 128
identity, cultural: American, 22–23; Sri Lankan, 66, 69–70
identity, mistaken, 202–203
identity, performance of, 45, 68, 167
Ihatha Atmaya, 128
Ill-Fated Lass, 99, 109, 129
image: action, 212, 231, 277n23, 282n10; affection, 212, 231, 277n23, 283n17; crystal, 186–87, 197; fact, 140–42; impulse, 212, 282n10; memory, 187, 225, 277n23; mimetic, 191; movement, 277n23; neorealist, 135–42; perception, 231, 277n23; recollection, 221, 226–28, 282n13; time, 160, 177–78, 186, 268n25, 273–74n57; virtual, 186–87
Image in a Mirror, 113, 114
images, optical and aural, 137–39, 143–46, 206
imagination, 139
Immigrant, The, 195–96
impersonator, 166, 167, 176, 177
impulse, mimetic, 189–90, 202
impulse, violence of, 213–16, 218–19, 221–22, 282n10
impulse image, 212, 282n10
"In Playland" (Agamben), 278n37
incest, 128
"incorporeal transformations," 177, 274n58
India Cabaret, 17
Indian cinema, 92–93, 116–17, 254n10; Sinhalese cinema and, 123, 127, 132; studies of, xiv
Indian Queen, The, 61
"indirect mediator," 160, 268n26
Indu (*A Bouquet for Indu*), 109
industrialism, 183
Induta Mal Mitak, 98
infinitive, 195, 197

influence, 266n9
inoculation, cinema of, 53
instinct, 84
intention, authorial, 25, 54, 126–27
interior narrator, 30, 256n26
International Centre for Ethnic Studies, 263
international trade, 65
intersubjectivity, 34–35, 167
intertextuality, 65
interviewing, xiii, 226–27, 233–34, 261–62(4), 271n29, 272n36, 284n7
intimacy, 27
Intolerance (Griffith), 17
intuition, 85–86
inventing the text, 54
invention, xii
Inverso, MaryBeth, 25
"irrational cut," 258n53
Islam, Needeya, 281n4
isolation, 131
Isolde, 169
Italian film criticism, 135, 139
Italian neorealism, 135–48

Jacka, Elizabeth, 26
Jade (*Do the Right Thing*), 235, 241
Jayamanne, B. A. W., 110, 117, 127
Jayamanne, Laleen, 251–52(2), 261–62(4), 263(6), 265n5, 269(12), 281n4; on *Row Row Row Your Boat,* 75–88; on *A Song of Ceylon,* 51–64, 65–74
Jean (*The Lady Eve*), 201, 203
Jeanne Dielman, 149–60, 223, 266n10, 267n18, 268n26
Jeanne Eagels, 61
Jedda, 10–11, 250n4
Jenkins, Henry, 279n44
Jewish barber (*The Great Dictator*), 202–203
Johanna (*Not Reconciled*), 155
Johnson, Colin (pseud. Mudrooroo), 11
joke, visual, 267n18
Judy (*Vertigo*), 59

Kadapathaka Chaya, 113
Kadawuna Poronduwa, 110, 117
Kafka, Franz, 285n17
Kali, 88, 126, 173
Kamala (*Another Man's Flowers*), 100–105
Kamin, Dan, 276–77n17
Kapurala, 67

Lukacs, Georg, 175
Lumière, 14, 42
lumpenproletariat mother, 128–31
Lyon, Lisa, 167–68, 169, 171–72

machines, 191–93, 201, 204, 279–80n45
MacKay, John, 274–75n1
Mad Wednesday, 200
Madeline (*Vertigo*), 58
madness, 27, 193; women and, 66–69, 72
Mafia, 232
Maggy (*Another Man's Flowers*), 101–104
magic, 182
Magnani, Anna, 8
Magritte, René, 169
Maland, Charles J., 276n14
"male dread," 203–204, 279n44
male slapstick body, 185, 195, 200, 204
male subject in extremis. *See* gendered subject in extremis
Mallawarachchi, Swarna, 94, 111–15, 264nn7,8
mambo dance, 168, 170
Mammen, Ashoka, 93
Mangolte, Babette, 267n18
mania, 270n13
Mann, Nick (*Blue Steel*), 214, 217, 219, 220
Maori, 39, 40, 41–42, 44–45, 47, 117, 259n63
Mapplethorpe, Robert, 167
Marbuk, 10–12
Marcus Aurelius, 224
Maria (*Humberto D*), 143, 159
marital conflicts, 94–100, 113
Mark (*Peeping Tom*), 81–88
Married Woman, A, 72
Martin, Adrian, 4, 14, 16–17, 91, 162–63, 271n29
Martin, Jeannie, 15
martyrs, 150, 151, 160
masculinity: Aboriginal, 11–12; Australian, 18–22; in *The Piano,* 44–46
masochism, 63
mass reproduction, 40–41, 193, 202, 279–80n45
Massey, Anna, 85
mass-media events, 13, 127, 203
Mast, Gerald, 276–77n17
maternal, figure of the: in family melodrama, 109–10; Jayamanne, Laleen, and, 80–88; in *Night Cries: A Rural Tragedy,* 4–9; Rodrigo, Anna, and, xiii–xiv; in surrealism, 172–77, 272n43, 273n47

maternal melodrama, 128–32
Mathilde (*Three Crowns of a Sailor*), 167–72
Matrix, 279n41
matrixed performing, 151–52, 266n6
Matthews, Grant, 254n3
maxim, 168, 272n38
McAlpine, Andrew, 254n5
McCrea, Joel, 200
McGrath, Ada. *See* Ada (*The Piano*)
McMahon, Melissa, 159, 261n77, 268n25, 284n4
Mean Streets, 43
meaning, generation of, 182, 190
meaning of life, 175, 273n53
meanness, 183
media events, 13, 127, 161
media performances, 18–19
mediation, 11–12
melancholia, 31–38, 162, 256nn31,33, 269–70nn8,13, 271n31, 272nn41,42,43
"melancholy of slapstick," 200, 279n41
Méliès, George, 62, 117, 119
Mellencamp, Patricia, 177
melodrama, 172; critical, 125–32; family, 92, 94–96, 111–12, 116–24; Gothic and, 24–48, 254n10, 257n44, 260n71, 261n77
Melodramatic Imagination, The (Brooks), 24
melodramatic-noir, 200
memory: allegory of, 172–78, 273n47; archive of, 207, 265n5; cultural, 172, 251n11; doubling and, 213; erasure of, 251n15; in flashback, 213, 216–20; involuntary, 272nn38,42, 273n55, 278–79n39; mimetic, 199, 278–79n39; as mnemotechnique, 269n1; in neorealism, 139, 143, 146; in sensory-motor action, 208
memory cone, 282n12
memory image, 187, 225, 277n23
Memory of Appearances, 269n1
memory traces, 27, 44
memory-work, 208, 281n6, 282nn12,13,15; in *Blue Steel,* 218–20; in *The Silence of the Lambs,* 225–28
Menander, 202
mentoring, 213, 215, 223, 226–28, 230
Messiaen, Olivier, 244, 285n15
metaphor, 165, 170; mimed, 189–90
method actors, 44
Michelangelo, 155
midgets, 99, 129

Psycho, 88
psychoanalytic paradigm: family melo-
    drama and, 118; feminism and, 52–53,
    262n5; in Peeping Tom, 81–82, 86; in The
    Piano, 28–30; in A Song of Ceylon, 67, 70;
    in Three Crowns of a Sailor, 173, 273–74n57
psychodrama, 14
psychopaths, 215, 224, 227
Public Enemy, 236, 242
public funding, 80
public reception, xiii, xv
Puerto Ricans, 243
punishment, 130
puppets/puppeteer: Bunraku, 151; The Cir-
    cus, 280n46; Paisan, 144; A Song of Cey-
    lon, 56, 58–60, 62, 70, 74
Purcell, Henry, 61
purism, cultural, 69–70
Pursuits of Happiness (Cavell), 200

Questions of Third Cinema (Pines and
    Willemen), 261–62(4)
Quilapayun culture, 164
quotation, 3, 51

race relations, 233–34, 240–41, 285n19
racism, 241–42, 285nn14,18,19
Radio Raheem (Do the Right Thing), 235,
    236, 239–40, 241, 242–45
Raffel, Carmel, 255n18, 256n31
Rainer, Yvonne, 152, 266n9, 267n18
Ramachandran, L. S., 109, 110
Ramslands, Marie, 269n1
Ran Salu, 105–108
rap music, 239–40, 284–85n12
Rape, The (Magritte), 169
rape scenes, 121; Blue Steel, 217–18, 218–19; in
    Image in a Mirror, 114; in The Piano, 40,
    47, 261nn75,77
Rathnavibhushana, Ashley, 264n8
rational thought, 182, 207
Raul Ruiz (Buci-Glucksman and d'Allones),
    269n1
realism: allegory and, 171; Bazin and, 135, 139,
    146–47; historical, 254n10; matrixed per-
    forming as, 151; Sinhalese cinema, 106,
    110–12, 113, 115; Sri Lankan cinema, 94, 116–
    17, 126, 127–32; of western melodrama, 120
reason, 182
reception, 13–19

recollection image, 221, 226–28, 282n13
reconciliation, 12, 250n6
refrain, 237, 242–45, 246
Rekava, 105
remarriage, comedy of, 200
remembrance, 173, 176, 272n42
rented mother, 172–77, 272n43
renunciation of life, 108
reparation, 250n6
repetition, 79, 191, 194–95, 196, 204
repression, social, 127, 129
rescue, 209
"rescue fantasy," 17, 225, 227–28, 252n13
Reservoir Dogs, 43, 44
Resnais, Alain, 156
Reutershan, Paul, 267n14
revenge, 201–202, 204, 213
revolving doors, 191, 197
"Rhizomusicosmology" (Bogue), 237
rhythm, 234–38, 244–45
riot scene, 236, 240, 244, 245–46
"Rise and Fall of the City of Mahagonny,
    The," 267n13
ritual, 196–99, 202
ritual drama, 61
Robbe-Grillet, Alain, 156
Robbins, Bruce, 223, 226, 283n21
Rodin, Auguste, 155
Rodowick, D. N., 268n22
Rodrigo, Anna, xiii; on Row Row Row Your
    Boat, 75–88; on A Song of Ceylon, 51–56,
    57, 61–63, 65–74, 261–62(4)
Roeg, Nicholas, 44, 62
Rohan (Floating Flower), 99–100
Rohdie, Sam, 135–37, 139–40, 142
Romero, George, 163
Rose, Barbara (The War of the Roses), 201
Rose, Oliver (The War of the Roses), 201
Rose, Tricia, 239, 284–85n12
Ross, Toni, 258n55
Rossellini, Roberto, 42, 136, 140–41
Roswitha (Occasional Work of a Female
    Slave), 78–79
Row Row Row Your Boat, 75–88, 263(6)
Royal Commission on the Film Industry, 132
"Royal Telephone," 6
ruins, 162, 272n42
Ruiz, Raul, xiii, 3, 161–78, 250n3, 269nn1,4,
    270n13, 271n29, 272nn36,38,41,43,
    273nn47,52,57

Russell, Theresa, 62
Rutherford, Anne, 64, 265n5
Rutnam, Brian, 285n15

Sabu, 76
sadism, 81–82
Sagara Jalaya, 113
sailors, 166, 168–72, 175–77, 274n58
Sal (*Do the Right Thing*), 236, 239–40, 243–44, 246–47
salsa rhythms, 243
Samiya Birindage Deviyay, 95–98
Saroja (*Golden Robes*), 105–108, 110
Sathsamudura, 112
Saturn and Melancholy (Klibansky, Panofsky, and Saxl), 270n13, 272n41
saudade, 172–73
Saxl, Fritz, 270n13, 272n41
Scheherezade, 174
Schindler's List, 254n3
Schubert, Franz, 62, 66
Schuman, Peter, 266n6
Schumann, Elisabeth, 66
Schumann, Robert, 27
Scola, Ettore, 44
scopophilia, 81
Scorsese, Martin, 43–44
Scott, Ridley, 33, 44
Scotty (*Vertigo*), 58
Screen, xiv, 118, 269n4
Screening of Australia: Anatomy of a National Cinema, The (Dermody and Jacka), 26
seagulls, 222–23
Searchers, The, 213
"second contact," 39, 41, 46
seduction, 93, 130, 223, 224
Self and Other, 70
self-preservation, 182
self-reflexivity, 143, 192, 272n38
semiotic, 277–78n25
"semiotic chora," 178
Senaka (*Golden Robes*), 107
Seneviratne, P. K. D., 105
Sennett, Mack, 184, 276–77n17, 284n9
sensory-motor action: in *Blue Steel*, 208, 209–10, 221–22, 282n10; in *Do the Right Thing*, 235–37, 243; in *Jeanne Dielman*, 159–60; in neorealism, 137–39; in slapstick, 184, 187–93, 277n23

Sentimental Bloke, The, 22, 253nn20,23
serial killers, 224, 225
Sesame Street, 232, 247
Seven Seas, 112
sex, unprotected, 18
sex industry, Thailand, 19–20
sex worker. *See* prostitute
sexual economy, 52
sexual relationships in cinema, 19–20
sexuality, female, 177, 283n21
Seyrig, Delphine, 149–60, 267n18, 268nn20,26
Shahani, Kumar, 3
shaman, 10–12, 182
Sharman, Jim, 26
Shaviro, Steven, 210, 281n4
Sheen, Martin, 260n70
Shelley, Mary, 256n26
Shimakawa, Karen, 22
shoe-gourmet meal, 189–90
shoot-out scene, 208, 210, 213
"Short Organum for the Theatre, A," 267n13
shudder, 188–89, 205
Sight and Sound, 26, 44
sight gags, 186, 189–90
Sigmund Freud's Dora, 53
sign, cinematic, 5, 141, 147, 150, 151
Sikuruliya, 99, 109, 129
Silence of the Lambs, The, 207, 211, 216, 223–31, 256n25, 283n21
silent cinema: film criticism and, 14, 118; slapstick and, 184–85, 186, 192, 200, 276–77n17, 279n41; *A Song of Ceylon* and, 63; Soviet, 136
Silent Clowns, The (Kerr), 276–77n17
Silva, W., 98
Silverman, Kaja, 82–83
Sin of Harold Diddlebock, The, 200
Sinesith, 112
Singleton, John, 234
Sinhalese cinema, 100, 102, 107, 114, 117; Indian cinema and, 93, 123–24, 127, 132; studies of, xiv
Sinhalese film criticism, 93
Siribo Aiya, 128
Sirisena (*Another Man's Flowers*), 101–102
Sirkean melodrama, 116
Sister, Your Permission, 98
Sister Act, 44
sisterly love, 109, 110

LALEEN JAYAMANNE is a lecturer in Cinema Studies at the Department of Art History and Theory, University of Sydney. She is also a filmmaker; her work includes *A Song of Ceylon* and *Rehearsing* and a dance video, *LAMA*. Her articles on her own film work and the work of other independent filmmakers have appeared in *Screen, Discourse,* and *The Australian Journal of Screen Theory*. She is editor of *Kiss Me Deadly: Feminism and Cinema for the Moment* and co-editor of *The Filmmaker and the Prostitute: Dennis O'Rourke's* The Good Woman of Bangkok (Sydney: Power Publications, 1997).